Women Filmmakers:

A Critical Reception

by

LOUISE HECK-RABI

The Scarecrow Press, Inc.
Metuchen, N.J., & London
1984

The author gratefully acknowledges those who granted permission to reprint excerpts from the following publications:

Abel, Richard. "Louis Delluc: The Critic as Cineaste," Quarterly Review of Film Studies, 1:2 (May 1976), pp. 205-44. By permission of the Redgrave Publishing Co. (89 Danbury Road, Ridgefield, CT 06877).

Barnouw, Erik. Documentary: A History of the Non-Fiction Film. Copyright © 1974 by Erik Barnouw. Reprinted by permission of Oxford University Press, Inc.

Barsam, Richard Meran. "Leni Riefenstahl: Artifice and Truth in a World Apart," Film Comment, Nov./Dec. 1973. Copyright © 1973 by Film Comment Publishing Corp. All rights reserved. Reprinted by permission of The Film Society of Lincoln Center.

Betancourt, Jeanne. Women in Focus. Dayton, Ohio: Pflaum, 1974. (Now available from Educational Film Library Assc., 43 W. 61st St., New York, NY 10023.) By permission of Jeanne Betancourt.

Cornwell, Regina. "Maya Deren and Germaine Dulac: Activists of the Avant-Garde," Film Library Quarterly, 5 (Winter 1971/1972). By permission of Jeanne Cornwell.

Cowie, Peter. Sweden 2. Copyright © 1970 by A. S. Barnes, San Diego, CA. By permission of Oak Tree Publications, Inc.

Current Biography, 1970 (1975). Copyright © 1970 (1975). By permission of the H. W. Wilson Co.

Curtis, David. Experimental Cinema. New York: Universe Books, 1973. By permission of Universe Books and Macmillan Publishing Co., Inc.

Dozoretz, Wendy. "Dulac vs Artaud," Wide Angle, Vol. 3, No. 1 (1979), pp. 47-53. By permission of Wendy Dozoretz.

Ford, Charles. "The First Female Producer," Films in Review, Vol. 15, No. 3 (March 1964), p. 141. By permission of The National Board of Review of Motion Pictures, Inc.

(continued on next page)

Library of Congress Cataloging in Publication Data

Heck-Rabi, Louise, 1931–
    Women filmmakers.

    Includes index.
    1. Women motion picture producers and directors--
Biography. 2. Feminism and motion pictures. 3. Feminist
motion pictures--History and criticism. I. Title.
PN1995.9.W6H4 1984   791.43'023'0922 [B]   83-20070
ISBN 0-8108-1660-1

(continued on next page)

Rosen, Marjorie. Popcorn Venus. New York: Coward, McCann, & Geoghegan, 1973; London: Peter Owen, Ltd., 1973. Copyright © 1973 by Marjorie Rosen. Reprinted by permission of Coward, McCann & Geoghegan, Inc. and Peter Owen, Ltd.

Rosen, Marjorie. "Shirley Clarke; Videospace Explorer," Ms., April 1975, pp. 107-10. By permission of Marjorie Rosen.

Sadoul, Georges. Dictionary of Films. Berkeley: University of California Press, 1972. By permission of the University of California Press. Copyright © 1972.

Scheib, Ronnie. "Ida Lupino: Auteuress," Film Comment, 16:1 (Jan. - Feb. 1980). By permission of The Film Society of Lincoln Center and Ronnie Scheib.

Slide, Anthony. Early Women Directors. New York: A. S. Barnes, 1977. By permission of Anthony Slide.

Young, Vernon. On Film. Chicago: Quadrangle, 1972. Copyright © 1972 by Vernon Young. Reprinted by permission of Times Books, a division of Quadrangle/The New York Times Book Co., Inc.

TO MY PARENTS AND HUSBAND,

who love me and understand that
I must write each day of my life

CONTENTS

ACKNOWLEDGMENTS

Librarians tend to be very helpful, but anonymous. To those many nameless information locators I extend my continuing appreciation. You guided me to indexes, audiovisual materials, and monographs that most likely would have remained unknown to me without your help at the Detroit Main Library, Henry Ford Centennial Library, and Purdy Library at Wayne State University. And you graciously tried to obtain the books and periodical articles I requested via interlibrary loan. Thank you.

Initially, Phil Smith and Margo Sasse of the University of California at San Diego replied to my request for help by sending their pamphlet Sharp Focus on Film and offering encouragement.

Jim Limbacher, Audio-Visual Director of the Henry Ford Centennial Library in Dearborn, Michigan, deserves a citation of merit from me for the advice and guidance he offered without being asked. In several instances he steered me in the right direction by coming up with a title or book that I needed when I needed it. As a busy author, editor, and instructor in addition to his full-time position as librarian, Jim always had time to help me (and many others, which I later discovered from those who benefited from his generous offers of help and materials).

I am grateful also to those who permitted me to quote from their reviews and books and to all women filmmakers everywhere. Their films--completed, unfinished, and not yet realized--have inspired this book.

ix

Women have worked in films since the inception of filmmaking as a viable industry in the 1890's. Not only have they written continuity (or scripts), edited, designed sets and costumes, photographed, and acted in films, but also they have produced, directed, and occasionally distributed films. In western Europe, England, and the United States, women have made films. When, in the early 1970's, it appeared that more women than ever before were making films independently or within the corporate structure, press notices heralded this flourishing incursion warmly, but as a novel phenomenon. Increasing numbers of women did indeed forsake the literary and fine arts, electing instead to plunge into the maelstrom of this seventh art, labeled variously the cinema, film, motion pictures, or movies.

However, this influx of women into the industry not as actresses or costume designers but in positions of artistic and technical decision, really calling the shots, was not a novelty, but the heightened progression of a lengthy tradition. Women have always made films. They were there at the starting line. In fact, Alice Guy-Blaché had a running jump on the starting line in France because she helped lay it down.

I didn't know these facts in 1973. I was attending a class dealing with the Image in the Media when I happened to read reviews in the Village Voice of several short films women had made and shown to audiences. I was intrigued! I wanted to know more. Who were these women who--all by themselves--could make films? What did one have to know to make a movie? Why, all of a sudden, were women trying to make films instead of writing novels or studying architecture? Were there women in times gone by who made movies? Could a woman find a good career in a TV station or film company now? Were there certain traits all women filmmakers shared? In 1974 I elected to do an independent study project on the women filmmakers with whom I had become acquainted in print. Sadly, I discovered that documentation equals reputation. I could study and write only about those women filmmakers whose film reviews and biographies were available to me. At the close of the eleven-week quarter session I had finished a 115-page paper which attempted to summarize the lives and films of 32 women. This became the first draft of this book. The criteria by which I chose the eleven women as subjects for a more comprehensive consideration were few and informal. Of course, I tried to pick the best! Again, I had to select those for which documentation was at least adequate, if not bounteous. Subjects chosen had to have a reasonable number of works in their filmography (no one-shot deals, however excellent, such as Barbara Loden's <u>Wanda</u>). Also, the filmography had to be a valid and memorable entry into the history of filmmaking. The woman herself was to be individual, in the richest meaning of that word, with her films bearing the impress of her own personality. The pleasant result was a roster of eleven women whose films have been viewed by audiences worldwide, with few exceptions, reviewed by critics in the popular and academic press, and may be considered historically important and interesting. My hope is that the timeline of women filmmakers, from Blaché to Varda, circumscribes the efforts of women everywhere in this twentieth century to make films, and encourages readers and audiences to view them.

Did I find any common denominators of temperament, training, or talents? Yes, I believe so. I base my observations, listed below, not only upon the eleven subjects of this book, but upon the total galaxy of women employed in films. For example, screenwriters June Mathis, Frances Marion, and Eleanor Perry, editor Dede Allen, and cinematographer Claudia Weill are included in my scope. I maintain files on over fifty women filmmakers and read everything I can to keep these up-to-date. Film critics, actresses who become directors, and costume designers and set designers for movies belong to the sisterhood. Some of those whom I have researched are Perry Miller Adato, Madeline Anderson, Gillian Armstrong, Carol Betts, Betty Box, Margot Benacerraf, Leigh Brackett, Mary Ellen Bute, Joyce Chopra, Vera Chytilova, Judy Collins, Judith Crist, Storm DeHirsch, Johanna Demetrakas, Joan Didion, Marguerite Duras, Lotte Eisner, Judit Elek, Cinda Firestone, Jane Fonda, Penelope Gilliatt, Joan Jonas, Pauline Kael, Fay Kanin, Nelly Kaplan, Anita Loos, Elizabeth Lutyens, Elaine May, Shirley MacLaine, Kate Millett, Lotte Reiniger,

Amalie Rothschild, Esther Shub, Susan Sontag, Joan Tewkesbury, Miriam Weinstein, Lina Wertmuller, and Joyce Wieland.

These are the characteristics that I believe women filmmakers tend to share:

1. Most are married or work in collaboration with men. The fact that men open doors into the film industry for women is well known. Men do encourage women to make films, provide access to finance and equipment, and introduce peers and superiors who can prove to be helpful.

2. Most are of short stature, are considered attractive, restless, dynamic, energetic.

3. Most have had previous training in the arts, *singer* especially dance.

15 4/5 in the making

4. Most have made, or want to make, films about women, or from a woman's point-of-view.

These common denominators aside, women agree that women who really want to make films will do so. Having guts is the basic ingredient, never mind stature and knowing men who will help you. If one really wants to do it, one will.

What options exist for gutsy women who want to make films now? There are several types of film enterprise to explore: the documentary, the feature-length film, pornography, the structural or "art" film, the women's film (usually feminist), expanded cinema, TV commercials, videotape, and cable TV production. A gutsy woman will fashion or find her own turf. Suzanne E. Bauman expresses this view about women in films: "Filmmaking is like life--men still run it. Great films often have the little woman behind them.... I have chosen to make tiny films myself rather than be absorbed by larger productions where I'm likely to be used to further some man's career" (from "Man's World, Woman's Place," Film Library Quarterly 5 [Winter 1971-72], page 27).

Financing a film is the hardest chore involved, as all women who make films concur. Since this financial picture is unlikely to improve, does it connote that women filmmakers will be forced to make short rather than longer works because brief films cost less to make? Not necessarily.

Karen Sperling affirms that filming can be done at near-zero budget levels. She made The Double Circle, she claims, with the first all-female, non-union crew in U.S. history. Her first picture was Make a Face. Filming in an abandoned hospital on Ward's Island, Sperling as screenwriter-director-actress will decide the final shape and length of her next film. She is using a cast of 150 non-actors playing characters who are alternately hospital patients and apartment dwellers. These characters talk directly to the camera, which functions as an immobile audience. Sperling is enthused about the feeling of co-operation and mutual respect throughout crew and cast. She is convinced that New York is the best place for women to make films, because Hollywood still excludes women from all levels of making films, except acting and costume design. Infiltrating the all-male ranks of union filmmaking is the next step.

As encouragement, TV stations do announce that they are Equal Opportunity Employers, although hiring women film crew members remains minimal. To film an independent documentary for TV and then getting it shown and sponsored at a local station is an extremely risky venture. Most women will not take that risk. Recently, women have been accepted into union membership as assistant film directors. This step forward probably was nurtured by the realities of women making more movies in the 1970's than ever before, assisted by the concurrent advances in the feminist movement.

Nancy Littlefield was the first union assistant director (AD) in New York. She joined Local 161 of I.A.T.S.E. with the experience of working as AD on thousands of TV commercials and specials. She claims that an overriding calm is the first requisite for the AD job. The secret of her success? She can handle difficult directors. Significantly, she adds that she is where she is today because of men, not women. Alice Bell, another AD in New York, describes the woman AD's work situation: "Let's face it, you have to prove you're not there because you're the director's latest little ..." (Patricia Bosworth, "Women Assistant Directors," Action 9 [Jan.-Feb. 1974], page 31).

Women working independently could consider traveling the pornographic or erotic film route. With vast distribution, the spicy sex movie makes money, or at least recoups costs. Stephanie Rothman's Group Marriage (1972) instances this fact. Stephanie has formed her own corporation, Dimension Films, a distributing company, and with her husband assisting continues to make films. Expanded cinema's best documented practitioner is Carolee Schneeman. Her film _Fuses_ contains all the elements of a "stag" film, but incorporates none of the dispassion and prurience usually associated with that type of film. She calls herself a pioneer intermedia artist who has experimented with happenings, environmental projections, and "kinetic theatre."

The underground film, as Sheldom Renan defines it, variously called independent or "art" film, will continue to appeal to women for a variety of reasons. It may make an artistic statement, as in the films of Marie Menken, or a personal statement, as in the films of Joyce Wieland. As a low-budget, non-union labor of love, this type of film will continue to be made by women. Inevitably, this is the initial form of the film a woman does make.

Videotape remains a glittering question mark as a film field for women to work in. Its technical capabilities are being explored. To date, a distributable and profitable video film product has not been realized on a regional or national basis. However, women interested in video production have had access to video-production houses and experimental television centers. They have learned to use video synthesizers and computers in their VT productions. Many women, most notably Shirley Clarke, are active in VT.

The popularity of cable television in the early 1980's may prove to be a bonanza for women seeking a local apprenticeship, hands-on training. The doors to cable TV are not locked, and this facet of the film industry may prove to be the most promising for women who want to get involved in the image industry.

I have intended this book as an introductory salute to the women who, in my judgment, have made the best, most memorable, films. To all of the women planning and dreaming about making films--and to those already filmmaking--I say, "Hello out there! Keep on making films! Someday I hope to join you! Carry on!"

1. ALICE GUY-BLACHE: PHOTOPLAY PIONEER

Born: July 1, 1875, Saint-Mande, Paris, France
Died: March 24, 1968, Mahwah, New Jersey

> "It has long been a source of wonder to me that many
> women have not seized upon the wonderful opportunities
> offered to them by the motion picture art to make their
> way to fame and fortune as directors of photodramas."
> [Richard Koszarski, Hollywood Directors. New York:
> Oxford University Press, 1976, p. 8.]

The film that tells a story was probably "invented" by Alice Guy.
She was "the world's first woman director and possibly the first director of either sex to bring a story-film to the screen."[1] Yet no
one recognizes her name and her accomplishments. Critical notices
of her films made in the United States are lean or lacking. Histories of the cinema have been published without her name.

Presently, there is accumulating documentation that the film
industry as we know it now, stemmed, branched, and developed
from one very short film made in Paris by Alice Guy in 1896.
Many historians claim that Guy shares this first film feat with her
contemporaries in the cinema, Louis Lumière and Georges Méliès.
Guy herself counterclaims precedence. Recognition of Alice Guy-
Blaché as a photoplay pioneer gradually developed after her death in
1968, almost a century after her birth.

There are several accounts, including her own, that chronicle Mlle. Alice's first foray into filmmaking. Francis Lacassin
met her, wrote to her, and researched her films in Los Angeles and
New York, according to his article, "Out of Oblivion: Alice Guy
Blaché," Sight & Sound 40:3 (Summer 1971), pp. 151-154.

Lacassin cites her birthyear as 1873, and birthplace as Paris.
Anthony Slide disagrees: "Madama Blaché's daughter assured me it
was 1875,"[2] and the birthplace was Saint-Mande, the outskirts of
Paris.

Alice Guy was born into a comfortable middle-class family,
the youngest of four daughters of a book publisher. However, Lacassin informs us that the Guy family "was bankrupted on three separate
occasions, once as a result of an earthquake."[3] The Guy family
moved to Chile when Alice was four years old only to return to Paris
two years later. Alice was convent-educated. When her father died,

1

Mlle. Alice was determined to gain her financial independence. She learned shorthand-typing, an unusual feat for young ladies in those days. Her mother organized several groups for charity work; at one of these gatherings Mlle. Alice met Leon Gaumont's family. After this encounter, Mlle. Alice became Leon Gaumont's secretary.

Gaumont manufactured film and cameras.

> One day in 1895 Gaumont was visited by a customer from Lyons, Louis Lumière, who wanted Gaumont to see his experiments with photographs of moving objects. As they were leaving the office Lumière said to Gaumont's secretary: "Mademoiselle Alice, if this gadget interests you, come along too. " She found the moving shadows Lumière's "gadget" cast upon a sheet as fascinating as Gaumont did. [4]

Alice Guy-Blaché recalls, in an autobiographical excerpt "Alice Guy: La naissance du cinéma, " Image & Son 283 (April 1974), pages 42-53, that the first public presentation of motion film by Lumière's "gadget" was in the cellar of the Grand Cafe, 14 Boulevard of the Capucines with a paying audience of 33 customers. Charles Ford describes subsequent events:

> Not long after the first public presentation of Lumière's Cinematograph (December 1895) Alice Guy urged Gaumont to let her try her hand at making simple dramatic or comic scenes and not just photographs of real life. Gaumont accepted on the condition that her secretarial duties should not suffer. Thus, early in 1896, long before George Méliès, Alice Guy produced her first film: La Fée aux Choux. She herself appeared in it as did two friends whom she had dragooned. ... " The picture was shot "in Leon Gaumont's garden in front of his villa"[5] and not, as some have claimed, in a vacant lot adjoining the Gaumont studio on the Buttes Chaumont.

Lacassin describes the products made by Gaumont which required demonstration films of the kind that Mlle. Alice took it upon herself to make. In 1896, Gaumont made a 60mm camera. In 1897, he manufactured a 35mm combined camera-projector.

> This was followed in 1898 by an inexpensive machine designed solely for projection: the "Gaumont Chronophotographe, " mass-produced and aimed at film exhibitors. As an accessory for demonstration purposes, Gaumont had hitherto produced a few reels of factual or news footage. The success of his new machine obliged him to provide customers with fiction films along the lines of those made by Pathé. He entrusted his active secretary with the organisation of this new branch. With no resources and no qualified staff, Mademoiselle Alice decided to tackle the job herself. [6]

Lacassin continues his sketch, in a humorous vein, of the historic moments when the short story-film was made. Mlle. Alice put in place a few backdrops (woodcut cabbages) and pressed into service two sisters who were her friends, Yvonne and Germaine Mugnier-Serand. A photograph shows Alice, smiling and trousered, with a pretty young lady to her right and left, as actresses in the film. "In a picture postcard vein of humour, it tells the story of a woman who grows children in a cabbage patch. "[7]

Lacassin remarks: "When I spoke to her, Alice Guy claimed that she had started making films before Méliès. It seems unlikely, however, that Gaumont would have envisaged producing fiction films before they started mass-producing their projectors in 1898; or, at the very earliest, their combined camera-projector in 1897. "[8]

Blaché realized the impediments met by the attempt to sell Gaumont cameras using 60mm film. The photographic equipment would sell only if pictures could be made to hold the attention of an audience, educate it, entertain it. Photographic stills were inadequate; something more, something else was needed to attract customers to purchase Gaumont's picture-making equipment.

I had done a little in amateur theatre, and I thought I could do better. . . . Gathering up my courage, I timidly proposed to Gaumont that I would write one or two short plays and make them for the amusement of my friends. If the developments which evolved from this proposal could have been foreseen, then I probably never would have obtained this agreement. My youth, my lack of experience, my sex all conspired against me. . . . [9]

Blaché describes her typical workday: secretarial duties in tandem with travel to her filming location and back again to complete office work before returning home in late evening. When Gaumont became aware of her commuting time, he established a filming studio for her behind a photo shop. Blaché observes that trade unions for film workers did not exist in 1896. Workdays were long and workweeks were six and seven days. It was under these conditions that she made her first film. She used costumes from sources available to her. She asked carpenters to cut out wooden rows of "cabbages" for scenery. She commandeered her friends, a bawling baby, a concerned-looking mother, and, at that moment, her initial effort, La Fée aux Choux (The Cabbage Fairy) saw the light of day. "It is now a classic; the negative is preserved by the Cinémathèque Française. "[10] Gaumont soon permitted her to relinquish her office work.

Blaché's daughter, Simone Blaché, recalls her mother's work experiences at Gaumont. A Turkish dignitary once visited Gaumont. He wanted a camera made of solid gold. Gaumont made it and sold it to him. An inventor himself, Leon Gaumont was receptive to the proposals and ideas of others. When the Lumière brothers' invention came to his attention, he had to inspect and investigate it him-

self. Then he made one like theirs, a mechanism that produced
motion pictures. He and his staff members experimented with it,
Simone Blaché reports. It appeared to her mother that Gaumont
and his associates couldn't find a purpose for it. They did not treat
the machine seriously.

One day, Simone Blaché continues, her mother asked permission of Gaumont to try to work the camera herself. A surprised
Gaumont agreed, sighing that it was like a toy for children. According to Simone Blaché, that was the day her mother "filmed the
fairy-tale of how children are born in cabbages."11

The question of precedence--who was the first to make a fictional film, Méliès, Blaché, Lumière, or others?--may remain in
dispute for lack of impartial documentation. There is no debate regarding Blaché's position as the world's first woman film director.
The debate pertains to the use of the motion picture as a storytelling,
fictional medium. That the lives and endeavors of Blaché and Méliès paralleled and may have merged in the creation of fictional filmmaking, each working independently, increases the difficulty of assigning the pioneer role.

> With a career spanning 1896 to 1920, her exploratory work
> in film as a storytelling medium parallels that of Georges
> Méliès (1861-1938), generally credited not only as the first
> great film fantasist but also as the first to develop narra-
> tive techniques.... Méliès' magic-trick films were imi-
> tated in England by G. A. Smith in 1898 and by the London
> maker of scientific instruments, Robert W. Paul, in 1899.
> Alice Guy, however, also began making fantasy films dur-
> ing this period, and she claimed that she had begun before
> Méliès.12

Richard Henshaw draws a historical parallel between Méliès
and Blaché also:

> Alice Guy was not merely the first woman filmmaker; she
> was in fact an authentic motion picture pioneer both in the
> expansion of a film aesthetic and in the development of the
> new art's technical possibilities.... The problems she
> faced were not unlike those of Georges Méliès, whose
> chronology in the years before 1900 was roughly parallel
> to Guy's. There were no studios in which to film "con-
> trived scenes." The possibility that an audience existed
> for such untested kinds of films was unknown; visually-
> oriented material was found only in some forms of theatre
> or variety (such as Méliès' magic shows); and aside from
> those forms, what was there in the realm of possibilities
> that could express the idiosyncracies of a new art to a
> pre-conditioned lay public? In France, the "contrived
> scenes" of Guy, Méliès, and Ferdinand Zecca of Pathé
> were the premier efforts in the establishment of a narra-
> tive cinema. Guy's importance in this regard should hence-

forth be understood and synthesized into the annals of film history, and Méliès' ultimate position as the more inventive of the two should not obscure Guy's prominence as an instigator of fictional film. ... [13]

Ephraim Katz, in his reference The Film Encyclopedia (New York: Crowell, 1979), comments that Guy's first film "preceded Méliès' story films by a few months, according to several authoritative French historians, although others claim that the film wasn't made until 1900 or even later. "[14]

What is certain is that Blaché and Méliès as contemporary cinematographers developed prominent careers for themselves remarkably similar in the imaginative use of the camera for capturing on film, with and without sound, what had never before been presented to the attention of an audience.

Gaumont allowed Mlle. Alice to forget her office tasks. "Between 1896 and 1901 she made dozens of little films for Gaumont. " Among these were The First Cigarette, The Sneak Thief, and The Courier of Lyon. Their average length was 75 feet. In The First Cigarette, Mlle. Alice concentrated on one actor.

Lacassin describes this film of 60 meters, released in 1904: "... Shows in semi close-up the reactions, as observed by his terrified sister, of a boy sneakily smoking a cigarette.... " Lacassin adds: "She advanced to longer and longer films with larger and larger casts. "[15]

Richard Koszarski capsules her accomplishments in this decade of work: "She established Gaumont's filmmaking arm, produced nearly all the films made by them through 1906 (specializing in the talking Chronophone films), and trained such future luminaries of the French cinema as Feuillade and Jasset.... "

From her first innocent effort, Mlle. Alice found herself directing films of all types with live performers. Lacassin categorizes them as fairy tales, fantasies, comedies, religious parables, trick films, myths, paintings coming alive. She hired acrobats, vaudeville performers, and famous clowns for her productions. Many of them were characterized by cinematic tricks, according to Charles Ford, "usually attributed to Méliès.... In Pierrot's Christmas she used masking and double exposure, and in A House Demolished and Rebuilt she ran film backward.... "

Blaché states that Gaumont's technical advisor Frederic Dillaye and her staff helped her discover, employ, and refine these tricks in her films. In amused accents, she recounts her trials and errors on the job, many of them uproariously funny. "... In experience acquired day by day, by mistake, by chance, I discovered small tricks such as: Film turned inside out allows a house to collapse and be reconstructed like magic. A person can tumble from a roof and go back up again instantly.... "[16]

Anthony Slide summarizes the start of Mlle. Alice's career in these words:

> Apparently, every motion picture produced by Gaumont until 1905 was directed by Alice Guy. In that year, needing additional assistance, Alice Guy hired Ferdinand Zecca as a director, Victorin Jasset as an assistant and Louis Feuillade as a writer. In so doing, it seems almost as if, with one almighty stroke, she had created the entire early French film industry.... "[17]

In 1901 Gaumont built a studio for making films up to 150 feet in length. An assistant named Denizot became a casting director for films with historical and religious themes. "In 1902 she produced Passion, which ran almost to the then unusual length of 2000 feet. Many historians have credited Passion to Victorin Jasset, ... but Passion was shown at the Société de Photographie Française under her name. "[18]

Blaché relates the mishaps and misunderstandings that occurred during the filming of Esmeralda (1905), based on Victor Hugo's novel The Hunchback of Notre Dame. The sets were painted incongruously; special effects worked improperly. Instead of a drama, her picture became a farce. All that had gone wrong was Mlle. Alice's fault.

The Life of Christ (1905), her next assignment, used 25 sets and 300 extras. That same year, Gaumont was manufacturing and marketing the Chronophone, which, in Slide's description, "synchronized a projector with sound recorded on a wax cylinder.... "[19] The talking picture had arrived, and Gaumont had always believed in films with sound. Lacassin describes this remarkable Chronophone as "combined sound recorded on a wax cylinder with the filmed image, and throughout 1906 and until the spring of 1907, Alice Guy was kept busy directing some hundred films for the Chronophone. Rarely more than a minute or two long, they mostly featured singers in performance or tableaux accompanied by choral singing. "[20] Charles Ford appends operational detail on the creation of these initial Gaumont-Guy mini-movies:

> Their first talking picture was made on the grounds of the Gaumont studio with Pedro Gailhard, who was then director of the Paris Opera. Other early sound films made by Miss Guy ... consisted of scenes from Carmen, Mignon, Manon and Les Dragons de Villars, and still others used such popular singers as Dranem, Polin, and Mayol.... "[21]

Just as Alice Guy pioneered in silent pictures, so "it fell to Alice Guy to pioneer 'talking pictures,' of which she directed more than a hundred during 1906 and early 1907. "[22] Surprisingly, Anthony Slide comments, "there appears to be doubt as to whether these early experimental films were successful. Certainly, it was not until December, 1910, that 'Filmparlants' were demonstrated, satisfactorily, to the Académie des Sciences in Paris.... "[23]

However, Mlle. Alice did not lose interest in making silent films.

> In 1906, eager to film the bullfights at Nimes, she de-
> cided to take advantage of the trip to film adaptations
> from Provençal literature. Feuillade ... was allowed to
> work on the direction of certain films (among them
> Mireille...) whenever the shooting involved practical dif-
> ficulties for a woman. Such as? "Climbing up into a tree,
> for instance," Alice Guy explains. Although the first nega-
> tive of Mireille was damaged, the month-long trip was
> both productive and agreeable. 24

An English cameraman of French descent, who had been in charge of Gaumont's London office, joined the film crew of Mirielle, hoping to learn film directing from watching Feuillade and Guy at work. In short order, Herbert Blaché-Bolton and Alice Guy met, a romantic rapport developed, and they were engaged to be married on Christmas Day, 1906. "Not long after this month-long location trip, she married Blaché. In 1907 she temporarily abandoned di- recting to accompany her husband to Cleveland, where he attempted to supply Gaumont products to American distributors. Alice Guy's replacement at Gaumont in France was Feuillade.... "25

Gaumont had sold the U.S. rights to the Chronophone to a pair of Cleveland, Ohio businessmen, and Herbert's task was to set up the branch office. When the Cleveland office failed, Gaumont re- claimed the U.S. rights and assigned the Blachés (who dropped the Bolton on their American arrival) to Flushing, N.Y., "where [Her- bert] bought a small factory and had it converted to a studio for the production of sound pictures. "26

Herbert Blaché's assignment was not to make films. Gau- mont's foreign branches were supposed to function as distribution agencies and laboratories. Blaché exhibited Gaumont films to Amer- ican exhibitors and took orders for them. Paris would send him the negatives and he would make as many copies as needed.

The unemployed Mme. Blaché, learning to speak English, gave birth to a daughter, Simone, in 1908. Sometime later, a son, Reginald, was born. In 1910, bored with domesticity, Mme. Blaché returned to the studio. "Since the studio was used only a few days a week Alice Blaché decided to produce silent pictures there with a staff she hastily recruited for the purpose. "27 Her recruits were Melville, an ex-U.S. Cavalry officer who could speak French; Henri Menessier, who had directed pictures for her under Gaumont; and an accountant, Mr. Bauries. While Herbert worked at the Gaumont office on Congress Avenue in Flushing, Mme. Blaché made movies, cowboy westerns, thrillers, historical romances, and mysteries, in the countryside nearby. With Melville's assistance, Alice Blaché made a few military movies using the resources of the U.S. Cavalry. These were sent to be developed and printed in the Paris laboratory of Gaumont also, proving to be so successful with audiences that Mme. Blaché was encouraged to start her own film studio.

Lacassin explains that Herbert Blaché was still under contract to Gaumont, this firm declining to finance filmmaking in the
United States, so that Mme. Blaché's sole path was to strike out
on her own. Where would her customers come from? Perhaps
they could be found among those Herbert contacted to rent Gaumont
films. Assigning herself the titles of president and director-in-
chief, Alice Blaché set up the Solax Company, with a blazing sun
as its trademark. The new firm's business director was George
A. Magie, with an office at 147 Fourth Avenue, corner 14th Street,
in Manhattan, open for business September 7, 1910.

Blaché had come to realize that the American public wanted
films catering to its specific tastes and acted by American artists.
Blaché was determined that the Solax Company's films would fulfill
this mission: in the four years of its existence, Solax released 325
films, of which 35 to 50 were directed by her. The remaining
were directed by Edward Warren and Harry Shenk.

Solax's first release was A Child's Sacrifice (1910), starring
Magda Foy, the "Solax Kid." Lacassin condenses the plot centering
on an eight-year-old girl:

> Her father is a worker out on strike and her mother is
> ill, so she tries to sell her doll to a junk-dealer. Seeing
> her distress, he buys the toy and then gives it back to
> her as a present. The little girl does not content her-
> self with bringing a few pennies into the starving house-
> hold; she also intervenes to prevent bloodshed in a quarrel
> provoked by the strike. 28

In Falling Leaves (1911), a young girl is once again the central character. In it, the child tries to arrest the death of her
older sister by tuberculosis by placing tree leaves back on branches
because she has heard her sister's physician speculate that her sister could die by autumn's end. In the Solax production Hotel Honeymoon (1912) the moon comes alive to smile at earthly lovers.

One Solax film definitely proved to be directed by Mme.
Blaché was The Violin Maker of Nuremberg (Dec. 22, 1911). A
pair of apprentice violin-makers dominate this romantic concoction.
Both love their instructor's daughter. When a contest is held "to
determine who will win the girl, ... the better apprentice of the
two, knowing that she really loves his rival, substitutes his violin
for his competitor's."29

A review of this film commends it as "a story of tender
sentiment told amid scenes of artistic quaintness. It carries a
simple sentimental thread in a skillful manner that never descends
to the commonplace, and, at the same time, holds the interest with
its dignity and artistic charm."30

Released April 10, 1912, and attributed to Mme. Blaché, The
Detective's Dog satirized melodramas of the day by focusing on a

dog running to rescue its master tied to a sawmill and threatened
with death.   In 1912, Solax ventured into the science-fiction film:
in its production In the Year 2000, women rule the world.   The director of this work remains undetermined.

At this time, there were 15,000 motion-picture theatres in
the United States, and Solax thrived, trying to maintain its production
levels.   Mme. Blaché decided to build a studio for Solax at Fort
Lee, close to the Pathé and Eclair studios.   Film reporter Hugh
Hoffman wrote in Moving Picture World,

> the entire studio and factory were planned by Alice Bla-
> ché, the presiding genius of the Solax Company.   The
> factory included carpentry shops, prop rooms, hotel-like
> dressing rooms, an area set aside for men (with pinochle
> table and cuspidors), a main floor large enough to accom-
> modate five stage sets, laboratories, darkrooms and pro-
> jection rooms. 31

The building was planned for a printing capacity of 16,000
feet of positive film a day.   A large studio in the building had two-
story high windows facing south.   At a cost of $100,000 to build,
the studio was located on Lemoyne Avenue, "slightly west of what
is today the Fort Lee Bridge Plaza. "32   It was probably the best
equipped moving picture plant in the world.

Why did she choose Fort Lee as the site for Solax's studio?
Of course, many film studios already were located there.   Calvin
Thomas Beck claims Fort Lee was initially selected as an ideal
site for filming serials, or "cliff-hangers. "   "Fort Lee was picked
as the site of these early cliff-hangers because the Jersey Palisades
provided one hell of a cliff to hang from. "33

Prior to opening her new studio building, Mme. Blaché presented a "special Solax evening on Broadway, attended by many New
York film personalities at Weber's Theatre. "34   The date was
February 12, 1912.   In this year she filmed two movies based on
operas: Fra Diavolo and Mignon, each consisting of three reels,
with accompaniment by orchestra.

A spate of thriller films issued from Solax in swift succession.   In The Sewer, set designer Henri Menessier dug trenches
and constructed pools in proximate undeveloped land as the locale
for an honest-to-goodness attack by live sewer rats on the hapless
hero.   The rats were first trained by an animal expert.   In a
scene for Mickey's Pal (March 1912), Mme. Blaché astounded viewers on the set with an unprecedented act: she set afire a three-
year-old Barracq automobile for a crime scene.   This scene was
directed by Edward Warren at husband Herbert's request.   Understandably, Herbert was alarmed at his wife's directing scenes involving acrobats performing on the struts of the Brooklyn Bridge
and setting off explosives herself.   Most frightening was Mme.
Blaché's use of a tigress Sarah (a photo shows Mme. Blaché ca-

ressing it) in a film, especially when Sarah escaped from her cage, roamed the countryside eluding its pursuers, only to seek shelter at a convent where the Blachés' daughter was a student.   Mme. Blaché herself coaxed Sarah back into the cage. [35]

How did Mme. Blaché conduct herself when she was not chasing tigers and setting fires?

> She quietly moves about the plant, unostentatiously and un-obtrusively energetic.   She carries with her an air of re-finement and culture, and her dark, modest clothes be-speak and emphasize her dignity....   Although Madame has decided ideas, and at times will obstinately insist that they be carried out, she is always too willing to listen to suggestions. [36]

She was liked, not susceptible to flattery, and ready to admit her own errors.

In her macabre thriller the Shadows of Moulin Rouge (1913), which she directed, wrote, and produced in four reels, bodies, dead and alive, were switched.   The Pit and the Pendulum (1913), based on Edgar Allan Poe's story, followed.   Actors who worked steadily for Solax appeared in it: Blanche Cornwall, Billy Quirk, Claire Whitney, and Darwin Karr.

Herbert Blaché directed another 1913 thriller, The Star of India.   The star is a precious gem removed from a Buddha's fore-head.   Each successive owner of the star meets with an unexpected and horrible demise.   This film was the first production released under the aegis of Blaché Features, Inc., which superseded the So-lax Company.   For some time, Herbert Blaché had asked to be re-leased from his tenure to the Gaumont firm.   Once again a free agent, he founded, in October 1913, the new company of which he was president and his wife, vice-president.   Solax ceased its pro-duction schedule October 31, 1914.   However, five films made un-der the Solax trademark were released by Blaché Features, Inc., the initial one being The Star of India.

In 1913, Edward Warren directed one of Solax's most suc-cessful movies.   The Beasts of the Jungle cost $18,000 and four weeks to make.   The studio became an East Indian locale "and the treasure-laden hills of the Transvaal....   A menagerie of jungle animals and birds was brought to Fort Lee.   This film was such a success that every studio copied the format. "[37]

With Mme. Blaché's penchant for animals, it appears natural for Solax to have made Dick Whittington and the Cat (1913).   This project required an army of rats, a cast of 200, and 26 sets.   The Equine Spy (1912), an historical horse movie, was made in the Fort Lee studio.   This Civil War drama starred "Don, " Solax's equestrian performer.

Herbert Blaché's specific plans for Blaché Features were to make only dramas, particularly adventure tales, in four reels or longer. But Blaché Features, Inc. enjoyed only a brief tenure; from November 1913 to November 1914 just fourteen films were made and released, nine of them directed by Mme. Blaché. These include The Monster and the Girl and Woman of Mystery. In the latter, a disembodied soul dictates a detective to perform acts of crime. In Dream Woman (1914) based on a Wilkie Collins' novel, a man dreams of a woman who threatens him with death.

By now, Mme. Blaché was a celebrity of sorts, even though she did not seek publicity. Once discovered by the press, she was photographed working on the set, megaphone in hand, a hood on her head to protect her from the sun. The "charming Frenchwoman whose gentleness on the set disguised such astonishing energy" was quoted and described in trade publications regularly, and addressed as Madame Blaché. [38] What she did not tell them was that she mingled with the audiences at her movies, incognito, to obtain first-hand reactions and criticisms. That longer films were both popular and profitable soon became evident.

Herbert Blaché formed a new company in April 1914, setting up the U.S. Amusement Company with $500,000. Mme. Blaché was vice-president and its managing director was Joseph Shear. The new company's purpose was to make longer feature films.

As Paul C. Spehr explains in The Movies Begin: Making Movies in New Jersey, 1887-1920 (Newark, N.J.: Newark Museum, 1977, page 82):

> In 1914, when longer productions were becoming popular, the Blachés organized a new company, United States Amusement Co., to produce feature films. These films soon proved to be more dominant in their production schedule than the short films which they had been making. As a consequence, they dissolved their own distribution system and began releasing their features through companies such as Pathé Exchange and Metro Pictures.

This time, Herbert documented the company goals in a

> ... manifesto entitled The Life of a Photodrama: the time had come to acknowledge the development of the cinema, to make it more of an art form and to produce masterpieces.... The company was proposing mainly to adapt plays which would be performed--and this was the innovatory part of the project--by actors who had successfully appeared in them on the stage.... [39]

Most of the U.S. Amusement Company productions were directed by Herbert Blaché. The initial venture was The Chimes, based on Charles Dickens' story. The Mystery of Edwin Drood was released next. Mme. Blaché directed only three films, all re-

leased in 1917: The Adventurer, based upon Upton Sinclair's novel;
The Empress; and A Man and a Woman, adapted from Emile Zola's
Nana.   Anthony Slide states that The Empress was released under
the label of Popular Players and Plays, yet another company founded
by Herbert, headquartered in New York.   Its films were released
through Alco, a subsidiary of Metro Pictures.

That the press was aware of Mme. Blaché's abilities is evidenced in warm, but brief, praise.   The New York Dramatic Mirror (March 3, 1917) commented on The Empress: "The direction
of this picture done by Madame Blaché further establishes her reputation as an able producer. " A review from The Moving Picture
World (March 24, 1917) asserts, "This reviewer has yet to see a
picture by Madame Blaché that was not sincerely and artistically directed and this, The Adventurer, one of her recent productions is
no exception. "

Her citation in Who's Who in the Motion-Picture World in
1915 credits the introduction of the longer feature film to U. S. audiences to her.

> Mme. Alice Blaché ... is probably the best-known woman
> executive and producer in the motion-picture world. ...
> [She] writes and directs practically all of her productions.
> She started the production of multiple reels in this coun-
> try, and to her the credit is due for many of the best-
> known features produced in the early days of feature pro-
> ductions. ... 40

Lacassin clarifies the dizzying procession of company names
under which Mme. Blaché directed her films.   From the autumn of
1914 to August 1917, she was in charge of producing a dozen films
directed by others, while directing ten five-reel movies herself.
From Solax to Blaché Features, Inc. to the U. S. Amusement Company to Popular Players and Plays, both Blachés worked without
respite.   Herbert was production director for the films The Girl
with Green Eyes (1916) and Shadows of a Great City (1915).   Alice
directed Spring of the Year (1917) on location in the Florida Ever-
glades, and films starring an actress with a Russian name (though
of British birth), Madame Olga Petrova.   The two women worked
together on The Tigress (1914) and The Heart of a Painted Woman
(1915).

Petrova met both Blachés in Lawrence Weber's office.   Weber was president of Popular Players and Plays.   "I liked them both
but was instinctively drawn to her. " Petrova admits she knew
nothing about making motion pictures.   That a woman film director
might be considered an oddity never occurred to the actress.   "I
asked if she might direct me and was told she would be pleased to
do so. "41

Petrova describes her first day at work, starting with a fer-
ry ride with her car and chauffeur across the Hudson River to Fort

Lee.   Upon arrival at 8:30 a. m. , Mme. Blaché greeted her warmly.
She was escorted to her dressing room and asked her preferences
on the lunch menu.   On the set, Mme. Blaché described what each
episode, or scene, contained in words and actions.   Although Petrova had read the story of the film before accepting the assignment
she recalled that it had had no dialogue with appropriate action in
it.   These basic elements were added by the director, Petrova discovered.   Speech and movement for the stage were surprisingly different from talking and moving on a movie set before the camera's
eye.   The large, massive cameras appeared to Petrova like huge
monsters.

Mme. Blaché's polite and softly-voiced directions maintained
serenity and a steady flow of photographic shots.   Even when an actor might change Mme. Blaché's instructions, she permitted it, as
long as the sense of the scene and story was not impaired.   She
corrected her cast members politely.   When the director was not
pleased with the rehearsals, the scene was repeated as many times
as necessary until she called "camera. "

When all the scenes on the set were completed, the close-
ups were done.   Under the burning Kleig lights, Petrova's eyes
teared, her skin flamed, and her hair bristled.   This concluded the
workday and, Petrova records, "Madame looked, and was, tired. "[42]
Mme. Blaché's firm-handed direction was sheathed in a silken glove.
According to Petrova, the director never lost her temper, argued,
or created tension or disagreement in her workforce.   Her working
manners never altered.

After a workday on movie sets, the Blachés' evenings were
consumed with writing scripts.   Mme. Blaché declared her own approach to creating scenarios as imaginative and tending toward fantasy, while her husband took a realistic view of their scripts, perceptive of their boxoffice merits.   They tried writing a script about
child labor and its horrors, pondering the production, casting, and
financial elements involved.   Whether the film was made or not is
unknown.

In 1917 Mme. Blaché was asked to lecture on film directing
to students and faculty at Columbia University.   She recommended
that her husband or a staff director fulfill the speaking engagement.
She felt her speaking knowledge of English was inadequate for the
occasion.   However, the university spokesperson wanted her because she was a woman.   She found an audience of 3, 000 waiting
for her lecture and temporarily lost her voice before she could begin.   Afterwards, students and instructors formed a ring round her,
asking questions and praising her film works.

Several acquaintanceships with professors developed, and Mrs.
Blaché discussed with them the possibility of founding a small movie
university at which the full spectrum of filmmaking would be taught
and exercised.   Although agreeing with the soundness of her concept,
no action was taken.

Mme. Blaché befriended a Columbia University sociology professor with a scandalous reputation. Prof. Rose Pastor Stock was a birth control advocate, provoking Mme. Blaché's interest and concern. When Blaché visited Prof. Stock at her small home, she found her in her garden working, carelessly dressed. Convinced of the merits of Prof. Stock's views, Mme. Blaché was determined to make a movie to promote the birth control cause. When Mme. Blaché took her concepts for this film to Selznick (she records no initial or first name), he laughed in her face. No movie was made.

The economic situation for independent film companies during World War I and its wake was treacherous and increasingly complex. An analysis by George Mitchell of the artistic and financial alterations in the movie business appears in Ciné-Tracts 2:2 (Spring 1979). "The Consolidation of the American Film Industry 1915-1920 (Part One)" and Part Two in the succeeding issue chronicle the shifts from small independents, like the Blaché's enterprise, to major corporations that engulfed them or drove them out of business.

Mitchell identifies the dynamic impetus forcing this grand-scale change "to concentrate production and profits in the hands of relatively few firms. "[43]

Longer feature films did cost more to make, but the longer movie, in itself, was not responsible for the cataclysmic mutation. Mitchell aligns costs of film production in specific years. "Using 1908 production costs, a 10-reel film running about two hours could be made for about $5000.... In 1914, however, the new Paramount Company was contracting with independent producers, paying them $25,000 per film plus a generous cut of the rentals. "[44]

By 1920, Mitchell observes, the average cost of a feature film ranged near $200,000. "This incredible inflation in the cost of film production was not a matter of longer films but of a much more expensive film, the Hollywood Style. "[45] Mitchell defines the Hollywood Style as the start of a plan assisting a few businesses to rule the international markets for movie entertainment. Mitchell attributes the startling increase in movie production costs from 1910 to 1920 to "the introduction, piece by piece, of a whole new kind of film. "[46]

Moviemaking had always been an extremely profitable enterprise. To reach the highest levels of profit required unlimited financial resources, expertly managed corporate structures, huge studios permitting shooting all year round, and, above all, in Mitchell's estimate, "solid control over production, distribution and exhibition. "[47] Any entrepreneur who could arrange this constellation of elements and work them would be assured of dominating the movie market to the point of radically diminishing all competitors' returns.

Mitchell quotes George Zukor, a leading producer, in a sum-

mation of the movie business scene in 1918:   "'... of 250 producers
it is said that only ten are making money; of these ten, four are
making millions.'"[48]

Earlier in the century, several attempts were made to dominate the movie market with patent claims, such as the Edison Company's well-publicized battle to control camera and projection equipment. Mitchell mentions a stronger and more complex monopoliza-
tion try by the Motion Picture Patents Company, which was formed
in 1909. The MPPC tried to regulate filmmaking by authorizing
only seven United States firms and two firms abroad the right to
make films, on the basis of filming patents. Small companies making movies, such as the Blachés' Solax and its successors simply
ignored the machinations of the MPPC. Exhibitors ignored it, too.
The fact that surfaced from this struggling and sparring for profits
was that some other technique had to be found "to lock up the
market, " in Mitchell's words.[49]

By identifying a film as a product of a specific studio, movie
audiences could be trained to expect and enjoy a certain type of entertainment. Using a director with a name and employing actors
and actresses were successful ploys to sell tickets. Identifying the
movie product--at the same time excluding newcomers from entering the moviemaking business--was achieved by advertising the personalities of those engaged in making the movies. As Mitchell concludes, magazines and newspapers flourished for the sole purpose
of whetting the audiences' appetites for films in which directors and
actresses and actors were personalities whose lives and loves were
chronicled and portrayed in photographs and glowing prose. This
movie press, of course, was amply supported by the expanding film
industry itself.

Mitchell concludes somberly that what the patent monopoly
efforts failed to achieve, the Hollywood Style movie and its production methods coupled with the hard-nosed race to rule the movie
marketplace did succeed in achieving. The Blachés and their competitors were forced out of business.

The Blachés' decline began when they rented the Solax studio
to Apollo Pictures in 1917. A few years later they sold it, and
the building was torn down in 1920. As Lacassin reports: "By
1917 it was already impossible for independents to survive and the
future belonged to the big companies, as the Blachés were to discover to their cost.... "[50] But Mme. Blaché continued to direct
films for other companies. From a scenario written by Agnes
Johnston, she directed Bessie Love in The Great Adventure for
Pathé. It was released March 10, 1918. For Popular Players and
Plays, she directed a movie based on a poem by Robert Service,
and two films based on novels, Michael Strogoff (1917) and What
Will People Say? (1917).

Many other film studios abandoned Fort Lee at this juncture,
moving west to more favorable climates, Southern California being
the chosen locale for surviving companies.

Tarnished Reputations (1920) was the last film Mme. Blaché
directed. Not considered a success, it was described in a review
in The Exhibitor's Trade Review as "five reels of anguish." Variety (April 9, 1920) noted that the screenplay by Leonce Perret
smacked of Parisian melodrama not favored by American audiences.
When Mme. Blaché was offered the job of directing Tarzan of the
Apes, she refused.

A curious and haunting fact is mentioned by Thomas Calvin
Beck in his description of the declining years of the Blaché partnership. They had helped Metro Pictures in its infancy by arranging
to have their pictures, from March 1915 to 1918, distributed by the
small firm which later became Metro-Goldwyn-Mayer: "a humble
and unintentional contribution to the birth of a giant."[51]

Sadly, the marital partnership of the Blachés disintegrated with
the collapse of their business and careers. Mme. Blaché, writing
a letter from Brussels to Films in Review (May 1964, page 137),
acknowledges: "In '22 the Trust offered to buy Solax but we refused because they wouldn't pay all cash. That was a great mistake.... " In that year, 1922, the marriage was dissolved. Her
daughter, Simone, declares, "When her marriage broke apart ...
I saw her almost on the point of committing suicide."[52]

Now she could find no work other than writing résumés of
movies for magazine publication. She returned to France with her
two children, seeking to establish herself in the film industry there.
But without prints of her films, as a no longer young woman, she
could not find a job. Her daughter recalls: "Mother was really
cherished in the United States.... The situation in France was
quite the reverse."[53] Herbert continued directing movies until the
advent of the talking picture. Mme. Blaché never made another
film.

In 1927, Mme. Blaché returned to the United States to
search for her films. She visited the Library of Congress and
several film depositories for evidence of her accomplishments--
only to find nothing. Regarding surviving films made by Mme.
Blaché, Anthony Slide maintains none of her Solax-label productions
have been preserved, except for a half dozen one-reel works in the
National Collection at the Library of Congress.

An undated program of The Museum of Modern Art Department of Film in New York, however, in an Early Women Directors
viewing, lists A House Divided (a 1913 Solax film) coupled with Her
Defiance (1916) directed by Cleo Madison and Joe King, a Universal/
Rex production. Program notes state that six Solax films directed
by Blaché, including A House Divided, presumably are preserved
in the Library of Congress's American Film Institute Collection.

Seven films by Alice Guy-Blaché were shown in a film festival according to "Movie Classics: Pacific Film Archive" in City
of San Francisco (February 4, 1976, page 46). Commenting that

Mme. Blaché quite possibly could have been the first person to "use the motion picture to tell a story, " the article also reveals that several Solax titles have been discovered in private collections of films. Charles Tarbox, of Film Classic Exchange, assembled six movies either directed or produced by Mme. Blaché: Her Double, Officer Henderson, Our Poor Relations, Idol Worshipper, The Marvelous Cow, and Hater of Women/His Better Self. These films date from the same time phase as A House Divided, the 1912-1914 period. Possibly, more Blaché films will be identified and shown as the work of film historians progresses.

In the late twenties, Mme. Blaché supported herself by producing several conferences at universities dealing with the subject of feminine psychology and filmmaking. She would report the proceedings of these to European newspapers. Whether these conferences were oriented toward a feminist point-of-view can only be guessed at. What is certain is that Mme. Blaché steadfastly held to the view that women had the right to a career and marriage, that she inspired many of her female contemporaries to begin careers of their own, and that, as a filmmaker, she was widely respected by the men who held positions of power in the movie business. Her daughter, Simone, has said that her mother knew she had to claim credit for her film work and that she devoted years of effort and energy to correct historians' records, and to assure herself of the place she had earned in the history of film.

In 1953, Mme. Blaché left her California residence to return to Paris. In her native city, at the age of 78, she was honored as the first woman filmmaker in the world, at the Cinémathèque Française. The program was broadcast and televised. At this ceremony of the Society of Authors and Composers she was made a knight of the Legion of Honor. "It was a very great day in her life, of course, "[54] Simone assures us.

Mme. Blaché made her home with her daughter, who worked as a secretary in American Foreign Service at posts in Brussels, various foreign cities, and Washington, D. C. In the capital, sculptor Gladys Moon Jones created a bust of Mme. Blaché. Upon Simone's retirement from the diplomatic service in 1964, mother and daughter settled in Mahwah, New Jersey. Four years later, Mme. Blaché died there in a nursing home, with no newspaper obituaries recording the fact, in the state where the second half of her career took place. She was 95 years old.

How many films did she actually make? What were her contributions to the film, as industry and as art? Accurate attribution may be out of the question: many of her films were cited as works by others. No one realized and tried to correct published errors more assiduously than Mme. Blaché herself. She anticipated that directing and producing credits for her films would be falsely assigned to her co-workers. She knew that her name, unintentionally or purposefully, would be omitted or ignored or demoted in the histories of French and American film.

Mme. Blaché instances the case of her co-worker Zecca's film The Misdeeds of a Calf's Head being mistakenly attributed to her! Lacassin corrects this: "For a long time this was the only film actually attributed to Alice Guy, although by her own account it was one of the few Gaumont pictures that she didn't make. The source of this historical error lies with the reminiscences of Etienne Arnaud.... "55

Mme. Blaché once approached film historian Georges Sadoul "and showed him documents by which I tried to persuade him that the films in question were my work. He promised to correct this in his next edition, which in all honesty he did so, but his list, once again, contained errors. "56

Lacassin reports that Esmeralda and The Life of Christ directed by Mme. Blaché are credited in most reference books to Victorin Jasset. Mme. Blaché explains the circumstances of this mistake: "M. Sadoul ... was poorly informed and in all good faith no doubt ... attributed my first films to those who were at the Gaumont studios as figureheads, ignoring my name.... "57

A look at Sadoul's most recent work supports her statement. Histoire de l'art du cinéma dès origines à nos jours (Paris: Ernest Flammarion, 1949) cites Alice Guy as secretary to Gaumont on page 58, and creator of the "cabbage film. " Peter Cowie in his Seventy Years of Cinema (New York: A. S. Barnes, 1969), states on page 17 among his indexing of cinema history for 1896: "As the late Georges Sadoul emphasized, Lumière may have founded the cinematograph, but Méliès established the cinema, and those are two very different things. " The name linking Lumière's invention with Méliès' institution is missing: Alice Guy-Blaché, who implemented the idea of a story on film.

Tardy, but very welcome, recognition of the work of Mme. Blaché is arriving. Her autobiography has been published. Francis Lacassin intends to write a book, tentatively titled, "Les femmes et la mise en scène de 1895 à 1930. " He lists Mme. Blaché's voluminous harvest of a quarter century's service to the silent and talking movie as

> ... approximately two hundred reels between 20 and 680 metres long ... up to 1906; more than 70 two-reelers and features between 1910 and 1920. She founded and directed, or contributed to the founding in the United States, of four production companies and one distribution company. She took on the Edison Trust, by braving their ban on productions over two reels long.... "58

Mme. Blaché was the first, or among the first, of fictional film makers who assisted in the creation of a new art form and an international industry based on imagery, simply by photographing herself and two friends in a cabbage patch, thereby capturing more than a few meters of mischief and a magical realm of make-believe.

FILMOGRAPHY

A. Films Made in France and Spain, 1896-1907*

The Cabbage Fairy (1896)

Black Maria (1897)

He (1897)

The Mummy (1897)

The Bewitched Fiancé (1897)

I Have a Maybug in My Trousers (1897)

The Pranks of Pierrette (1897)

Moving out in the Night (1897-1906)

Ballet of Monkeys (1897-1906)

Pierrot's Christmas (1897-1906)

Midnight (1897-1906)

The Enchanted Bean (1897-1906)

Delightful Rustle (1897-1906)

Legend of St. Nicholas (1897-1906)

The Dangers of Alcohol (1899)

The Dance of the Seasons... (1901)

Cavalry Officers and Shopgirls (1901)

Passion (1902)

The Willing Sacrifice (1903)

Thugs Are Not Lucky (1903)

The First Cigarette (1904)

Assassination of the Courier of Lyons (1904)

Infants' Abduction by Gypsies (1904)

The Crime on Church Street (1904)

Baptism of a Puppet (1904)

Young Painters (1904)

The Small Cutters of Bois-Vert (1904)

Relubitation (Rehabilitation) (1904)

Paris Night (1905)

The Crinoline (1905)

*Several films of this period have no specific year cited for release, thus two years or the entire time phase is given.

A Wedding at Lake St. Fargeau (1905)

Vendetta (1905)

Esmeralda (1905)

Faust and Mephisto (1905)

The Life of Christ (1906)

Spring Fairy (1906, in color)

Mireille (1906, with Louis Feuillade)

Dreams of an Opium-Smoker (1906, with Victorin Jasset)

The Descent into Mines at Fumay (1906, with Victorin Jasset)

Midnight Mass (1906)

Cakewalk of the Clock (1906)

Carmen (1906-1907)

Manon (1906-1907)

Mignon (1906-1907)

Ballets of the Opera (1906-1907)

The Bells of Corneville (1906-1907)

The Dragons of Villars (1906-1907)

Madame Angot (1906-1907)

The Canteen Manager (1906-1907)

FanFan the Tulip (1906-1907)

Sisters' Mantle for Worldly Dancers (1906-1907)

The Knife (1906-1907)

B.   Films Made in France and Spain 1896-1906.   No specific re-
      lease dates are available.

Closed Lips

Flight of the Bohemians

Frozen Lovers

The Hat

He Leaves for the Holidays

A House Demolished and Rebuilt

In Search of an Apartment

It Is Father Who Takes the Plunge

Lilliput and Gulliver

The Mattress

Ogre and Tom Thumb

On the Telephone

One Wedding for Robinson

The Paralytic

A Priest's Conscience

The Prison Van

Professor of Living Languages

The Scared Glutton

The Sentry

A Shelter for the Night

The Sneak-Thief

Tea at the Concierge's Home

To Do a Moonlight Flit

C.   Films Made in the United States 1910-1920*

A Child's Sacrifice (Oct. 21, 1910)

Rose of the Circus (1911)

The Doll (1911)

Greater Love Hath No Man (June 30, 1911)

Violin Maker of Nuremberg (Dec. 22, 1911)

A Man's a Man (1912)

Dublin Dan (1912)

The Equine Spy (1912)

Mignon (opera) (1912)

Falling Leaves (1912)

The Million Dollar Robbery (1912)

The Sewer (1912) (A. G. Blaché was producer only)

A Face at the Window (1912)

Bloodstain (1912)

Phantom Paradise (1912)

Playing Trumps (1912)

---

*Attributions to Alice Guy-Blaché and Herbert Blaché overlap and become confused, particularly in the span 1915-1920. Errors in attribution and dates of release are readily acknowledged.

The filmography here has been compiled from all lists and articles about the Blachés' careers in the motion picture industry.

Fra Diavolo (1912)

The Detective's Dog (April 12, 1912)

Canned Harmony (Oct. 9, 1912)

The Girl in the Armchair (Dec. 18, 1912)

Mickey's Pal (1912) (with Edward Warren)

Hotel Honeymoon (1912) (with Henri Menessier)

In the Year 2000 (1912?)

Her Double (1912-1914)

Hater of Women/His Better Self (1912-1914)

The Marvelous Cow (1912-1914)

The Sewers of New York (1912-1914?)

Our Poor Relations (1912-1914)

Idol Worshipper (1912-1914)

Officer Henderson (1912-1914)

Fortune Hunters (1913)

Beasts of the Jungle (1913)

The Rogues of Paris (1913)

A Terrible Night (1913)

The Little Hunchback Tailor (1913)

Dick Whittington and His Cat (1913)

Shadows of Moulin Rouge (1913)

A House Divided (May 2, 1913)

Matrimony's Speed Limit (June 11, 1913)

The Star of India (Nov. 17, 1913)

The Pit and the Pendulum (1913)

Kelly from the Emerald Isle (1913)

The Yellow Traffic (1914) (with Herbert Blaché)

The Ragged Earl (1914)

Hook and Hand (1914)

Dream Woman (1914)

The Tigress (1914)

The Monster and the Girl (1914)

Michael Strogoff (1914)

A Fight for Freedom or Exiled to Siberia (1914)

The Lure (1914)

Fighting Death (1914)

Woman of Mystery (1914)

Beneath the Czar (1914)

House (or Castle) of Cards (1914)

The Shooting of Dan McGrew (1914)

The Heart of a Painted Woman (1914)

My Madonna (1915)

The Vampire (1915)

The Sea Wolf (1915)

The Eternal Question (1916)

What Will People Say (1916)

Woman's Fight (1916)

The Adventurer (Feb. 15, 1917)

Whoso Findeth a Wife (1917)

The Empress (March 11, 1917)

Behind the Mask (1917)

Spring of the Year (1917)

A Man and a Woman (1917)

When You and I Were Young (1917)

The Soul of Magdalene (1917)

The Auction of Virtue (1917?)

The Great Adventure (March 10, 1918)

A Soul Adrift (1918)

Social Hypocrytes (1918)

The Divorcée (1919)

Out of the Fog (1919)

The Brat (1919)

Tarnished Reputations (March or June, 1920)

D.   Films Made in the United States 1910-1920.   No Re-
      lease Dates Cited.

Dreadnaught

Way of the Sea

Honeymoon

Eyes That Could Not Close

Snake Temple

NOTES

1. Ephraim Katz, The Film Encyclopedia. New York: Crowell,
    1979, p. 319.
2. Anthony Slide, Early Women Directors. New York: A. S.
    Barnes, 1977, p. 15.
3. Francis Lacassin, "Out of Oblivion: Alice Guy Blaché, " Sight
    & Sound 40:3 (Summer 1971), p. 151.
4. Charles Ford, "The First Female Producer, " Films in Review
    15:3 (March 1964), p. 141.
5. Ibid. , p. 141.
6. Lacassin, p. 151.
7. Ibid.
8. Ibid.
9. Alice Guy Blaché, "Alice Guy: La naissance du cinéma, "
    Image & Son 283 (April 1974), p. 42.
10. Ibid. , p. 43.
11. Calvin Thomas Beck, Scream Queens: Heroines of the Hor-
    rors. New York: Macmillan, 1978, pp. 34-35.
12. Ibid. , p. 33.
13. Richard Henshaw, "Women Directors: 150 Filmographies, "
    Film Comment 8:4 (Nov. -Dec. 1972), p. 33.
14. Katz, p. 319.
15. Lacassin, p. 152.
16. Helma Schlief, Gertrud Koch, and Eva Hiller, trans. , "Alice
    Guy--die erste Filmemacherin, Auszüge aus ihrer Autobi-
    ographie, " Frauen und Film 12 (June 1977), p. 30.   This
    excerpt was translated from Alice Guy Blaché, Autobiogra-
    phie d'une pionniere du cinéma.   Paris: Denoël Gonthiers,
    1976.   The Musidora Association sponsored this book publi-
    cation, for which Francis Lacassin compiled the filmography.
    My efforts to borrow or buy the book in this country were
    unsuccessful.
17. Slide, p. 15.
18. Ford, p. 142.
19. Slide, p. 15.
20. Lacassin, p. 153.
21. Ford, p. 142.
22. Slide, p. 15.
23. Ibid. , p. 17.
24. Lacassin, p. 153.
25. Beck, p. 35.
26. Ford, p. 143.
27. Ibid.
28. Lacassin, p. 153.
29. Slide, p. 22.
30. Ibid.
31. Marc Wanamaker, "Alice Guy Blaché, " Cinema no. 35 (1976),
    p. 12.
32. Beck, p. 5.
33. Ibid. , p. 2.
34. Ibid. , p. 36.
35. Schlief, Koch, and Hiller, p. 34.

36. Slide, p. 20.
37. Wanamaker, p. 12.
38. Lacassin, p. 154.
39. Ibid.
40. Beck, p. 39.
41. Slide, p. 26.
42. Ibid. , p. 27.
43. Mitchell, p. 31.
44. Ibid.
45. Ibid.
46. Ibid. , p. 32.
47. Ibid.
48. Ibid.
49. Ibid.
50. Lacassin, p. 154.
51. Beck, p. 39.
52. Ibid.
53. Ibid.
54. Ibid. , p. 40.
55. Lacassin, p. 152.
56. Alice Guy Blaché, p. 47.
57. Ibid.
58. Lacassin, p. 154.

2. GERMAINE DULAC: MOTHER OF SURREALISM

Born: November 17, 1882, Amiens, France (Charlotte Elisabeth Germaine Saisset-Schneider)
Died: July 22, 1942, Paris (Vichy), France

"The existence of an inner life rendered palpable in images, by movements, is the whole art of the cinema.... The cinema is marvelously useful for expressing the manifestations of our thoughts, of our hearts, of our memories...." [Georges Sadoul, Histoire générale du cinéma. Paris: Editions Denoël, 1975, t. 5, vol. 1, p. 117.]

Consider the situation of the cinema in France in the post-World War I era. Cinema was not yet a full-grown industry, destined to be nationalized as were most film industries in the European nations. It was not an art, but a craft exercised and pursued by a few firms and free-lancers who grappled with its piquant possibilities.

Most artists and craftworkers were immersed in or influenced by Dadaism, which had thrown up its dark umbrella during the "war to end all wars," to adumbrate all artistic impulse and imagination for almost a decade. This Dadaism was "a movement of young writers and artists in Paris during and after World War I, which attempted to suppress the logical relationship between idea and statement ... with the admittedly destructive intent of perverting and demolishing the tenets of art, philosophy, and logic and replacing them with conscious madness as a protest against the insanity of the war...."[1]

Inspired by Tristan Tzara, the Dadaist movement waned in the early twenties in France, metamorphosing into the Surrealism first espoused by André Breton in his Manifeste de Surréalisme (1924). "The movement took over from Dada, making aesthetic and political formulations of that movement's random attempts to shock...."[2]

Contemporary with the Dadaists of the War decade who developed into the Surrealists of the twenties was a small group of French filmmakers who gathered, in April 1919, to name themselves Impressionists and to identify the meaning of their central concepts. Impressionism then infused all six of the arts (notably painting, poetry and drama). Film entrepreneurs Marcel L'Herbier, Abel Gance, Germaine Dulac, and Jean Epstein added cinema, the seventh art, to this roster. These Impressionists of the cinema agreed with the movement's chief theoretician, Louis Delluc, that their films should be thoroughly French in style and spirit.   The Impressionist slogan demanded that "French cinema should be cinema, and French cinema should be French. "[3]

In this year of 1919, Delluc scripted and Dulac directed La fête espagnole in which Delluc's wife-to-be, Eve Francis, appeared. The film was Delluc's first, but it was Dulac's seventh, for she had been writing and directing her own films for many years.   Delluc worked in a hyperactive lifestyle as editor of Le Film magazine (1917-1919) while contributing articles in which he debated standards for criticism of the seventh art to film journals and newspapers. With Louis Moussinac he had established a school of independent film criticism, clearly indicating the necessity of recognizing the film as an art form whose significant traits were "its rhythmical and lyrical elements. "[4]

From the War's inception, Dulac had grasped the primordial elements of the silent film and tried to fuse them into significant sound and image form; after the War, she put her acquired capabilities and Delluc's precepts to test.   Dulac's empirical and Delluc's theoretical approaches to film were merged into one work, La fête espagnole.   Because both filmmakers were very much products of their time and place, a parallel timeline of their films and ancillary activities will be aligned in anticipation of as accurate and vivid a delineation of Dulac as possible.

In 1919 when Delluc and Dulac collaborated on La fête espagnole she was 37 years old, a married and presumably childless matron, who would divorce her husband, Albert, after 15 years of marriage in the next year.   Delluc was 29.   In the four years before his death in 1924, he wrote and directed several films, married actress Eve Francis, published two books on the cinema, and articulated an assimilated theory of film.   So emphatic was Delluc's command of the Impressionists' circle, which included Dulac, and so enduring the impact of his films that the Prix Louis Delluc has been awarded each year since 1937 to a top caliber French film. Delluc and Dulac were friends bound to a working partnership, their affinities expressed in strong-voiced dissensions and exhilarating agreements.   Today their credos and films appear first to complement each other, then run tangential, occasionally intersecting, and, finally, stand opposed.   But there was no dispute regarding the overriding importance of this new "seventh art": Delluc and Dulac devoted their lives to it.

Born in Amiens in 1882 of middle-class family employed in the manufacturing industry or in the military, the young Germaine Dulac was cast in the role of a soldier's daughter.   "Knocked about from town to town ... the little girl's life in the garrisons of her father, a cavalry captain, was dominated for many years by transience.... "[5]   Placed in her Parisian grandmother's household, the adolescent was instructed in the arts.   Most of her energies she applied to the study of music and singing, and she was fond of Wag-

ner's operas, though she became engrossed in photography for a
time.   Married to Albert Dulac in 1905, she turned to journalism
for employment.   She wrote for La Fronde and she became a drama
critic for La Française; both were feminist publications.   In 1908
she wrote a play, L'Emprise, at the same time renewing her interest in photography.

In 1911 Dulac became acquainted with dancer Stasia de Napi-
erkowski.   Together they went to Rome to watch scenes of Caligula
being filmed.   Dulac's reaction to this viewing was intense and immediate: she formed Delia Film, her own production company,
with her husband as administrator, and poet-novelist Irene Hillel-
Erlanger as scenarist.   At this time, women workers were accepted,
even encouraged, in the film industry. 6

The first five films released by Delia Film, and distributed
by Pathé, were conventional and commercial products, judging from
the available fragmentary descriptions of them.   They were titled
Soeurs ennemies (1915), Geo le mystérieux (1916), Dans l'ouragan
de la vie, also known as Vénus victrix (1916), Le bonheur des
autres (1919), and Ames des fous (1917).   Dulac met Delluc while
making this last film.

Having seen the film, Delluc declared that

> the modernity of the film is striking.   The personages
> are of today, that today which still barely exists. ...   We
> have the impression of being received in the salons on
> the screen.   This is rare in film and yet indispensable.
> The theatre never succeeds in giving us the impression of
> being on the stage, and not in the audience.   At a film we
> must be and live in the setting of the drama as complete-
> ly as the actors themselves. 7

Then formulating his critical theory of film, Delluc hypothesized this "seventh art" as both a commercial object and a superla-
tive means of communication, intended for direct experience not
contemplation, through its arts of suggestion, detail, simplification,
movement, and precision.

Dulac herself had this to say about Ames des fous:

> This film made me realize that over and above precise
> facts and events, atmosphere is an important emotional
> factor.   I realized that the value of a film was more tied
> to the subtleties coming out of its atmosphere than the
> mere action in the film.   I further appreciated the fact
> that even though the acting in itself was important, it
> could only attain fullest intensity operating in conjunction
> with the play of images.   Light, camera angle and editing
> were more important elements than the straight acting out
> of a scene only following the laws of drama. [Donald H.
> Blumer, "The Camera as Snowball: France 1918-1927, "
> IX:2 Cinema Journal (Spring 1970) page 33.]

Donald Blumer is convinced that Dulac did not share Delluc's "concern for unity" in a film. "What was for him a quest for laws unique to the cinema as a total experience became in the hands of others an exploration of technical trickery.... " So, Blumer posits, Dulac tended to strive for atmosphere in her films, resorting to "technical trickery" to do it, sacrificing the cohesiveness that Delluc declared was the filmmaker's most pervasive priority. With others, Dulac bore the malaise of form severed from content in her work. Her discovery of atmosphere "led her work in the wrong direction. In her later films, the concentration was completely on the atmosphere, to the exclusion of both the story line and the acting. Actors became props and ludicrous plots were mere pretexts on which to hang long strings of technical effects ... " (Blumer, pp. 33 and 35).

Charles Ford (in Femmes cinéastes, Paris: Editions Denoël, 1972, pp. 7-8) agrees with Blumer:

> With Ames de Fous (1917) the critics, who were preoccupied with clear and forthright articulation of plot, had already become uneasy by what they considered her excessive emphases on editing, lighting and the creation of atmosphere through visual means, all of which were becoming more important operative elements in film to Dulac than competent acting.... "

Dulac's next film, La bonheur des autres (1918), displayed similar inclinations toward the establishment of mood.

The merger of Dulac's direction with Delluc's script probably accounts for the significant singularity of their collaborative enterprise, La fête espagnole (1919). It "established her name as one of the strongest forces in the French impressionist school.... "[8] Delluc helped Dulac direct in the latter portions of the film and this brief training, along with the consolidation of his published hypotheses on the nature of the film, propelled him into making six films in the next four years. La fête espagnole was a pivotal hinge in both their careers.

Richard Abel's "Louis Delluc: The Critic as Cineaste, " in Quarterly Review of Film Studies, I:2 (May 1976), pp. 205-244, offers the most complete description of the film's plot, photography, and production process.

> ... the narrative runs as follows: Soledad (Eve Francis), a wealthy young woman, refuses to choose between two young suitors, Real (Gaston Modot) and Miguelin (Jean Toulout), and instead suggests out of boredom that she will marry whichever [sic] returns from a duel. While they go off to a wood to consider this, Juanito (Robert Delsol), a young man from the city, passes her villa and persuades her to accompany him to the city festival in progress. There Soledad is transformed by the excite-

ment and her past memories of dancing and love. That
night she has to be carried home and over the bodies of
the two suitors who have died at her gate.   Embracing
Juanito as they enter the villa, Soledad does not even see
them.... "

The irony inherent in this outline of action stems from Delluc's literary leanings; Abel points to the selection of the Spanish
setting for an "appropriately exotic atmosphere. " But, "It is
strongest in the parallel plots that culminate with Soledad's obliviousness to the suitors' bodies and in the mysterious old woman,
Paguien (Anna Gay), who witnesses the parallel journeys of Juanito
and the suitors and also the latter's deaths.... " What was the
central concern of the film? Abel asks. "... The tragic passion
of the suitors, the dramatic change in Soledad, or the ambience of
the festival itself?... " He replies to the question quoting "another
filmmaker working alongside Germaine Dulac ... Henri Fescourt.... "
And the reply's essence is that Delluc groped along uncertainly,
trying to integrate the designated three created components mentioned into a unified composition.

The film [he says] began with a series of shots designed
to suggest Spain on holiday. These details multiplied, in
fact weighed down and slowed the beginning. But at the
same time they established the atmosphere.... So that
when the principal character appeared on the screen he
seemed less presented than incorporated in the flow of
picturesque events.... If I had been able to realize my
intention, the action--that is, the story--would not have
emerged, at least, not by my making it do so. The details which constitute the story would not dominate to the
detriment of the others. Mixed with the other details
they would swirl about in the whirlpool of the festival.... "

And while reviewers liked Delluc's script, they claimed that
Dulac's rendering of the Iberian landscape in Louis Nalpa's studio
in Nice lacked veracity. Judging from the scenario, Abel found
"some rather sophisticated cutting for a French film in 1919" but
does not key the artist responsible for this excellence. Cutting is
used effectively, producing "a clear articulation of simultaneous
action occurring in two or more places at once, which eventually
emphasizes the irony of the parallel plots. " The vivid fusion of
tenses, past and present, is portrayed by Soledad's losing herself
in the mood of the festival: "... her memories of the past came
to life in her present actions--she is reborn.... " As Abel re-
capitulates, "The power of environment and memory is no more
positive in La Fête espagnole than it will be in Le Silence Fièvre,
La Femme de nulle part, or L'Inondation. " The importance of La
fête espagnole then, in the careers of Delluc and Dulac, appears to
be that it embodies several advances of the filming art never before
accomplished in France, and that these advances--subordination of
all elements toward a meshed unity, parallel plots employing characters who undergo emotional alterations while recollecting the past

and confronting present time, evocation of moods--correspond to
Delluc's announced critical insights into the nature of film.   For
Dulac, the film "... appears to be her first really important
work. ... "

The fact that Dulac could not have escaped the knowledge and
influence of Delluc's considerations of the cinema's structure and
style while partnered with him in their filmmaking venture cannot
be debated.   To appraise her films after this fateful co-operation
with Delluc requires a summary of Delluc's exposition of the nature
of the cinema.   Abel admirably captures Delluc's concepts in his
article, all of which begin with Delluc's study of the American films
of three directors: Thomas Ince, D. W. Griffith, and William S.
Hart.

For Delluc, the dominant trait of the cinema was its realism,
the intensified materiality of life.   But cinema possessed a trans-
forming power (he termed it a "lyric force") that could--better than
literature, painting, music, and sculpture--represent the phenomenal
flux of human consciousness in all tenses, most especially the confrontation of the past (fantasy-memory) with the present (realism-
immediacy).   The scenario should "spring naturally from the contemporary world, from the real lives of common people ... its sequential signification should be governed by a single, original idea
... the scenario writer and director should be one and the same,
the true auteur of the film.... "9

In contrast, Dulac's commentaries on her films reflect a
hard-nosed practicality rooted in work experience with which she
tried to capture human thought and feeling as images in black and
white.   Philosophical abstraction was less related to her temperament than the mastery of the camera's techniques governing the moving images that the silent cinema offered its viewers.   The theoretician Delluc

> went on ... to film his own original scenarios, while Du-
> lac continued, for the most part, to film material taken
> from theatre and literature, experimenting with that ma-
> terial by way of soft focus and special lighting, prisms
> and distorting mirrors, screen panels for split screen ef-
> fects, and fast and slow motion as the integral technical
> means in her quest for a visual cinema....   She was one
> of the first artists to use the screen panel, along with
> prisms, distorting mirrors and other similar effects.... "10

In his essay "Experimental Film in France, " Jacques Brunius
partitions the film's avant-garde movement into four phases.   The
first is labelled Delluc, and only Delluc. 11   Its start is undated.
The second phase begins in 1920 when La fête espagnole was released and films by Dulac, Gance, Epstein, and L'Herbier are
bracketed into the years 1920 to 1924.   Phase three overlaps the
second in 1923, continuing the films of these and other filmmakers,
while phase four, tagged "Dissolution of the Avant-Garde" dates from
1928 with the appearance of the talking picture into the thirties.

In the second phase, Brunius gives his impression of Dulac's filmwork:

> After a rather dull start, Germaine Dulac had made a
> brilliant flash in the pan under the wing of Delluc when
> she directed his script, La fête espagnole (1920). This
> style she abandoned in her ensuing films, and turned
> towards the new trend ... which can be defined pretty
> well like this: any anecdote from a novel, however vul-
> gar, may be accepted or chosen as long as it is disguised
> by an exuberant ornamentation of technical effects to
> "look visual. " A further outstanding characteristic of
> this school: total lack of humour.... [12]

Dulac's colleague Jean Epstein, however, commended her
evocative use of detail to advance the action and to enrich the mood
of the characters in her films La cigarette (1919), for which she
co-wrote the script, and Malencontre (1920).

Dulac was interviewed during the filming of La cigarette by
a reporter who approached her with deference and curiosity. She
smoked without pause throughout the session. Her urbanity impressed the journalist as much as the jewelry she wore: several
rings on her fingers, a bangle on her wrist, and a bracelet of gold
on one ankle. She also used a walking stick, he noted. [13]

Charles Ford remarks on page 32 in Femmes cinéastes that
"In La cigarette ... she envelops her main character, the superb
Gabriel Signoret, in a silken atmosphere so delicate and ethereal
as to satisfy the most demanding of lovers of poetic photography.... "

As a corollary to his Impressionist film credo, Delluc proposed the formation of ciné-clubs, a term he coined, for the public
viewing of experimental films, then defined as specialized and non-
commercial, small-scale projects. In the final months of 1920,
Delluc founded, with Ricciotto Canudo, the first ciné-club, the Club
des Amis du Septième Art (Club of Friends of the Seventh Art), or
CASA. Delluc and Canudo issued a manifesto-like essay which appeared in Cinéa May 13, 1921, "... in which the cinema, the seventh art, is defined as the modern synthesis of all arts 'sculptures
of light, figures in rhythmic motion, trembling stillness.... ' "[14]
While Delluc and Canudo were engaged in organizing and publicizing
CASA and beginning a lecture series on film, Dulac filmed La belle
dame sans merci (1920). With J. H. Rosny presiding at the third
lecture session in the CASA series, the lectern was offered to Dulac, who talked informally about this film.

La belle was biographical but contained few extraordinary
events. Rather, it recorded the emotional impacts and intimate
movements that occur in love and affection. It seems that Mme.
Erlinger expressed her doubts about the appeal of the film because
Dulac rebuts her negative comments. Erlanger's argument held that
the plot failed to develop, that stasis enveloped the action, the atmosphere, and the characters. Not so, Dulac protested.

A film work, in order to be exhibited throughout the country, has to shun talking about adultery; on the other hand, if the film can be allowed to show in sparkling impressionism what the principal action is with a group of characters, then theme and action fuse in parallelism and continuity.... "15

The film enthusiast can appreciate how hard it must have been to make a movie about adultery while refraining from "talking about" it in the subtitles and photographing illicit physical relationships. Dulac's choice of story reflects her awareness of the twin-edged dilemma artists face in their work: to fulfill their individual creative credos, while satisfying the public with appealing offerings.

Speaking from the lectern, Dulac continued to explain why she made La belle as she did: She tried to render an atmosphere of elegance, charm, and grace so that both the scenic design would simulate real life and an accumulation of swiftly seen details would be such as those perceived in life, without significance attached to them. Dulac explained how and why she tried to create an effervescence of emotion by the presence of La belle's heroine, Lola. "I tried to express the essence of life. If I wanted to tell lies to please my audience, then I'd risk being misunderstood. "16

Dulac's analysis of La belle was published in Cinéa, May 20, 1921, as Sadoul cites, continuing to comment: "Dulac wanted domestic and foreign distribution of all films, including her own, in exchange for certain concessions.... "17 Then he relates the plot of La belle which begins with the arrival of a celebrated actress, Lola, in a small town where she meets a long ago lover and is reunited. Their reunion pushes his son into committing suicide, and his wife into the arms of a lover. The situation returns to normal when Lola departs. Sadoul remarks that Delluc liked the film's fluid direction. In fact, Delluc is recalled by La belle to the work of Manet and Renoir, and Sadoul quotes two brief paragraphs from Delluc's warmly appreciative criticism. However, Jacques Brunius warns that the Second Avant-Gardists overindulged themselves in aping the painterly styles of the French masters of the canvas.

As for the use of soft focus and gauze, the less said the better. Everyone took to vying with Turner and Claude Monet without rhyme or reason. These effects soon became as irritating as the inevitable orange-tinted and purple-toned sunsets in mass-produced films.... 18

To Delluc, Dulac's camerawork was not irritating. He believed La belle surpassed in several significant qualities La fête espagnole and La cigarette. How Dulac reacted to his films is unknown.

A photograph dated 1921 of Dulac with D. W. Griffith suggests that she visited the United States to meet him and other film-makers, and to inspect their workplaces and equipment as well. 19 Only the lower half of her face can be seen--and a strong, square

jaw is outlined clearly--under her hat.   She appeared to be of medium height and weight.   In another small photograph, her large,
dark expressive eyes are directed not at the viewer but to one side;
besides her eyes, her high-bridged straight nose and short dark
hair parted on the left are predominant. [20]

Whether Dulac filmed La mort du soleil before or after this
trip abroad is uncertain.   Sadoul quotes her discussing her dynamic
camerawork in filming it.

> In Death of the Sun ... I started to use what I call acro-
> batic techniques to give the impression of inflated size,
> great depths, super-imposition of one mask upon another,
> all giving the suggestive values of a musical measure.
> The public is not accustomed to these techniques and some
> parts of the film had to be excised. ... [21]

A memorable scene in this film is described by Lionel Landry.   A permanently paralyzed man tries to find a cure for his
tuberculosis.

> We see Dr. Faivre stretched out full length upon his bed,
> his body rigid, only his eyes moving.   The background
> enlarges following his increasing anxiety, while his stare
> is fixedly attached to the shadows of trees which move on
> the curtains; that shade is an image of the life ahead for
> this scholar, placing a symbol in his heart with its game
> of realistic light.   But these are evocations.   In flux, in
> a dull illumination, a woman appears leading her children
> along the street.   He watches ...; the light triumphs. [22]

Dulac's emphasis on and exploration with effects of light to
create seen and symbolic images of light is assuredly explicit here.
Assuredly, too, she and her Impressionist colleagues would agree
that the camera's capturing of light and the filmmaker's penetrating
its properties of abstraction, expansion, contraction, and distortion
were the most creative challenge of this seventh art.   Dulac's own
ever-experimental efforts to move the camera, change the lighting,
adjust the lens, appear to have been paramount in her direction of
thirty-odd films.

Working in unrecorded circumstances in interior sets--no
mention is made of going "on location"--Dulac knew that a director's
signature was inscribed by his or eye-staying feats: the impact of
light upon the retina and on into memory.   Light was non-verbal
symbol, metaphor, simile, statement, query, equivocation, reply.
Did she work with a written script?   Or merely block out the movements of the actors from an outline and write the subtitles later?
Delluc's scripts La fête espagnole and Le Silence are "available in
scenario form, " as Abel asserts (page 206).   Not one of Dulac's
scripts has been discovered and identified.   Luckily Dulac's dis-
courses on her own films and the nature and state of the cinema
were published in the ciné periodicals managed by Delluc and others.

Dulac began in 1922 but did not finish Werther, based on Goethe's novel. Simultaneously, Delluc was filming La Femme du nulle part on location, a challenging deviation from the normal course of shooting a film. Excerpting from Abel,

> Although his scenario was set on the plains above Genoa
> in Northern Italy the filming took place ... in the region
> of Arles and the Camargue where Andre Antoine had shot
> his L'Arlesienne one year earlier. The light was softer
> but the landscape no less arid than that around Nice on
> the Côte d'Azur and their expressive plasticity was per-
> fect for the dramatic theme of the film... [p. 223].

On January 2, 1923, Dulac took part in a reunion celebration of the Committee for the Defence of French film. The Committee resolved that a minimum of 25 percent of French films should be exported and that the nationalities of foreign films be specified when they were imported. It demanded taxation of foreign films to pro- tect the domestic cinema product. The power of the Committee can be judged by the results of its published resolutions. Important film distributors (Leon Aubert, for one) approved and implemented them.

The film to which Sadoul attaches "masterpiece" designation in his Dictionary of Film-Makers (Berkeley: University of Cali- fornia Press, 1972, p. 70) was a sensation when first shown in 1923. The 3200-foot length film, The Smiling Madame Beudet (1923), is called Dulac's "best" film by Sadoul in his Dictionary of Films (Berkeley: Univ. of California Press, 1972, p. 350). He says there that the film is

> ... derived from a play by Andre Obey and Denys Amiel,
> the exponents of the "theater of silence" involving for-
> malized, mimetic staging. Its theme is clearly theatrical
> but also very cinematic. The action, set in a dreary
> provincial town, takes place in the back-shop living quar-
> ters of [a] couple. The style is set by Dulac's impres-
> sionistic camera and by metaphors established through
> editing devices--the angry Monsieur Beudet becoming an
> ogre or Madame Beudet's romantic daydreams of streams
> and ponds as she plays Debussy on the piano.... Objects,
> too, (the vase that the wife, then the husband, keep moving
> about) are used to express the domestic conflict but are
> not "symbols." Germaine Dermoz as the wife gives a
> sensitive performance, unforgettable in the shot in which
> her ravaged face is reflected by three mirrors....

Sadoul mentions here and in his Histoire de l'art du Cinéma (Paris: Ernest Flammarion, 1955, page 172) that Dulac used all of the resources of a highly respected film by Karl Mayer, Le Kam- merspiel, likening these to the qualities of chamber theatre. But, considering the climate in which Dulac worked, Sadoul affirms that in Dictionary of Films it was quite unlikely that Dulac was aware

of Le Kammerspiel and that her realizations of the actions in Madame Beudet's inner eye on the screen, as well as the psychology
portrayed, stemmed from her own talents, not an adaptation of another filmmaker's concepts. Urged on by her restless and seeking
personality, Dulac was ever alert to new trends. She determined
what she could or could not use, alter, or dismiss, and quickly
left behind what she had already tried. In Beudet, which she adapted
from the play, the portrayal of an unhappy wife who fantasizes killing her husband is subject material perfectly suited to the "theater
of silence," one factor for its unusual excellence. Sadoul, however,
does find reciprocal influences between Beudet and La Nuit de la
Saint Sylvestre.

Marjorie Rosen, in Popcorn Venus (New York: Coward, Mc-
Cann & Geoghegan, 1973, p. 378), signifies the importance of the
ambience of French filmmaking work atmosphere in which Dulac
could and did make a film of vibrant feminism. If this encouraging
environment had not existed, Rosen is convinced the film could not
have been made. Just as meaningful, Rosen declares, is the fact
that in Beudet Dulac moved completely into the convictions of the
avant-garde aesthetic.

> In this film she very literally illustrates the fantasies
> and inner frustrations of a romantic middle-aged woman
> who feels neglected and abused by her insensitive husband.
> The woman is sitting at her piano playing Debussy--the
> screen dissolves into a mass of sparkling highlights (pho-
> tographed off water). When her husband sings opera to
> himself, costumed actors depict the various roles. As
> Madame Beudet reads a magazine, an advertisement for
> a tennis racquet sparks off a fantasy in which a handsome
> young player leaps from the pages in slow motion and
> carries off her husband (rather inaccurately suggesting his
> replacement in her affections). Later she sees him beat-
> ing the piano in fast motion displaying his anger. Unfor-
> tunately the trick photography creates such clichéd situa-
> tions that they can only seem comic today....

Jeanne Betancourt explains how Dulac denotes the passage of
time to underline Madame Beudet's longing for freedom from a man
she despises.

> Much of the imagery ... is based on Madame Beudet's
> feelings of imprisonment by her surroundings and the regu-
> lated order of time. Clocks and calendars are always in
> evidence; Beudet is ever looking at his watch. Madame
> Beudet looks out the window only to see the courthouse
> and local jail. She approaches what seems to be a win-
> dow, but it is a mirror reflecting her sorrowing face.
> As she wakes up to a new day, a long shot of her sitting
> up in bed is superimposed by an animated pendulum.
> Taking her head between her hands, she moves back and
> forth, keeping time with the seconds marked by the pendu-

lum, forcing herself into the order. It is only in her
imagination that things appear in fast or slow time. Her
real life will not allow any deviation from the norm....

For Betancourt, Dulac's technique of "revealing the psychological
state of the characters through purely cinematic devices ... "23 and
her "feminist perspective" are reasons for the singular success of
Beudet in spite of a conventional storyline.

The theatrical origin of Beudet can be traced from its initial exposition, its strengthening momentum of conflicting action,
the climactic scene in which Mon. Beudet aims his revolver at his
head, and the denouement embodying a just-as-before sadness.
Betancourt outlines this for us.

As the film progresses, you sense Madame Beudet's
mounting oppression from her coarse, bourgeois mate,
who blissfully lives as master of the house. He exercises
his authority so blatantly that when his wife refuses to go
to the opera Faust with him, he locks her piano and takes
the key so that she can't have her one private pleasure.
When he crushes the head of a decorative doll, he ...
says, "So fragile, just like women. " Madame, never
smiling, watches as her husband repeats a well-worn joke.
When something disturbs the husband, he puts an unloaded
revolver to his head and pulls the trigger.... Need I
say more about the attempted murder except that it back-
fires. When Monsieur Beudet picks up the revolver (now
loaded), he points it at his wife, saying, "I should shoot
you. " (She hadn't kept the household records accurately!)
When the revolver goes off, the shocked Beudet is so
oblivious of his wife's wrath that he thinks she loaded the
revolver to kill herself. "You wanted to kill yourself.
What would I do without you?" She stares at the camera
with a stolid, unflinching expression. Her act of courage
is unrewarded; she must go on. The closing shot is of
this couple greeting a local priest as they walk through
their small town.... 24

The subject and style of Beudet speaking as they do for the
liberation of women made it a "must" inclusion in the First Festival
of Women's Films held in New York City, in September 1972. Reviewing several of the films shown, Joan Braverman, in her article
"The First Festival of Women's Films, " Artforum, XI, 1 (Sept.
1972, pp. 87-92), responds to the photographic and metaphorical
skills that fashioned the film.

Its simple narrative (Dulac called the story "nothing, a
surface only") involves the domestic strife of a petit
bourgeois French provincial couple and its ensuing psychological ramifications for a smiling Madame Beudet, who,
in fact, never smiles. The husband ... is portrayed as
a capitalist male supremacist in the best spirit of today's

movement. And the absolute isolation, alienation and con-
finement of his wife is rendered palpable through the use
of elaborate masking and lighting techniques, superimposi-
tion, split-screen, prism and graphic effects that include
some of the most radical uses of the filmic frame of the
period. Dulac's continual projection and shattering of
theatrical illusionism call into question the most basic assumptions about the film form...."

Braverman describes one of the final "ironically undercut"
scenes which underscores Madelaine Beudet as a "proto-feminist
revolutionary."

As we watch ... Mme. Beudet staring blankly into the
camera as she is embraced, a superimposed curtain is
lifted within the large wall mirror above them to disclose
a Punch and Judy couple recapitulating their actions below.
And if we have not understood the implicit joke of the
mirror's double illusionism as an autonomous object we
are certainly convinced when the word "T-H-E-A-T-R-E"
materializes on that mirror frame, which is a frame
within the cinematic frame...."

Much of the success of the film is attributed to the acting of
Germaine Dermoz in the leading role. Dermoz asked director Dulac to tell her how to project the intensity of her role. Dulac replied: "Only think, only experience your reactions without moving
a muscle in your face. You must be like glass in your acting, as
one with the rhythm of the images and with your thoughts...."[25]
Since Sadoul calls the film "No action, or just a bit: the life of a
soul," we are assured that Dermoz ably conveyed with her immobile
facial muscles the misery and monotony of her uxorial existence
dominated by a loathsome spouse. If Dulac is remembered--and
she should be--as a filmmaker, Sadoul declares it will be for this
film.

Beudet was made under the aegis of the Film d'Art company,
which came under new management shortly before contracting with
Dulac to make the film. Film d'Art, as Braverman explains, adhered to a crowd-pleasing formula for filmmaking. Nevertheless,
"At that time ... serious developments and innovations came by way
of the commercial film industry.... Dulac's ... Beudet stands as
a remarkable testimony of this ... one of the few historical exceptions in the Film d'Art stable...." Cornwell clarifies Dulac's
acknowledging and acting upon the commercial considerations inherent in film production after the success of Beudet.

Rather than pursue, as she had in ... Beudet, psychological probings through the visualization of what could not
be spoken and of what Dulac explicitly did not want to convey in the conventional subtitle, she contracted to direct
the serial, Gossette. Her conviction was that even in
such a popularized work it was possible to strike a com-

promise without forfeiting one's principles.... In essence, Dulac felt that she could still work intelligently
within an ostensibly commercial framework and yet achieve
what she desired toward the evolution of the art of the
film... [p. 33].

That Dulac strove to fuse popular appetite and personal taste
in Gossette ("street urchin, " 1923) is affirmed by Sadoul also.

When after Madame Beudet she contracted for a serialized
novel such as Gossette, she intended, in this assignment,
to familiarize the public with her avant-garde researches,
as she explained in a conference of the Friends of the
Cinema in a session on the film-novel. "Two basic situations require comment: 1. The bandits kidnap a young
girl while she is asleep. 2. How to make real the
psychic reality of the young girl's martyrdom. "

Then Dulac must have pondered aloud on her methods of shaping the
material.

"Motion alone is the basis of my psychological technique:
roads which are distorted, trees that are lengthened, one
movement within another movement, objects which multi-
ply themselves, impressions of fantasy, the translation of
a spiritual state: the heart of a young girl with her fears,
her frankness. The theme of the action: an emotion...."26

Wendy Dozoretz, in her article "Dulac versus Artaud, " 1:3
Wide Angle, 1979, p. 47, describes Gossette as "a very popular
serial film about the adventures of a girl who is rescued from the
clutches of hooligans, taken in by a wealthy family and finally returns to her life in the circus. Events around her include assas-
sinations, mysterious deaths, and disappearances.

While Dulac was making Gossette, Delluc was working on his
last film, L'Inondation, which bore the influences of Scandinavian
film directors Sjostrom and Stiller. It was released in 1924, the
year of his death.

With Delluc gone, Dulac worked faster. She completed Le
diable dans la ville, a study of fanaticism in the Middle Ages.
Jacques Brunius assigns 1926 as the release date in his negative
reflection on Dulac's use of superimpositions of images in it: "Dulac doubled the image to indicate violent emotions in one of her
characters ... vision of this sort on the screen conveys nothing at
all to me... " [p. 84].

A "superproduction" is what Dulac tackled next. Working
for a consortium named Westi, Ame d'artiste (1925) mirrored the
declension of the British aristocracy in grand style. Dulac collaborated with a Russian immigrant, Volkoff, on the script, which
was based on a novel by Christian Molbech. Huge sets that evoked

a "thousand and one nights, " Scheherazade-like atmosphere reminiscent of Cecil B. DeMille film sagas, furnished the background for
a plot intertwining the lives of a lord and a lady, a genial poet,
and an actress.

In this same year, Dulac founded and became first president
of the Federation of Ciné Clubs, Parisian and provincial, while
making a well publicized and half-successful try at synchronizing
music and images in La Folie des vaillants (1925). She adapted
Gorki's novel to the screen, trying to reconstruct the lives of fishermen on their boats in the Black Sea, knowing that she had to appeal
to public tastes even while she created a "visual symphony employing
the rhythm of images and their sounds. "27   But she recollected the
following after the film was made.

> I didn't know how to approach the goals of my concept.
> The visual symphony will be realized some day, a faroff
> day alas, and it will be made with several scenes and
> characters, there will be games of light in it, collision
> and union of objects, and fleeting impressions, bypassing
> all literary logic as it plays like a musician with emo-
> tions. This concept is what I investigated in La Folie des
> vaillants, an expression of a life of the spirit in cadence
> with the rhythm of images and their duration, their dra-
> matic or sentimental intensity, depending on the passivity
> or the violence born in the mind of my heroes. And I
> am discouraged when I realize how far the reality of my
> experiment is from my ideal of a visual symphony. 28

Sadoul appends Dulac's admission of dissatisfaction if not
downright failure to achieve the sight-sound mesh she had planned
with a description of the film from Ciné-Magazine December 25,
1925, which characterizes it as a "film-poem. " It continues:

> A superimposition [perhaps similar to the technique used
> in Le Diable dans la Ville] of the themes of a melody ap-
> pear above the violin of a musician: paths, clouds, for-
> ests, fields of flowers were added to the content of the
> film, the scenario does not hold a place of importance;
> it is a hymn to liberty, to the grandeur and beauty of
> runaway roads. 29

After two films that were accounted more failures than suc-
cesses, Dulac found herself in financial difficulties which imposed
hardships on her "esthetic. " Brunius records that she lectured,
presumably under the sponsorship of CASA, on The Cinema's Fetters, in 1925: "Our ideal exceeds by far our realizations. We
have to help liberate the cinema from its fetters, and create the
pure cinema" [p. 70]. She added, "Sadly, filmmakers presently
do not have the right to express themselves, they place their sensibilities in service to their work which the public will recognize,
that is, the form of the films as it is now. Among viewers, some
will love in the cinema its future possibilities. Which should be
understood. . . . "30

A surmise of the nature of "pure cinema" as Dulac would define it can be hazarded, helpfully perhaps, at this juncture, some ten years after her first film was made and in the midst of growing pains of the silent film as it struggled to mature and discover itself. Even as the cinema sought to free itself from the encumbrances of related arts, its identity reposed uneasily in proximity to, and was itself a synthesis of, all of them. Everyone had a personal definition, as Brunius informs us: "'Cinema is painting in movement,' wrote Louis Delluc. 'Cinema is the music of light,' said Abel Gance. 'Rather mime than theatre,' thought another .... "[31] Indeed, a majority of Dulac's colleagues felt strongly about releasing film from the doctrines of the theatre. Because her films derived from novels and plays, our safest guess is that her choice of script was a commercial concession within which she hoped her own doctrines could be seeded to germinate and grow. Her own doctrines peg movement and light as basics in a grammar of cinema in concordance with Delluc, Gance, and others. Nothing cataclysmic in this. But Dulac urgently needed the technology of sound incorporated within her films to get the synesthetic effect she wanted: sound structures linking visual images that would stimulate a never-before-experienced sensation as response in the listener-viewer. This previously unknown response to a sight-and-sound film which indulged in irrational, time-defying, non-storytelling, freeform frolicking even as it sustained a deliberate harmony to the seen and heard, would be, Dulac believed, confirmation of the attainment of pure cinema. Pure cinema required the sound motion picture. As indicators that the film industry was approaching its inception were the controversies about the uses of the subtitles and musical accompaniment.

Distributors added subtitles to French versions of U.S. made movies, Brunius recounts, "and even French films were not spared .... "[32] A film without a single subtitle was made in Germany by Lupu Pick and Karl Mayer: La nuit de la Saint Sylvestre (1924). There were also imitators in France. Brunius reports the cautionary judgments of critic Lionel Landry on the meaning and function of subtitles. Landry considers subtitles necessary to clarify action. Their elimination would leave the viewer confused, their omission would be impractical. Subtitles must be endured as operative, though flawed, clarifiers. As for the suggestion that subtitles be artistically lettered and integrated into the film--Landry pooh-poohs this as impractical. Subtitles are not to look at lingeringly. They are to be read quickly. The subtitle is a basic element in the silent film, he concludes. Without it, film would show a fresh subservience to mime and a truly unsophisticated scenario.

Brunius cites 1924 as the year in which musical scores were first written for films. Customarily played by a symphony orchestra, the film score superseded the piano player's aural emotional embellishments to the pictures seen. As with subtitles, whirlwinds of contention and debate circled here, too, spewing forth more questions than answers. Why was musical accompaniment needed? Wasn't it redundant? Shouldn't the cinema be free of music, liberated from literature, etc. ?

Brunius explains that music accompanying a film is meant to engage the ears while the viewer's total attention is addressed to seeing the film.   More to the point, the music pleasantly blocks the operational sounds of the film projector and audience noises. Music for a film is an acoustic device enhancing the enjoyment of the viewer.

Brunius aligns the research and published essays of Dr. Paul Ramain on the similarities and differences of music and film to Dulac's published articles and experiments.   Ramain, for instance, looked for rhythmic patterns in cinema akin to those in musical composition.   He hypothesized that the structure of a good film and a concerto were alike.   He was aware of the fact that two arts simultaneously occurring can cancel out each other, or clash, weakening the impact upon the appreciator.   Ramain conjectured that when a film's musical score calls attention to itself, the vision of the film is eroded.   If the film is too engrossing, the music is muted.   Brunius concludes that Dulac, musically gifted as she was, probably sought and found the basic kinship of music and film that Dr. Ramain observed: The white and black of a musical composition matched the white and black of a film, complete with rhythmic patterns including rests and syncopated notes.

> [Dulac's] writings on the relationship of film to music were very much of her time. . . . Unlike those who reacted strenuously against sound, pronouncing it the death of cinema, Dulac was open, but reserved about its possible uses and sceptical of its abuses. In "Jouer avec les Bruits" written in 1929, she explained that she was against the talking cinema meaning at that time the "all-talkie," but for the sound cinema, that is the discrete use of sound which would reinforce the visuals. "Outside of all that there is room only for silence," she wrote. . . 33

From this all-pervasive colloquy, Dulac's designs for pure cinema were readied and refined.   However, her opportunity for making these purist films had not yet arrived.

In 1926 her film Antoinette Soubrier was released by Paramount.   She had adapted Romain Coolus' play to the screen.   Sadoul tells us only that it was "permeated by a chilly modernism. . . " and that it was made in a truly sumptuous style, its decor contemporary. 34

Le cinéma au service de l'histoire (1927) stands as Dulac's first "montaged" film, what we now call a documentary.   From the sparse descriptions of it, we gather that it was a newsreel of current and past events adroitly edited by Dulac herself.   This cutting, selecting, and arranging film from Actualités-Gaumont studio was relatively new and untried in France.   Brunius says, "The first attempt . . . seems to have been made by Jean Epstein with Photogenies (1925). " Dulac, with Albert Guyot, completed Mon Paris (1928) and these two factual works served as her entry into the newsreel-type product she made in the last decade of her life.

In 1927, Dulac made her most controversial film, La Coquille et le Clergyman (The Seashell and the Clergyman). Signaling
the high tide of French film impressionism and Dulac's joining the
second avant-garde movement, as Cornwell and Sadoul document,
La Coquille is regarded now as the first surrealist film. Apart
from this historical designation, the film generates excitement now,
as then, for many salient reasons, the most important being the
subject and style of the film and the percussive relationship of its
co-architects, Antonin Artaud and Dulac.

Two paragraphs from The Oxford Companion to Film (1976,
p. 670) reveal the length of the film as 45 minutes, and its cast of
three characters: Alex Allin in the priest's role, Gerica Athanasiou
as the woman, and Bataille. Artaud is cited as scriptwriter.

> Artaud had intended to direct and play the lead ... de-
> veloped as a collaboration between Artaud and ... Dulac,
> but Artaud withdrew and repudiated it. When Dulac pre-
> sented the film as "un rêve d'Antonin Artaud" ... the af-
> fronted Surrealists stormed out of the cinema, leaving the
> lay audience, who were totally baffled by the film, in a
> state of uproar. In Britain it was refused a certificate
> by the censors on the grounds that "this film is so cryptic
> as to be almost meaningless. If there is a meaning, it
> is doubtless objectionable. "... La Coquille ... is now
> recognized as an enduring example of avant-garde film: in
> addition to its imaginative qualities it has a technical ease
> attributable to Dulac's experience in commercial cinema
> . . . .

Sharon Smith, in Women Who Make Movies (New York: Hopkinson and Blake, 1976, p. 12) edges further into the Dulac-Artaud
connection: La Coquille '[e]xposes male sexual fantasies, a frustrated man of the cloth pursues a white-robed woman in weirdly
shifting surroundings suggestive of Freudian symbolism.... Artaud
denounced Dulac for having 'feminized' his script...."

The International Encyclopedia of the Film rates the film:

> A rather self-conscious, but to a certain extent effective
> essay in Freudian sexual symbolism made at the Studio
> des Ursulines. Unfortunately it lacked the forceful per-
> formance Artaud could have given the role of the priest
> had he not been too unwell to play the part intended for
> him. . . .

Marjorie Rosen in Popcorn Venus capsules the achievement
of La Coquille:

> [Dulac] presented a boldly surrealistic anticlerical diatribe
> which--two years prior to the masterful Buñuel-Dali col-
> laboration Le Chien andalou, in which a razor blade gouges
> across an eye--she used trick photography to split a hate-

ful general's head down the middle and audaciously showed
a tormented priest masturbating under his cassock.   That
both Antonin Artaud, père to the Theatre of the Absurd,
and the prestigious Cinémathèque Française credited Dulac
as the mother of surrealism is fitting in view of her brilliant originality... [p. 378].

Brunius observes that the film "had been spoilt by Alex Allin's poor acting and drowned in such a deluge of technical tricks
that only a few admirable shots could struggle to the surface.... "35

La Coquille and Beudet share the same flaws in David Curtis' critical gauge (Experimental Cinema, New York: Universe
Books, 1973, p. 20).   "The same oversimplified pictorial conception
detracts" from both films.   La Coquille is

> an equally literal translation of an infinitely superior
> scenario written by ... Artaud [who] was very much in-
> volved in the cinema.   He acted parts in two major movies
> in the late twenties ... and according to reports very
> much wanted to play the clergyman in Dulac's film....

Artaud's scenario is historically significant, Curtis asserts,
for being the first of a kind, and for radically differing from the
René Clair fantasies or the "pure" films made by Fernand Leger
and Hans Richter at this time.   Curtis read the Artaud script which
was published after the release of La Coquille and his criticisms
and conclusions stem from his study of it.   "Artaud deliberately
delved into the ugly depths of the subconscious, and allowed his
plot to embrace the full extent of the chaos he found there. "

Key scenes from the scenario as it appears in Experimental
Cinema are quoted.

> The main protagonists are the clergyman, an officer, and
> a young woman.   The clergyman is in a ballroom and has
> just been confronted by a woman's ghost.   The apparition
> seems to terrify the clergyman.   He lets the breastplate
> fall and it gives off an enormous flame in breaking.
> Then ... he gathers his clothes to him.   But as he grasps
> the skirts of his cassock to draw them around his thighs,
> these skirt-tails seem to stretch out, forming an endless
> road into the night.   The clergyman and the woman run
> desperately through the night.   This race is interspaced
> with hallucinating sequences with the woman in different
> guises: now with her cheek prodigiously swollen, now
> with her tongue sticking out, stretching out infinitely, with
> the clergyman hanging on to it like a rope ... the clergy-
> man emerges in a passageway with the woman swinging
> in a sort of cloud behind him....

Curtis then connects the character of La Coquille to the character of the Artaud-Dulac collaboration.

> The images have no narrative meaning, they are rather a series of visual stimuli intended to create a psychological drama within the viewer, rousing the mind by osmosis without verbal transposition. Dulac's cinematic transposition is not always helpful. Her sense of pictorial design and too-well-measured editing (visual rhythm) detract from the essential realism of Artaud's vision. When the film was premiered ... Artaud apparently denounced Dulac's production and was supported in his attack by his Surrealist friends; but the circumstances suggest that they may have been more in anger at his exclusion from the cutting rooms than through any basic disagreement over the visual conception, as has sometimes been suggested . . . . "

That Dulac misunderstood Artaud's intentions in his scenario and that she "betrayed her total incomprehension of the surrealist viewpoint on film" in La Coquille is the conclusion of J. H. Matthews in Surrealism and Film (Ann Arbor: University of Michigan Press, 1971, pp. 78-80).

> When adapting his scenario to the screen ... Dulac included among the credits the words "a dream of Antonin Artaud. " This reference to Artaud's text was made in violation of contract ... it amounted to distortion of the script's nature and purpose.... [An angry Artaud] asked the surrealist group to undertake a "punitive expedition" against the movie and its director. During the premiere performance, he led the protest from the auditorium....

Sadoul referred to this walkout "as one in which Mme. Dulac was found guilty of having 'deformed and betrayed' a surrealist script" and he quotes Artaud's publishers on this matter. Artaud wanted to take part in making the film but Dulac didn't want him. Later, Artaud "disavowed ... Dulac's adaptation, which he accused of being a solely oneiric interpretation of his scenario.... " For Artaud, the framework of a dream was false: his intentions were to portray psychic reality. He attempted "to transpose action to a plane on which it makes its effect 'almost intuitively on the mind ... I will not seek to find excuse for its apparent incoherence through the facile loophole of the dream....' " If La Coquille was only a dream, then it lost its potency. His intentions in his own words were "to display the motives of our actions 'in their original and profound barbarity, ' and to transmit them visually.... "

Dulac and Artaud had embarked on a collision course in their proposed partnership. Neither could have foreseen the conflicting consequences. Dulac "had called his script 'mad. ' Now he countered, calling her 'a cow. '... " Matthews assesses La Coquille as

> a remarkably fluid cinematographic movement sure to find favor with contemporary exponents of vanguard technique ... although she made a determined effort to conceal its

"madness, " she did not succeed altogether in emptying
Artaud's scenario of surrealist content.   For this reason
alone, her Coquille ... deserves mention among the first
surrealist films....

The most detailed and accurate explication of La Coquille and
its reception by the premiere audience who were aware of the
stormy Artaud-Dulac relationship is made by Wendy Dozoretz in
"Dulac versus Artaud, " Wide Angle 3:1 (1979), pp. 47-53. Dozoretz clarifies critic Georges Sadoul's role in establishing the reputations of Dulac and La Coquille, a role of unwitting confusion,
omission, and correction.

In Sadoul's Histoire de l'art du Cinéma, La Coquille is "poetic and psychological in context, a bit too stiff, too formal....
[p. 109]" In his Dictionary of Filmmakers, he adds, "Her later
features were so hampered by commercial restrictions that she
joined the second avant-garde with her La Coquille.... [p. 70]"
Not a word about the dissension between Artaud and Dulac.

Dozoretz explains Sadoul's silence on this matter.   The film
had

opened on February 9, 1928....   As the credits appeared
Andre Breton yelled "Mme. Dulac est une vache, " and a
demonstration typical of the Surrealists ensued, ostensibly
protesting Germaine Dulac's treatment of Antonin Artaud's
script.   Robert Desnos, Louis Aragon and Georges Sadoul
prevented the projection of the film by screaming pro-
fanities at Dulac and by throwing objects at the screen.

Dozoretz writes that Sadoul believed that he was protesting Artaud's
work, not Dulac's!   "He realized he had been wrong fifteen years
later. " Dozoretz affirms that Sadoul disfavored La Coquille for
thirty-four years, when he was asked, in 1962, to reappraise it.
Doing so, Sadoul discovered it was "a classic of the Surrealist
cinema. "

In his Histoire Générale du Cinéma (Paris: Editions Denoël,
1975, t. 6, v. 1, p. 348), Sadoul remarks that the film is better
known and shown more often because Henri Langlois, head of the
Cinémathèque Française, "rediscovered" it in 1962.   La Coquille,
with its inhibited priest in ironic pursuit of an ideal woman, wrest-
ling with an officer whom he views as a rival, appeals to Sadoul as
a successful parody of the priesthood, in general terms.   In one
acerbic episode, the priest in a long frockcoat, shatters a hundred
glasses in an underground cellar-like cave, having first poured out
their contents, red wine.   Then, with no transitional shots, he
makes his way, crawling on his hands and feet on Paris streets.

Sadoul expresses the belief that it was this crawling scene
that revolted Artaud, but he supplies no supportive evidence for his
supposition.   In addition, Sadoul affirms that the film has aged

gracefully, its power intact after forty years, thus earning a place
among the classics of surrealist cinema.

Dozoretz's description of the film's reception and Sadoul's
errors serves as introduction to the theme of her article: "The
Seashell and the Clergyman must now be considered not simply as
a mockery of Artaud's work, for which Dulac has too long been re-
proached, but as the unique product of two incongruous minds. "[36]

Dozoretz traces the artistic concepts of scenarist Artaud
and director Dulac as shared incompatibility. "Clearly Artaud's
violent conception of the spectator/screen relationship opposes Dulac's romantic theory of moving light. "[37] The genealogy of their
partnership on Seashell is gleaned from Artaud's letters to Dulac.
Initially, Artaud and Dulac trusted each other. He wrote the script.
He did not want to direct the film, but in a gradual transition, he
changed his mind, as shown in his letters when he made suggestions
and sketches for the film, and involved himself in its production
problems. "After two-and-a-half-months, Artaud wrote a letter to
express his irritation for having been excluded from the shooting
and editing of the film. "[38]

Dozoretz admits that, since Dulac's letters to Artaud are
not available, "perhaps the film can be seen as a subversion of
Artaud's misogynist attitude towards women evident in his script. "[39]
The strongest criticisms of Dulac as director were "Dulac's use of
optical tricks and her 'feminization' of the script. "[40] But the use
of optical distortions is inherent in the script, as Dozoretz indicates,
and, yes, Dulac probably did soften the harsh brutality in Artaud's
scenario.

There was still another basis for conflict. Artaud expected
to play the clergyman's role, but Dulac, as director, selected another actor. As Artaud wrote the script,

> the clergyman represents Artaud in Seashell.... Dulac's
> choice of Allin rather than Artaud to play the clergyman
> shatters the positive value Artaud gives to the role....
> Artaud's obsessive identification with the protagonist must
> be understood as the crucial issue in his denunciation of
> the film. Whereas Artaud saw the powerful male ego suf-
> ficient unto itself, Dulac exposed and criticized this con-
> ception by ridiculing the dominant representation of man. [41]

Following a summary of the action of Seashell, Dozoretz
posits the film's theme as Artaud's "search for himself, a quest
that involves three sides of his sexuality; the feminine, the masculine, and the neuter. "[42] It is obvious that misogynist Artaud and
feminist Dulac could not be in accord and that Seashell is, indeed,
in Dozoretz's terms, "the unique product of two incongruous
minds. "[43]

In 1927, in the wake of La Coquille, Dulac faced a dilemma:

she lost her faith in her ability to make films that would please everyone--producers, audiences, herself. She decided, before it was too late, to make pure films, her visual symphonies. L'invitation au voyage (1927) was first. Baudelaire's poem was placed in a musical mesh with the "orchestration of images" and the "play of light" (these are Dulac's phrases) producing a mosaic of sensuous splendor. Several pages of Chopin were "illustrated" in Disque 927 (1928). Thèmes et variations (1928) wove classical airs into a tapestry of light and shade. In a fourth short "visual symphony, titled Etude cinégraphique sur une arabesque (1928) Dulac integrated portions of Debussy into moving shadow and light: mirror-like music. As Ford summarizes: "It is in the making of these ... small films, without literary subjects, that the essential creativity of Dulac in her truest esthetic preoccupation can be discovered."[44]

She did make one last commercial film: La princesse mandane (1928). This was her "swan song" Ford says, and her last important feature film. She adapted her script from Pierre Benoit's novel L'Oublie: the film chronicles the picaresque adventures of a bewildered soldier seemingly oblivious to the circumstantial consequences of the Russian Revolution. Dulac's scenario stressed the lack of will of the hero as he endures the caprices of his destiny.

After completion of La princesse, the course of cinema history changed and, in Ford's description, Dulac was reduced to accepting secondary tasks and abandoning her director's role, a status she had enjoyed for fifteen years. The Oxford Companion to Film attaches a differing significance to this abrupt alteration in Dulac's career:

> Ill health and her apprehensions regarding the expense and
> inhibiting effect of working with sound halted her career
> as a director, although she continued to work on news-
> reels in an advisory capacity.... [p. 211]

Trying to understand Dulac's interest in making news films and scientific documentaries, Cornwell writes,

> Two seemingly disparate attachments ... her love and re-
> spect for the Lumière brothers, and her affection for an
> experiment ... shooting single-frame, Germination d'un
> Haricot (Growth of a Bean Plant) ... seek to explain her
> interest.... With this influence understood, her move-
> ments from the avant-garde to the scientific and newsreel
> film merge into one.... [p. 36]

These provided channels of hope for her in the thirties--fresh corridors of creativity in film.

A plurality of film-related activities supplanted her film direction, scripting, and production. In 1930 she made the documentary Les 24 heures du Mans and was named a Chevalier of the Legion of Honor for her activist role in the evolution of film as an

art form. Because talking pictures stopped independent film production at this point, Dulac took a final step toward recognition of
this reality: she became head of Actualités-Gaumont, best known
for its fact films on current affairs and news events.

In 1927 and 1928 Dulac had been instrumental, with Louis
Lumière, in establishing a filmmaking school named L'Ecole Technique de Photographie et de Cinématographie de la Rue de Vaugiraud
in Paris where she taught for many years. She tried publishing a
magazine, Schémas, in 1927, which failed after only one issue.
Ever inventive and ingenious, and urged on by a barely concealed
instinct for survival, Dulac managed to support herself with a tremendous variety of jobs in spite of the ill health which plagued her.

She continued to make known her reactions to film. News-
reels became popular in the thirties; talking pictures became an international industry; and the French film industry--the avant-gardists
having vanished with Dulac--tried to get out of its rut (as Brunius
phrases it) as a new and young generation of filmmakers arrived at
the film studios looking for employment.

> ... Speech and sound may be considered as an accompani-
> ment, a splendid projection of the image, but they have
> nothing to do with its essential form ... speech and sound
> being indispensably complementary. Movement in all its
> truth is the scientific and artistic significance of the cine-
> ma. "[45]

This was Dulac's conviction as she voiced it in a speech.

In 1932 she made a montaged film, Le Picador, with Jaquelux as a scene designer. No doubt she continued to be responsible
at Actualités-Gaumont for several tasks--editing, we are certain--
until her death on July 22, 1942. She was involved with the Cinémathèque Française, too. One source conjures a picture of Dulac
trying to salvage the films in the Cinémathèque's depository from
war damage, "exerting herself for it in the most tragic hours ... "
perhaps during the fall of Paris. [46]

With only Beudet and La Coquille extant, what can the film
student conclude about the value of Dulac's film work? Film historians who mention her tend to view her endless energetic efforts
darkly. Richard Roud, for example, sounds his regret in these
words.

> Dulac ... I found very disappointing. I suppose she had
> to do her symphonies of flowers just to teach us all that
> it was a path not worth pursuing. And La Coquille ...
> was really proof that ... well, that Un Chien andalou was
> authentic. You would have thought how two films could be
> lumped together, but they can't, because one is genuine
> and the other is sheer coquetry.... [47]

In Women and Film, 5/6 (1974), pp. 55-61, William Van
Wert characterizes "Germaine Dulac: First Feminist Filmmaker"
in these words:

> Most important and prolific French director between 1920
> and 1930. Her film style proceeded from psychological
> realism and symbolism through surrealism to documen-
> taries and attempts at transposing musical structures to
> film. . . .

Pending discovery and identification of the factual films she
worked on in her last decade, and a reassessment of her filmography and published commentaries, an honor already awarded Louis
Delluc, our most valid view now of Dulac is as an intrepid impro-
viser and experimenter in film form. Dulac assisted in the au-
thorship and articulation of the film form. She was Mother of Surrealist Film. She was there.

FILMOGRAPHY

Les Soeurs ennemies (1915)

Geo le mystérieux (1916)

Vénus victrix (1916)

Dans l'ouragan de la vie (1916) ⎱ (Probably same film)

Ames des fous (1917) (also script)

Le bonheur des autres (1918)

La fête espagnole (1919)

La cigarette (1919) (also co-script)

Malencontre (1920)

La belle dame sans merci (1920)

La mort du soleil (1921)

Werther (1922) (unfinished, also script)

Gossette (1923)

La souriante Madame Beudet (1923) (also script)

Le diable dans la ville (1924)

Ame d'artiste (1925) (also co-script)

La Folie des vaillants (1925) (also script)

Antoinette Soubrier (1926) (also script)

La coquille et le Clergyman (1927)

L'invitation au voyage (1927) (also script)

Le cinéma au service de l'histoire (1927)

Germination d'un haricot (1928)

Mon Paris (1928) (with A. Guyot)

La princesse mandane (1928) (also script)

Thème et variations (1928)

Disque 927 (1928)

Etude cinégraphique sur une arabesque (1928-29)

Les 24 Heures du Mans (1930)

Le Picador (1932) (with Jaquelux)

Le cinéma au service de l'histoire (1937)

NOTES

1. William Flint Thrall and Addison Hubbard, revised and enlarged by C. Hugh Holman, A Handbook to Literature. New York: Odyssey Press, 1960, p. 130.
2. Liz-Anne Bawden, ed., Oxford Companion to Film. New York: Oxford University Press, 1976, p. 670.
3. Paul Monaco, Cinema & Society. New York: Elsevier, 1976, pp. 68-69.
4. Bawden, p. 184.
5. Charles Ford, Femmes cinéastes. Paris: Editions Denoël, 1970, p. 25.
6. Ibid., p. 28.
7. Eugene C. McCreary, "Louis Delluc, Film Theorist, Critic and Prophet," Cinema Journal XVI/1 (Fall 1976), pp. 14-35.
8. Georges Sadoul, Dictionary of Film Makers. Berkeley: University of California Press, 1972), p. 70.
9. Richard Abel, "Louis Delluc: The Critic as Cinéaste," Quarterly Review of Film Studies I:2 (May 1976), p. 210.
10. Regina Cornwell, "Maya Deren and Germaine Dulac: Activists of the Avant-Garde," Film Library Quarterly 5 (Winter 1971/72), p. 32.
11. Jacques Brunius, "Experimental Film in France," in Roger Manvell, ed., Experiment in the Film. London: The Grey Walls Press, 1949, p. 84.
12. Ibid., p. 79.
13. Georges Sadoul, Histoire générale du cinéma. Paris: Editions Denoël, 1975, t. 5, v. 1, pp. 107-108.
14. Ibid., p. 54.
15. Ibid., p. 108.
16. Ibid.
17. Ibid.
18. Brunius, p. 85.
19. Jeanne Betancourt, Women in Focus. Dayton, Ohio: Pflaum, 1974, p. 123.
20. Charles Ford, "Germaine Dulac," in Anthologie du Cinéma, vol. 4 (Paris VII, 27 rue Saint-André-des-Arts, 1968), p. 46. The name of the anthology's editor or compiler is not cited.

21. Sadoul, Histoire général, p. 110.
22. Ibid., p. 111.
23. Betancourt, Women in Focus, p. 121.
24. Ibid., p. 122.
25. Ibid.
26. Sadoul, Histoire général.
27. Ibid., p. 119.
28. Ibid.
29. Ibid., pp. 119-120.
30. Brunius, p. 70.
31. Ibid., p. 73.
32. Ibid.
33. Cornwell, p. 34.
34. Sadoul, Histoire générale, p. 120.
35. Brunius, p. 99.
36. Dozoretz, p. 46.
37. Ibid., p. 49.
38. Ibid., p. 51.
39. Ibid.
40. Ibid.
41. Ibid., p. 52.
42. Ibid., p. 50.
43. Ibid., p. 46.
44. Ford, Femmes cinéastes, p. 42.
45. Cornwell, p. 30.
46. Ibid., p. 36.
47. "Memories of Resnais, " 38:3 Sight and Sound (Summer 1969),
    p. 126.

3. LOIS WEBER: MORALIST MOVIEMAKER

Born: June 13, 1882, Allegheny, Pa.
Died: November 13, 1939, Los Angeles, Calif.

"During two years of church army work I had ample opportunity to regret the limited field any individual worker
could embrace even by a life of strenuous endeavor.
Meeting with many in that field who spoke strange tongues,
I came suddenly to realize the blessings of a voiceless
language to them. To carry out the idea of missionary
pictures was difficult. " [Anthony Slide, Early Women Directors. New York: A. S. Barnes, 1977, p. 35.]

When Lois Weber died in Hollywood, screenwriter Frances Marion
paid her funeral expenses. The New York Times obituary (Nov. 14,
1939, 23: 2) states that Weber died after a long illness caused by
a stomach ailment. Not stated was the fact that Weber's first husband, Phillips Smalley, with whom she shared the larger portion of
her career in Hollywood films, had died, a "bit" player, six months
earlier, on May 2, also in Hollywood. Her death notice nods briefly at Weber's lengthy and all-inclusive Hollywood roles: acting,
writing, directing and producing, set-designing, and editing, as well
as "discovering, " coaching and advancing the careers of starlets
Anita Stewart and Claire Windsor. The notice omits the name of
Frances Marion, whose long screenwriting career began under the
tutelage of Lois Weber, Weber's lengthy career in silent pictures
rivalled Marion's in tenure, taking its beginning in 1907.

Christened Florence Lois Weber, the child's primary interest in the arts was music. She had been born, a second daughter,
to George and Mary Matilda Weber, who were the descendants of
Pennsylvania Germans who settled in the western area of the state,
many of them preachers. "... The Weber home was one of strict
religious observance.... "[1] Young Lois sang at church and played
the piano. She toured as a concert pianist at sixteen. Her venture
onto the concert stage ended abruptly during one southern junket
when a piano key broke off in her hand, an incident that "broke my
nerve" as she recalled.[2] Forsaking the piano, she resumed her interest in singing.

[As] a Christian Home Missionary she sang hymns on
streetcorners and worked in the industrial slums of Pitts-
burgh ... she left the group after a short time. "It gave
life a bitter taste for a while, " she recalled later....

By now family problems forced her to go out and earn her own living. . . . "3

An uncle offered advice.   "'As I was convinced the theatrical profession needed a missionary, he suggested that the best way to reach them was to become one of them, so I went on the stage filled with a great desire to convert my fellowman. . . . ' "4

A short stint as a soubrette in the touring Zig Zag Company proved to be too superficial for her altruistic aims.   In 1904 she joined a road company production of Why Girls Leave Home, a melodramatic show more to her taste.   In it she "'sang two very pretty songs very effectively, ' a reviewer reported, 'and won considerable applause. ' (Boston Globe, Sept. 27, 1904). "5   Phillips Smalley was actor-manager of this company.   He and Weber were married in Chicago, May 1904 after only one week's acquaintance and courtship.   Although the Smalleys tried to work together, their touring schedules separated them constantly during their first two years of marriage.   In 1906 Weber stepped down from the stage into a housewife role, setting up housekeeping in New York City.

While her husband was on tour, Weber sought employment and found a job acting in the Gaumont Studios.   The year was 1908 and the reasons that prompted Weber's entry into film acting, instead of returning to the stage, are debatable, Koszarski ponders:

> Legitimate actors despised the movies in those days and
> only appeared in them under duress. . . .   So something
> special pushed Weber into films; something more than
> boredom, and perhaps even more than money. . . .   Lois
> Weber sensed early the emotional power of the cinema,
> its unique ability to dramatize an issue and drive home a
> moral. . . .   "I find at once the outlet for my emotions
> and my ideals, I can preach to my heart's content, and
> with the opportunity to write the play, act the leading role,
> and direct the entire production, if my message fails to
> reach someone I can blame only myself, " she wrote a few
> years later. . . . 6

Weber's enthusiasm was contagious.   "'I wrote the story for the first picture, besides directing it and playing the lead.   When Mr. Smalley returned [from tour] he joined me and we co-directed and played leads in a long list of films. ' "   For the next ten years the Smalleys signed joint contracts.   ". . . They made their debut in a series of experimental 'talking' films--two decades before the successful coming of sound--for the Gaumont Company; Miss Weber wrote the brief scenarios and the dialogue, which was recorded on phonograph records and synchronized with the action. . . . "7   In their article "Women Directors, " 1 Films in Review (Nov. 1950), p. 9, Joseph and Harry Feldman affirm this priority: ". . . she, together with her husband, Phillips Smalley, with whom she usually collaborated, produced the first talking picture for Gaumont back in 1908. . . . "

The Smalleys worked for a swift succession of employers: Gaumont, Reliance, Rex, Universal, Bosworth, Universal again, and ultimately, Lois Weber Productions. The year 1911 found the couple at Rex then owned by Edwin S. Porter, director and producer of The Great Train Robbery for Edison, whose employ he quit to form his own Rex Studios, "... and evolved for it a trademark with a rim of stars--the same stars which the public sees today on the famous trademark of Paramount...."[8] Weber's experience was extended and refined at Rex where she helped write, edit, act, and direct most of the Rex films released. Thus, in 1912, when Porter decided to direct films for Adolf Zukor, then at the helm of Famous Players, he left the Smalleys in charge of Rex, by now "one of the satellite companies of the New York Motion Picture Corporation, which in 1912 became a subsidiary of Universal Pictures. At Rex, Miss Weber acted, assisted her husband ... cut the film, and if necessary turned the camera and developed the negative...."[9]

At the now-named Universal workbase, Weber's skills were refined by an unrelenting production schedule; two two-reelers each month were spun out by the Smalleys in the period 1913-14. Each was co-directed, co-acted, and scripted by Weber. Included in this small company was cameraman Dal Clawson, who remained with Weber until 1921. In the years cited, "she churned out footage at a feverish rate," Koszarski states, "between two and four hundred titles according to her own estimates, although less than 50 have been positively identified...."

> His Brand, released Oct. 2, 1913, concerned a cowboy who brands his wife on the breast and whose son is born with the mark of the brand. The Jew's Christmas, released Dec. 18, 1913, demonstrated how race prejudice was conquered by parental love. The Leper's Coat, released Jan. 25, 1914, indicated that "science has proven that fear of disease will produce its symptoms more surely than contagion, and that thought governs the body." The Career of Waterloo Peterson, released May 10, 1914, was a comedy of studio life, in which many Universal personnel appeared. A comedy was unusual for ... Weber, for as The Universal Weekly (Nov. 29, 1913) noted, "Miss Weber's plays are always thoughtful and thought compelling, deeply understanding of human nature and soul-searching in their revelation of truth."[10]

Described as of medium height, compactly built, with dark hair and decisive in manner, Weber's authoritative manner undoubtedly helped her become elected as mayor of Universal City in 1913. In that year she addressed the Woman's City Club of Los Angeles and presented her conviction that social improvements could be inspired and implemented by films (hers), and that films could serve as a vanguard to develop many necessary social reforms. Weber's commanding personality gradually assumed dominance of the Smalleys' working arrangements. "In the early part of their career the

creative chores had been split between the two, but by 1914 Weber
seems to emerge as the dominant partner.... "11

        In 1914, although Weber was very popular at Universal (best-
known as an actress), the Smalleys moved on to the Bosworth Company for an eight-month period. Their shared ventures at Bosworth
included Hypocrites (1915) in which viewers were treated to "The
Naked Truth" in the form of a nude young woman, representing
hypocrisy itself. Koszarski dubs it,

> a thinly disguised sermon on the corruption of modern
> society, but the film's copious frontal nudity brought riot-
> ing crowds to New York's Strand Theatre. Variety (Nov.
> 6, 1914) enthused: "There is no other picture like it,
> there has been no other, and it will attract anywhere. "12

        What actress performed "The Naked Truth"? Slide claims
there is a definite resemblance between the actress and director
Weber. "Some contemporary sources state she is portrayed by an
actress named Margaret Edwards, but I can find no record of such
a player. Other sources claim that Lois Weber, herself, played
the role.... "13

        Finding and fostering female thespic talents was a role as-
sumed by Weber as the careers of Mildred Harris (who later became Mrs. Charlie Chaplin), Clara Viola Kronk (who was renamed
Claire Windsor), Lois Wilson, and Esther Ralston gave testimony.
In the case of Frances Marion, the skills that Weber nurtured
evolved into writing not acting. Marion herself graphically portrays
her first interview for a job with Weber, having been introduced to
the filmmaker by a phone call from Adela Rogers St. Johns.

        Marion arrived on the set when the Versailles was being
seized. When the scene was completed

> the whistle blew, the mob dispersed, and the director left
> the set. "Sit down, my dear, " Miss Weber said when
> taut nerves made me rise stiffly....   "I'm very happy
> you came to see me. I'm sure Mrs. St. Johns told you
> why I was interested in you. One of the fascinating side-
> lights in the art of making motion pictures is the search
> for new talent.... I believe in taking amateurs and teach-
> ing them all I have learned.... I have a broad wing,
> would like you to come under its protection.... "

When told that Marion was not an actress, but could do publicity,
"... Her laughter silenced me. '... If you don't want to work before the camera ... I'll find plenty for you to do.... ' Thus I entered the Bosworth Studio as: Frances Marion. Actress, Refined
Type. Age 19.... "14 Although Marion was then a divorcée of 24
and acted as an extra in many films, her forte resided in the typewriter, not in being type-cast, and many of the Mary Pickford and
Lois Weber films bore her byline.

The success of Bosworth film releases made by the Smalleys
advanced the salary ratings of the pair.   Charles Ford[15] attributes
the merits of such films as False Colors (1914) especially, Sunshine
Molly (1915), and It's No Laughing Matter (1915) to Weber's directing them from the female lead's point-of-view.

> By 1915, she had become a popular celebrity whose work
> was as characteristic to audiences as that of Griffith or
> De Mille.   A Weber film could be expected to tell a
> story with a moral, and often in these years to swing
> from documentary-like realism to dream induced allegory.
> Her films took themselves very seriously indeed, but
> Weber did not lack the showmanship to bring in the audi-
> ence. . . . [16]

Returning to the Universal Studios, Weber was ensconced as
a director earning $5,000 a week.   She had been acting for seven
years--played Portia to her husband's Antonio in The Merchant of
Venice (1914) with good notices--and no longer wished to take part
in each operational phase of moviemaking.   Instead, she wanted to
and now could concentrate on overseeing the entire work of filming
and leave on-the-set acting roles to her protégées, serving her
most urgent motivation: making morality message movies with a
shrewd recognition of box-office values.

Jewel (ca. 1915) was Weber's first release at Univeral, although it is not listed in Film Directors: A Guide to Their American Films (Metuchen, N. J.:   Scarecrow, 1974, pp. 412-413), by
James Robert Parish and Michael R. Pitts.   Weber's script was
adapted from a novel by Clara Louise Burnham titled, Jewel: A
Chapter in Her Life, and she enjoyed the Christian Scientist flavor
of the story so much that she filmed it a second time in 1923, ap-
propriating the subtitle of the novel as its title.

Weber then made the film--considered a choice assignment--
which introduced Anna Pavlova and the Ballet Russe to American
film audiences: The Dumb Girl of Portici (1916).   But "there was
little to interest her in the elaborate production, and neither critics
nor audiences were satisfied. . . . "[17]   Two months of filming Pavlova
and her group, who were performing at the Midway Gardens in Chicago, were followed by another month's shooting on the set in Universal City.

Weber's anti-capital punishment film, The People vs. John
Doe, in which Weber took her last acting role, elicited this reaction
from the New York Dramatic Mirror: "It is by far the most effective propaganda that has been seen in quite some time ... " (December 23, 1916).   The film was renamed God's Law.   Shoes (1916)
"possibly the finest film she made"[18] analyzed and agitated against
child labor and poverty.   With its revelatory name, Hop, the Devil's
Brew (1915) waved an anti-saloon banner.

In 1916, at the peak of her success, Weber told a reporter,

"'I like to direct because I believe that a woman more or less intuitively brings out many of the emotions that are rarely expressed
on the screen.   I may miss what some of the male directors get,
but I will get other effects that they will miss.'"[19]

        The lesson intended for audience consumption can be gleaned
or guessed from the titles of Weber's films in her peak year, 1916:
Idle Wives, The Flirt, and Saving the Family Name.   Not as self-
evident was the film title which rocketed Weber's name to larger
audiences, bigger box-office returns, and an even higher annual income: Where Are My Children?   Released in 1916 closest in chronology to Dumb Girl of Portici, this film vibrated with not one but
two inflammatory themes: Abortion is a crime and birth control is
necessary.   Weber wrote the script from a story by Lucy Payton
and Franklin Hall.   So explosive was this double-barreled message
that it used a two paragraph preface to prepare the audiences for
its bold tale.   Anthony Slide quotes the opening of this film (probably written by Weber), which advocated an adults-only audience,
perhaps an initial instance of self-imposed censorship by an American filmmaker:

        The question of birth control is now being generally dis-
        cussed.   All intelligent people know that birth control is
        a subject of serious public interest.   Newspapers, maga-
        zines, and books have treated different phases of this
        question.   Can a subject thus dealt with on the printed
        page be denied careful dramatization on the motion picture
        screen?   The Universal Film Mfg. Company believes not.
        The Universal Film Mfg. Company does believe, however,
        that the question of birth control should not be presented
        before children.   In producing this film the intention is to
        place a serious drama before adult audiences, to whom no
        suggestion of a fact of which they are ignorant is con-
        veyed.   It believes that children should not be admitted to
        see this picture unaccompanied by adults, but if you bring
        them it will do them an immeasurable amount of good
        [pp. 41-42].

        The plot is simple realism.   A district attorney learns that
he is childless because his wife's pregnancy has been aborted.   According to Richard Koszarski, "After calling her a murderess, he
forgives his wife; but throughout the years with empty arms and
guilty conscience she must face her husband's unspoken question:
'where are my children?'"   He continues,

        While arguing "that birth control might be advantageously
        applied among the needy," most of the film dealt with the
        issue of "race suicide"--abortion on demand as practiced
        by a group of vapid social butterflies.   Weber made clear
        distinctions between charitable humanitarian issues and
        what she saw as slackening moral standards, and to the
        end of her career championed the ideals of Christian
        fundamentalism. [20]

Marjorie Rosen brackets the film with Hypocrites and The Hand That Rocks the Cradle (1917) as Weber's "most interesting." In each of these Weber focused on a substratum of deception perceived as an injustice and then created a visual sermon--reproving in tone and a call to the conscience in concept--to flesh out her fable. For Rosen the most biting and memorable of this triad of films is Where Are My Children? which

> melodramatically emphasized the nobility of motherhood, yet while its conservatism corresponded to popular sentiment, the film boldly, even audaciously acknowledged abortion as an alternative. The story concerns rich women who prefer not to bear children and consult an abortionist without their husbands' knowledge. When the doctor is caught and sentenced to fifteen years of hard labor, he tells the prosecuting attorney to "see to your own household." The lawyer returns home, and on finding his wife with her childless friends, tells them: "I have just learned why so many of you have no children. I should bring you to trial for manslaughter, but I shall content myself with asking you to leave my house."

His wife cannot answer to the question he asks her. In the years following, according to the picture's plot, this

> murderess ... tries to change, but we are told that "having perverted nature so often, she found herself physically unable to wear the diadem of motherhood." Everywhere she goes, she gazes longingly at tots playing. ... In the final scene the couple are seated unhappily in their parlor, and Weber superimposes tiny youngsters crawling all over them, as in a dream. ... [21]

Amid swirls of controversial discussion and calls for imposition of censorship on the film, Universal earned three million dollars. Weber had read the pulse of her audience and struck home at its heart: she defused an explosive human concern. Reaping profits with an equivocal message, by sensibly setting forth the positive and negative aspects of intentional abortion in a film which evoked cries of sensationalism and vulgarity, Weber deftly supported motherhood while questioning its inevitability. She offered her audiences, perhaps for the first time, a sober scrutiny of motherhood's alternative in everyday dress, with appealing feminine characters and believable male actors playing, not overacting, their roles. The district attorney does not take refuge in lofty rhetoric; the abortionist is not a blackguard with dirty hands.

> It is not often that a subject as delicate as the one of which this picture treats us is handled as boldly yet, at the same time as inoffensively as is the case with this production. It succeeds in making its point, in being impressive, in driving home the lesson that it seeks to teach without being offensive. This is largely due to the capable

direction of the Smalleys and the superb acting of Tyrone
Power, aided by an excellent cast.

This is the poorly worded opinion of the New York Dramatic Mirror
(April 27, 1916). 22

        Observes Sharon Smith in Women Who Make Movies (New
York: Hopkinson & Blake, 1975, p. 11): "... Weber's advocacy of
birth control made her a figure of controversy, but she never backed
away from this issue and in fact made four more films on the subject.... " Smith does not name these; maybe one of them was The
Hand That Rocks the Cradle (1917).

        The inevitable next step for Weber was a film studio of her
own. In 1917, with Universal financing, Weber remodeled an extensive property at 4634 Sunset Boulevard, according to Koszarski,
or 4634 Santa Monica Boulevard, according to Slide. Diametrically
opposed to the colorless, assembly-line warehouses native to most
filming companies, including Universal, Lois Weber Productions
exuded the leisurely ambience of a private country estate. The
fact that the Smalleys lived and worked there may be held at least
partially accountable.

        "Visitors were greeted by landscaped gardens, giant pepper
trees, and 'dancing flames in the fireplace.' She had designed the
'inspiring and delightful environment' of the studio to fit her own
ideas of creativity, and was able to closely supervise all aspects
of her productions. "23 Significantly, she could shoot films in sequence, a matter of first importance to Weber. In an interview,
Weber pointed out,

        One thing which I have never been able to do before and
        which I shall do now that I have my own studio is to have
        every set needed in a picture ready before I begin to take
        a scene. In that way I shall be able to take my whole
        picture practically in sequence. I think the inability to
        do that has been one of the greatest difficulties under
        which both actors and directors have labored.... 24

After explaining the confusion and constraints of discontinuities of
filming, she continues,

        If I am able to carry out that one thing it should go a
        long way toward knitting a picture into a more plausible
        and connected whole. And I have several kindred experi-
        ments which I shall give a fair trial.... "25

        As for what she considered the best basis for a film work,
Weber replied: "I pin my faith to my story, for all the sumptuous
settings in the world and a cast of two dozen stars will not and cannot carry a bad story to a legitimate and pronounced success. And
I pin my faith to that story which is a slice out of real life. "26

As her own administrator, Weber enjoyed shooting in sequence and building up a stock company of players, technicians, and writers.   But her independent stance evoked a complete change in the type of film she wanted to make.   In place of reform and social criticism she now wanted to portray the social status quo, instead of slaying dragons she would now caress kittens.   The heavy hand of movie-made justice gave way to a light tap on the wrist, and the products labeled with her logogram, an Aladdin's lamp in a circle, were akin to pacifiers enclosing a medicinal pill   This type of woman's movie, which would later be euphemized as soap opera shows, was still a profitable enterprise, but a surprising shift in subject matter.   In the absence of documentation, one wonders if the switch from strong appeals to conscience to inoffensive nostrums concerned with matters of etiquette and class distinctions was a written or unwritten agreement in Weber's contract with Universal.   Even while working under her own company's aegis, in the studio grounds and structures she designed herself, Weber remained under contract to Universal   Of the filmographies consulted, none of her films listed are designated as Lois Weber Productions.   Yet, Weber herself may have tired of crusading, choosing to work in a markedly different subject area.

"... Her new contract emphasized fewer and better pictures, with Weber earning $2500 a week plus one third of the profits of her films, the most important of which were sold as 'Universal Special Jewels. '"27   Henshaw cites a number of "Jewels" in Weber's filmography: The Price of a Good Time (1917), For Husbands Only (1917), The Doctor and the Woman (1918), A Chapter in Her Life (1923) and The Marriage Clause (1926). 28

The first of Weber's "fewer and better pictures" was To Please One Woman, which introduced Claire Windsor in a leading role.   Although a half year was consumed making the film, the result was ho-hum mediocrity:

> Essentially a drama of human errors, ... To Please One Woman shows how perverted womanhood brings unhappiness into the lives of many, causing the unwary to commit mistakes that result in their own ruin.   The poison of this woman's selfishness infects almost everyone with whom she comes in contact.   On account of her, her husband takes his life, the other man almost sacrifices the love of a good woman, a girl's heart is broken, and a young boy takes a dangerous ride that results in his death.   Thus, the story has rather a doleful trend, and in its introduction of the deathbed scene of the boy-hero, is unnecessarily morbid.   The acting during this emotional scene, and directly after, would be more effective if more restrained, and the whole would be more balanced if a saving scene of humor had left its trace here and there. 29

The New York Times (Dec. 20, 1920, 11:2) reconstructs the plot, adopting a benevolent wait-and-see attitude toward Weber's work.

> To please the woman in question, her husband futilely
> robs a bank or something and then achieves his ambition
> by committing suicide; a country doctor of apparent im-
> peccability falls out with his sweetheart ...; a silly girl
> sees her smoking and ... borrows a dime from her swain
> to buy a box of cigarettes, and this young rustic, not
> having the dime, steals it from his employer's cash
> drawer.... The picture might be subtitled "In Imitation
> of Griffith. " Mr. Griffith can take such trite, homiletic
> stories of small-town virtue and corrupting vampires and
> by the magic of cinematography sometimes give them life,
> but Lois Weber ... evidently has not his talent or knack.
> Occasionally her picture shows flashes of inspiration,
> which may be evidence that with more responsive material
> she could make a sufficient number of dramatic moving
> pictures to compose an exceptional photoplay, and this
> seems the more likely because of similar evidence in
> some of her earlier works. So, perhaps, the production
> that fulfills the promises made for each of Miss Weber's
> pictures is to come.... "

Sadly, this initial Weber try at fewer and better proved not even up
to the caliber of her earlier efforts.

In contrast, the New York Times (March 10, 1919, 9:3)
beams warmly upon A Midnight Romance, a fun-for-fun's sake film,
completed by Weber nearly two years earlier and prior to her Universal contract. With a transparent plot--boy meets and gets girl--
or millionaire's son meets a princess-in-disguise, the prime attraction of the movie must have been its sun-surf-sand background.

> Despite the story, there are some beautiful scenes in "A
> Midnight Romance, " pictures of surf and rocks and sand,
> with Marie [Anita Stewart] like a mermaid, among them
> .... To Lois Weber, the director, it is assumed, should
> go the principal credit for the pictures, and also the re-
> sponsibility for a mass of conversational sub-titles that
> try to be poetic and bright.... "

In 1920, Weber signed an even more advantageous contract
with Famous Players-Lasky, which awarded her $50,000 for each
picture and half the profits. Of the five films she completed to
fulfill this contract, The Blot is typical in that it poses the kind of
conflict closest to Weber's typewriter and camera: the dilemma of
a family's inability to properly entertain visitors because it does
not own a proper tea service. Koszarski discerns "an obsession
with the details of middle-class life, with proper form and correct
behavior ... " in these post-1920 films. [30]

Anthony Slide calls The Blot

> a distinctive example of Weber's best work ... it con-
> cerns itself with the very unglamorous subject of "genteel"

poverty among schoolteachers and clergymen.... The simple plot of the film concerns the professor's family's fight to stave off the threat of poverty, the equally humiliating threat of charity, and the daughter's ... gentle wooing by the student, the wealthy neighbor's son, and the impoverished clergyman. Weber handles her subject in a simple, yet sensitive manner, and with her typical concern with detail. Unlike most other productions of the period which would end with the hero and heroine in a love clinch, Weber ends The Blot with a close-up of the heroine, staring after the clergyman she has apparently rejected in favor of the wealthy college student.... 31

The Blot was submitted to a multistep process of restoration to preserve it, with four other Weber films, in the Library of Congress. Although, Slide says, contemporary judgment found the film unappealing (Photoplay's phrase was "rather tiresome"), "It was recently enthusiastically applauded by film festival audiences in Nashville and Chicago.... "32

The year 1920 may have been the one producing Weber's highest income, but it also marked the first step of her descent from appeal to audiences, as The Blot evidences, and from filmmaking. The four Weber films released subsequent to The Blot no longer addressed public taste or topical affairs: to post-World War I viewers they were out-of-date, obsolete, old-fashioned. Films which criticized "free" behavior, smoking in public, and new modes of speech and dress were not welcomed by moviegoers who themselves endorsed the departures from conventions long obeyed. Koszarski coins Weber's films' failures: "... [they] died at the box office, deserted by audiences who found the films' virtues anachronistic.... "33

More exasperation than enthusiasm is expressed by The New York Times (Nov. 14, 1921, 18:1) review, not at all intrigued by discovering the reply to the query in Weber's film title What Do Men Want? Sadly, the film was not what the audience wanted, the critic implies. "... Why does Miss Weber devote the really worth while time of herself and her staff to those simplified sermons on the screen which make a transparent bluff of dealing wisely with problems of human nature but get nowhere at all?"

In approaching a common enough marital exigency, the critic complains, why did Weber concoct an artificial plot, then cap it with a garrulous overextended resolution? Weber's filmed reply to the query "why do good men leave wives for other women ... does not take into account the human need for intensification of life which the good home so often fails to provide.... "

Complimenting the cast, the review finds "the photoplay arrives at a scarcely impressive conclusion after such verbally explicit explanation of the obvious and considerable wandering through a made-to-order plot that becomes theatrical at times to suit the

predetermined purpose of the story.... " Patience exhausted, the
review asks, "Why don't all these sufficiently competent people concern themselves with telling a good, straightforward story and let
whatever moral it has take care of itself?"

Charles Ford asks the same question regarding this film:
"Why does Miss Weber dedicate herself, her time and her equipment to the construction of simple sermons?"[34] Her overstated
style verged upon condescension, her moralistic messages had not
been refurbished to incorporate the freshly emerging worldliness
and social sophistication which moviegoers brought with them to
movie theatres.

Changes in public taste, as Koszarski suggests, "had little
to do with the intrinsic merit of the works, but instead reflected
only their success at reading the barometer of public taste.... "[35]
Weber's contract was voided by Famous Players-Lasky after three
of her films were released and failed at the box office.

Marjorie Rosen poses questions about the causes of Weber's
dismissal from her contract, the failure of her films:

> Did the Roaring Twenties and the rising sun of bedroom
> farces ... diminish her power as one of Hollywood's lead-
> ing directors? Or did the growth of big studios limit not
> only the material she was permitted to work with, but
> also her own usefulness? Unfortunately Weber's decline
> resists analysis because of the scanty documentation of
> her career....

Contributing factors may have been these facts:

> By 1920 motion pictures were the nation's fourth largest
> industry.... Already women were on their way out. It
> was an excision which would occur with startling rapid-
> ity.... [36]

The decline that Weber experienced in the early twenties
was cataclysmic: her personal and professional lives disintegrated
simultaneously into a divorce on June 23, 1922, a nervous breakdown, and the loss of her company. Instantaneously, it would
seem, Weber's whole world of marriage, movies, and individual
fulfillment vanished. Known for her wholesome withstanding of the
pressures of moviemaking, Weber's health deteriorated swiftly under this triple thrust of misfortune. "Adela Rogers St. Johns remembers that she never seemed very dynamic.... "[37] Yet, Carl
Laemmle at the helm of Universal issued this considered judgment
of her:

> I would trust Miss Weber with any sum of money that she
> needed to make any picture that she wanted to make. I
> would be sure that she would bring it back. She knows the
> motion picture business as few people do and can drive her-
> self as hard as anyone I have ever known. [38]

What the hiatus of four years--virtually a blank space in
Weber's life occupied only by rumors of her attempted suicide and
rehabilitation from mental depression--signified in terms of self
and sustenance no available record shows. From the year of her
divorce until 1926, the year of her marriage to Captain Harry Gantz,
a retired Army officer, Weber ostensibly "retired" from public life.
And it was Gantz who assisted her back into the work she loved
after several years of despondent bitterness.

Return she did in 1926, to Universal where she made two
films. The first, starring Billie Dove with Francis X. Bushman,
was The Marriage Clause, which revolves around the marital pro-
hibitive clause in an actress's three-year employment contract.
Several faults are evidenced in the film, as pointed out by The New
York Times (Sept. 26, 1926, 30:2). Subtitles were glaringly mis-
matched to the action; one such was: "Galling memories of his vanished leadership ran like poison through his mind." Bushman was
miscast as Townsend, a theatrical director; besides, his motivation
is not credible and the ease with which he encounters trouble shows
he had no common sense. Mordaunt Hall, the reviewer, suggests,
"To the casual observer it seems as though the hero and heroine
might have pursued their happy relations if the motion picture producer had not stepped in with all the conventional twists to create
a vexatious triangle...."

Marjorie Rosen believes that these Weber films were her
"best received and possibly least interesting ..." and goes on to
recapitulate the trite plot:

> A modern romance about an actress and her lover who
> are deterred from wedded bliss first by a clause in her
> contract stipulating she must not marry, then by a re-
> negotiating of contracts in which the lover is fired and
> forced to seek work elsewhere ... it knew a modest suc-
> cess but came nowhere near fulfilling the potential the di-
> rector had shown between 1914 and 1918...."39

Sensation Seekers (1927), again with Billie Dove, drew de-
murely phrased praise from The New York Times (March 16, 1927,
28:2) even though Weber's plot, based on the novel Egypt by Ernest
Pascal, was another too transparent triangle story of a society girl
known as "Egypt" Hagen, who "seems to be well qualified to become
the bride of Ray Sturgis, a young man of wealth, who, when he is
not making merry in a night club, is quenching a terrific thirst
aboard his yacht...." Egypt visits the Rev. Norman Lodge and
"asks the minister whether he will give up the church...." Egypt's
response to his negative rejoinder is her decision to marry Sturgis,
"at the first port the yacht touches. But the motion picture producers have willed otherwise, and therefore one has to face the sight
of turbulent waters, a groaning vessel, and a rescue...."

Weber's small-scale or "table" photography of the shipwreck
and a flood were unrealistic, the review complains: "The miniatures

are very obvious and the sea at intervals looks extraordinarily
calm...." However, the naturalness of Weber's directing is complimented even though the storm-tossed yacht scenes were anything
but:

> [T]he action rumbles along in a fashion so natural that
> many other directors would do well to study Miss Weber's
> style. She makes the most of her characters and the
> players are not posed at the opening of the scenes...."

Yet Koszarski discerns in these two films

> a scarcely veiled contempt for jazz-age moral standards.
> "It is disconcerting to watch the young girl of today grow
> into manhood," says the hero of "The Sensation Seekers,"
> while in "The Angel of Broadway" a cabaret dancer bur-
> lesques the innocence of a Salvation Army girl--an
> oblique, but bitter allusion to Weber's own early days in
> Pittsburgh....40

The Angel of Broadway was made when Cecil DeMille "invited her to direct a film based loosely upon the life of Texas
Guinan. Subsequent to her two films made for Universal, Weber
was offered a Topsy and Eva property to write and direct. Offended by the racial bias inherent in this popular stage piece, Weber
departed from the studio which had been her "home" for so long--
the site of her own best work and highest affluence.

A ridicule of religion permeated Angel, released in 1927, and
the outcome is a parody of the Salvation Army, with Weber "sparring to give and take in the story" with her scenarist, according to
the criticism in The New York Times (Nov. 1, 1927, 21:1). The
contention lay between Weber's seriocomic tale embodied in her subtitles and the eye-grabbing scenes of "exaggerated costumes" and
"startlingly arrayed chorus girls." The action is initiated when
Babe Scott, popular nightclub entertainer, visits a Salvation Army
meeting "for the purpose of gathering local color to serve her in
the jazz parlor.... Although this yarn ends in Babe becoming a
fervent member of the Salvation Army there are some scenes that
are not in good taste...." The reviewer did not appreciate the
obvious overlay of emotion throughout the film, ranging from high
hysteria to a retarded lethargy. "... Toward the end the agony
is accentuated by artificial actions coupled with tears and actions
...."

In 1930 Weber was reported to be managing an apartment
building in Los Angeles. Divorce ended her second marriage on an
unrecorded date. Presumably alone, Weber accepted short-term
jobs and the lengthy periods of unemployment which now prevailed.

> Unable to find work as a director, she free-lanced for a
> while as a script doctor, then was given a charity job at
> Universal interviewing and screentesting potential starlets.

Finally, in 1934, she contracted with a poverty row outfit to direct "White Heat, " an exploitation film. Shot on location in Hawaii, it was quickly dismissed as "a humorless account of the amorous difficulties of a young sugar planter. "41

White Heat (1934) was Weber's first--and last--talking picture, perhaps a symbol of the comeback she hoped for. A "triangle" story once more, The New York Times (June 16, 1934, 20:2) review (signed A. D. S.) recognizes Weber's dependence upon well-worn emotional exigencies in the plot, frayed by an adherence to the decency code then in force.

> White Heat is effective for a few scenes while it is describing the gradual degeneration of the young wife under the monotony of island life.... Narrowly escaping an affair with a handsome native boy, she finally turns in desperation to an old admirer ... who is visiting the islands. The husband returns to his native mistress. This is by no means a trivial theme, although the film ... cheapens it by applying a routine motion picture code of behavior to its principals....

Surprisingly warm, The Film Daily (June 15, 1934) admits, "Among independent productions, this rates way up near the top of the division.... It has been written and directed by those who quite obviously are familiar with the unusual background of the melodrama. "42

No further opportunities to direct came her way. Weber ventured into the promotion of audiovisual aids as teaching tools, using her own scripts, at the public educational level. Her failure at this ahead-of-the-times scheme was her final try at working in a film-related job. The subsequent silence continued until her demise in 1939, a near-penniless nonentity, forgotten by her peers. Frances Marion was the exception.

Matter-of-factly, Koszarski relates the fate of Weber's works and her reputation. "Those few historians who know Weber's work today are divided on its stylistic merits, while feminists cringe before her more reactionary excesses.... " She was not a cinematic wizard--like Riefenstahl--nor did she have a muliebrious ideology à la Dorothy Arzner. "Her films lie scattered in vaults across the country.... "43

Slide ticks off Weber's merits, forgotten now or never recognized: "When she began directing in 1907, Lois Weber brought to the cinema an intelligence and a commitment that was rare among filmmakers. " In fact, Slide compares her to Griffith: "... along with Griffith, Lois Weber was one of the cinema's first totally committed filmmakers.... "44

Undeniably a strong scriptwriter who may never have com-

pletely mastered the technical prowess required of photographing
creatively, Weber managed to show stamina, staying power, and a
sky-high ambition to make her moralistic stories come alive in
motion pictures. Her storylines were strong: when consonant with
public taste, her achievements were good investments and good
ideologies. Never idolized or acclaimed as an actress or director,
and never judged by her peers to be more than a zealous, competent
worker, Weber nevertheless did write and produce many more films
than we shall ever be able to identify and view, all of them suf-
fused with her own style and personal conviction.

Koszarski's query remains to be answered: "what is to become of poor Lois, who so much wanted to speak to the world
through moving pictures?"45 Just as her films lie waiting in re-
positories to be identified and restored for our retrospective regard
and reappraisal, so the facts of her roller-coaster ride through life,
plunging forward into unremitting work while hitting highs and lows,
remain to be discovered and documented. Then the true Lois Weber
will be reflected from the movie screen.

FILMOGRAPHY

His Brand (1913)

The Eyes of God (1913)

The Jew's Christmas (1914)

The Fool and His Money (1914)

The Merchant of Venice (1914)

False Colors (1914)

The Hypocrites (1914)

It's No Laughing Matter (1914)

The Leper's Coat (1914)

The Career of Waterloo Peterson (1914)

Sunshine Molly (1915)

A Cigarette, That's All (1915)

Scandal (1915)

Jewel (1915)

The Flirt (1916)

Discontent (1916)

Where Are My Children? (1916)

The French Downstairs (1916)

Alone in the World (1916) (short subject)

The People vs. John Doe (retitled God's Law) (1916)

The Rock of Riches (1916) (short subject)

John Needham's Double (1916)

Saving the Family Name (1916)

Shoes (1916)

The Dumb Girl of Portici (1916)

Idle Wives (1916)

The Hand That Rocks the Cradle (1917)

Even as You and I (1917)

The Mysterious Mrs. Musselwhite (1917)

The Price of a Good Time (1917)

The Man Who Dared God (1917)

There's No Place Like Home (1917)

For Husbands Only (1917)

The Doctor and The Woman (1918)

Borrowed Clothes (1918)

When a Girl Loves (1919)

Mary Regan (1919)

A Midnight Romance (1919)

Scandal Managers (1919)

Home (1919)

Forbidden (1919)

Too Wise Wives (1921)

What's Worth While? (1921)

To Please One Woman (1921)

The Blot (1921)

What Do Men Want? (1921)

A Chapter in Her Life (1923)

The Marriage Clause (1926)

Sensation Seekers (1927)

The Angel of Broadway (1927)

White Heat (1934)

NOTES

1.   Edward T. James, Janet Wilson James, and Paul S. Boyer,
      eds. , Notable American Women 1607-1950.   Cambridge,
      Mass.: The Belknap Press of Harvard University Press,

1971, vol. III, p. 554.
2. Richard Koszarski, "The years have not been kind to Lois Weber, " Village Voice 20 (Nov. 10, 1975), p. 140.
3. Ibid.
4. Ibid.
5. James, James, and Boyer, p. 554.
6. Koszarski, p. 140.
7. James, James, and Boyer, p. 554.
8. Terry Ramsaye, A Million and One Nights: A history of the motion picture. New York: Simon & Schuster, 1964, p. 496.
9. James, James, and Boyer, p. 554.
10. Anthony Slide, Early Women Directors. New York: A. S. Barnes, 1977, pp. 37-8.
11. Koszarski, p. 140.
12. Slide, p. 38.
13. Ibid.
14. Frances Marion, Off with Their Heads! New York: Macmillan, 1972, pp. 12-13.
15. Charles Ford, Femmes cinéastes, ou le triomphe de la volante. Paris: Editions de Noël Gonthier, 1972, p. 87.
16. Koszarski, p. 140.
17. Ibid.
18. James, James, and Boyer, p. 554.
19. Koszarski, p. 140.
20. Ibid.
21. Marjorie Rosen, Popcorn Venus: Women, Movies and the American Dream. New York: Coward, McCann & Geoghegan, 1973, pp. 372-73.
22. Slide, p. 42.
23. Koszarski, p. 140.
24. Richard Koszarski, Hollywood Directors 1914-1940. New York: Oxford University Press, 1976, pp. 52-53.
25. Ibid., p. 53.
26. Ibid.
27. Koszarski, "The years have not...," p. 140.
28. Richard Henshaw, "Women Directors: 150 Filmographies, " Film Comment 8:4 (Nov./Dec. 1972), p. 34.
29. Slide, p. 46.
30. Koszarski, "The years have not...," p. 141.
31. Anthony Slide, "Restoring The Blot, " American Film vol. 1 (Oct. 1975), p. 72.
32. Ibid.
33. Koszarski, "The years have not...," p. 140.
34. Ford, p. 88.
35. Koszarski, "The years have not...," p. 140.
36. Rosen, p. 374.
37. Slide, Early Women Directors, p. 47.
38. Ibid., p. 51.
39. Rosen, p. 373.
40. Koszarski, "The years have not...," p. 140.
41. Ibid., p. 141.
42. Slide, Early Women Directors, p. 50.

43. Koszarski, "The years have not...," p. 141.
44. Slide, "Restoring The Blot," p. 71.
45. Koszarski, "The years have not...," p. 141.

4. DOROTHY ARZNER: AN IMAGE OF INDEPENDENCE

Born: January 3, 1900, San Francisco, California
Died: October 1, 1979, La Quinta, California

> "Why should I be pointed out as a strange creature be-
> cause I happen to be the only woman director? Intelli-
> gence has no sex.... It puzzles me--why more women
> don't deliberately set out to become directors.... Of
> course, there are going to be many of them sooner or
> later.... In getting where I am, I suffered a good deal.
> It was not much fun then.... I know all I need to know
> to direct.... There is no question that can come up that
> I will ever have to bluff on...." ["Woman Among the
> Mighty, " The New York World Telegram, Nov. 21, 1936,
> p. 7 (magazine section).]

The undisputed achievement of Dorothy Arzner is that she was the
only woman director of films in Hollywood who linked the silent and
sound moviemaking eras, making a career for herself of twenty-five
years' tenure in the film capital. "A couple of women had preceded her as film directors, but she was the first to emerge from
the silents and make a successful career at it in Hollywood. " So
states Lee Margulies in "Tribute--1975, " Action v. 10, no. 2
(March/April 1975), p. 15, reporting the testimonial tribute con-
ferred upon Dorothy Arzner by the Directors Guild of America on
January 25, 1975.

A packed audience welcomed her with a standing ovation. The
first woman member of the DGA saw clips from nine of her movies.
Ida Lupino narrated a presentation of stills from Arzner's movies
and sets. Arzner was given a keepsake book of photographs and
memorabilia distilled from her films. She expressed her appreciation: she had in her possession no scripts, no stills, no scraps of
evidence from any of her works.

The revival of interest in Arzner films stems from the ambience of cultural nostalgia in the seventies, which encouraged reviewing and reassessment of old movies, and more strongly from
the strident tides of feminist activism characterizing the post-Vietnam
War years. As tangible evidence of both trends--nostalgic and fem-
inist--was the creation of the First International Festival of Women's
Films, which took place in the summer of 1972 in New York City.
"It offered 14 narrative films, 3 feature-length documentaries, and
about 100 shorts--all by women. "[1] Arzner's first sound film for

72

Paramount, The Wild Party, was viewed. Four years later, a Second Festival was held in the same city during which a retrospective program of Arzner's films (and Ida Lupino's) was shown. The Festival was accorded no press coverage by newspaper or periodical journalists.

Contemporary criticism of Arzner films by qualified professionals barely exists. The most dependable roster of commentary is that in The New York Times: unsigned or initialed reviewers have issued brief paragraphs capturing the graces and shortfalls of her films when originally released. Feature stories appearing in print about the lady director are gossipy and humorous, much given to physical description and Arzner's famous low-key directorial style in action. Reading what is available, the film student forms an image of Arzner as competent and talented, and most assuredly unique, ascending as she did with deliberation and dedication through apprenticeships in the disciplines that coalesce to make movies. As Arzner herself says, "I seemed to know I was going to be a director.... I loved every piece of work I was given to do which I think was partly responsible for my advances."[2]

However, making films was not Arzner's first career choice, as an "authorized interview" with Arzner by Gerald Peary and Karyn Kay reveals.[3] Arzner's father, Louis, owned the Hoffman Cafe in Hollywood, to which many film stars--Mary Pickford, Mack Sennett, and Douglas Fairbanks among them--came to dine. "I had no personal interest in actors because they were too familiar to me. I went to the University of California and focused on the idea of becoming a doctor." After sampling a summer working in a surgeon's office and electing courses in art and architecture, "I became a so-called Drop-Out." Still, with the onset of World War I, Arzner's interest in medicine inspired her to join a women's volunteer ambulance corps. Regrettably, she was not assigned to a post abroad. With the War's end, she was free to go back to her medical studies, but in the meantime she had gone with a party of friends on a sightseeing tour of a Hollywood studio. Thenceforward the cutting room took the place of the dissecting laboratory in her plans for the future. She determined to become a motion picture director. "For, " she reasoned, "the greater part of the motion-picture audience is feminine. Box-office appeal is thought of largely in terms of the women lined up at the ticket window. If there are no women directors there ought to be."[4]

Arzner recognized the need for a multifaceted training for the job. There are several accounts of her beginning at the bottom --typing scripts, for fifteen dollars a week. "When an opportunity presented itself for a manuscript reader, Dorothy Arzner was on the spot and got the job. When she felt she had learned enough about plot construction and dramatic climaxes, she was ready for the next logical step--the work of script girl. " Film cutting and editing followed, and subsequently the writing of film continuities and stories. "Then an executive made her an assistant director. It sounds fairly exalted but means no more than serving as a flunky for the director, seeing that stars reach the set on time, scampering for their lunches and such. "[5] The first film that Arzner directed was Fashions for Women starring Esther Ralston. "Into it she incorporated her own system of directing, working with the writer, then directing the picture and supervising the cutting, making the picture an Arzner product throughout.... "[6]

How did Arzner get her first directing assignment? From her insistence upon "saying goodbye. " As Arzner tells it, she had worked for Paramount for seven years. "I had been writing scripts for Columbia, then considered a 'poverty row' company.... I had told Jack Bachman ... that the next script I wanted to direct or 'no deal'.... I had an offer to write and direct a film for Columbia .... "[7]

Arzner was leaving Paramount in late afternoon to take her director's job at Columbia. Impelled to "say goodbye to someone after seven years and much work" she tried to see B. P. Schulberg. He was in conference. His secretary told Arzner that she could not wait to see him. Arzner then caught sight of Walter Wanger. She told him goodbye. Surprised, Wanger phoned Schulberg who appeared on the scene in three minutes. They couldn't believe she was leaving. They cajoled, "Now, Dorothy, you go into our scenario department and later we'll think about directing. " She resisted, finally stating her terms. She was offered a French farce, "The Best Dressed Woman in Paris" to write and direct. This was re-titled Fashions for Women. Arzner became a director by insisting upon it, by refusing to keep the job she had.

If there was a mentor, a good guide, and a role model for Arzner, his identity isn't hard to determine: James Cruze. He knew Arzner from the Hoffman Cafe days. Impressed by her editing of Blood and Sand starring Rudolf Valentino, he asked her "to edit his next production, The Covered Wagon. "[8] She edited three more Cruze films: Ruggles of Red Gap (1923), Merton of the Movies (1924), and Old Ironsides (1926). Her chores on this last film expanded, Arzner reports. She not only edited but wrote the script, kept the script (continuity), was of general assistance, and cut the film "all of which I did for more salary. "[9] Arzner is all admiration for the character of Cruze himself. She views him as one of the kindest and best men in the movie business, with no biases at all. He appreciated Arzner's abilities and praised her to others.

When asked what her training in film directing was before Fashions for Women, Arzner replied candidly, "I had not directed anything before. "[10] In fact, she'd never given anyone orders to do anything. But she had watched many directors at work while employed as continuity girl and editor, and learned the trade. In an aside, Arzner recalls that she kept the script in The Secret Doctor of Gaya, starring Nazimova. It was directed by Herbert Blaché. Arzner never met Mme. Blaché, although she'd heard of the "directress, " as she was called.

Arzner's work attitude in her apprentice years was an amalgam of willingness to learn, financial independence, and no false pride. "Sometimes, I think that pride is the greatest obstacle to success. A silly false pride, that keeps people from being willing to learn.... "11 Was she forced to make changes in scripts she directed at Paramount? She had her way, Arzner affirms. No one interfered with her picture making. She did not have to work for a living. If she was displeased she could have stepped aside. She is convinced that her independent stance was responsible. "I believe this was why I sustained so long--twenty years. "12

Reviews of Fashions for Women included Arzner's name.

The production is the first offering of Dorothy Arzner, Paramount's new woman director. She seems to have been over-eager [sic] to direct, and some of the scenes show this in their lack of spontaneity. The action is directed, rather than natural, but as a whole the novice has done well. She has produced a colorful background and introduced bales of charming frocks. Between dress and undress the play should please both sexes. "13

The New York Times review (March 28, 1927, 26:4) observes in garment industry language,

Whether this story is exactly the type of yarn for Miss Arzner is questionable. She undoubtedly has an eye for attractive costumes, but her incidents are cut off abruptly in some cases, and there are episodes that are too fractious even for this style of story.... Brooks Atkinson commented: "If fashion pictures must be made, let Dorothy Arzner make them. "14

This silent pic was followed by another film, starring Esther Ralston, titled Ten Modern Commandments (1927). "Describing this tale of a maid in a theatrical boarding house as 'flashy, ' The Moving Picture World (July 27, 1927) noted, 'the story is a bit thin as to plot, yet it is well laid out to get and hold attention, and is more true to the life than many backstage yarn [sic]. ' "15

The film was well received at the Paramount Theatre in New York City. The unsigned New York Times reviewer states:

If the spectators had realized, as they probably didn't, that the film is the work of a new director, and a young woman at that, their interest undoubtedly would have been even keener.... The unmistakable enjoyment of the film by those in the house was an unconscious, and therefore unalloyed, tribute to Arzner's work. 16

The terminal work in Arzner's trio of silent pics starred Clara Bow in Get Your Man, released on December 7, 1927. In Anthony Slide's words, "the film was intended as a follow-up to

the star's immensely successful Hula.   It was amusing, but in no
ways as good as its predecessor.‾17‾ Centered upon the antics in a
waxworks show in Paris, The New York Times (Dec. 5, 1927, 26:2)
points out that "Dorothy Arzner ... has at least succeeded in con-
juring up some amusement out of a few of the wax effigies, which
are in most cases portrayed by flesh and blood players.... "

From the review of Manhattan Cocktail in The New York
Times (Nov. 26, 1928, 30:2) it is hard to discover what the film
was about.   With Nancy Carroll, Richard Arlen, and Paul Lukas in
the cast, a backhanded acknowledgment of Arzner's camera skills
is tendered in this paragraph:

> There are some outstanding photographic feats in "Man-
> hattan Cocktail"....   Out of an impressive screen prologue
> of Crete and the Labyrinth comes the theme of the story:
> back to the provinces....   This city is introduced in an
> expert cinematic fashion, as if one were in an airplane,
> passing over the skyscrapers....   When the modern nar-
> rative bursts forth, one has to be content with the manner
> in which Miss Arzner has filmed the subject ... scenes
> are so ridiculous that one wonders that Miss Arzner, who
> demonstrates her ability in this particular feature, was
> willing to picture them as they were set forth in the
> script.

It was with Clara Bow and Fredric March in The Wild Party
that Arzner unluckily touched bottom in sound film.   The New York
Times review (April 2, 1929, 28:4) although affirming that "Miss
Bow's voice is better than the narrative ... " does not mention Arzner and issues a downbeat verdict: "This production is intended for
dwarfed intellects.... "

Viewed at the First International Festival of Women's Films,
The Wild Party brought cheers and whistles from the audience with
this scene: "Hiding in the woods from a gang of drunks, college
professor Fredric March looks deeply into the eyes of his cheeky
student, Clara Bow.   Armed with a stick to do battle, he chides:
'If you paid any attention to me, you'd find I spent a lot of time in
the jungle.' "18

David S. Hull takes a historically cool stare at this reputedly
thermal film:

> [The Wild Party is] an excellent example of the "flaming
> youth" cycle of the period ... the personality of the "It"
> Girl comes across strongly today.   Perhaps in the last
> analysis this little picture is better sociology than enter-
> tainment, recording some college customs which are
> (fortunately) long gone.   Made before the clean-up period,
> some of the situations are unusually racy and Miss Arzner
> contributes some extremely odd direction.   Definitely a
> curiosity piece, but not without period appeal.... 19

In 1930, Arzner was asked to help Robert Milton, a stage director, to co-direct Behind the Make-Up and to finish the film The Constant Wife with Ruth Chatterton, which Milton was unable to complete. Arzner explains: "I don't believe I took a screen credit on it. I merely helped with technical work. He directed the performances. I blocked the scenes for camera and editing."[20]

Working with Chatterton probably was an agreeable task; Arzner selected her as the principal of her next completed film, Sarah and Son. The New York Times (March 13, 1930, 22:4) relates the plot and renders an opinion of the film based on Timothy Shea's novel of the same name.

> [Sarah and Son is an] intelligently directed narrative of a young mother whose infant son is given to the care of a wealthy family by her ne'er-do-well husband.... Dorothy Arzner, who recently has been producing films with Robert Milton and alternating in the credit for them, is set forth as the director of this production. Every performance is restrained.... A little less attention to pathos and a little more attention to cheer would have made this even a better film than it is.

When Arzner was asked by Gerald Peary and Karyn Kay in their "Dorothy Arzner Interview" about Ruth Chatterton and the effect of Sarah and Son upon the latter's career, she replied: "When I made Ruth Chatterton's first motion picture at Paramount, Sarah and Son, it broke all box office records at the Paramount Theatre in New York. Chatterton became known as 'The First Lady of the Screen.'"

Women film directors of the seventies should take note: If you believe your films with an all-female (or nearly) crew is pioneering at its freshest, be advised that Arzner's Sarah and Son was close to a full feminine work complement. "Stars, author (Zoë Akins), director, supervisor (Elsie Janis), business manager, and cutter all were women. The camera was operated by a man and the producer was Al Kaufman." So states The New York World-Telegram, July 24, 1936, p. 8 (in the first section).

With Chatterton starring, Arzner filmed Anybody's Woman, based upon a Governeur Morris story. The August 16, 1930, review in The New York Times (8:3) is lackluster gray.

> In her direction Dorothy Arzner reveals no little care, but there are many moments when the incidents lack imagination. It becomes a case of preaching during many of the scenes.... The picture "favors" coincidences that are absurdly unconvincing....

Ten directors are listed for the Paramount on Parade musical extravaganza which was made, according to Arzner, "to exploit Paramount and its directors and stars and to show off the studio."[21] She directed "The Vagabond King" segment in it.

Arzner saw and liked Ginger Rogers in the stage production of Girl Crazy enough to request her for a small part in her next film Honor Among Lovers. "Paramount gave me about everything I wanted after Sarah and Son and Anybody's Woman, so I imagine they offered her much money. She could also continue playing in Girl Crazy at the same time.... "22 With the leads played by Claudette Colbert and Fredric March, The New York Times (February 28, 1931, 15:2) barely records that the film was based on a story by Austin Parker and was exceptionally well cast. Neither Arzner nor Rogers is named. An outline of the plot can be had from the "Dorothy Arzner Interview" in which the movie is described as dealing with a married woman taking an ocean voyage with a man who is not her husband.

Working Girls, released in 1930, included Frances Dee, Paul Lukas, and Stuart Erwin in the cast. It was written by Zoë Akins, who had written the two Chatterton vehicles, and who was to write the script for Christopher Strong, one of Arzner's best films. Arzner's decisions to choose the best talent available to work with and to continue the collaborations is evident from a study of Arzner's film casts and credits, most notably the names of actors (March and Lukas) and actresses (Chatterton, Bow, Ralston, and, later, Billie Burke). Arzner's wish to cast Marlene Dietrich in a film was unfulfilled.

The last film Arzner made for Paramount starred Fredric March and Sylvia Sidney in Merrily We Go to Hell (1932). The New York Times (June 11, 1932, 9:3) states: "Miss Arzner ... has evidently been handicapped by the script." In this depiction of the Prohibition era, March portrays an alcoholic reporter with whom a bored socialite falls in love.

Why did she leave Paramount after this picture? Arzner admits, "The departments were geared to give a director what he wanted if he knew exactly what he wanted.... "23 But then there was a complete turnover of executives. Everyone was apprehensive about the success of Merrily We Go to Hell to the extent that the studio heads wanted to shelve it. Arzner insisted that her film be released. She was sure it would be a success. When it gained audiences and made money, Arzner observes, the executives asked her to make another movie just like it, 'but by that time I wanted to freelance."24 Arzner stresses that Paramount placed no pressures, no impediments on her work. It was the lack of confidence in her work that impelled her to go it alone.

David Selznick asked her to direct an Ann Harding film at RKO. She agreed. Then Ann Harding had to be replaced. Arzner chose Katharine Hepburn, whom she'd seen in the studio. "I felt she was the very modern type I wanted for Christopher Strong...."25

The film was made with Hepburn, and Leslie Howard was replaced by Colin Clive. Zoë Akins' script was based on Gilbert Frankau's novel of the same name written about the life of Amy

Johnson, the English counterpart of Amelia Earhart. "It was the
story of an aviatrix who falls in love with a married man, becomes
pregnant, and kills herself by pulling off her oxygen mask while
breaking the altitude record at thirty thousand feet. "[26]

A grudging admiration slides into the guarded praise emitted
by The New York Times (March 10, 1933, 19:2):

> It may not be a weighty story, but Zoë Akins ... and
> Dorothy Arzner ... have accomplished their respective tasks ...
> with marked intelligence and also they have dodged shrewdly the
> usual stereotyped ideas, with the result that the unexpected often
> happens.... Besides its other pleasing qualities, this picture is
> beautifully staged....

An inside look into the making of the film is found in Kate:
The Life of Katharine Hepburn by Charles Higham, in which three
problems surfaced. The first, of course, was the script. "Arzner
was working daily with Zoë Akins at Akins' house in Pasadena ...
but Akins' husband, a British artistocrat, was in an oxygen tent,
stricken, and the author was painfully distracted. A page took days
to complete, and Kate never saw anything approaching a finished
script. "[27] The second problem encountered took form as the cameraman, Bert Glennon: "Arzner fired him when he refused to shoot
the setups she had ordered and replaced him with Sid Hickox. "[28]
Thirdly, when shooting the film began in the rainy winter of 1932,
Hepburn did not enjoy it at all. Rapport between Hepburn and Arzner started and finished at zero levels.

> At first, Kate was fascinated by the idea of making a pic-
> ture with a woman director. But she was rapidly disill-
> lusioned. Both very strong-willed, the two women had a
> somewhat awkward relationship from the outset.... For
> Arzner, making the picture was a challenge. As a woman
> in a man's business, she dared not have any failures; she
> would have been "let out of the club. " This made her
> directing of the film purposeful and grim; she took little
> or no time getting to know Kate on a personal level; they
> didn't really hit it off. [29]

Hepburn was used to high humor and jokes while making films.
Arzner's filming ambience was somber, proceeding in a funereal
tone.

> ... Arzner insisted on a cathedral hush, with everyone
> talking in low-pitched voices--no hammers, no saws, no
> laughter--as she instructed Kate and the rest of the cast
> in a subdued, level, sometimes almost inaudible voice.
> The point of the near inaudibility was to force everyone
> to attend to every word. Nobody ever dared call Miss
> Arzner "Dorothy"--let alone "Dotty. " And she addressed
> Kate as "Miss Hepburn" throughout.

Several outdoor scenes were filmed in torrents of rain at the
old Van Nuys airfield. Kate developed influenza.

Arzner drove her very hard, and the two women frequently
quarreled. Miss Arzner says, "I remember one night I
was working on a shot of a truck and a motorcycle col-
liding. The actual collision would have been too difficult,
so we had to have the drivers barely miss each other,
then cut to give an impression of an impact. Hepburn
was watching, and each time the drivers came closer and
closer to hitting, she'd cry out, "That's it!" She was
concerned for the safety of the players.... After the
fourth time, she yelled out, "You can't get any closer than
that!" She was directing, you see. And when I ordered
another take, she said to me sharply, "I'd heard you were
a cruel woman. Now I know it!"[30]

Hepburn collapsed after three weeks' work; shooting the film
stopped, then resumed, although "She recovered, but played the last
scenes listlessly. " Her performance shows signs of strain, and
Dorothy Arzner's direction looks stiff and conventional today. However, the reviews were excellent. Regina Crewe wrote in the Journal American, of Hepburn's performance, "She is a distinct, definite,
positive personality--the first since Garbo. "[31] However,

Christopher Strong was not a success at the box office;
the audience was put off by the strained, artificial script
written under such duress by the unfortunate Zoë Akins,
and by the evident lack of emotional rapport between actress and role.... Arzner abandoned her immediate plan,
to do another Zoë Akins screenplay, Morning Glory, for
Kate. [32]

Another appraisal of Hepburn's performance concurs.

[C]ritic William Boehnel lamented in the New York World
Telegram: "She leaves some of us who cheered her along
during her marvelous performance in A Bill of Divorce-
ment aghast at the amateurish quality of her histrionics.
For the first half of the film, she shrieks her lines in an
unduly affected voice; for the rest of the time, her diction
is so raspish, it jars the nerves...." Despite its inadequacy, Hepburn's performance as Lady Cynthia Darrington,
the free-willed aviatrix, provided the first stage in her
development of the screen's independent woman.... Critical opinion was mixed at best. Both The New York Times
and the Times of London reviewed Hepburn's performance
favorably but public reception was disappointing. "[33]

Hepburn, the strong-willed actress, sent this telegram of
congratulation to Arzner, the strong-willed director, on the occasion of the tribute to Arzner some forty years later: "Isn't it wonderful you've had such a great career when you had no right to have
a career at all?"[34]

Gerald Peary and Karyn Kay describe Arzner's characterization of men and women as unchanged in her films. From Fashions
for Women in 1927 to Christopher Strong in 1933, the personalities
of male and female roles remain fixed. Arzner's women are "dash-
ing, flashy women-on-the-go characters, "35 from Esther Ralston's
aggressive cigarette girl to Katharine Hepburn's Cynthia, an ambitious and daring aviatrix. Arzner's men, in pointed contrast, are
overconfident, think too highly of themselves, and attempt to make
the women in their lives accede to their demands. And, of course,
the overriding mood of Arzner's films is sympathetic to the women
characters who struggle to advance their own ambitions even as
the men in their lives oppose or destroy them.

Destruction of a deadly kind is keynoted by Pauline Kael in
her appraisal of a bedroom scene in Christopher Strong.

> ... as soon as they went to bed together, he insisted,
> late on the very first night, that she not fly in the match
> she was entered in.... I don't know of any other scene
> that was so immediately recognizable to women of a cer-
> tain kind as their truth.... The heroine's acquiescence
> destroyed her.... It is the intelligent woman's primal
> post-coital scene, and it's on film; probably it got there
> because the movie was written by a woman, Zoë Akins,
> and directed by a woman, Dorothy Arzner. 36

Kael hones her critical gears to a more acute point:

> Though the only word for what the man did to Hepburn's
> aviatrix in Christopher Strong is "emasculation, " it was
> perfectly well understood in 1933 that her full possibilities
> as a woman, as a person, were being destroyed.... In
> movies, the primal scene of Christopher Strong has never
> been played out satisfactorily--at least, not from the wom-
> an's point of view. She always gives in.... And not
> solving this problem is a major factor in the gradual im-
> poverishment of human relations on the screen since the
> war years.... Movies are full of depersonalized sex, but
> in terms of sexual love between equals nobody's flying,
> both sexes are grounded. 37

Just as David Selznick chose Arzner to film Christopher
Strong, Samuel Goldwyn chose her to do Nana. Goldwyn returned
home from Europe, saw Christopher Strong, and was so favorably
impressed by it that he called it the best picture of the year. He
selected Anna Sten to star in Nana because he wanted an actress to
contend with Dietrich and Garbo. Arzner was not enthused. " 'I
wanted a more important script. ' "38 Aware of the script situation,
Goldwyn ordered endless revisions. The script Arzner finally received was the fiftieth revision. The barely mentioned notice in
The New York Times (February 2, 1934, 20:3) is not a review.
The film is remembered only as Anna Sten's American screen debut.

In stunning contrast, Arzner's next effort was showered with
varieties of praise. She directed and designed, though did not produce, the film based on the Broadway hit Craig's Wife (1936). Arzner chose Rosalind Russell for the lead role because she wanted an
actress the audience would not immediately like. Arzner had seen
Russell, then an MGM bit player, an unknown, in the studio. "She
was what I wanted. "39 The film elevated Russell to stellar status.
Happily, the Arzner-Russell relationship was amicable. Russell,
who was supposed to be temperamental and "did not want to play the
part to begin with, willingly worked through lunch and dinner,
limped around ten days on a sprained ankle. "40

Joan Crawford, who admired Craig's Wife and wished she'd
had the role, was cast in Arzner's next film. (Crawford played the
lead in a remake of the film Harriet Craig, released by Columbia
in 1950.)

The three excerpted reviews of Craig's Wife appearing in the
Motion Picture Review Digest, vol. 1, p. 18 (1937), award the film
a single plus mark which equals "good" on a scale of double plus
for exceptionally good to double minus for exceptionally poor. A
summary of the film precedes the reviews.

> Realistic, sometimes almost grim, it is a vivid story of
> the working of a selfish, self-centered woman's warped
> mind. Loving only her home, seeking always to bend oth-
> ers to her will, she causes unhappiness to relatives and
> friends and finally drives her husband from her side.

From the Hollywood Reporter, p. 3, Sept. 11, 1936, came
this opinion:

> Essentially a character study, lacking practically all the
> components of orthodox cinema, the box office fate of this
> will remain a mystery until the last booking is checked,
> depending, as it must, strictly on artistic merit, of which
> it has plenty. Well-directed, well-acted, handsomely pro-
> duced, it is a deviation from the run-of-the-mill stuff that
> we believe will pay off, and on which any exhibitor should
> take a chance.

According to the Motion Picture Daily, p. 2, Sept. 12, 1936:

> A radical departure from the regular run film merchandise
> is made here.... It is a woman's picture. The film
> places in the hands of exhibitors many things outside of
> the usual formula.... If possible, the film should be seen
> before being presented to get ideas for stimulating busi-
> ness.

And from Variety (Hollywood), p. 3, Sept. 11, 1936, came
these comments:

To put so much of general audience appeal into what has
been regarded as a play of limited class interest, and to
do the job without distorting its essential character, is a
token of sound showmanship in Columbia production ranks,
a credit to the adapting writer and a fine feather in Dorothy Arzner's directorial cap. Picture may stand alone in
the discriminating spots and will complement with distinction on any program.

Last, heavy bell-ringing praises pealed from The New York
Times (Oct. 6, 1936, 29:3):

> Hollywood appears to have found the magic stone for con-
> verting good plays to better pictures.... Mary McCall,
> Jr. has retained all that mattered of the original lines,
> Dorothy Arzner ... has given them a full beauty without
> sacrificing camera mobility, and a supple cast ... has
> translated the whole into a thoroughly engrossing photoplay
> which has a point to make, keeps it constantly in view and
> drives it home viciously at the end.

In Popcorn Venus, Marjorie Rosen ruminates on Arzner's
"feminist foothold in filmmaking."[41] Her circumspect hypothesis is
stated on page 375: "If the body of Arzner's work reveals little of
an avant-garde or elevated consciousness that might have helped
divest the screen's female mythology of its potency, perhaps it is
because she was a product of American society and was also required to conform within the studio system." Inside those limits
however, Rosen indicates to us, Arzner "utilized her authority to
effect subtle, mitigating nuances, nuances open to interpretation as
'feminine sensibilities.'" Rosen appends a happenstance in the making of Craig's Wife which for her illustrates Arzner's appreciation
and expression of the feminine point of view, as opposed to the
masculine. In Arzner's words, on page 376:

> In Craig's Wife there was a crucial moment when Rosa-
> lind Russell was left alone with her house. The audience
> hated her up to that point, and I had only one close-up
> left with which to turn their emotion to sympathy. Rus-
> sell did it so perfectly that in movie theaters handkerchiefs
> began coming out, and many women cried as they moved
> up the aisle.... It was the regeneration of Mrs. Craig.
> But in talking to George Kelly who wrote the play, I told
> him I was following it as faithfully as possible in making
> the movie, but that I believed Mr. Craig should be down
> on his knees to Mrs. Craig because she'd made a man of
> him.... Kelly rose to his six-foot height and said,
> "That's not my play. Harriet Craig is an SOB and Craig
> is a sweet guy." So there you are--a woman's point of
> view vs. a man's....

The Cinema column in Time magazine (Oct. 12, 1936, p. 32)
purrs euphorically at the brilliance of Craig's Wife, in which the

star "loses her husband through psychopathic selfishness." John
Boles, as Mr. Craig, rebels when an accident

> makes it clear that his wife would rather see him accused
> of murder than let herself be touched by a scandal. ...
> The screen version exhibits to good advantage the talents
> of two ladies. Her brilliantly vitriolic portrayal as Mrs.
> Craig is likely to be a turning point for actress Rosalind
> Russell. ... The work of Dorothy Arzner, Hollywood's
> only woman director, is equally distinguished for giving
> pace without apparent effort to a picture that might, with
> less expert treatment, have seemed pedestrian.

The columnist continues with the physical description and career
résumé and work habits of Arzner: "... She whispers on the set--
every one else ... does too!... Shows small interest in food,
takes roughage for lunch. She has never married, goes out little,
and is now making Mother Carey's Chickens for RKO."

The fate of this last film is indeterminate in Arzner's career. What is certain is that she took a vacation year of rest after
the triumph of Craig's Wife and her credits do not include the RKO
film. Returning to work, Arzner moved, as a free-lancer, from
the Columbia studios to MGM, excited about the prospect of making
a film from an unpublished play by Ferenc Molnar, titled The Girl
from Trieste. But Arzner's early expectations were disappointed
by unpleasant conditions attending the making of the movie. The
story dealt with a former prostitute who tries to reform. Luise
Rainer was to act this leading role, but she was replaced by Joan
Crawford. The Molnar play was rewritten as a less realistic,
brighter script titled The Bride Wore Red. Arzner did not care
for the script. She felt unsettled while working at MGM. Then she
was ordered to use huge sets and scenery already constructed in her
picture. "Arzner considers The Bride Wore Red rather synthetic,
not a favorite of her movies."42

The New York Times review (October 15, 1937, 18:4) says
as much: "The film pretends to a sophistication which the material
obviously lacks ... it reduces Dorothy Arzner's direction to mere
manipulation of a group of decorative puppets."

When the filming of Dance, Girl, Dance began, it was weighed
with afflictions and without Arzner. Initial impetus for the film
came from Erich Pommer, former head of UFA Studios in Germany.
He had exiled himself in Hollywood to continue his career as a producer. After the first week of filming, Pommer replaced the original, unnamed director with Arzner. She revised the script before
directing it, focusing on the conflict "between the artistic, spiritual
aspirations of Maureen O'Hara and the commercial huckster gold-
digging of Lucille Ball."43

Released in 1940, the film elicited a pointedly critical jab
from The New York Times (Oct. 11, 1940, 25:2) writer signed

T. S. Maureen O'Hara was miscast. And the film was "pretentiously staged ... just a cliché-ridden, garbled repetition of the story of the aches and pains in a dancer's rise to fame and fortune. It's a long involved tale told by a man who stutters ... it isn't art.... " Further, the film contained "some of the season's more inane lines and situations.... "

Yet, it is this film, with Merrily We Go to Hell, which invites analysis of Arzner's "touch": the instilled strong-willed quality always apparent in the heroines of her films. Claire Johnston defines the critical strategies she has formulated to properly assess Arzner's films, focusing upon these two films in some detail. Johnston warns the film student, "To understand the real achievement of her work, it is necessary to locate it within the constraints imposed by the Hollywood studio system and in relation to the patriarchal ideology of classic Hollywood cinema. " In Arzner's films, a woman "determines her own identity through transgression and desire. " These last two terms are used in the psychoanalytic, not the conventional, sense. In her films, "Structural coherence is provided by the discourse of the woman. "[44]

Pam Cook, in Approaching the Work of Dorothy Arzner, finds the Hollywood film using a system of representation based upon a patriarchal ideology.

> The films of Dorothy Arzner are important in that they foreground precisely this problem of the desire of women caught in a system of representation which allows them at most the opportunity of playing with the specific demands that the system makes on them. This concept of play permeates every level of the texts: irony operates through the dialogue, sound(s), music, through a play on image, stereotype and nature and through complex patterns of parallels and reversals in the overall organisation of the scenes.... [45]

In Cook's judgment, Dance, Girl, Dance "provides the clearest example, by its play on stereotypes and reversals, of ironic method.... " She posits that the earlier film Merrily "displays the seeds of the method which is so rigorously and economically articulated in Dance, Girl, Dance" and she continues with a meticulous dissection of Merrily We Go to Hell to illustrate her hypothesis.

Arzner's last film did not fare well with the critics. She observes: "I don't think people were very enthusiastic about my last picture. It was made too late. The war was over, the Norwegian invasion was over, and people didn't want war pictures.... "[46]

First Comes Courage (1943) was the movie version of Elliott Arnold's novel The Commandos. Starring Merle Oberon and Brian Aherne, The New York Times review, dated Sept. 3, 1943, 15:3, and signed T. S. again, categorized it as

a modestly satisfactory romantic melodrama ... its authors and director have failed to stamp it with any distinction or depth of conviction to lift it above the level of
a dozen similar mediocre war films ... emerges as a
sort of emotional strip-tease dressed up in noble motives.

Joseph and Harry Feldman present a mixed verdict on Arzner's artistic and technical abilities, her career, and her last film,
First Comes Courage, in their article "Women Directors: Seem to
Go More Often Than They Come," Films in Review 1 (Nov. 1950) pp.
9-12. With reluctance, they acknowledge that Arzner is the only
woman director of any importance. "Though feminists always cite
the fact that Dorothy Arzner was as capable as any man and proved
that a woman could safely be entrusted with the directing of a film,
we must, at the risk of seeming ungallant, declare that she has no
real claim to distinction." More generously, the Feldmans admit,
"Her films ... were clever, efficient, and commercially competent;
but these are qualities shared by a throng of other directors...."
Now the surprise: "Her last work, First Comes Courage, however,
was far from mediocre, although in conception and execution it owed
much to Marcel L'Herbier's The Citadel of Silence." They draw
several parallels of character and action in the two films, then, "To
this theme and conception Dorothy Arzner brought such technical
proficiencies as crisp cutting, swift tempo, sinuous camera work,
exquisite lighting, effective gestures, and a brilliantly handled chase
sequence at the end. They almost matched the impeccable crafts-
manship of L'Herbier himself...."

First, the Feldmans seem to imply, Arzner is only as good
as other directors--but not good enough. Second, the use of another film as a model they frown fiercely upon--as if it were il-
legal. Yet, the Feldmans conclude, "The significance of her achievement lies not so much in the quality of her works as in the fact that
she was able to direct at all."

This film flagged the goalpost for Arzner. Asked why she
stopped making films, Arzner candidly revealed,

> Because pictures left me, really ... I was off for a year,
> having gotten pneumonia at the end of First Comes Cour-
> age. And I never did make any effort very much to get
> a job. I never hired an agent; I got one after I got the
> job and had to go in and ask for a salary I wanted, be-
> cause I didn't like to talk salary. So I think they just
> naturally left me.... And ... I had had enough. Twenty
> years of directing is, I think, about enough. [47]

Marjorie Rosen's succinct summary of Arzner's retirement
activities affirms that films may have left her behind, but she did
not stop being interested in films.

> During World War II, she directed the Woman's Army Training
> Films and has since then set up a professional studio movie-

making program at UCLA and a Motion Picture Department at the Pasadena Playhouse....

At the Playhouse, Arzner began teaching the first filmmaking course on a non-existent budget, instructing her students with a single camera and a tape recorder.

> She has also hosted a radio program You Were Meant to Be a Star, and ... she filmed fifty Pepsi-Cola commercials in three weeks at the request of Joan Crawford. [48]

Rosen credits Arzner with the improvisation of the first moving microphone. She told her sound technicians at Paramount to attach a microphone to a fishing pole balanced on a ladder "and thus follow Clara Bow about the sound stages in The Wild Party...."

In the seventies, Arzner resided near the College of the Desert in California, where she was hard at work writing a historical novel about early Los Angeles and its settlers.

On the evening of her tribute, January 25, 1975, Arzner appeared much as she had in her prime, a slender five feet four inches, suited, low-voiced, with her once dark hair now honey-blond, still worn in the slicked back style. The evening's eulogies for her unique career were coined in glowing words: "Tremendous talent ... distinguished ... great ... glorious leader ... changed my life." Four years later, at 79, Arzner died in La Quinta, California.

Critical citations aside, the Arzner literature can be scanned for clues to her longevity and conjury in the realm of cinema. The Literary Digest 118:12 (Nov. 3, 1934) reports biographical tidbits only: Arzner was barred from going to France during the War because she was only 17. Her corps director introduced her to William de Mille who hired her for her first movie job. Paul Rotha in his compendious The Film Till Now (Feltham-Middlesex, The Hamlyn Pub. Group Ltd., 1967), p. 212, devotes one sentence to her: "Dorothy Arzner is a clever woman director who at one time wrote scenarios, took up editing (The Covered Wagon) and finally made a picture called Fashions for Women."

Paul Harrison captioned his article in The New York World-Telegram, July 24, 1936, p. 8, section 1, "Hollywood's Only Woman Director Never Bellows Orders Herself." Arzner was bossing Craig's Wife, but as Harrison clarifies,

> "Bossing" may not be quite the word, for all the directorial bellowing of "Quiet!" and "Let's Try It Again!" and "Action!" comes from Miss Arzner's assistant, Art Black .... She goes about her job very quietly ... when she sits by the camera to watch the ensuing action, a visitor might mistake her for a script girl. A nod from her and Black gives the orders. When something goes wrong she says "Cut!" in a voice scarcely audible.

Wittily, Harrison captures the cause of Arzner's non-talking direction. "Practically all successful directors are dominant people who know when to do a bit of outright bullying, and how. Players might not take kindly to bullying from a woman; they'd call it nagging. And so there's only one woman director in Hollywood.... "

But Arzner's silence-steeped film guidance did include frequent consultation with the filmwriter, according to an article in the very same New York World-Telegram later that year (November 21, 1936, p. 7, magazine section):

> Usually, she asks to have the writer of a picture on the set with her, to suggest dialogue changes and discuss changes she herself may think of. Nine out of ten other directors make arbitrary decisions and will endure no one on the set except their personal errand-boys. This makes Dorothy Arzner popular with the screen writers.

Arzner voiced her own belief in this collaborative policy: "If a moving picture is bad, the director should be blamed and no one else.... If he accepts a bad script, it's up to him to work with the writer to make it a good one. "

As Lee Margulies' "Tribute--1975" article reports on Arzner's acceptance of the director's responsibilities as first and final voice on a film,

> Arzner maintained a fierce independence, believing the director should have the final word on the film, and she often threatened to walk off a picture when that belief was challenged. Directors Guild President Robert Wise was Arzner's editor on Dance, Girl, Dance in 1940 and he told the audience that his strongest memory of the film is watching Arzner firmly and consistently stand her ground against feisty producer Erich Pommer. "I want to commend her to our guild for this sort of stand she took in those days, " Wise said. "It's something we've fought for all these years. We're making headway on it, but you were one of the pioneers in that area of the director having the say in the control of his film. Thank you very much for that. "

"[E]diting experience is ideal training for direction. Dorothy Arzner, following her years as an editor, became Hollywood's most successful woman director.... " Kevin Brownlow in The Parade's Gone By (New York: Knopf, 1969, p. 286) quotes Arzner herself on this major phase of her self-styled apprenticeship:

> I was a very fast cutter. I cut something like thirty-two pictures in one year at Realart, a subsidiary of Paramount. I also supervised the negative cutting and trained the girls who cut negative and spliced film by hand. I set up the film filing system and supervised the art work on the titles. I worked most of the day and night and loved it.

Brownlow continues with an Arzner anecdote reporting her entry into film history. Arzner cut, edited, and kept script for Valentino's Blood and Sand.

> Paramount planned to spend $50,000 on a double-exposure process to matte Valentino into the Madrid Bull Arena. As a temporary solution, Miss Arzner cut the three bull-fights from existing stock footage. She then asked to shoot some close-ups of Valentino to match the long shots. The result was so effective that the picture was released with Miss Arzner's bullfights intact.

Arzner herself recalls,

> I was running Blood and Sand in the projection room when Jim Cruze passed through to reach the adjoining theatre. He paused to watch. Suddenly I heard an exclamation. "My God, who cut that picture?" I wasn't sure if this meant approval or disapproval, but I quietly admitted I did. When the lights went up, he asked me if I would cut his next picture, The Covered Wagon.

Brownlow concludes,

> It was her association with The Covered Wagon that brought Miss Arzner's name into the film history books-- the only editor from the entire silent period to be official-ly remembered.

Arzner is compared to Lois Weber by two film historians. In Hollywood in the 20's, ". . . Arzner was a . . . director less social-ly committed than Lois Weber, but certainly more talented." Com-menting only upon her silent films: ". . . her silent films were so-cial comedies, now valuable as period studies of feminine psychol-ogy."49

A totally different personality from Lois Weber, Charles Ford agrees, in Femmes cinéastes. 50 Arzner was not a comedienne. She knew cinematic technique from the bottom up, experiencing good luck in several ways: being in Hollywood when it was possible to learn the basics as she did, being in Hollywood when it was possible for women to direct films and also to span the silent and sound eras. Ford credits Arzner on her editing abilities with this opin-ion: "The intelligent, perhaps wise, montage of Dorothy Arzner con-tributed much to several great films made by Paramount. . . . Al-though none of her films can be considered a masterwork, each bears the impress of the indisputable dexterity of the filmmaker." Ford indexes the strip-tease dance sung by Lucille Ball in Dance, Girl, Dance as especially admirable.

Cinema literature expert and film history professor Richard Henshaw claims Arzner's talents more richly endowed in the pro-cesses of editing than in the director's role. In "Women Directors:

150 Filmographies, " Film Comment 8 (Nov. -Dec. 1972), p. 34, he
views Arzner in historical perspective and agrees with Brownlow's
appraisal of Arzner the editor as superior to Arzner the director.
"Arzner ... entered films through the story department--script
typist to reader--and then transferred to editing, where she was to
make an impact (considerably more of a one than as a director)
on some important films. "

Henshaw then appraises Arzner's directorial efforts with a
close-up lens:

> As a director, Arzner was more interesting thematically
> than stylistically. She concentrated on strong independent
> female characters, and her choice of stars, or in some
> cases their choice of her, reflects this. Clara Bow, Ruth
> Chatterton, Claudette Colbert, Sylvia Sidney, Katharine
> Hepburn, Rosalind Russell, and Joan Crawford were per-
> sonalities linked by a common spirit of independence in
> the face of oppressive movie-men. Arzner was the only
> director who worked with all of them....

Arzner's character delineation and camera prowess is ex-
amined and explicated:

> In Arzner's films, a reversal of some common traits in
> films directed by men takes place. Scenes involving wom-
> en are generally complex, thoughtful and multi-dimensional,
> whereas her male characters are relatively barren and
> played with considerable ham. As a matter of fact, Arz-
> ner's films are invariably uplifted when she takes her
> camera outside the house and becomes involved with ob-
> jects, landscape, and movement. In these cases, where
> cutting is not dependent on lines of dialogue, her strength
> as an editor surfaces....

The director herself corroborates the Brownlow-Henshaw
posit that her reputation as a film director was supported by the
superb sense of pace and place required of the film editor. "I
learned more about pictures in the cutting room than anywhere else
.... " Arzner is quoted in Anthony Slide's Early Women Directors
(New York: A. S. Barnes, 1977), p. 93. On page 95 she acknowledges that she learned a lot from male co-workers who never confronted her with objections or obstacles in the course of making
films.

Francine Parker backstops the praise of Arzner as a sound
technician in her article "Approaching the Art of Arzner, " Action 8
(Sept. -Oct. 1973), p. 8. In Arzner films she finds

> relationships between women ... intriguingly explored....
> Her women are multi-dimensional, placing all the charac-
> ters on an even footing.... She is a master of comic
> business.... Her flair for the zany, both structurally and

visually, however, is combined with an extraordinary
realization of the technical detail in establishing illusions
of special backgrounds and milieus....

Arzner's consistent trait was her exemplary sound treatment, Parker
observes, citing a few of Arzner's alignments of sound and image.

Marjorie Rosen debates the question of women in positions of
decision in films, in opposition to Arzner's claim that men were
helpful to her. "Curiously, the history of women in film-making
reeks, if not of conspiracy, then of vaguely defined obstacles.... "
Rosen cites the fact that the film industry was the fourth largest in
the United States in the 1920's and that

> females were phased out of decision-making positions ...
> too much money, power, and prestige were at stake....
> Only one woman managed to maintain a major foothold in
> film-making during Hollywood's booming years: Dorothy
> Arzner ... and although Arzner denies that her gender
> was responsible for any professional difficulties, she did
> write me recently: "Of course there are problems in
> being a director--problems for the man as well as for the
> woman. But I never saw them as caused by being a wom-
> an.... I ... observed that not many women came forth
> to support me. No one was handing me wonderful stories
> to make.... I'm fully aware that my sex did not enter
> into my work.... " If that is true, Arzner is certainly the
> exception, not the rule.... 51

Arzner was an exceptional woman who prevailed as a film
director because her unique work approach yielded a popular com-
petently-crafted product. Her method of indirection (the assistant
director yelled when needed), the totality of her vision, her willingness to rewrite with the author, her insistence on the director taking complete responsibility for the film together with final decisions
and final cut, her editing expertise, meshed with a completely
new use of feminine discourse, the result being a demolishment of
the stereotypical female film characters and instead an acceptance
of self-determined, strong-willed women (this was called "the Arzner touch") in her films. It is no wonder that Arzner could establish a new image of woman in films. The "Arzner touch" was Arzner herself.

FILMOGRAPHY
(Feature films only)

Fashions for Women (1927)

Ten Modern Commandments (1927)

Get Your Man (1927)

Manhattan Cocktail (1928)

The Wild Party (1929)

Sarah and Son (1930)

Anybody's Woman (1930)

Working Girls (1930)

Paramount on Parade (1930--one segment)

Honor Among Lovers (1931)

Merrily We Go to Hell (1932)

Christopher Strong (1933)

Nana (1934)

Craig's Wife (1936)

The Bride Wore Red (1937)

Dance, Girl, Dance (1940)

First Comes Courage (1943)

NOTE: In The Filmgoer's Companion, revised and expanded edition
        (New York: Hill and Wang, 1977), p. 43, Leslie Halliwell credits
        two additional films to Arzner: Alias French Gertie (1931) and
        Lost Squadron (1932).

NOTES

1. Elenore Lester, "At Last: A Festival of Women's Films, "
    Ms. 1 (October 1972), p. 26.
2. Marjorie Rosen, Popcorn Venus. New York: Coward, Mc-
    Cann & Geoghegan, 1973, p. 374.
3. "Dorothy Arzner Interview, " Cinema 34 (1974), pp. 10-17.
4. "Distaff Side Director, " The New York Times, Sept. 27, 1936, X,
    4:4.
5. "Woman Among the Mighty, " The New York World-Telegram,
    Nov. 21, 1936, p. 7 (in magazine section).
6. "Distaff Side Director. "
7. Gerald Peary and Karyn Kay, "Dorothy Arzner Interview, "
    Cinema 34 (1974), p. 12.
8. Anthony Slide, Early Women Directors. New York: A. S.
    Barnes, 1977, p. 93.
9. "Dorothy Arzner Interview, " p. 10.
10. Ibid., p. 13.
11. Slide, p. 92.
12. "Dorothy Arzner Interview, " p. 14.
13. Slide, pp. 94-95.
14. Kevin Brownlow, The Parade's Gone By. New York: Knopf,
    1969, p. 286.
15. Slide, p. 95.
16. New York Times Film Reviews, July 11, 1927, 23:4.
17. Slide, p. 95.
18. Marjorie Rosen, "Women, Their Films, and Their Festival, "
    Saturday Review (Aug. 12, 1972), p. 31.

19. Film Society Review (March 1966), p. 18.
20. "Dorothy Arzner Interview, " p. 14.
21. Ibid.
22. Ibid.
23. Ibid., p. 15.
24. Ibid.
25. Ibid.
26. Charles Higham, Kate: The Life of Katharine Hepburn. New York: Norton, 1975, p. 41.
27. Ibid., p. 42.
28. Ibid., p. 44.
29. Ibid., p. 43.
30. Ibid.
31. Ibid., p. 44.
32. Ibid., p. 45.
33. Alvin H. Marill, Katharine Hepburn. New York: Galahad Books, 1973, p. 23.
34. Variety 277 (Jan. 25, 1975), p. 7.
35. Gerald Peary, "Dorothy Arzner, " Cinema 34 (1974), p. 4.
36. Deeper into Movies. Boston: Little, Brown, 1972, p. 341.
37. Ibid., p. 346.
38. "Dorothy Arzner Interview, " p. 17.
39. Ibid.
40. "Woman Among the Mighty, " p. 7.
41. Rosen, Popcorn Venus, p. 275.
42. "Dorothy Arzner Interview, " p. 18.
43. Ibid.
44. Claire Johnston, ed. , The Work of Dorothy Arzner: Towards a Feminist Cinema. London: British Film Institute, 1975, pp. 2-8.
45. Pamela Cook, "Approaching the Work of Dorothy Arzner, " in Claire Johnston, ed. , The Work of Dorothy Arzner: Towards a Feminist Cinema. London: British Film Institute, 1975, pp. 9-18.
46. Lee Margulies, "Tribute--1975, " Action 10, 2 (March/April 1975), pp. 14-18.
47. Ibid., p. 18.
48. Rosen, Popcorn Venus, p. 377.
49. David Robinson, Hollywood in the 20's. New York: Paperback Library, 1970, p. 118.
50. Femmes cinéastes, ou le triomphe de la volante. Paris: Editions Denoël Gonthier, 1972, pp. 90-92.
51. Rosen, "Women, Their Films, and Their Festival, " p. 34.

5. LENI RIEFENSTAHL: A CRYSTAL GROTTO

Born: August 22, 1902 Berlin (Berta Helene Amalie Riefenstahl)

"Film will become art only when--by the means that are possible only in film--it creates the artistic experience that no other art form can give us: the harmonious fusion of optical, acoustical, rhythmical and architectonic factors --then film will become the king of all arts. " [Film Culture, No. 56-57, Spring 1973, p. 197.]

Rarely have the resonant forces of history and politics so vibrantly pervaded and congealed in the work of a filmmaker with percussive dissonance as in the instance of Leni Riefenstahl. The brief tenure of the Third Reich dominated by Adolf Hitler encloses the era of Riefenstahl's best films, and the history of Germany during a dozen infamous years, 1933-1945, has integrated with Riefenstahl's private and public lives so inextricably that it has become nearly impossible to discuss her films as cinematic entities apart from an extremely emotional bias--one either likes Leni's films or one doesn't--and an imperative historical context. Yet, this chapter is aimed at the following goal: a dispassionate approach chiefly to the films directed by Riefenstahl and a spectrum-wide view of the critics' considerations of her film work. By doing so, film students may then define and put a name to their own apperceptions of Riefenstahl's reputation and filmography.

A substantially large accumulation of literature surrounds Riefenstahl: one approaches it chronologically to appreciate the growth of the legend which she has become; one ingests it with as temperate a taste as can be had. A sequential and stabilized orientation to Riefenstahliana is commanded by the kaleidoscopic keys struck in documenting her four careers: dancing, film acting, film direction and production, and still photography. Reportage, rhetoric, interviews, refutations and allegations, antagonistic appraisals matched with apologetic essays--of these there are an abundance. Few in number and harder to find are criticisms of her films when first made, and responsible extended analyses of the two films which are considered in the one-and-only category--(classics, perhaps): Triumph of the Will (1935) and The Olympiade (1938). At the core of this body of literature is the kinetic coil of quicksilver energy from which Riefenstahl created her careers, her legend, and her irresolvable predicament. This quicksilver quality is addressed in this chapter. The heinous historical matrix of World War II and the Holocaust, with the years prefacing and following, will serve as

a support structure for the dates and deeds of Riefenstahl's timeline.

Wunderkind, child of wonder, is the aptest description of her
earliest years. She was a precocious infant born to Alfred Riefenstahl, affluent proprietor of a plumbing and heating business who
wanted his only child to take his place as proprietor. Bertha
Riefenstahl insisted that Leni, with "her great shock of yellow
hair..." ("Leni Riefenstahl," by David Gunston in Film Quarterly
14:1 (Fall 1960), p. 54) "might not be interested in the ... business. Bertha Riefenstahl was exactly right.... The young Leni
showed a natural talent for painting.... Later, however ... her
interest turned from art to dancing. 'When I was six or seven
years old I saw Swan Lake in the theatre,' Riefenstahl said, 'and
from that moment I only wanted to dance.'"

Encouraged by her mother, the young Leni took dancing lessons. Upon discovering this fact, her father was horrified. His
riposte was to send Leni to the best Russian ballet school in Berlin. He was sure she had no talent. "After the very first lesson
it was evident to teacher Jutta Klammt that her new pupil had a
great talent."1

Current Biography (May 1975, p. 37) cites 1919 as the year
in which Leni studied classical ballet with Eduardova and Klammt,
and modern dance with Mary Wigman. Leni's father had planned a
career for her in commercial art. To settle the career question,
he promised to pay for his daughter's dance recital if she would consent to forget a career in dance if she were unsuccessful. Leni
agreed.

Success was hers. As a solo dancer (modern, not ballet)
she created each detail of her stage appearances--the costumes,
choreography, music, publicity--in Dresden, Munich, Frankfurt,
Prague, Cologne, and, of course, Berlin. She toured Germany with
her mother and her pianist Herbert Klammt, though unable to fulfill
the deluge of requests for her performances. Her professional debut in 1923 was seen by Max Reinhardt, who engaged her for his
Deutsches Theatre in Berlin. Then she toured under his sponsorship.

Leni's adolescent years concurred with the growth and development of the German cinema. Predictably, her reactions to
movies were typical of an upperclass Berliner. Films were entertainment for commoners. To work in the film industry, even to at-
tend movie showings, did not require an educated taste. The cinema was not intellectual or artistic, good reasons for the literati
and artists to ignore it. Riefenstahl did--until she met Dr. Arnold
Fanck, geologist-turned-moviemaker pursuing the realization of a
new type of movie, the mountain film. Having suffered a knee in-
jury that required surgery, Riefenstahl saw Fanck's film Der Berg
des Schicksals (Peaks of Destiny) (1927) while convalescing. So enthralled was she, so indelible an impression did Fanck's film en-
grave upon her mind, that Riefenstahl decided she wanted to partici-

pate in the exhilarating experience of shooting a film in the geo-
graphically hazardous locations required.   She arranged an introduction to Dr.   Fanck, "who immediately realized that she would be a
definite asset on the screen.... "[2]   He had been looking for a woman dancer for his next film Der Heilige Berg (Holy Mountain).

Delighted by the fast healing of her knee, Riefenstahl faced
three options.   Producers in several European cities offered her
contracts for dance performances.   Max Reinhardt offered her the
role of Penthesilea in a drama with this title.   And Dr.   Fanck offered her a contract to appear in Der Heilige Berg.   Which should
she choose?

Many years later she admitted that her training as a dancer and her ability to paint had helped her to achieve success in the cinema when at last she turned to it.   "These
two elements, dance and painting, played a role in forming the style of composition and editing images that were
mine, " she said.... [3]

She signed Fanck's contract.   At once, the filming was be-
deviled by mishaps.   Leni learned to ski and broke a bone in her
foot.   She wore a cast for a month.   Another actor became ill.
Weather worsened.   Financers of the film withdrew their support,
alarmed at these setbacks and the extension of time required.
Fanck asked his crew and cast to defer salaries and to pay their
own expenses.   They did.

From the beginning, Riefenstahl observed and studied Fanck's
photographic and production methods.   She cast herself into the role
of pupil, asking questions, working in all phases of filmmaking.
Then a light exploded in her face and burned her cheek.   She had
been watching how to film in darkness.

As the filming progressed her foot and her face healed.
When the film was released and viewed, it was a success: audiences were enchanted by Leni, although her acting was awkward.
Dr.   Fanck seemed not to have understood that his avid pupil who
offered suggestions and debated his directions had in fact determined
to become a film director herself.   In a rapid series of audience-
pleaser films, Riefenstahl improved her acting, skiing, mountain
climbing, and, in her self-styled subterranean manner, her filmmaking skills.   She played the leads in Der Grosse Sprung (The
Great Leap) (1927); Das Schicksal Derer von Habsburg (The Fate of
the von Hapsburgs) (1929); Die Weisse Holle von Piz Palu (The White
Hell of Pitz Palu) (1929); Sturme über Mont Blanc (Storm over Mont
Blanc; also known as Avalanche and her first sound film) (1930), and
Die Weisse Rausch (The White Frenzy or The White Ecstasy) (1931),
a skiing comedy.   With these five films behind her, Riefenstahl
terminated her Svengali-Trilby relationship with Dr.   Fanck to make
a film on her own, titled The Blue Light.

Even after establishing the Leni Riefenstahl Studio Films en-

terprise in 1931, she starred in a Fanck mountain epic.   No actress
with the required athletic abilities and physical strength was available for a strenuous role in Fanck's S. O. S. Eisberg (S. O. S. Ice-
berg) (1933), filmed in Greenland. Riefenstahl recorded her experiences on location in a book published in 1933, Kampf in Schnee und
Eis (Struggle in Snow and Ice).

   Logically enough, her entry into independent moviemaking
was with a mountain film, but quite dissimilar from Fanck's brand.
From a dance titled "The Blue Flower" that she had successfully
performed, and based upon a romantic Italian folk tale, she developed
a script, collaborating with the Hungarian writer-director Bela Ba-
lazs, who assisted her in directing it.

> The story line was based on a legend from the Dolomites
> ... on nights of the full moon a blue light shone from the
> mountain and lured young men from the villages below to
> their deaths.   Riefenstahl plays Junta, a mountain girl,
> who alone of the villagers knows that the blue light on
> Mount Cristallo is a glimmering beam emitted when moon-
> light strikes the crystalline rocks in a grotto.   When oth-
> ers try to follow Junta as she climbs a secret path to the
> grotto, they fall to their deaths or are lost.   Eventually
> Vigo, an artist ... successfully follows her up the path.
> When he discovers the valuable crystal rocks, he tells the
> villagers about them in the belief that they will stop con-
> sidering Junta a witch and persecuting her.   But the vil-
> lagers greedily strip the grotto of the valuable rocks....
> Junta, convinced that her lover has betrayed her, leaps to
> her death from the top of Mount Cristallo.... 4

   Glenn B. Infield juxtaposes the idealism of this plot with the
opportunism of the filmmaker in achieving this film.   He calls it
her "blue light, " namely "her determination to direct and produce
her own film ... she was willing to go to practically any length to
achieve this dream ... just as she was later, during the Third
Reich, in an effort to fulfill her craving for recognition in the film
world. ... "5

   A perennial career-shaping trait first figures prominently
here: Riefenstahl's talent for obtaining and maintaining friendships
with men capable of and agreeable to helping her make films.   Many
of them were former romances, would-be fiancés, and warm chums
who admired her.   For Das Blaue Licht she raided Fanck's film
crew without compunction.   Hans Schneeberger was her cameraman
and Walter Trout her production supervisor.   Heinz von Jaworsky,
camera assistant, is quoted, "We all just loved what she did. "
Riefenstahl enlisted the help of Guzzi Lantschner, a world champion
skier; Harry Sokal, who financed her company; and Germany's great
screenwriter Karl Mayer, who polished her script--even Fanck himself!   She showed Fanck her script before filming began.   ". . . He
told her it would be impossible to infuse mysticism into Junta's
climbing of Mount Cristallo unless she had a large studio and a lot

of money, and didn't use outside arc lights...." But Riefenstahl's
Trilby triumphed over Fanck's Svengali. "... I got the idea that if
I make the mountain full of fog and she climbs through this fog it
will add the unrealistic effect that I want.... I decided to use
smoke bombs.... They put the whole mountain in 'fog'...."6

This type of triumph was repeated in a disagreement between
Riefenstahl and Schneeberger. The topnotch cameraman refused to
use a green filter with a red one, assuring her that no picture at
all would develop. She insisted. He tried it. "... The combination of filters resulted in the new, unexpected magical effect that
made Das Blaue Licht so different...."7

Added to her facile working relationships with men was a
diamond-hard determination to attain perfection, plus a tireless propensity for improvisation and innovation. Suffuse these elements
with Riefenstahl's hyperenergetic strength, an audacious intensity
which remains incredulous, and a total submergence of self into the
created object and one feels the fierce fire of her ambitions and an
admiration for her quicksilver--unknown and glimmering--quality of
getting whatever she wanted. The operative method for The Blue
Light, inculcating everyone's help and her own abundance of talents,
became a prototype for each film project following. Her commanding-
collaborating style suited her creative temper and was acceptable to
her colleagues.

The New York Times Film Reviews (p. 1058) devotes a paragraph to a plot summary in its review of The Blue Light, then appends two sentences: "A summary of the story gives no adequate
idea of the beauty of the action and the remarkable camera work,
especially in connection with the light effects. The sparse dialogue
is in German, Italian and the local dialect...."

"Although The Blue Light had only a modest success in Germany, it received a gold medal at the 1932 Venice Biennale and enjoyed a long run in Paris and London...." Glenn B. Infield describes the film's reception as "an outstanding success...."

Riefenstahl's own recollection of the movie's reception is
given in Rena Andrews' article "Hitler's Favorite Causes a Controversy in Colorado, " The New York Times Biography Edition (15
Sept. 1974), p. 1320:

> "'The Blue Light' was only a modest success in Germany, "
> Miss Riefenstahl told me. "The film was a sensation in
> France and England. It played 50 months at the Rialto in
> London. It won second prize--a silver medal--at the first
> Venice Festival. "

In a literary prologue, The Blue Light opens with this statement:

> "We, the people of the Dolomites, far from the strife and

turmoil of the outside world, dwell primitively in the
rugged wilderness and magnificence of the Italian Tyrol.
We are a simple peasant folk and strange legends have
come down to us through the centuries, casting shadows on
the peace of our lives.   Above all do we cherish the legend of Junta, The Mountain Girl, whose story we have
reverently engraved for future generations. "   Riefenstahl's
athletic brunette beauty, juxtaposed to the film's magnificent scenery, made DAS BLAUE LICHT a hit. [8]

    Film Comment 11:1 (Jan. - Feb. 1975), pp. 13-14, supple-
ments this quote with taglines from reviews in the New York press:

> "One of the most pictorially beautiful films of the year.
> Leni Riefenstahl--author, director, and star--is an expert
> climber as well as a handsome woman" (unsigned review,
> The New York Sun, May 9, 1934); ". . . for sheer pictorial
> beauty, is perhaps unexcelled.   Told with absorbing in-
> tensity. . . . [sic]   How flawlessly this girl, who plays the
> lead and also wrote and directed . . . " Marguerite Tazelaar,
> The New York Herald Tribune, May 9, 1934); ". . . majes-
> tic and impressive" (The New York World- Telegram, Sep-
> tember 26, 1934). . . .   Few critics of that period noted
> Nazi overtones in the mountain films: reliance on intui-
> tion, nature worship, cultivation of myth, glorification of
> youth. . . .

    After World War II, however, several critics appear to agree
that the mountain epics in which Riefenstahl starred earlier, as well
as her own film The Blue Light, expressed pro-Nazi attitudes.
Siegfried Kracauer, in From Caligari to Hitler (Princeton, N. J. :
Princeton University Press, 1947) specifies these attitudes as, most
prominently, a glorification of the earth's elements and forces and
a scorn for civilization viewed as vile and contaminated.

    A Newsweek article, "Misguided Genius, " dated September
16, 1974, links, on page 91, the filmmaker's visit to Telluride,
Colorado, to receive an award to her first independent film.

> It was an extraordinary fusion of art and life.   The story
> on-screen took place in the 1930's in a remote village . . .
> and it told of a wild vagabond girl who was persecuted as
> a sorceress because she alone knew the secret of a mys-
> terious Alpine blue light.   The events off-screen took place
> . . . in Telluride . . . a hamlet high in the mountains, and
> they concerned Leni Riefenstahl, the legendary outcast di-
> rector of "The Blue Light" who was once Hitler's favorite
> filmmaker and was making her first U. S. appearance in
> ten years. . . .

    Telluride audiences were thrilled by her films.   "'The story
of that girl and that village, ' Riefenstahl told Newsweek's Martin
Kasindorf, 'is nearly the story of my life.   But I didn't know that
until later. ' "

Among those who admired The Blue Light was Adolf Hitler. Their first meeting vibrated with mutual appreciation. She was flattered by his praise for Das Blaue Licht ... " and she "saw an opportunity to further her ambitions through her friendship with Hitler. ... " Hitler warmed to her praise and her expressed anticipation of "the wonderful things she knew he would do for Germany . . . . "9

She applied for membership in the Reich Film Association. This was granted after a search of her lineage back to her great-grandparents to ascertain the absence or presence of Jewish ancestors. Three of eight great-grandparents who were Jewish rendered an individual Jewish. Riefenstahl was judged Aryan and a membership card was granted to her. Then Hitler asked her to photograph the Nazi Party Congress in Nuremberg. Although "her instincts were to continue in the romantic vein that had just brought her great success and that appealed to her essentially childish nature..." namely, The Blue Light, she agreed to the assignment and completed the film. 10   Titled Sieg des Glaubens (Victory of the Faith; 1933), it was and remains a relatively unknown work.   It was never publicly viewed, and no prints of the film have been found.

Film Comment 11:1 (Jan. -Feb. 1975), p. 14, observes "the film revealed masterful editing" and continues with a quoted paragraph from The Observer, December 3, 1933, of London: "'Chancellor Hitler and the whole German Cabinet, including General Goering, attended the world premiere last night of the film, THE VICTORY OF THE FAITH, which depicts the NSP Congress held at Nuremberg in September. The film is one long apotheosis of the Caesar spirit, in which Herr Hitler plays the role of Caesar while the troops play the role of the Roman slaves. It is certainly to be hoped that this film will be shown in all cinemas outside Germany, if one wishes to understand the intoxicating spirit which is moving Germany these days. Herr Hitler handed Leni Riefenstahl a bouquet at the end of the performance. ' "

Infield reports that "the film of the 1933 Party congress, although short, was excellent. ... Titled Sieg des Glaubens (Victory of Faith), it was premiered on the night of December 2, 1933, and revealed masterful editing of the sparse footage" (p. 63).

The film was the first of her trilogy of Nazi centered documentaries: as Robert Gardner in his article "Can the Will Triumph?" in Film Comment 3:1 (Winter 1965), p. 29, categorizes it, "... Victory of Faith was only a sketch of her later major document, Triumph of the Will. ... " Riefenstahl and Dr. Goebbels, who was Hitler's Minister for Peoples Enlightenment and Propaganda, were adversaries. Her completion of the film was aggravated by deliberate obstacles placed in her path by the Propaganda Minister. Gardner gives us the filmmaker's reaction to Goebbels' impediments: "... So painful was her experience making the ... film ... that Riefenstahl left immediately upon its completion for Spain, where she intended making a new feature. However, once in Spain, she collapsed and spent two months in a Madrid Hospital. ... "

For causes unknown, Riefenstahl's Tiefland (Lowland) based on an operetta by Eugen D'Albert, was left unfinished after only the barest of beginnings. Riefenstahl returned to Germany in a few months' time. Gardner affirms that Tiefland was insured by Lloyds (p. 29) suggesting no monetary loss was incurred. She was approached by Hitler who asked her to make another film, this time of the 1934 Party Rally in Nuremberg. Riefenstahl paused and demurred. She had never made a full length documentary. She desired the greatest distance possible between herself and Dr. Goebbels. She asked veteran filmmaker Walter Ruttmann "to create an opening sequence that would show the Nazi rise to power.... "11 Once her request was known to Hitler, he pointedly insisted that he had requested her, not Ruttmann, to make the film. She finally agreed to the assignment only after Hitler agreed to three conditions she imposed: ". . . one, that funds be arranged by her rather than by the Party; two, that no one, including Hitler, but especially Goebbels, be allowed to see the film until it was finished, and three, that Hitler never ask her to do a third film.... "12

This third concession was abruptly canceled when several Army generals asked Riefenstahl while she was editing the finished Triumph of the Will if Army footage was included in the film. She said No--there was no need for it. (Army scenes had been shot in the rain and could not be used.) The generals then complained to Hitler who then asked her to reconsider. When she refused to comply, she offered instead to make a short film solely about the Army. A year later, Day of Freedom, which she had shot in one day with six cameramen, fulfilled her promise. She says of this film that it was "an experimental short using a montage technique both pictorially and aurally to create what must be a dazzling as well as deafening impression of military force.... "13

Which came first, the Rally or the film? This query surfaces again and again from the clouds of controversy still swarming above the realization of the 1934 Party Rally film. Was the Rally filmed as a tool for propaganda? Or did it objectively document an historical event? If Riefenstahl knew that the Rally took place for her cameras then surely she was Hitler's handmaiden, assisting the political platform of the National Socialist Party. If this was not the case, then would Riefenstahl be less guilty? Innocent of all charges? The passage of time has distilled no provable conclusions from this quandary.

According to Current Biography, May 1975, on page 38, Riefenstahl has expressed both views. Interviews in the early 1970's relate that Hitler named her film Triumph of the Will, an unbiased record of the Congress. She declares an opposing view--that the Congress was planned for her photographic prowess--in her book Hinter den Kulissen des Reichsparteitag-Films (Behind the Scenes of the National Party Congress Film, Munich, 1935).

Georges Sadoul in Dictionary of Films (Berkeley: University of California Press, 1972), page 383, in his annotation of the film quotes Riefenstahl from her book as saying,

"The preparations for the Party congress were made in
concert with the preparations for the camerawork. " (This
comment on the willingness of the Party to fit their plans
in with hers has often been taken to mean that the congress was actually staged for the purpose of making the
film. There is no factual basis for this supposition,
which is a little like suggesting that moon shots are staged
only for television....

Erik Barnouw details the Herculean labor and complex organization of equipment and personnel required of Riefenstahl to prepare for filming.

Thirty cameras and four sound trucks would be in operation. Twenty-two automobiles and their drivers were assigned to her, along with uniformed field police. She felt
they must all live together in Nuremberg, location of the
rally, for constant coordination through the week of scheduled events--September 4-10, 1934. But all hotels were
booked. More than a million people were expected in
Nuremberg, tripling its population. Leading Nazi official
Julius Streicher owned a large Nuremberg building and
offered it.... 14

With the on-site improvisation which characterized her photographic prowess, Riefenstahl ordered ramps, towers, and bridges
built for her camera positions. She planned to place a photographer
on an elevator built to ascend a flagpole; other camera crewmen on
a second-floor scaffold, on a firetruck's ninety-foot extension ladder,
on rooftops and in ditches, all wearing elite-troop uniforms. She
rehearsed them in these vantage points, with wide-angle and tele-
scopic lenses operating. She would tell them what to shoot and how
and why. Heinz von Jaworsky graphically tells what it was like to
work with her. "She would rush around from one cameraman to
the other like a maniac and say--How are you doing, how are you
doing?.... Screaming and hollering--oh, she was an absolute maniac, she was wild.... "15 Although Jaworsky refused to work with
her on Triumph he did join her crew for The Olympiade, having
shared filmwork with her from the Fanck mountain epics.

The extraordinarily impressive opening of Triumph dominates
the majority of the discussions and reviews of the film.

In the film's prologue Hitler descends from the clouds like
a Messiah to the masses awaiting salvation. His plane
lands to the accompaniment of a bombastic commentary:
"On 5 September 1934, twenty years after the outbreak of
the Great War, sixteen years after the beginning of the
German people's humiliation, nineteen months after the
German nation was reborn, Adolf Hitler was flying.... "16

As the September 1, 1934, edition of the Nazi controlled newspaper Volkischer Beobachter announced, the "political mission" of the

film was "to show Germany ... 'the order, unity and determination
of the National Socialist movement'.... " Further, "It was essential
to show the Party's strength to the people as a whole, and the means
to this end was 'a documentary record of the unanimous loyalty to
the Führer and so to Germany which would be at the same time a
resounding demonstration to the whole world of the peaceful intentions of the German people as embodied in the Führer....' "17

Hitler's speeches and promises of loyalty from his supporters
and the masses comprise the rhetorical text studded with exclama-
tion points of only tertiary importance in judging the film. The total
texture of sound figures second to the excellence of the visual composition demonstrated in frame after frame during the two hours'
running time of Triumph. Riefenstahl's control and design of each
element appearing in each frame of Triumph, augmented by her per-
fectionist editing, is the core from which the success of the film as
a film radiates.

Erwin Leiser discerns that Triumph's image compositions,

> to a considerable extent modelled on Fritz Lang's monu-
> mental silent epic The Nibelungen, show Hitler as a new
> Siegfried and his supporters as extras in a colossal Wag-
> ner opera, an anonymous mass completely under his sway.
> When the Labour Service parades, detachments of youth
> from every region stand ready "to lead Germany into the
> new era. " In chorus they shout that "though we have not
> been under heavy bombardment, we are still soldiers. "
> Time after time their God is revealed to them. The
> figure of Hitler is outlined in solitary glory against the
> sky.... He poses as the prophet of a new religion, as
> the grand master of a mystical order, as an animal train-
> er who has disciplined his beasts of prey.... The Pied
> Piper of Nuremberg--an intimidating spectacle for those
> who were still undecided on the sidelines.... 18

A definitive description of the beginning of Triumph appears
in The German Cinema by Roger Manvell and Heinrich Fränkel (New
York: Praeger, 1971), on page 79:

> The Führer approaches through the clouds, his plane
> weaving through the white masses. The music is soft and
> romantic, the effect godlike. Nuremberg appears below.
> The Horst Wessel Nazi anthem starts. The shadow of
> Hitler's plane passes up a long line of marching men in
> the street below. Shot by shot, we descend nearer to the
> earth and the city full of marching columns....

Returning to Sadoul, we find much the same flavor in his
paragraph on Triumph:

> The Führer descends from the clouds like a Messiah ar-
> riving for the second coming. From the clouds he makes

his way through the streets amid scenes of quasi-religious adoration. This is followed by processions, by day and by torchlight, men staged against the architecture like statues, and endless speeches by the Führer. Some of the most revealing sequences of the film are those behind the scenes: the SS and Hitler Youth with their naked chests, their apparent gaiety only thinly covering their animal ferocity.... [19]

Program notes written by Marshall Lewis after a showing of Triumph in New York City on June 27, 1960, attest to the sway of the film--which remains undated and fresh--and to his judgment that that the rally was staged for the film.

> ... Riefenstahl's major problem was to take the staged display and create a quality of spontaneous action and coverage in her material. Every sequence was carefully planned in advance, and only the most thoroughly experienced technical eye even today can detect the fabrications so expertly staged. One, for example, occurs near the end of the film as Hitler stands reviewing a five-hour parade of his followers. It is no accident that Riefenstahl photographed the black-uniformed troops of the S. S. in the falling shadows of the later afternoon ... and the effect is chilling ... while the Sixth Congress was held, on the surface, as a convention, the real reason for the gathering ... was solely for the making of the film.... Be that as it may, the resulting TRIUMPH OF THE WILL is a fantastic film, a unique achievement in the documentary genre.... Riefenstahl never allows a static moment. TRIUMPH's greatness as a film, then, is because of this woman who, before our eyes, constructs a world out of nothing and imbues it with an essence of reality so authentic that many times we are forced to shake ourselves out of the visual trance her superb virtuoso editing style places us in, and staggeringly accept the truth that the world we see was built out of segments of film and a powerhouse of cinematic talent. Even the most jaded professional critic must admit that TRIUMPH OF THE WILL is a brilliant technical tour de force. The succession of faces, symbolic images and juxtapositions of Hitler as the omnipresent and omniscient mystical soul of this nation are worthy of comparison with, as Paul Rotha suggests, the powerful editing of Pabst and Eisenstein.... [20]

Without question, the keenest dissector holding the most balanced views of Riefenstahl's films is Richard Meran Barsam, who defines the theme of Triumph as "the apotheosis of Adolf Hitler over the mass of ordinary Germans ..." tagging it with a triad of sub-themes: "(1) the German heritage in the Nazi order; (2) the importance of communal work and cooperation; and (3) the mysticism of the Nazi Party.... [21]

As for the staging concept Barsam draws a fine line which may rest as close to the truth as it is possible to reside. "This annual event was not staged for Riefenstahl's cameras, but all evidence indicates that an extraordinary degree of cooperation existed between those who planned it and those who filmed it. The film does not preserve a chronological record of the meetings, rallies, and speeches.... " The essence of Riefenstahl's accomplishment in Triumph

> is a cinematic expression of the Nazi mystique. A masterly blend of light, darkness, sound, and silence, it is not just an achievement in cinematic form. It has other essential elements--thematic, mythological, narrative, psychological, and visual interest--and it is in the working of these elements that Riefenstahl transcends the genre limitations of either the documentary or the propaganda film....

This transcendence involves Riefenstahl's relating

> Triumph to the Western epic tradition ... she does attempt to create myth.... Although Triumph shares many characteristics with the epic literary form, it varies in the one essential ingredient: the hero. Its central figure is demonic, not heroic ... Riefenstahl presents Hitler, a figure of national importance, as a leader of great historical significance to the destiny of Germany.... [22]

Instead of the supernatural forces inherent in epic art forms, Riefenstahl works with ritual and ceremony and "develops the heroic elements with restraint, although one idea recurs throughout: that Hitler will restore Germany to heights of ancient heroism and grandeur.... " Earlier in this essay, Barsam states flatly that "The film suggests that the party is the legal and spiritual heir to the legacy of the German nation.... "[23] This bonding of Hitler to Germany, and the Nazi Party to epigones of a Teutonic inheritance, and the linking of these four as a basis for a greater-than-ever-before Germany is the shocking and superbly shaped import of the film.

Barsam describes this import. "The effectiveness of Riefenstahl's interpretation of German myth relies on the interplay of the heroic visual image and the heroic musical score.... " Barsam describes composer Herbert Windt's subtly evocative film score which mixed Wagnerian operatic themes, German folk tunes, and Nazi Party songs: "Windt suggests the continuation of an ancient musical tradition. More important, he awakens a racial and cultural memory in the filmgoer's consciousness.... "[24]

As for the heroic visual image, Barsam continues by placing Riefenstahl's work in a historical perspective which suggests that the filmmaker drew upon her memory of films she had viewed in addition to those she had participated in.

In the Russian tradition of Eisenstein and Pudovkin, and
in the German adaptation of that tradition in Walther Ruttmann's Berlin: The Symphony of a Great Day (1927), Triumph of the Will demonstrates the power of the rhythmic
montage to provide multileveled impressions of each scene
. . . . This retains the viewers' attention; moreover, it
creates the excitement and anticipation that give the film
its essence. . . . Riefenstahl not only takes viewers to the
events, but she also makes them a participant in them.
The circular and symbolic structure of the film may become apparent after several viewings, but the immediate
effect of the film is to immerse the viewer in the dynamic
reality of the events it records. . . . "25

        In his Nonfiction Film: a critical history (New York: Dutton,
1976, p. 85), Barsam states:

        The film records the actual spectacle of the 1934 Nazi
        Party congress in Nuremberg, but its real purpose is the
        deification of Hitler as spiritual leader of the Germans.
        It is a solemn, symbolic film, beautifully photographed
        and edited with a sense of structure and rhythm that make
        it the rival of its Russian masters. It should be studied
        not as propaganda only, but also as art of the highest
        order; no film has been more vilified for its subject mat-
        ter, yet no film has been more misunderstood. Triumph
        of the Will and Riefenstahl's Olympia are among the great-
        est nonfiction films of all time. . . .

Testifying to the wonder and terror generated by this film
which too few actually were permitted to see, is this opinion of
filmmaker Robert Flaherty quoted by Vernon Young:

        "Hitler was a very clever fellow. . . . He spared no effort
        to make films and use them . . . wonderful films made by
        Leni Riefenstahl, but terrifying like her Triumph of the
        Will. Here was a film made in 1934 in which you saw
        even then that the Nazis were a psychopathic case with
        whom to reason was impossible. But that film, which be-
        cause of its revelation could have had a vital influence on
        subsequent events, was suppressed. . . . "26

Actually, Triumph was premiered on March 29, 1935, and
instantaneously declared a masterpiece. It was awarded three
tributes: "Germany's Staatspreis in 1935, the gold medal of the
Venice Biennale in 1936, and the Grand Prix of the Exposition In-
ternationale des Arts et des Technique at Paris in 1937. " David
Gunston, from this quoted source (Current Biography, May, 1975,
p. 38), ". . . called the film a 'historical document of utmost importance' but added that 'it could never have been made by anyone
not fanatically at one with the events depicted. ' "

Yet, Barsam differs with Gunston in his judgment of the necessity of the filmmaker's ideological immersion in the film's "message. " "Triumph of the Will is surprisingly free of reference to the specific evils which we associate with the Nazi doctrine.... In short, Triumph ... like Birth of a Nation, embodies an overwhelming contradiction: it is cinematically dazzling and ideologically vicious.... "27 And in his Filmguide to Triumph of the Will, p. 67, Barsam reiterates: "Today, we too acknowledge Triumph ... as a superb example of political propaganda even as we are repelled by its vision.... "

The contemporary consensus of Triumph is one which likens it to a vile and evil body in an embellished and eye-catching display case: a despicable political doctrine cloaked in a stunning mantle. "... With its infectious scenes of mass enthusiasm and adulation is a unique example of art completely, blatantly and yet successfully serving a political idea.... "28

In his book Tower of Babel (Philadelphia: Chilton, 1966, p. 52), Eric Rhode insists,

> The movements of the Nuremberg Rally were mostly arranged so that the film could be made.... Triumph ... is a case, not of history being rewritten, but of history being faked as it takes place. In its disdain for all truth, it is a premonition of a nihilistic future. The beautifully modulated camerawork and the pageantry are as empty as writing on the air.... Its purpose is to make converts to Nazism and to influence people.... "

True, Glenn Losey agrees, in "The Will Triumphant, " After Dark 8 (March 1976), p. 28: "... Her Triumph ... is very close to being the product of an evil genius. " Observing that this film convinced Riefenstahl's detractors, especially Goebbels, of her unique genius, Losey commends the film which "remains a landmark in propaganda documentary film. Many of the visual effects Frau Riefenstahl achieved were previously inconceivable, but no expense, no technical innovation was spared which might give the footage the greatest possible impact.... " Losey then muses on an eventuality which no one else has expressed. "Perhaps, had Triumph been merely a shoddy, noisy, Nazi newsreel--which it could quite easily have become--it might have been mocked and dismissed as the failure of a woman trying too hard to succeed doing man's work. Unfortunately for Frau Riefenstahl's career after World War II, however, Triumph was all too effective.... "

Although Charlie Chaplin's The Great Dictator (1935) is acknowledged as a parody of Hitler in Triumph no extended critical comparison of these two filmworks has been made. Jill Caldwell ruminates upon "Propaganda--Militant/Non-militant, " in Film Library Quarterly, 9:1 (1976) in her line-up of parallels and differences between Listen to Britain (1941) and Triumph (1935). The latter is militant, while the British film is non-militant.

As proof of the continuing critical responses to Triumph and
the controversial imports which still fulminate within them, is their
division into three basic views, for the purposes of study, by Barsam, who outlines them thus:

> First, there are the critics whose moral and political
> convictions prevent them from appreciating the film; sec-
> ond, there are those who understand the film, and even
> appreciate it, in light of its mission as propaganda; and
> third, there are those who appreciate the formal beauty
> of the film in spite of its politics. And, indeed, there
> are some critics who might agree with all three view-
> points.... 29

Siegfried Kracauer, whose view has influenced a generation
or more of film critics, historians and viewers, and is espoused by
contemporaries David Gunston and David Stewart Hull, takes the first
position toward Triumph. His binary stand against the film assumes
that the rally was arranged and held for the purpose of filming (in-
correct, Barsam interjects) and, most meaningfully, "Through a
very impressive composition of mere newsreel shots, this film
represents the complete transformation of reality... "30 and the
emphasis is Barsam's.

John Grierson takes position two, non-supportive of the political aspects of Triumph, but appreciative of the aesthetic and
technical marvels in the film. Kevin Brownlow and Robert Flaherty
concur with Grierson, who is, as Barsam points out, "the founder
of the British documentary movement.... "31

The third stance is a formalist one, as expressed by Ken
Kelman. Form is paramount over content. And "a propaganda film
must transform politics into art.... " Kelman tenders this tribute
to Triumph:

> However, Triumph ... did come to surpass Potemkin as
> the ultimate in cinema propaganda. This is for one es-
> sential reason: Triumph is a true documentary, complete-
> ly made up of "actual" footage--the ultimate in incontro-
> vertible credibility. The wonderful paradox here is that
> under any conditions but this absolute reportorial truth,
> the propaganda itself would be quite incredible.... 32

The emphasis, again, is Barsam's.

Barsam tempers his triad of critical responses with the cau-
tion that "none offers more than partial answers.... "33

The admittedly anti-Leni Paul Rotha with his position one
critical response shapes the highest eulogy to Riefenstahl's attainments in making Triumph. In his compendious The Film Till Now
(New York: Funk & Wagnalls, 1949), on pages 590-91, Rotha refers to Kracauer's statement that "This film represents an inex-

tricable mixture of a show simulating German reality and of a German reality manoeuvred into a show. '' Rotha then comments,

> The triumph here was due to the fact that the mixture
> really was inextricable, except to the eye of the experi-
> enced analyst, and that it had been cast into the melting
> pot by a talent which we must, however reluctantly, recog-
> nise as one of the most brilliant ever to be concerned
> with films, that of Leni Riefenstahl ... this woman's
> knowledge of the power of editing images was profound,
> nearly as profound as Pabst's or Eisenstein's ... the
> ideological artillery of America has yet to demonstrate
> that it can destroy, by matching, the psychic world which
> she created out of nothing with camera and shears.
> Nazi Germany is no more, but the challenge stands.   It
> has not been met.

As Barsam confirms, ''... it has not been imitated directly, nor has its footage been successfully used against it. ''34   Segments of Triumph have been extensively used in anti-Nazi propaganda films with a wide range--zero to the top--of success.   In the United States, Frank Capra's series of films Why We Fight, are best known.   Erik Barnouw lists all of them. 35

Triumph was used by enemies of the Third Reich purportedly to defeat it.   ''... No film has been more widely used by opposition forces.... ''36

Riefenstahl remains indignant and angry about any use, partial or total, of Triumph by such institutions as the Museum of Modern Art in New York City, without any arrangement for payment of royalties to her.   She has stated again and again that Triumph (and Olympia as well, which has been repeatedly exhibited in the United States in the past thirty years) is her property, made by her own film company and that she plans soon to enlist an American attorney to settle this question of her rights.

> ... She comments on the completion of the film: ''It is
> not important to get everything on the screen in the right
> chronological order.   The structural outline demands that
> one finds the road to unity by instinct, influenced by the
> real experience of Nuremberg, so that the film takes shape
> in a way that, scene by scene, impression by impression,
> makes an overwhelming impact on the viewer and listener.
> I try to discover the inner dramatic force of this retro-
> spective structure....   So ... there rises a film about
> the German present--a triumphant progress of the knowl-
> edge, the courage, the strength to fight and win for our
> German people.   A heroic film of facts--in the will of
> the Führer his people triumphs.... ''37

There are critics and commentators whose views of Triumph defy Barsam's classification scheme, from whose published opinions it is impossible to tag their positions.   Film history teacher William K. Everson attaches bland praise for Triumph in his brief essay included in Lewis Jacob's The Documentary Tradition (New York: Hopkinson & Blake, 1971, pages 138-140):

> One of the greatest documentaries of them all, certainly one of the most pictorially eloquent, and one that still influences documentary-makers today.... One of the highlights ... is a brief, almost imperceptible vignette lasting less than a second. The mob roars approval of one of Hitler's speeches. Even he is a bit surprised at the enthusiasm. There is ... a suggestion of a smile which says, more clearly than reels of film, "Boy, I've got them just where I want them!" Of such moments is the real truth of history, and some of the most valuable moments of film documentary, composed.

B. Ruby Rich adheres to the second and third positions in Barsam's categorization besides bringing to Triumph provocative insights regarding Riefenstahl's feminist orientation in the Nazi hierarchy and her use of Romantic tenets in the film.   Rich contends that Riefenstahl's films have never been thoroughly dissected and studied.

> The lesson of Riefenstahl demands a reexamination of the nature of romanticism and its entire legacy of mystic illusionism, a rethinking of the function of myth, and an analysis of the roles open to women living under a patriarchy. 38

Rich fulfills this mandate, at least partially, by concentrating on Triumph and the two queries it prompts: (1) Is Triumph documentary or propaganda? and, (2) Can art and politics be sifted one from the other?   Rich replies to (1) that Triumph does messenger the truth of its subject on Riefenstahl's terms, rendering it documentary.   She answers to (2) that art and politics can serve each other, can be so mingled as to resist filtering.   In Triumph "the principles of Romanticism [were] subjugated to the Nazi mythology by means of specifically Romantic pictorial devices. "39

How could the ideology of Fascism so smoothly permeate the contemporary cultural values of German society?   Rich wonders. She posits that a study of the romantic aspects of Triumph lay the groundwork for comprehending "the ideological nature of cinema in our society today.... "40   Using Modern Painting and the Northern Romantic Tradition by Robert Rosenblum as a guide, Rich identifies the Romantic images and ideals in Triumph as epitomizing all of Germany's history in the grammar of its national Romantic style.

In Triumph, Riefenstahl the Romantic associates Hitler "with a Faust-turned-Archangel access to a state of natural grace. "41 From her reading of Rosenblum's text, Rich finds this type of godmaking a common pursuit in Romantic paintings.

A saintly Hitler flying in from cloudy space, contrasted with the medieval architecture of a calm Nuremberg, always considered a spiritual center in Germany, "neatly dovetails two accepted representations into a single mythology of limitless power incarnated in Hitler. "42

Referring to the quest for order by the Romantics which led them, according to Rich, to "'fearful symmetry,' the imposition of an archaic and artificial structure onto the universe of the work, translated into Triumph as the massing of crowds and the geometric precision of the spectacle. "43   The absence of middle ground, the angles of vision, and the lighting of major figures, especially Hitler (noted by others) from below and behind, in Triumph ally its images with those painted in the Romantic tradition.

Rich tries to pinpoint the reason why Triumph inevitably engulfs and sweeps away its audiences whenever shown.   Riefenstahl used yet another trait from the early German Romantic painters. This was the use of unknown "faceless beings" whose nameless presences drew viewers to enter into the painting and to participate in gazing with interest on the object or major scene in the painting. Thus, a lone viewer would no longer be what Rich names a third-person audience but instead be a first-person participant in the painting.   Translating this shift of perspective from a Romantic painting to the film Triumph occurs because the pluralistic cinema audience easily identifies with the crowds of German citizens in the film.

The angled shots that were used to magnify the stature of the speakers serve the dual function of leading the audience to identify with their ground-level point of view and therefore with the masses there listening.   It's no wonder that the film entrances, for the theater audience ... becomes its reflection, the rally crowd, swept up in the visual pageantry and ... hailing Hitler with the rest. "44

Riefenstahl as a token Amazon accepted into the Nazi patriarchy because she adopted its values cannot be viewed as a feminist. She did not, could not, build a power base from which other women could rise to a position similar to her own, Rich concludes.

The most definitive, detailed shot-by-shot examination of Triumph is conducted by Steve Neale in "Triumph of the Will: Notes on Documentary and Spectacle, " in Screen XX: 1 (Spring 1979), pages 63 to 86.   Criticisms of Triumph, Neale observes, have not been probing or profound, merely falling into the contentions of art versus history or Nazi propaganda vehicle versus film masterpiece.   The film has never been accorded the painstaking and meticulous study it deserves.   To reach a comprehensive and correct understanding of the genius of Triumph as film "an examination of the film's textual organisation and discursive systems" is required.   From this study, "conjectural analyses can proceed" (page 63).   Neale's essay does indeed attempt to address Triumph with this kind of procedural dissection, giving particular attention to spectacle and looking, both of which are responsible, in Neale's judgment, for the film's "cinematic and its ideological power. "

Cloud formations, which "signify spectacle itself" (page 67), are "important and indicative" in luring the eye to the aircraft flying Hitler to Nuremberg.   In turn, these clouds are seen from the aircraft. The alternating of shots between Hitler and the crowds responding to him in a rhythmically satisfying manner is one key to Triumph's success.   This rhythm is established in the opening of the film, particularly in a sequence of shots numbered by Neale 15 to 23, in which views of Hitler's plane switch to views of the city below with its expectant crowds and uniformed troops, and back again.   These two types of shots enfold each other "integrating the two into a common diegetic space itself heavily marked by the instance of spectacle (the troops on parade), leads on to a shot ... which initiates a system of looking that runs throughout the remainder of the film and that dominates its visual articulation" (page 69). Neale describes this shot as one showing a crowd looking up right, ostensibly at Hitler's arriving plane, with a pair of Nazi guards before it.   "It is at this point that the activity of looking is inscribed into the diegesis itself, and that its privileged object begins to be established" (page 69).

Thirteen shots later, Hitler appears.   This first segment of Triumph, Neale theorizes, sets up the "political relationship between the crowd and Hitler" (page 69).   Hitler is targeted as "the privileged object of the gaze" (page 69) of the audience.

Neale agrees with B. Ruby Rich on Riefenstahl's adroit use of illuminating Hitler's head and body to mark him as the central focus and "privileged object" of the film.   Neale selects shots numbered 47, 59, 61, and 85 as those in which Hitler is successively given a halo round his head, then a halo round his head and shoulders, then Hitler moves from darkness into light enveloping his entire body, and, last, a circle of light radiates about his head once again.   This highlighting of Hitler with singular effects of brightness "is one of the film's most insistent, most evident and most important" techniques (page 73).

Neale posits that two constructs of "repetition/difference, the one crossing the other" (page 81) are established in Triumph.   The first construct is of "sequencing the images as such" (page 81), changing from views of Hitler to shots of the crowds.   "Here the repetition lies in the alternating pattern itself, varied only at the point at which two shots of the scene rather than the usual one intervene between shots of Hitler" (page 81).   The second construct involves the images themselves, the contrasting of shots of Hitler with shots of the scenes around him, each shot differing from the others in variations in distance, gesture, angle, etc.   This economical and patterned use of repetitions with marked diversities is held by Neale to be a characteristic of the very best, if not classic, films.

Neale quotes Raymond Bellour's "'The Obvious and the Code,'" Screen 15:4 (Winter 1974-75), pages 15-16.   Bellour asserts that "A 'profound tendency towards repetition,' but a tendency that is countered by 'powerful' differences--precisely that economy of process ... is the mark, par excellence, of classical cinema... " (page 82).

Neale resolves that Triumph is a "classic of propaganda" (page 83) and "cinematic poetry" (pages 85-86), as well as a triumph not only in title, but of "vision and the visible" (page 86).

Even as the sound of applause for Triumph was thinning Riefenstahl suggested to UFA (Universum Film Aktiengesellschaft) a new project for herself: A film record of the 1936 Olympic Games to be held in Berlin.   UFA demurred.   Another company, Tobis, agreed to back the film.   On her own initiative, Riefenstahl came to terms with the International Olympic Committee because, as Barsam phrases it, "she wished to avoid official sponsorship...."   These terms involved obtaining consents from all national committees and from each participating contestant.

Not surprisingly, Riefenstahl submerged herself into Olympia (sometimes named The Olympiade), which developed into two films, with her accustomed strenuous and frenzied approach fueling her penchant for recalling an infinite number of facts and details in a complex organization of personnel, equipment, restrictions, and economics, her comprehension of the total organization necessary for filming and the delegation of tasks to those whose abilities could succeed in their completion.   Riefenstahl as producer appears to have been every bit as inexhaustible and inspired as Riefenstahl the scripter-director-editor always was.   As producer she sought to solve anticipated conflicts, or forestall them, before they could impede or embarrass her.   Once again, Goebbels was her adversary: how ridiculously comic it seems now to realize that he and his Propaganda Ministry were planning to produce their own Olympics film! Once again, Goebbels was virulently antagonistic toward her and her filmwork; Riefenstahl has repeatedly said that she managed to make Olympia over his protests and planned impediments.

In the making of Triumph the big question was one of staging. With the making of Olympia the big question was one of financing: did or did not the Nazi officaldom eventually pay for the film to be made? Riefenstahl claims the film was made independently of any government support.   Hans Barkhausen claims not.   This debate has been documented, as has been Leni's so-called harassment by Goebbels and his aides.   No verdict on either the financial or harassment issues has been documented which satisfies a majority of film critics and individuals on the scene who witnessed some of the filming, its aftermath, and the lengthy preliminaries.

Preparations for filming the Olympic Games were more cumbersome, elaborate, and extensively detailed than those experienced by Riefenstahl and her crew in making Triumph.   Limitations were more rigid, and the scale of operations grander. Riefenstahl's own "Notes on the Making of Olympia (1958)" which appears in Richard Meran Barsam's Nonfiction Film: theory and criticism (New York: Dutton, 1976), pp. 323-341, tersely outlines a "work program" for the sixteen days of the competition. All kinds of technical improvisations are described--a catapult camera for one--a summary of the restrictions imposed upon her by the International Olympic Committee, plus an addendum of some thirty itemized facts with which she has tried "To explain things that are generally not known to the public. There is legal documentary evidence for all the following statements ... " (p. 330). These "things" include the financing of the film and Goebbels' interference during its filming.

The improvisatory techniques used in Olympia to obtain filming positions engendered as much activity as the actual shooting. "Cameras were mounted on steel towers, on balloons, in trenches, and in rubber rafts.... "45 Current Biography (May 1975, p. 38) describes Riefenstahl's ingenious methods of filming. The sound of the cameras that followed the athletes was muted. To partially record a race, Riefenstahl mounted a camera in a cage which was moved along a track. Yet another camera was placed atop shock-resistant materials and attached to a saddle.

Riefenstahl herself records this frenzied period of preparation:

> Every day was a new ordeal for all concerned. These camera-men ... found themselves placed in a paradise for any camera-man. They had not only to define their own personal impressions in a way never experienced before, they had also to work with lightning speed in order to lose no valuable second. Dripping with perspiration they rushed to and fro untiringly with their heavy cameras. 46

Heinz von Jaworsky was one of her crew and he remembers his work on Olympia:

> After a 16-hour day's work ... she would get the whole gang together around a big table. We were all falling asleep. She had been with us all day long. But that woman was full of energy. She would assign you to your position.... She would go into minute detail--and no contradictions, you do this.... 47

The filming crew worked seven days a week, arguing and planning late into the night.

Olympia begins with an aerial scene just as Triumph did. "She had the opening of the games photographed from the Zeppelin Hindenburg. Automatic cameras were sent aloft via free balloons, with attached instructions for returning the film to Leni Riefenstahl.... "48

As Barnouw details this opener (on page 109), it ".... has

an extraordinary Wagnerian opening, reminiscent in its mythic overtones of Triumph of the Will and of ... Riefenstahl's early 'mountain
film' career...." And, of course, Herbert Windt composed an apt
music score echoing the sonorities of Wagner and Mahler and Bruck-
ner.

The allocation of film footage (or metres) to specific sports
in both halves of the film is listed in The German Cinema (pp. 97-
98). It reveals thirteen segments in the first film and eleven in
the second, and is inserted here, with deletions as a frame into
which critical responses can be inserted.

"I Fest der Völker" (Festival of the Nations)

Opening sequence

Opening sequence concluded

Throwing the discus (women)

Hurdles (women) Throwing the Hammer.   100 metres.

High jump (women).   400 metres.

Putting the weight.   800 metres.   Hop-skip and jump.

Long jump.   1500 metres.

High jump.   Hurdles.

Throwing the javelin.   1000 metres.

Pole vaulting.

400 metres relay (women) 400 metres relay.   1600 metres
relay.

The Marathon

The Marathon concluded.

"II Fest der Schönheit" (Festival of Beauty)

Opening sequence and march past ceremony at the Stadium

Mass physical training and gymnastic exercises (men and
women)

Yacht racing

The Pentathlon (riding, pistol shooting and cross country run
only shown)

Finals hockey.   Polo.   Association Football.

Three days riding.

100 kilometres road race.   Final of double sculls.   Coxswain-
less Fours and Eights.

The Decathlon (to the middle of the pole vaulting)

End of Decathlon.   Diving (women) 200 metres breast stroke.

100 metres free style. 100 metres free style (women). Diving.

End sequence.

Infield (on p. 189) cautions that "It is very difficult to list
the order of sequences ... because there are numerous versions of
the film...." True. Although Riefenstahl didn't rearrange the
sports events neither did she follow the real-life sequence of their
performances. Repeating the fate of Triumph, exhibitors and editors
have altered the film to their own tastes.

An intense assurance exudes from Riefenstahl's replies to
Gordon Hitchens' questions about Olympia in an interview in 1964:

> She stated that most sports films are dull because the
> subject is very difficult ... she decided from the start to
> make two films and that "the form must excite the content
> and give it shape." Most important, she said, "remember
> that beauty is not names." The editing ... was ...
> planned ... before the shooting. "I had the whole thing
> in my head" and "I was like an architect building a house
> .... The law of film is architecture, balance. If the
> image is weak, strengthen the sound, and vice-versa; the
> total impact on the viewer should be 100%.... You must
> alternate tension with relaxation for both sound and picture:
> when one is up, then the other must be down...."[49]

The secret of Olympia's success, Riefenstahl reveals, is the
sound,

> ... the three months of mixing. "No general crowd
> noises ... no synchronized sound but all made by us in
> the studio" (demonstrating footsteps); even horses breath-
> ing and runners panting because "people cry too much"
> ... 70% of the shooting was useless....[50]

The first film opens with "fifteen minutes of pure visuals
without dialogue" but with musical background,

> suggesting a misty, primitive world. Soon we see a run-
> ner carrying a torch across rugged landscape; architecture
> and coastline tell us this is ancient Greece. We briefly
> see nude athletes and dancers training--one of them is
> Leni Riefenstahl. Then we see the torch handed from one
> runner to another, as they carry it from ancient Greece
> to modern Germany, and into a vast stadium presided over
> by Adolf Hitler. The sequence seems to tell us that the
> torch of civilization has been carried from its ancient cen-
> ter, Greece, to modern Germany, watched over by a pan-
> theon at whose apex is Hitler....[51]

The torch scene climaxes

in the lighting of a huge brazier high in the stadium. The next major sequence shows the parade of participants before Hitler and his entourage, some of this cut in the usually circulated prints. The remainder of the first film is devoted to track and field events, and recorded for posterity the great performance of the nineteen-year-old Jesse Owens. The second film ... starts with the sequences in the Olympic village and continues with ... other events of games.... 52

A more specific and subjective description of the films appears in The Nazi Olympics (pp. 262-3):

> Opens with a sort of visual metaphor of creation. To grand orchestral music, clouds, rock masses, and then off-focused architectural masses gradually sharpen. The buildings are those on the Acropolis at Athens and then the fallen column drums of the temple of Zeus at Olympia. This part of the film clearly reveals Leni's debt to the mountain movies.... We have some lyrical, slow-motion scenes of running males and some slender females--all presumably evocations of the Greek athletic spirit--who appear to be offering their beauty to the sun. The scenes fade to a solitary runner who carries a torch.... He becomes part of a relay. A final runner in the series gradually approaches a vast public square, packed with people who are clearly National Socialists (they wear swastikas) in Berlin. Then we see Schilgen, the last blond runner, climb the steps at the Olympic Stadium to light the sacred fire....

The surprising and spectacular championship of the black Jesse Owens is captured by cameras intent on his concentration of effort in mind and body.

> What is most surprising about movies of this fabulous individual is that as we examine his physical perfection we divine the intensity of his psychic effort. The deeply cut lines separating the muscles of his thighs, the pulsing arteries at his temples, the slight pout of his lips--all reveal inner gathering for the abstract pursuit of supremacy .... As Jesse breaks the records the camera leads us to ponder the deep power of his perfect grace, not the crass evidence of stopwatches. In Riefenstahl's films as at the Games themselves, Jesse Owens receives more lavish attention than any other individual.... 53

Vernon Young's breezy yet profound reaction to Olympia I is recorded on page 36 in his anthology On Film (New York: Quadrangle/Times Books, 1972):

> A naked youth apotheosized to carry the torch in relay. Leisurely cutting, as a succession of beach boys trots

across the Grecian landscape, down to the verge of the
sea, and then, by way of "dissolves," up through the ages.
The four elements--air, earth, fire, and water. Inevitable? All the same it's pretty damned impressive. Within five minutes you're more enthralled than patient; within
twenty minutes it dawns on you that if this keeps up you're
seeing one of the very great cooperatively made fact films
on record.... And it keeps up....

Young describes these introductory scenes as "imposing,"
"Siegfriedian," recording individual shots so strikingly that we can
see them, with him, as we read. One such is the placement of the
cauldron (which the runner ignites with his torch), "where the sun
will set directly behind it ... and there is one stunning shot of the
flames licking and consuming the molten star as it sinks: a terrifying conceit when you recall the date--1936. Morgen die Welt!..."
Another such is "the release of about a million doves (what a
touch!)...." More of these are "Jesse Owens' jaw muscle tightens
... the man in the white coat (he looks like a village butcher) warns
.... 'Fertig!' Runners up on their toes and fingertips ... The
gun goes off ... [pp. 36-37]."

The kaleidoscopic acrobatics of the cameras are chronicled,
too:

With unflagging variety of witness point, reporting their
subject--competition.... You're overhead, underneath,
running parallel, out in front.... Cameras pan, swivel,
tilt, track, or just wait....
    Most of the music ... sounds like Richard Strauss
(even when it's good) and the rest like the Mars movement
of The Planets Suite by Holst, most effective where it ac-
companies the flight of the javelins....

And Young focuses on the ubiquitous "public intrasexual hugging and
kissing." A girl athlete, after crossing the finish line, is embraced by another girl. Then night approaches. The cauldron
burns on. The stadium is empty. "Dissolve to a tolling bell, from
the bell to the caldron, from the caldron to the flags of all nations,
revolving, ascending, and descending.... The Olympics flag with its
linked circles.... Trumpets...."

Olympia II is prefaced with "coming alive" scenes of which
Riefenstahl must have been overfond, fitting as they--"dewey leaf
and birds caroling"--are. Once the stadium is filled, Young continues, "the preliminary exhibition is an unstinting display of Kultur.
This a gymkhana with a vengeance. Battalions of German man-
and womanhood (but you can barely tell women from men without a
program) perform a joyless if intrepid ceremony of calisthenics...."

Just as the camera recording of Jesse Owens' prestigious
feat in Olympia I forms the peak of viewer excitement and high caliber photography, so do the diving sequences in Olympia II oblige us.

These scenes are unparalleled miracles of documentation, still unsurpassed, particularly those photographed underwater and those

> taken with the lens half-submerged. For some of the se-
> quences of the 10-meter diving competitions, the camera
> followed the athlete from his take-off, down the 33 feet to
> the water to trace his bubbling change of trajectory be-
> neath the surface, and finally emerged with him from the
> pool. This trial for camera and technician required sev-
> eral abrupt changes of lens opening and even a rapid chang-
> ing of lenses under water. Naturally the final filming in
> August was preceded by a great deal of rehearsal work be-
> fore the athletes gathered for their actual event. Some
> athletes even graciously repeated their performances for
> Leni after the Games were over.... 54

Riefenstahl's feat of supremacy--these diving scenes--is analyzed for film students by Lincoln F. Johnson in Film: Space, Time,
Light and Sound (New York: Rinehart and Winston, 1974, pp. 76-
86): "The interdependence of space, movement and time intervals
can be seen with almost paradigmatic clarity in one of the most famous short bits of film history, the 'Diving Sequence' from Olympia
(1938)...."

Johnson sketches in language as pictorial as Young's how
Riefenstahl leads into the diving. First we see the pool and the
audience. Then the routine movements of diving follow: the walk
to the end of the board, the spring into air, the plunge into the water, the climbing out of the pool, the cross to the ladder, and the
walk to the end of the board. Now our expectations are shaped--
only to be surprised. The magic begins when the diver's identity
changes at the ladder, but a feeling of unbroken motion is maintained.

> At appropriate moments close-ups of the audience are
> interpolated ... to reveal their reactions; usually, the
> camera focuses on a person of the same ethnic background
> or nationality as the diver of the moment. Throughout this
> section the camera maintains a position on a level with the
> subject, the disposition of forms is generally architectonic,
> the close-ups of the divers and spectators are very nearly
> frontal, and movements occur horizontally or vertically on
> the screen. The effect is of journalistic completeness and
> classical order....

Then, Johnson explains, three changes are introduced: the cutting
rate is altered, time condensed, and the angle of vision is switched
"regularly and rhythmically. "

This contraction of time and creation of mood in space "continues through the sequence, until at the end all the spectator sees
are brief shots of divers suspended in air ... alternating in the direction of their movements, silhouetted against the clouds, soaring
in an infinite space that seems unrelated to the earth.... "

Riefenstahl's camera retards the movements in the swan dive
to achieve a floating glide.   Then it reverses the motion or the
image appears unside down!   This molding of motion by the camera
attaches an aesthetic sensibility to the "least dramatic" and most
non-competitive of the Olympic sports, for, as Johnson asserts,
"The basis of judgment is a matter not of time, distance, or points,
but of aesthetic quality.   Nevertheless, this sequence develops as
drama. ... "

The encompassing effect toward which Riefenstahl directed
was one of liberation and release through beauty in motion.   This
unfettered, free-from-earth mood is described by Johnson as one of
dissociation.

> As the film progresses, the divers are gradually disso-
> ciated from the spectators, from the Olympic pool, from
> any national grouping, and from earth as well, trans-
> formed into soaring silhouettes.   More than a documentary
> report, the sequence becomes a paean to physical strength,
> skill, and human aspiration, a freeing of the spirit through
> a freeing of the body ... an apotheosis of man as a con-
> queror of space....   The spectator, like the diver, is re-
> leased--from the confinement of real time and real space
> . . . .

The theme of <u>Olympia II</u> for Erik Barnouw is

> not politics, but the magnificence of the body in action.
> Dropping earlier attention to victories and statistics, she
> composes sequences of unforgettable splendor--moving, as
> she explained to interviewer Gordon Hitchens, from "real-
> ity" to "poetry."   The high point of this comes at the
> climax of the diving events, in a sequence based on a
> simple but brilliant editing idea.   In a series of dives
> ... she gives us only the flight through the air, eliminating
> the climactic splashes.   We see a long succession of such
> dives, sometimes overlapping via dissolves.   The impres-
> sion is one of total victory over gravity, as body after
> body tumbles through the air, in choreographed patterns of
> stunning beauty, without ever being brought to earth.   Few
> lovelier sequences have ever been put on film. ... [55]

Vernon Young comes up with airborne responses to the divers' ballet above water, prefacing his elation with a sober reflection:

> ... objectivity falters; the provocation for a sortie of ex-
> pressionism was too strong....   You no longer know or
> care who is diving for what team or with what score.
> Surely these flexed and soaring figures are meant to poise
> themselves, step tiptoe, bounce, jackknife, twist in half
> gainers, spiral, swallow-flight and swan eternally, with
> trumpets to herald their abrupt ascent and plummeting fall.
> The camera as Wagner? ... [56]

Young records the remaining sports feats noting, "There is no breaking of stride in this cinematic ingenuity.... "[57] The yacht races on the Kiel Canal, the shell-racers, the cross-country bicycle competition, ever aware of the camera's position because it is his--and the spectators'--own. Then, at last, the finale, with swirling flags.

Young overheard a member of the audience say afterward,

> "With all those cameras, you couldn't miss!" The hell
> you couldn't and the hell they don't! Try to find an equal
> five minutes in the billion feet you've seen of Fox Movie-
> tone, Pathé.... You saw nothing like this. Olympiad,
> 1936 is not a newsreel; it is history, estheticized.... Did
> Adolf the Hammer ever realize that Olympiad, 1936 was
> an act of treason? The redemption of the adrenalin cor-
> tex by the creative eye? The vindication of mass by per-
> spective?... 58

Judgments of the total film educe the critics' political appraisals as well as their artistic criteria perhaps because the Olympic Games have been declared international in intention but nationalistic in execution. Riefenstahl has perennially emphasized that Olympia was apolitical "and cites the fact in her favor that Olympia was accepted as the official film of the Olympic Committee, which awarded her a diploma and gold medal for her work in 1948 at Lausanne.... "59

Opposing this apolitical view is Ulrich Gregor, a leftist critic, who claims the films are "still outspokenly fascistic in spirit. The films celebrate sport as an heroic, superhuman feat, a kind of ritual ... apparent in the narration, which constantly resounds with words like 'fight' and 'conquest'.... "60

Dissenting from Gregor's views is American filmmaker Robert Gardner:

> Neither Triumph nor Olympia could have been made by a
> propagandist pure and simple. They are self evidently the
> work of an artist, even if an artist of an immensely naive
> political nature ... the two Olympia films, which everyone
> said could not be made, were an even more brilliant suc-
> cess than Triumph ... Jim Card, head of the film collec-
> tion at Eastman House, asserts that Olympia might be the
> best film ever made. 61

> Sportswriters who saw the film acknowledged that athletics
> had been rarely better recorded. One correspondent for
> the United Press called Olympia "the finest motion picture
> I have ever seen" and said that at times "it was all I
> could do to keep from rising in my seat and yelling." A
> French critic stated that the film was one of the "summits
> of the cinema. "62

Current Biography (May 1975, pp. 38-39) asks and attempts
to answer the perennial question assigned to a Riefenstahl film: Is
it pro-Nazi propaganda? Olympia does document the winners of
competitions, regardless of race or nationality. To date, critics
can't find proof that Riefenstahl slanted her film toward the Nazi
party-line. If there is a critical consensus its substance is this:
Each viewer of Olympia can decide as a private matter its political
nuances. As a film, Olympia is a superb work. No one denies
this assertion.

The dispassionate evenness of Barsam's appraisal admits,
however, that "the Nazi message comes through. " The film is
lengthy but never bores.

> It concentrates too much on track and field events, but
> this is relieved by the often humorous coverage of other
> events, such as horseback riding and jumping. And the
> diving sequence is one of the masterly achievements in
> all cinema.... The darker elements are there, nonethe-
> less, for the last faces we see before diving begins are
> Aryan ideals.... Riefenstahl knows kinetics and she
> knows memory, and she relies on these sequences to sug-
> gest, however subtle that suggestion may be, that it is
> the blond, muscular German who will soar into limitless
> time and space.... This diving sequence is all cunning
> artifice, but it creates an entity that transcends more than
> time and space. Like all great art, it defies simple ex-
> planation. [63]

Even though Olympia is beautiful because of content, Sadoul
opines, "Riefenstahl's use of slow motion and telephoto lenses" in
other portions of the film are

> ridiculous, such as the sequence in which Riefenstahl com-
> pares the naked bodies of athletes to Greek statues [it pro-
> vides strange glimpses of the Nazi mystique and about its
> idealization of the young male body whose implications may
> seem disturbing today.... More than a hymn to the glory of
> athletics, its compelling beauty remains only a monument to
> the Nazi ideal of Kraft durch Freude [i. e. , art through
> joy].)[64]

As Lewis Jacobs, editor of The Documentary Tradition (New York:
Hopkinson & Blake, 1971) annotates respected critic Parker Tyler's
pronouncement, it is a "retrospective appraisal" (p. 136) from Tyler's book Classics of the Foreign Film published in 1962.

> Olympia survives as one of the grandest documentaries
> in the world film archives and it undoubtedly is the most
> impressive film ever to deal with field sports. Regarded
> aside from its political function, it provides a fascinating
> study of its innate content: whole-souled, harmless phys-
> ical competition....

Tyler bows to Riefenstahl's effort--successful, he says--to make her film as "classical" as possible, and affixes a phrase--"homerically scaled collective piece of filmmaking" to underline the fact. His tribute to Riefenstahl is couched in his last sentence: "Nazified Germany, in having to grant athletic supremacy to the United States in the 1936 Games, could mark up one supreme conquest of its own: the by-lines on this film. "

If any sports documentary can come close to, or match, Olympia, for beauty and technique it is Ron Ichikawa's filming of the Tokyo Olympics in 1964. A comparison of the use of slow motion in the two film chronicles of the Olympic competitions is Dai Vaughan's "Berlin versus Tokyo" in Sight & Sound 46 (Autumn, 1977), pp. 210-15. Limiting his analysis only to the marathons and pole-vaulting portions in both filmworks, Vaughan comments, apart from his dissection of style and content, on the political import of Riefenstahl's Triumph and Olympia.

> It seems to me ... that whereas Triumph of the Will may be construed in an anti-Nazi sense, as exposing the tedium of ceremonial, much of the Olympics film fails to take on full meaning unless we are prepared to invest in our own perception of it certain at least near-fascist values....

With the games done and filming completed, the 400, 000 meters, estimated variously at 1, 300, 000 feet, of camera film were sent to the laboratory for developing. Then Riefenstahl and the nucleus of her crew looked at all of the film in a projection room. Then, "During the winter, ... Riefenstahl dispersed her crews and began what she envisioned as her special contribution. "65 Editing was her responsibility alone, and her workplace and the conditions obtained there for the next two years are described in several sources. She wore a white coat in a white laboratory

> with many back-lighted opaque screens for the examination of individual frames with a magnifying glass. She entered into a close association with that precious footage, eliminating, repeating, compressing, combining, and dubbing in order to compose and orchestrate the film that was to be the artistic distillate of a modern sporting festival. 66

Her goal was to attain "a sort of difficult creation most analogous to the writing of symphonic music. In her recollections of her editing, she unaffectedly uses the terms 'melody, ' 'harmony, ' ... and, most particularly, 'rhythm. ' "67 Here is Leni relating how she lived while editing Olympia:

> I lived in the editing room for a year and a half, never getting home before five o'clock in the morning. My life was tied to the material and the film.... I had glass partitions built, on each side of which I hung filmstrips that went down to the floor. I suspended them one to the other, in order to look at them, compare them, so as to

verify their harmony in the scale of frames and tones.
Thus in the long run, as a composer composes, I made
everything work together in the rhythm.[68]

In eighteen months of editing, 18,000 feet of film were selected from the 1,200,000 or 1,300,000 shot. During this interval
the international situation had deteriorated. Completing the editing
on February 21, 1938, Riefenstahl's final cut measured 6,151 meters
(close to the 18,000 feet mentioned above). Olympia was premiered
on Hitler's birthday, April 20, 1938. Nazi reviewers liked it.
Even Goebbels liked it: he sent her a congratulatory telegram when
Olympia won the Staatspreiz. It won the Grand Prize in Paris, the
Polar Prize in Sweden, and the Mussolini Cup at the L M. P. Festival in Venice pushing Walt Disney's Snow White and the Seven
Dwarfs from first place. Leni sailed on the Europa to the United
States, arriving in New York harbor November 4, 1938. When she
arrived in Hollywood for a private preview of Olympia she was boy-
cotted--Walt Disney alone extended hospitality and showed interest
in her and her work. Although the film was not widely exhibited before World War II in the United States, Great Britain or Germany,
it had accomplished its festive purpose.

According to Current Biography (May 1975, page 39), Olympia
was deemed as one of the ten best films ever made by a group of
Hollywood filmmakers. It was released in four language versions,
and in what Sadoul names as "several differently edited versions."[69]

Still, Leni had not yet finished her Olympia assignment. She
compiled and wrote a book Schoenheit im Olympischen (Beauty in the
Olympics), published by Deutscher Verlag A. G. in Berlin, 1937,

> containing several hundred excellent photographs, captions
> in five languages, and her Foreword in praise of sports,
> youth, and physical beauty. The Foreword mentions,
> among others, the two famous American athletes, Jesse
> Owens and Glenn Morris. The book contains many photo-
> graphs of nude male and female bodies and Greek statuary
> from Olympia's opening sequence ... contains many photo-
> graphs of Riefenstahl and her crew rehearsing equipment
> .... [70]

For the records, Riefenstahl has attended every Olympics
event since the early fifties. She is fully aware of her Olympia
film's enduring fame, and its exhibition all over the world in a variety of forms. On September 29, 1968, Olympia was the subject of
a BBC-1 Omnibus television program. Norman Swallow, Executive
Producer of the Omnibus program series, visited Riefenstahl in her
Munich apartment to work with her for a week to prepare the show.

Swallow writes in "A Visit to Leni Riefenstahl," in Listener
80 (Sept. 19, 1968), pp. 358-59, that he sensed his own "ambivalent attitude" toward her, replying graciously to the inevitable questions about her early films. As for Olympia Swallow believes that

it "can only be described as Nazi propaganda by those who are determined to find what they seek. " Swallow quotes from and agrees
with American critic Andrew Sarris' assessment of Olympia:

> The film as a whole is distinguished from most other docu-
> mentaries by the power of its unifying idea. This idea of
> the transcendence of the human spirit over all physical
> obstacles, over the universe, over nature, is, by implica-
> tion at least, an elitist view of the world ... whether you
> agree with its sentiments, or its ultimate implications or
> not, it does flourish coherently as a work of art.

At the twenty-sixth Olympiade in Montreal, Riefenstahl was
there, taking still photographs. The Canadian Jewish Congress had
telegrammed its protests at her presence. "The Montreal press, on
the other hand, couldn't have been nicer. Or less informed. "

W. Aitkin's "La grande dame blonde aux petits gants blancs, "
in Take One V/4, October 1976, page 15, reports the customary
question and answer session, focusing on the dominant query perennially posed about her Olympia: Did she make it independently or
not? She addressed the focal question on the war years in Hitler's
Germany to an unidentified reviewer in the Montreal Star (20 July
1976): She'd gone to court over 50 times since World War II to get
an apology from a newspaper that called her a Nazi (which she never
was) and also to prohibit "pirate prints" of her films being shown
without her permission, and without royalty payments.

Did Riefenstahl say Yes to Hitler's request to film Berchtesgaden, his mountain retreat, following the Olympia (1938) films,
publicity tour, and book publication? She has denied making it, suggesting that Hitler's mistress Eva Braun concocted it. Her name
does not appear on the fifty-minute documentary Berchtesgaden über
Salzburg (Berchtesgaden above Salzburg). Richard D. Mandell in
Nazi Olympics (page 271) claims she made it "as a favor to Hitler
... in 1938 she quickly assembled a crew ... to shoot footage which
she edited into a fifty-minute lyric to the rugged scenery around
Hitler's new mountain retreat.... "

"A Review of a Lesser Riefenstahl Work, " by James Manilla
appears in Film Comment 11:1 (Jan. - Feb. 1975), p. 23. He saw
the documentary on November 4, 1958, and claims the overall effect
is one of dullness. Without narration or dialogue,

> it is perhaps her worst picture ... typical of Riefenstahl
> in many respects ... big, lush Wagnerian-type music-
> track. It opens up with dawn scenes ... there are some
> wonderful shots ... there is some good cutting. Had it
> been kept to eight minutes or less, this might have been
> many times more interesting ... the music score is un-
> distinguished and the opticals ride.

For many years Riefenstahl had hoped to make a film based

upon Heinrich von Kleist's tragedy <u>Penthesilea</u>, about the Amazon
queen who is slain by Achilles when she comes to the aid of the
Trojans after Hector's death. Leni planned to act this leading role
as well as write, produce, and direct. The declaration of war in
1939 required postponing this project. "She was, in fact, taking
part in the invasion of Poland in September 1939 as a uniformed
war correspondent when she witnessed the massacre of twenty-eight
Jews by German troops. She abruptly quit her film unit, protested
to General Walter von Reichenau and eventually to Hitler, but to
no avail. "71

In Infield's account of this episode of horror the date is September 5, the place is the Polish city of Konsky, the victims numbered thirty-one, and Riefenstahl returned to Berlin. Whether she
resigned her status as correspondent or became involved in other
activities is unknown. According to her account, "Goebbels wanted
her to make political propaganda films, but she refused.... "72

She has said that she had her own school before and during
the War and that teaching camera techniques was easy, while teaching film directing was not easy.

<u>Current Biography</u> fixes the year as 1940 for her resumption
of work on the film <u>Tiefland</u> started in Spain. Starring as the young
Spanish gypsy girl and directing with the help of G. W. Pabst,
Riefenstahl finished the film in 1944 in Prague. Not released until
ten years later, this drama of oppressed peasants in conflict with
their landowners, has not been viewed in the United States and bona
fide criticism of the work is not readily accessible. Apparent from
descriptions of its source material is its theme, a favorite and
familiar one for Riefenstahl: simple and natural folk in hilly terrain are contrasted to the tense and self-indulgent "civilized" inhabitants of (flat, level country) urban centers. If this simple synopsis
sounds reminiscent of <u>The Blue Light</u> and the Fanck mountain films,
then the film student's surmise is correct.

By mid-1944 nearing the end of <u>Tiefland</u>, Riefenstahl's
strength failed her, and she directed a few final scenes from a
stretcher. Fellow filmmakers Pabst and Veit Harlan shot some
scenes for her without credit. In August 1944 her father died. A
few days after his demise, she received news that her brother had
died in battle. Her husband, Major Peter Jacobs, whom she married in 1944 and divorced in 1946, was then stationed on the Italian
front.

In October she had recuperated fully and was ready to work
even while Allied Forces were closing in on Germany. By year's
end, with editing yet to be done, she put aside <u>Tiefland</u> and returned
to her home in Kutzbuhel, Austria. She was there on April 30,
1945, when Hitler, Eva Braun, Goebbels and his family killed themselves in an elaborate bunker near the Chancellory in Berlin. The
following month, the American Army seized her lakeside villa "for
use as a rest center for the Forty-second Division.... "73 Leni

was imprisoned by French authorities who confiscated her films and equipment. The ensuing four years were consumed by her efforts to rid herself of her reputation as an activist in Hitler's hierarchy. She insisted that she had never been a Nazi, that she knew nothing of the atrocities committed, and that her friendship with Hitler was a professional relationship.

In 1948 a denazification court ruled that Leni was a follower not an active member of the Nazi Party, but she was still blacklisted by Allied occupation authorities as a filmmaker. Another four years of testimony and investigation elapsed before a second verdict was handed down in Berlin in 1952, supporting the 1948 decision. Riefenstahl had "engaged in no political activity in the Nazi state which warranted punishment.... "74 Her papers, films, and equipment were returned to her and in 1954, some twenty years since its inception, Tiefland was released, attaining only a modest success with audiences. After a tour of Austria and Germany to show Tiefland, Riefenstahl withdrew it from further exhibition.

Painfully, she discovered that her classification as a "sympathizer" carried an unexpected stigma. When her final clearance was obtained and widely publicized, all Germany was in a seething uproar.

Infield presents an excerpt from a Dusseldorf newspaper article:

> Frau Riefenstahl experienced in Berlin the triumph of her own will. She has achieved her atonement exactly like the circle of persons to which she belongs, who were presumably nonpolitical but never opponents of Hitler. The release of her confiscated villa in Berlin-Dahlem--peacetime value 140,000 DM--confronts no more Nazistic condemnation. Frau Riefenstahl also now has her peace for further work, for renewed entry into the large film industry.... 75

In the early fifties, Leni developed at least a half dozen film projects, all of them aborted. Most poignant of these was her friendship and correspondence with Jean Cocteau, who had written the subtitles for Tiefland's French version. In a letter appearing in Film Culture (Spring 1973), p. 90, Cocteau wrote to Riefenstahl: "I have sent a cable to Germany asking for your Tiefland to be shown at the Cannes Festival. I hope to get a positive answer from the appropriate ministry in Bonn.... " The collaboration of Cocteau and Riefenstahl on a film titled Friedrich und Voltaire (Frederick and Voltaire) was terminated by Cocteau's death; shortly afterward, Riefenstahl's ex-husband died, and she suffered a nervous collapse.

Another film project, Drei Sterne am Mantel der Madonna (Three Stars in the Robe of the Madonna), was to star Italian actress Anna Magnani. Die Roten Teufel (The Red Devil) never progressed beyond the paperwork. Ewige Gipfel (Eternal Summit), Tanz mit

dem Tod (Dance with Death), and Sol y Sombra (Sun and Shadow)
bear mute testimony to Leni's untiring efforts to resume her filmmaker career.   She resisted the realization that her official clearance papers were virtually meaningless when financing for films
was impossible to find, when film trade unions refused her membership, and when technical and artist union members refused to work
with her.   The London home where she stayed while working on an
English language version of The Blue Light was smeared with swas-
tika signs.   "Her films were blacklisted or censored by the new
democratic Germans.... "76

     Finding herself unwelcome, scorned and insulted, really re-
garded as an untouchable, she decided in 1956 to travel in Africa
as a still photographer.   Returning to London, she submitted a script
for a documentary film on slavery to the Anti-Slavery Society there.
Titled Schwarze Fracht (Black Cargo), the film was intended to document the prevailing slave trade, but an auto accident in Nairobi ne-
cessitated her hospitalization for broken ribs, lung damage, and a
fractured skull.   She subsequently continued to film the persistent
slave traffic from east Africa to Arabia, in the Sudan.   When she
sent her film to be developed, the laboratory processor used an im-
proper chemical solution thereby ruining all of it.   Of this film,
The Oxford Companion to Film states: "Her unfinished Schwarze
Fracht ... begun in 1956 in Ethiopia, was ostensibly planned as an
anthropological study, but in its treatment of human beings as objects it harks back to her films of the thirties.... [p. 593]"   From
this, one guesses that portions of the film are available for viewing
and for critical assessment.   And one may ask why Riefenstahl became interested in Africa in the first place; aside from the position
of finding in this "Dark Continent" a refuge from her own reputation
as Hitler's girlfriend and a fresh locale in which to work.   She
could have migrated to Asia or South America, but, more than just
the proximity of Africa to her home in Munich, why Africa?   She
saw a photograph and she read a book.   The prospect of capturing
on film native Africans still living in a traditional manner far from
the co-ordinates and currencies of urban civilizations appealed to
her.   On numerous visits to Africa in the late fifties and early sixties she came to love its climate, its peoples, and its promise of
a fulfilling personal and professional life for herself.

     Riefenstahl's intense enamorment with Africa, where she now
resides intermittently and plans to build a home, took root one
sleepless night in the mid-fifties when she read Ernest Hemingway's
Green Hills of Africa.   She "was soon caught up by an enthusiasm
that was to dominate her life from that point on.... "77   Her love
affair with Africa was not dimmed by the auto accident injuries she
suffered and about which "doctors were fairly despondent about her
eventual recovery. "78   Two days after her hospital release she records how she registered a more fervent attraction for Africa.

          ... now I find myself more enchanted by the African scene
          even than hitherto.   I have fallen under its spell.   Africa
          has been epitomized for me by two Masai warriors striding

with their swinging gait beside the roadside.   They wore
head-dresses of black ostrich feathers, and they were
carrying shields and spears.   ... they took no notice of
us at all.   It was the first time I had seen Africans in
their tribal dress.   I could not take my eyes off these
figures until they disappeared in the dust of the road-
way. 79

Her convalescence and this glimpse of warriors solidified her
resolve to imprint the resonance and rituals, colors and customs of
a native African people.   She wanted to discover an isolated group,
unvisited by missionaries or safaris, that would fit her preconcep-
tions.   She found what she wanted in a photograph captioned "A Nuba
of Kordofan, " then ten years old, taken by a British photographer,
George Rodger, and printed in a periodical.   Arrow-like, this photo
directed her to her desired project.   She later said, ". . . that photograph persecuted me. "   For six years she read voraciously and
voluminously everything she could find about the Nuba peoples and
the fabric of their lives.   Then she joined a German expedition
which planned a safari in the vicinity of the Kordofan highlands, near
enough for Riefenstahl, with dependable guides, to make an initial
incursion into the Nuba home territory.   When she learned that the
Nuba were inaccessible, and not Islamized or mixed with their
northern neighbors, she was convinced that her search for a perfect
subject for filming was fulfilled.

But several impediments faced her from officialdom.   De-
parting from a rainswept Munich in October 1962, she arrived a
few hours later in a sun-blazed African airport.   She was told the
Kordofan district was closed to even the best-intentioned of travel-
lers.   Circumventing this obstacle, local advisors said she would
meet with roadless stretches of Sudanese land without water, land
which would be mired in mud during the rainy season.   Then, too,
the new Arab rulers of the Sudan disapproved of nakedness, and the
Nubans were naked.

Overcoming all of these objections, Riefenstahl and her group
started their safari and reached El Obeid, the capital of the province
of Kordofan.   When shown the Rodgers photograph, the police chief
told them they were ten years too late.   "They are wearing clothes,
working on plantations and have increasingly given up their old tribal
life. "

Riefenstahl's party pressed on into the territory bereft of
animals and water, a wasteland geography graced only by rocks and
trees.   Two days later they observed circular houses on the nearby
hilltops.   They caught sight of a lovely nude girl who was terror-
stricken when she saw them and fled.   Then they saw tall unclothed
men, and women carrying baskets on their heads.   These were the
Mesakin Nuba.   Riefenstahl remained with the Nuba, while the expedition continued without her.

During each of many trips in the seven-year period 1962-

1969, Riefenstahl gained the friendship of the Nuba, lived with them, and became--almost--a Nuba, chronicling their lives in motion and still pictures. Still photos have appeared in periodicals, and in 1974 a book, The Last of the Nuba (New York: Harper & Row), was published and warmly received.

Critic and filmmaker Susan Sontag detects a fascist aesthetic throughout all of Riefenstahl's film work, including the Nuba photographs. In "Fascinating Fascism, " appearing in Movies and Methods: An Anthology by Bill Nichols (Berkeley: University of California Press, 1976, pp. 31-43), Sontag "makes a powerful case for the consistent indivisibility of fascism and beauty in the work of Leni Riefenstahl. . . . " Others have said that Riefenstahl's portrayal of the Nuba is an act of atonement for her fascistic films.

In 1972, Olympia was scheduled for showing at the Ufa-Palast-am-Zoo "where Triumph des Willens had first been shown to Hitler. " Such a mass of protests was received that the viewing was cancelled "and Riefenstahl was warned to leave the city immediately because her life was in danger. . . . "80

Riefenstahl completes free-lance photographic assignments while continuing her forays into the land of the Nuba. With the passage of time, she has become disillusioned with them.

> She has returned several times to Africa ... only to find
> to her despair that the life of the Nuba people has changed
> considerably. She found that they have been exposed to
> money and to material comforts, that for the first time
> they know what it was to kill and to steal, and that many
> of their simple ways have been destroyed by their contacts
> with technology. Nonetheless, she does not rush to com-
> plete her film, spending her energies, instead, on minor
> photographic assignments, on scuba diving ... and on her
> raveled business interests. 81

She contributed a segment to the Olympic games in Munich incorporated into Pieces of Eight (1972). She was commissioned to complete a photo-essay on rock star Mick Jagger. In September 1974 she went to Telluride, Colorado, to be awarded a silver medallion for her excellence in contributions to the cinema. Her home is an apartment in Munich, a depository of her collected tributes and photographs and slides, legal papers and letters, a gallery of documentation enclosing a protean career. She does not plan to write her memoirs. She is too busy creating fresh photographic challenges for herself, and fulfilling them.

Having finished her Nuba book, Riefenstahl discovered another tribe of Nuba at Kau. These Kau Nubans were unspoiled, untouched by commerce, adhering to inherited customs and ceremonies. The Kau were worshippers of beauty. In Riefenstahl's book of photographic essays, The People of Kau (New York: Harper & Row, 1976), she records the amazing masking rituals that Kau warriors undergo,

once, sometimes twice, daily. The Kau paint their faces, in this
ritual, in bright abstract bizarre patterns. The Kau also tattoo
themselves. No quotidian chores are represented by Riefenstahl's
typewriter and camera: Riefenstahl the Romantic brings to the be-
holder images of heroic figures, tribal dances, and "the bloody
ballets" of warriors. [82]

To accusations that her book on the Kordofan Nubans celebrated "Fascist esthetics, " Riefenstahl denied it vigorously. The
People of Kau elicited similar criticisms. Riefenstahl negates the
entire catalogue of charges against her art: she did not canonize
the physicality of the Nazis, the perfect bodies of Olympic athletes,
the beautiful Nuban beings. "'I'd like to see the critics try to draw
a parallel between the Third Reich and my next book--which will be
on underwater photography. ' "[83]

At 71, she did learn to dive, determined to capture on film
the coral growths in the Caribbean and Red Seas and those in the
Indian Ocean.

Her book Coral Gardens (New York: Harper & Row) did appear in 1976, a polychromatic assemblage of photographed underwater
plants and animals. Riefenstahl did the layout of the book herself.
The year 1976 was when Glenn B. Infield's biography of her appeared,
decidedly anti-Leni in substance and import. Riefenstahl responded
to this biography as to an attack; she would get an injunction against
the distribution of the book in "any German edition. "[84]

> All lies ... I was fascinated by Hitler but took no political
> position. I have always been a romantic and loved beauty.
> People have been stoning me for years to destroy me.
> There is a Mafia-like international conspiracy against
> me. [85]

The paradoxical puzzle presented by Riefenstahl's character
and artistic achievements may well be insoluble. The legendary
Leni eludes in numerous accounts the correct order of her given
names and descriptions of her appearance vary. In Current Biography (May 1975, page 37), she is Berta Helene. In Infield's biography (page 12) her name is Helene Berta. Current Biography (page
40) describes Leni at 73, as a "trim, handsome woman with penetrating blue eyes and blonde (formerly titian) hair ... dresses mod-
ishly and appears decades younger than she is.... "

Other sources claim that in her prime she was a dark-haired
woman with dark brown eyes, heavy-lidded, and with a decided
squint. Rather tall, she had a swagger in her walk. The chameleon-
like legendary Leni will remain exactly that--legendary.

Her cinematographic reputation rests upon her quartet of finished films: Triumph, Olympia, The Blue Light, and The Lowland.
Barsam ably capsules her attainment in these.

With the monumental exception of Triumph, Riefenstahl's
films are concerned with a fanatically romantic vision of
the good and simple life, of physical strength and spiritual
purity.... From the crystal grotto of The Blue Light, to
the pure spectacle of human flight in the diving sequence
of Olympia, to the shepherd's victorious fight with the
wolves in Tiefland, and finally to the primitive rituals of
the Nuba tribe to be seen in her forthcoming film, Riefenstahl has transcended both time and space, as a visionary
poet, to create a world of her own. Triumph is an aber-
ration that will always stain her reputation, but it should
not be allowed to obscure the beauty and strength of what
remains in her achievement. 86

FILMOGRAPHY

The Blue Light (1932)

Mademoiselle Docteur (1933); unrealized film project

Victory of the Faith (1933)

Triumph of the Will (1935)

Day of Freedom--Our Armed Forces (1935)

Olympia (1938)

Weekly Military Review (1939); unrealized film project

Penthesilea (1939); unrealized film project

Berchtesgaden Above Salzburg (1939); questionable attribution to L. R

Van Gogh (1943); unrealized film project

Three Stars in the Robe of the Madonna (1950's); unrealized film
    project

The Red Devil (1950's); unrealized film project

Eternal Summit (1950's); unrealized film project

Dance with Death (1950's); unrealized film project

Sun and Shadow (1950's); unrealized film project

Lowland (Tiefland) (1954)

Frederick and Voltaire (1955); unrealized film project

Black Cargo (1956); unfinished film project

Pieces of Eight (one segment of) (1972)

The Last of the Nuba (1973); unfinished film project

NOTES

1.   Glenn B. Infield, Leni Riefenstahl: The Fallen Film Goddess.
     New York: Thomas Y. Crowell, 1976, p. 13.

2. Ibid., p. 24.
3. Ibid., p. 16.
4. Ibid., p. 45.
5. Ibid., p. 30.
6. Ibid., pp. 31-32.
7. Ibid., p. 33.
8. "Biographical sketch of Leni Riefenstahl, " Film Comment 3:1 (Winter 1965), p. 13.
9. Current Biography, May 1975, p. 38.
10. Infield, p. 74.
11. Ibid.
12. Robert Gardner, "Can the Will Triumph?" Film Comment 3:1 (Winter 1965), p. 29.
13. Ibid., p. 30.
14. Erik Barnouw, Documentary: A History of Non-Fiction Film. New York: Oxford University Press, 1974, p. 101.
15. "Henry Jaworsky ... interviewed by Gordon Hitchens, Kirk Bond, and John Hanhardt, " Film Culture 56-57 (Spring 1973), p. 122.
16. Erwin Leiser, Nazi Cinema. London: Secker & Warburg, 1974, p. 25.
17. Ibid.
18. Ibid., pp. 26-27.
19. Georges Sadoul, Dictionary of Films. Berkeley: University of California Press, 1972, p. 383.
20. "Triumph of the Will, " Film Comment 3:1 (Winter 1965), p. 22.
21. "Leni Riefenstahl: Artifice and Truth in a World Apart (1975), " in Nonfiction Film: Theory and Criticism, ed. Richard Meran Barsam. New York: E. P. Dutton, 1976, pp. 256-257.
22. Ibid., p. 257.
23. Ibid.
24. Ibid.
25. Ibid., pp. 257-258.
26. "Monologue on a Nazi Film, " in On Film: Unpopular Essays on a Popular Art by Vernon Young. New York: Quadrangle/Times Books, 1972, p. 35.
27. Richard Meran Barsam, Filmguide to 'Triumph of the Will.' Bloomington: University of Indiana Press, 1975, pp. 17-18.
28. Infield, p. 217.
29. Barsam, Filmguide, p. 68.
30. Ibid., p. 69.
31. Ibid., p. 70.
32. Ibid.
33. Ibid., p. 71.
34. Ibid., pp. 71-72.
35. Barnouw, p. 105.
36. Leiser, p. 137.
37. Ibid.
38. B. Ruby Rich, "Leni Riefenstahl: The Deceptive Myth, " in Sexual Stratagems: The World of Women in Film by Patricia Erens. New York: Horizon Press, 1979, p. 202.
39. Ibid., p. 207.
40. Ibid., p. 205.
41. Ibid.

42. Ibid.
43. Ibid., p. 206.
44. Ibid., p. 207.
45. Hans Barkhausen, "Footnote to the history of Riefenstahl's 'Olympia', " Film Quarterly 28:4 (Fall 1974), pp. 8-13.
46. Richard D. Mandell, Nazi Olympics. New York: Macmillan, 1971, pp. 259-260.
47. "Henry Jaworsky ... , " p. 122.
48. Barnouw, p. 108.
49. David Stewart Hull, Film in the Third Reich. Berkeley: University of California Press, 1969, p. 132.
50. Ibid., p. 133.
51. Barnouw, p. 109.
52. Hull, p. 134.
53. Mandell, p. 263.
54. Ibid.
55. Barnouw, p. 110.
56. Vernon Young, On Film: Unpopular Essays on a Popular Art. New York: Quadrangle/Times Books, 1972, p. 40.
57. Ibid.
58. Ibid., p. 41.
59. Ibid., pp. 42-43.
60. Ibid.
61. Hull, p. 135.
62. Ibid., p. 136.
63. Richard Meran Barsam, ed., Nonfiction Film: Theory and Criticism. New York: Dutton, 1976, p. 259.
64. Sadoul, p. 383.
65. Mandell, p. 261.
66. Ibid.
67. Ibid.
68. Ibid.
69. Ibid.
70. Sadoul, p. 383.
71. "Biographical sketch of Leni Riefenstahl, " p. 15.
72. Mandell, p. 271.
73. Infield, p. 180.
74. Ibid.
75. Infield, p. 238.
76. Ibid., p. 218.
77. Leni Riefenstahl, The Last of the Nuba. New York: Harper & Row, 1974, pp. 9-11.
78. Ibid.
79. Ibid.
80. Infield, p. 227.
81. Barsam, ed., Nonfiction Film, p. 261.
82. Paul D. Zimmerman, "Leni's Triumph of the Will, " Newsweek 88 (November 29, 1976), p. 72.
83. Ibid.
84. Ibid.
85. Ibid.
86. Barsam, ed., Nonfiction Film, p. 255.

6. MURIEL BOX: "LET ME ENTERTAIN YOU"

Born: 1905, Surrey, England

"I am often asked: "When did you first begin to direct
films? ... I give the year as 1950 or my age as forty-
five. Neither is strictly true. Both refer to my entry
as a director only into feature films; I started with documentaries much earlier.... My chance to direct in the
documentary field would not have come but for the scarcity
of male directors in wartime."[1]

Collaboration of two sorts is integral to the accomplishment of the
performing arts. Requiring hundreds of individuals, a theatre or
film company's enterprise is premised on the successful integration
of numerous diverse talents and skills to produce a play or film.
Supplementing this type of giant-size co-operation are the grain-size
groups or teams of complementary talents achieving what a lone
artist cannot or will not do, in many instances fulfilling one another's inadequacies, to complete a satisfactory artistic whole. Both
collaborative forms operate simultaneously, especially in moviemaking.

The question of credits is presented by the creative group or
partnership: Who did what? To whom is the fame or blame assigned? How can a critic or reviewer be fair to all contributing
creators? Because no one, after the fact, can correctly attribute
segments of a performance to a team member, the query stands beyond debate. The proper response to the collaborative composition
is best-informed criticism of the performed product.

Such a response will be tried in this scrutiny of the films by
the Box team: the partnership of Muriel and Sydney Box that
spanned 30 years, generating more than 70 stage plays, numerous
documentary films during World War II, and a roster of feature
films in the two decades after the War.

The Box team's venture into the film industry stemmed from
their abilities as playwrights. Their screenwriting credits led to the
roles of film entrepreneur and producer for Sydney and director for
Muriel. Those critical reviews and circumstances, biographical and
financial, attendant upon the feature films written and directed by
Muriel Box will be considered here.

After a jill-of-film-trades apprenticeship, Sydney Box's sister

Betty rose to the role of film producer, on occasion working with
Muriel and Sydney on a film, then expanding the Box team to three.
Betty Box has created a prestigious career for herself as producer
of a roster of well-known and applauded films. However, it was
Muriel who was prime mover of these three careers. There would
have been no Box team, no careers for three industrious and
talented young people in the English cinema were it not for the initial forays into the realms of stage and film by Muriel Baker.

Violette Muriel Baker was born in Surrey, England, some
sources citing New Malden, others Tolworth, in 1905. Her earliest
memories were of her parents' quarrels about money. Her father
enjoyed gambling. Her mother was a teacher. By age 10, Muriel,
as she was called, was a weekly student-boarder at Holy Cross Convent in Wimbledon. There she "took an impish delight in bursting
into outrageous mime, "[2] which evoked boisterous laughter from her
classmates. So often did she indulge her mimetic skills for effects
of hilarity and disruptive mischief that she was asked to leave school.
Her ebullience and inclination toward argument were intolerable,
while her propensity for verse writing may or may not have con-
tributed to her unacceptable behavior. Each chapter of her autobiography Odd Woman Out (London: Leslie Frewin, 1974) is captioned
by her own poetry.

Enrolled in Regent Street Polytechnic she prepared to enter
Surbiton High School, although by 16 she'd already decided she
wanted to be in moving pictures. Luckily, she met Joseph Grossman of Stoll Pictures on a train trip. Warmly informed of her film
ambitions, Grossman gave her crowd work as an extra. At 17
Muriel enrolled in ballet lessons, receiving a certificate from bal-
lerina Adeline Genée, even though she failed an intermediate ballet
exam due to a cold that developed into rheumatic fever. Recovering,
she left home, tired of endless family arguments. She left her parents a terse farewell note: "Gone to the devil, "[3] and moved in with
her sister's mother-in-law.

Continuing her independent studies, Muriel took singing lessons, joined a choral society, and enrolled in a half-year's course
in acting from Ben Greet, a Shakespearian actor-manager. She
acted in the Mary Ward Settlement theatre group. Playing a lead
role in Milestones, a play by Arnold Bennett and Edward Knobloch,
Muriel Baker's performance was favorably reviewed by A. B. Walk-
ley, a well-known drama critic.

Having completed shorthand and typing classes at Pitman's
College, she worked as a secretary at Barclay's Corsets. Her
friend, actress Flora Robeson, was employed near the corset factory
as a firm's Staff Entertainments Organizer. Muriel arranged a tango
for Flora in an amateur play she was rehearsing. The play was performed sometime in 1925 in Welwyn. Renewing her activities in
amateur dramatics broadened Muriel's knowledge of acting techniques
and play production methods. Seized by a desire to write a play,
she did so. Hearing that a shorthand-typist was needed at the

Scenario Department at British Instructional Films, she applied for
and got the job.

Her employer, like most film producers, was then--it was
early 1929--in the worrisome period of changing from production of
silent films to talkies. The largest nub of anxiety formed about the
need for dialogue which scenario writers were not trained to write.
As Muriel points out in her autobiography, she occasionally typed
scripts for scenarists who accepted her helpful hints when a dry spot
appeared. In this guise, she learned how to structure plots and
write appropriate dialogue in scripts, a job bonus she was quick to
appreciate.

However, she was soon jobless. British Instructional Films
ran out of funds. She found a position with Joseph Grossman, who
was now with British International Pictures. With friends, she
visited George Bernard Shaw at Ayot St. Lawrence. Shaw gave the
group permission to perform his play How He Lied to Her Husband
and Muriel was continuity girl for the production. Becoming knowl-
edgeable about the practices of the film industry, Muriel learned
that workers were hired only for one film, always getting a termina-
tion notice about a week before filming finished. Workers could be
re-hired for the next film, of course, and sometimes were not.

In this tenureless capacity, Muriel worked for 18 months.
She earned five pounds each week. She was script girl for Anthony
Asquith on his first picture. But she found herself traveling long
distances to studios, and working irregular hours, including Saturdays
which were considered normal workdays. Sundays, when worked,
were paid an extra pound. They were overtime days. Determined
to find a permanent position, Muriel applied for work in London at
Michael Powell's small independent film firm. She was hired as
secretary to Powell and his American producer, Jerome Jackson.
Her workload was enormous. In addition to her dual secretarial
duties she was assigned a long list of chores, including budget reviews, typing of cast lists and other schedules plus scripts, doing
continuity for each picture done, and reading plays and stories submitted and completing a form in which she evaluated their suitability
for a film adaptation. For these duties she was paid four pounds
each week. She preferred a pound less in wages in order to gain
London residence and job permanence.

Her ambitions in high gear, Muriel auditioned for the Royal
Academy of Dramatic Art and failed. She tried writing plays again
and attended the theatre often. She saw Murder Trial, a one-act by
Sydney Box, which had won the Welwyn Cup in an annual drama competition. This was the summer of 1932. Intrigued by the play, Muriel
asked the playwright for a copy of his script. After reading it she
re-typed it for him and returned it. Their friendship was formed
and warmed, although Sydney Box was married, a journalist with two
published plays.

When Sydney Box began divorce proceedings, he was a Fleet

Street reporter and Muriel a permanent continuity girl at Gaumont-British Studios.   The couple settled into housekeeping together, Muriel recording candidly in her diary that she enjoyed the excitement of their partnership.   She counted herself lucky to have met Sydney and sensed that their co-operative work efforts would be prolific and satisfying.   Their compelling love of literature and the stage proved to be the foundation of their friendship while their personalities were opposed: Muriel saw herself as a pessimist, and Sydney as an optimist, a stabilizing force.   They worked and wrote well together.

From their photographs, Muriel and Sydney Box appear to be physical opposites as well.   On the fair side, Sydney looks like a portly business executive with a fleshy face and receding hairline. With dark hair, large eyes, straight nose, and a determined jaw, Muriel appears to be an attractive petite-sized woman of purpose and ambition.

Their partnership began in earnest when Sydney secured a contract from Harraps for a book of half a dozen one-act plays with all-women casts, due in three months.   This book Ladies Only met the deadline, yielding large royalty checks.   So began a writing partnership of some thirty years.   One-acts by the Box team were in demand and a second volume, Petticoat Plays, was published.

The Boxes' playwriting path turned to screenwriting when someone asked Muriel to recommend a writer for a documentary film.   Muriel recommended Sydney, who wrote the film's commentary.   More work was offered to him, while the team continued writing stage-plays, more than fifty of them by 1939.

Because of a threatened lawsuit involving Sydney's prizewinning play Not the Man, an attorney advised the Box team to marry. Now divorced and paying alimony, Sydney married Muriel on May 23, 1935.   Subsequently, they moved to a house in Highgate where a daughter, Leonora, was born November 5, 1936.

In 1935, the Box team collaborated on their first screenplay, Alibi Inn.   The British National Film Catalogue summarized the plot: "Inventor breaks jail to prove jewel thieves framed him for killing watchman. "   In the years before World War II, the busy Boxes wrote three-act plays, and the librettos for several projected musical shows.   Sydney authored a book on Film Publicity while Muriel compiled Vigil, an anthology of prayers.   Using the pen name Evelyn August, her poems appeared in The Christian Herald.   Next, she published an anthology of jokes, puzzles, games, and aphorisms titled, The Black-Out Book, which became a bestseller.   When an offer came from play publisher Samuel French, the Box team sold the copyrights for all their plays for £1,000.

Looking back on the years of World War II, Muriel Box determines the effect of the 1939-1945 time period upon her own life as one of suspenseful waiting.   The first half of her life was before

the war, and the second half subsequent to it.   Yet, it was during
the war years that Muriel became a director of documentary films.
Although she directed her initial feature film at age 45, she had directed documentary films during the war.   The dearth of male film
directors provided her the opportunity for directing assignments.

In 1940, Sydney, Muriel, and Betty Box were working for a
company with failing revenues.   Sydney refloated it as Verity Films.
In less than a year, Verity was the biggest company in Britain making documentary films.   In fact, its production level was so high,
and rapidly increasing, that technicians were in short supply to produce the ever greater number of films scheduled.   Betty was already working in an assistant production capacity, while Sydney assigned Muriel to direct a film, titled The English Inn, for the British Council.

Muriel's first encounter with job discrimination swiftly arrived.
A documentary she had written, Road Safety for Children, was assigned to a male director.   However, her experience as director of
shorts ended not because of discrimination but because Sydney Box
was asked to make a feature film, and he agreed to produce it.
The film was On Approval, based on a Frederic Lonsdale play.   At
this juncture, there were ten units headed by able directors at Verity
Films making documentaries connected with the war effort for several Ministries, such as Health and Air, Bomb Disposal, and the Ad-
miralty.   Betty Box was in charge of four or five of these units and
coming to be known as a shrewd executive.   By the end of World
War II she was responsible for helping produce around 200 propaganda films.

So, with documentary film production in good hands, Sydney
revised the script of On Approval with Muriel, which he planned to
film concurrently with another film, The Flemish Farm.   An aggregate of conflicts in the production processes of both films had to be
solved, a major one being an inadequate director assigned to On
Approval.   As a result, Sydney and Clive Brook co-directed it,
while Muriel assisted in editing and choreographing a dream sequence
in the film.

The war's end signified the end of Verity Films' production
of documentaries for the Government.   The Box team ventured into
the production of their first jointly-written feature film, 29 Acacia
Avenue meeting financial problems head-on.   Sydney had moved to
Gainsborough Pictures, and Muriel followed him, becoming the head
of the Script Department.   There she grasped two realities.   Just
as the start of the war produced a dearth of film technicians, now
the end of the war resulted in a scarcity of competent screenwriters.
And, to meet production schedules, there had to be three stand-by
scripts for each one filming in the studio in case of accidents.

Excellent dramatic writers were too expensive to hire.
"Thus we were forced, more often than we would have liked, to
settle for second best."4   The Boxes revised scripts "in order to
meet the minimum standard required...."5

The omnipresent financial conflicts which Sydney Box's wizard-
ry strove to solve began with the production of 29 Acacia Avenue, in
which Muriel and Sydney had invested all their savings. Several
thousands of pounds had to be borrowed to complete the film. When
viewed by Arthur Rank, he believed it was immoral. The lesson to
be learned from 29 Acacia Street, Muriel discerns, is that it was
hard then, and remains hard now, to get a picture of this type, a
frothy British comedy film, distributed properly.

What was this comedy film about, having to overcome financial and censorship problems both, before becoming a hit with viewers? The British National Film Catalogue labels it a comedy.
"Youth falls for married flirt and his sister has trial marriage."

Based on a story by Denis and Mabel Constanduras, the New
York Times (Oct. 31, 1949, 20:2), reviewer found it

> one of the season's most pleasant surprises ... this gay
> little package of nonsense ... finds Sydney and Muriel Box
> writing at the top of their form and spilling double en-
> tendre in dialogue and situations in a spirit of mischievous-
> ness which must have given our censors pause ... the
> truth is that "The Facts of Love" hasn't much in the way
> of a straight story.

With its American title, The Facts of Love, according to
Variety 176:22 (Nov. 2, 1949) relates the "Story of two love affairs
and quiet marital relations of an elderly couple ... told with
aplomb by a highly capable English cast." It is when the middle-
aged couple presumably leaves for a sea voyage that "the newly engaged couple start taking matters into their own hands.... Sudden
arrival back home of the parents prevents it from becoming 100%
bedroom farce, but it's the next thing to it."

Noting a choppiness in the film suggestive of pruning the
film after its arrival in the United States, Variety concludes:

> British producer Sydney Box, long known in England for
> turning out boxoffice-wise product, has a real sleeper for
> the American market in "Facts of Love." It is a case of
> English film-makers trying their hand at frothy farce and
> whipping up a good comedy dish.

In the concurrent style required by film production schedules,
the Boxes were solving funding problems for their first film while
writing the script for their second. Muriel reports on the genesis
of Close-Up, later titled The Seventh Veil, revealing the close co-
operation she and Sydney employed in shaping what proved to be one
of the Boxes' most popular films.

While still producing documentaries for Verity, which Sydney
Box later sold, he was approached with a query about making a film
on remedial measures employed on servicemen home from the war

who were mentally depressed, or neurotic, or shell-shocked. Sydney informed himself on these remedial techniques and discussed them with Muriel at the dinner table. One technique caught her interest. This was the use of drugs which helped psychiatrists discover their patients' unconscious doubts and apprehensions so that a cure or relief could be given. She suggested a storyline for a film about the use of drugs and supportive therapy upon an artist or dancer or musician. Sydney agreed with her concept and urged her to start writing a script.

Muriel proceeded, changing to a pianist because a film on Paganini was planned by another company. Ann Todd was approached: was she available and could she play the piano? Arthur Rank was approached for backing. "The script was read by Rank's board of directors (all scripts had to be submitted and approved in this manner) but failed to get a unanimous verdict on its merits. "[6]   Rank then gave it to his wife who liked it, and he agreed to finance the film.

Although cash was not available at the start, The Seventh Veil was filmed from mid-December 1944 to February 23, 1945, with Sydney adroitly manipulating bookkeeping matters. Even with Arthur Rank as a backer, Sydney appealed to Alfred Shipman, who had rescued 29 Acacia Avenue at the most crucial moment, for £40,000 which was loaned after Shipman viewed parts of the movie.

The sound track was continually plagued by the whine of V-2 rockets which unexpectedly exploded near the studio. Shrapnel falling on the studio roof caused rain to drip onto the sets in the studio. Black-outs and bomb-craters, the demolition of proximate damaged buildings and the unpredictable sounds of sirens and alarms delayed production. "We often despaired of ever being able to finish shooting the picture. "[7]

Labelling it a "romance, " The British National Film Catalogue capsules the plot: "After psychiatric treatment, a suicidal pianist prefers cruel guardian to artist or band leader. " The second edition of Halliwell's Film Guide (New York: Scribner's, 1979, p. 675) tacitly agreed to the Romance category. "A concert pianist is romantically torn between her psychiatrist, her guardian, and two other fellows. A splendid modern melodrama in the tradition of Jane Eyre and Rebecca, it set the seal of moviegoing approval on psychiatry, classical music, and James Mason, and it is the most utter tosh. "

The National Board of Review 21:2 (February 1946), pp. 7-8, takes an unexcited view of the young lady concert pianist's mental ills being treated by hypnosis and narcotics. "It is while under the influence of these devices that the psychiatrist draws from her the story of her life that led up to her mental seizure and, incidentally, gives to the film its none too original form of the flashback. "

The heroine is Francesca, played by Ann Todd, orphaned early, reared by her cousin, a wealthy bachelor played by James Mason. Discovering her extraordinary musical talent, Nicholas

> makes it his life work to train her to be a great artist.... After years of intensive study on her part and of tyranny on his, including the smashing of one love affair and an attempt to smash a second, the now famous pianist runs off with a painter. But an auto accident ends that and lands the girl in a hospital with burnt hands and a mental disorder.

Herbert Lom as Dr. Larsen recommends complete self-revelation as the cure.

> He uses the rather fanciful figure that a person is like Salome and her famous seven veils.... It is the task of the mental doctor to induce her to drop the last veil in order that he may bring to light the thing that causes the trouble, make her realize it and hence dissipate the fear that is the base of her illness. "

The review applauds the use of concert music in the film "without letting it get in the way of its action, " and it is the first to note the Ann Todd-James Mason relationship as similar to Trilby and Svengali in the George duMaurier novel Trilby.

The British newspaper reviews refused to be impressed by the intended seriousness of the film. The Spectator 175:383 (Oct. 1945) found it to be "An example of the intelligent, medium-priced picture made with great technical polish which has represented for Hollywood the middle path between the vulgar and the highbrow. "

The Daily Mail agrees in one sentence: "A popular film that does not discard taste and atmosphere. " Richard Mallett in Punch calls it "An odd, artificial, best sellerish kind of story with reminiscences of Trilby and Jane Eyre and all their imitations down to Rebecca. "

The Times, October 22, 1945, review on page 8a recites the plot in lofty tones arriving at total nonjudgment:

> The heroine's history is disengaged, episode by episode, from her confessions made during a hypnotic trance. It appears that she is a famous pianist who ever since she was caned at school has dreaded injury to her hands and now believes, mistakenly, that they are injured.... Her guardian, a rich man with perfect taste, some undefined complications of his own, and manners which are either exquisite or brutal, has turned her from a shy, pig-tailed schoolgirl into a great artist. He has prevented her marriage to a cheerfully vulgar young dance band leader; he tried to dissuade her from becoming the mistress of a rich

painter and, being told to mind his own business, lashes at the key-board with a walking stick, fortunately missing her hands.

Once cured, Francesca must decide whom she will marry, and considerable suspense is created by her decision process.

The least likely choice is, of course, the man whose polished brutality has made her leap from Waterloo Bridge: precisely why she chooses him is not clear. But he is played by Mr. James Mason, who succeeds in making the solitary attractive in spite of his aberrations and suggests a passion for art that is strong and selfless. ... Miss Ann Todd, whether at the piano with the London Symphony Orchestra in all great opera houses or in the very depths of despair, lends elegance to genius.

British critic James Agate harshly reproves the filmmakers for making the film! He compares the plot of The Seventh Veil to an unnamed Hollywood product admittedly trite, with an improbable plot. Perhaps, he ruminates, this film inspired the weavers of The Seventh Veil.

Whereupon our English concocters of masterpieces, moved by the spirit of emulation, produced The Seventh Veil. ... Now both these stories are tripe and the trouble is that Hollywood makes bigger and better tripe than anything we can manage in this country.

Agate suggests that the English moviemakers make documentaries for which they have talent and temperament for "our natural taste instinctively avoids sentimentality. "[8]

Moving across the Atlantic, the film fared much better in North America than at home, a curious but welcome precedent established for Box team films. The Seventh Veil proved to be overwhelmingly more popular and lucrative in the United States, more favored by critics also, than in Britain, a fact Muriel Box records without explanation.

Film Reports, available in libraries as a movie guide, regularly evaluated domestic and foreign films exhibited in the United States. Published by the Film Estimate Board of National Organizations, it was printed on Green Sheets and was called the Joint Estimate, being a consensus of evaluations. The Joint Estimate for The Seventh Veil asserts: "Estimates agree. This successful psychological drama, directed with skill and ably enacted, has dignity and depth although the denouement is not quite clear. ... " The rating was "Mature" and for family viewing.

The New York Times (Dec. 26, 1945, 15:1) critic A. W. deemed it "a genuinely intriguing offering to the film scene" and "both an intelligent and engrossing case history and an example of

the adroit blending of the pictorial and musical media. " Despite a
few too-long, convoluted episodes, the film is "a suspenseful and
unusual treatment of a challenging theme. . . . "

The New Yorker 31:47 (Jan. 5, 1946), p. 49 urbanely admits
it is charmed by The Seventh Veil, identifying its central character
Francesca as "our old friend Trilby in modern dress and that she
has a Svengali, a crippled misogynist who serves as her guardian.
The du Maurier idea, however, still wears well, particularly since
the acting and the musical accompaniment . . . are excellent. " The
attraction between Francesca and Nicholas, her guardian, is per-
plexing though. "In the end . . . it becomes apparent that Mr. Mason
loves his Trilby, but just why she decides, after a few bouts with
the psychiatrist, to reciprocate his affection, I'm not at all certain. "
John McCarten, the critic, then credits Eileen Joyce as "the unseen
soloist who runs superbly through everything, from Chopin to Rach-
maninoff, when Miss Todd is simulating at the keyboard. "

Both Time and Life stress factors of influence operative in
the Anglo-American movie industries:

> The Seventh Veil is handsomely photographed, elegantly
> produced and acted with full romantic flourishes. It is
> a typical exhibit in Britain's current campaign to beat
> Hollywood at its own game. 9

Noting that the film utilizes a new technique--narcohypnosis--to implement a traditional film convention--the flashback--, the review
suggests that "American audiences may note that the psychiatric
theme used in Hollywood's recent Spellbound has been more intelligently filmed by the British. "10

"The British movie industry's current campaign to sell its
products to the U. S. public has just received heavy reinforcements
with a picture called The Seventh Veil. " This admission of a "war"
between British and American films in the post-World War II years
is the opening statement of the film's review in Life 20:4 (Jan. 28,
1946), pp. 65-68. Calling it "an absorbing film, " Life asserts that
"It is also an extremely successful attempt to sell two new English
stars to the American public. " Deeming the film "an excellent vehicle" for James Mason's talents, including a sneer "the best to turn
up since Basil Rathbone's, " because

> its story is told with economy and its characters are force-
> ful. The dialog, unlike much of Hollywood's, resembles
> normal human conversation. The result of such intelligent
> movie making is a picture which is currently successful in
> New York where critics, while praising it, warned that it
> was definitely for adult minds.

The newspaper critics' reviews appearing in the New York
Motion Picture Critical Reviews 2:46 (1945), pp. 57-59, are adula-
tory, with nitpicking nearly nil. Rose Pelswick of the Journal-

American, Dec. 26, 1945, considers it "One of the best of the recent British imports" citing "A brilliant performance by an actress
named Ann Todd. ... " The musical selections are meticulously
named: "the Chopin Prelude no. 7, Beethoven's Pathetique Sonata,
Grieg Piano Concerto in A Minor, Mozart Sonata in C Major, Rach-
maninoff Piano Concerto in C Major and the Overture from 'The
Merry Wives of Windsor.' "

John T. McManus of PM, Dec. 26, 1945, praises all but the
close of The Seventh Veil: "will probably provide more adult satisfaction per foot of the film than any of its Christmas Day rivals--
up to the last reel, that is. At that point it seems as if some one
may have been in a hurry to end matters and permitted an unconvincing ending to be applied to a story which is otherwise quite compelling, superbly acted and distinguished by a whole repertory of
fine music built into the plot. " However, when Francesca tries to
select from her suitors the one she loves best, "that is where I
got off. "

Muriel Box clarifies the ending of the film for us by revealing that she and Sydney "spent many a night working on three alternative endings which were kept secret till the last day of shooting, for
diplomatic reasons. Even then, none of the four was quite certain
who was going to get the girl!"11

Another reason was the planned departure of Mason to the
United States the day after the film's shooting was to be completed.
The misty effect which partially obscured Francesca's choice of
suitors in the final frame "was due to our inability to re-shoot it
the following day when we noticed the flaw in the 'rushes. ' "12

"Outstanding cinema, " is Dorothy Masters' term for the film
in her Daily News, Dec. 26, 1945 review. "In addition to being a
skillful probing of mental neurosis, the film is excellent for suspense, rich in drama and endowed with magnificent performances. "
James Mason's "Uncle Nicholas" role is heaped with praise, and his
neurosis considered deserving of psychiatric aid. "But for the fact
that Francesca has straight away been established as the moribund
patient ... Nicholas would appear to have been a likely candidate. "

Eileen Creelman of The Sun sounds lukewarm in her Dec. 26,
1945, review, listing her reservations amid the best elements of
the film. "At its best when at its most musical ... " and "Interesting, although somewhat episodic and leisurely. " Creelman objects
most to the transformation of Nicholas from surly guardian to romantic hero. "This switch is decidedly not successful. It is too
much like announcing that the Witch of 'Hansel and Gretel' is really
Whistler's Mother after all. " But Ann Todd "with a fine taste in
music and a terrible taste in men" is "sad and lovely. "

Suggesting a "bit of cutting" and lamenting that "it has a tendency to spread its moments of high drama over too much material"
Otis L. Guernsey, Jr. in his New York Herald-Tribune review,

dated Dec. 26, 1945, rates The Seventh Veil as "entertaining melodrama" that "combines good music and good mental portraiture into
an interesting motion picture. "

In her short, but high-spirited, article, Irene Thirer (New
York Post, Dec. 27, 1945) refers to the film as "a rather intriguing
modern-day Svengali story. " Thirer confides: "We don't like to
boast, but it was obvious in reel one that the pretty pianist's meticulous mentor ... was the man she preferred over all others.... "
She agrees with Ann Todd's choice, concluding (and prophesying correctly) "We do very much like James Mason. Hollywood'll get him
yet!"

William Hawkins' view is that of a "mature and authentic picture, made out of elements which ... would lead you to expect one
of the hokiest movies in the world. " His New York World-Telegram
review of Dec. 26, 1945, dubs it "a Trilby story, a psychiatric
study and a generous display of concert music technique, " the performance of Ann Todd being its best asset.

Without exception, Eileen Joyce was credited as the "ghost"
pianist responsible for the keyboard performances in the film. Initially declining credit, Joyce later was persuaded to list her name
as the pianist performing with the London Symphony Orchestra.

The emotional appeal and dramatic values infused in The
Seventh Veil by the piano solos with orchestral backing are properly
assessed in Film Music Notes 5:7 (March, 1946), p. 20. Attributing
the score to Ben Frankel the review iterates that "settings and photography are noteworthy and the recording the best of any British
film to date. " No pun was intended in the use of the word "noteworthy, " thus we may read it as a double entendre with a smile;
recalling the difficulties Muriel Box records dealing with bothersome
environmental noises, we wonder what miracle was wrought to
achieve the fidelity of the soundtrack.

> Moreover, the use of classical music beautifully cued in
> and performed, adds further distinction.... The piano
> playing of the concerto ... has real virtuoso feeling, a
> plus rarely conveyed in a picture. There is nothing arti-
> ficial either about the entrances ... the drudgery of prac-
> tise is cleverly suggested--the waltz which Francesca as-
> sociates with Peter is charming--then comes the gradual
> change to the bravura type work. The montage of the
> continental study required for a concert artist is marvelous-
> ly conceived and executed. There is a feeling of being
> backstage.... With the playing of the Beethoven Pathetique
> Sonata the story enters another phase and at the end we
> share in the suspense of the four men as they await Fran-
> cesca's verdict....

The admirable integration of classical music with romantic
story elements into a case history with a happy ending was respon-

sible for the broad appeal and box office profits of The Seventh Veil.
Melodrama, yes.   But such satisfying, memorable melodrama!   The
film won the 1946 Academy Award for Best Screenplay and the Top
Moneymaker prize in 1945.   It is unique because it led to a stage
play.

As the Box team notes in the Foreword to the three-act play
with the same title: "So far as we know, this is the first time a
successful film has been translated into a stage play. "   Dedicated
to Ann Todd, who played Francesca again, the play was "presented
by Henry Sherek at the Princess Theatre, London in March, 1951
. . . ."13

Reviewing the play for the New York Times (April 15, 1951),
W. A. Darlington admits he did not see the film but judges the play
"a botched piece of work. "   The reason?   "Because the authors had
not realized how different is the approach in the two cases. "

Considering the lengthy and lucrative playwriting career the
Box team had, this is difficult to understand. Darlington continues:
"They told their stage story in the same order and with many of the
same technical tricks as they had used for the film and it did not
seem to have occurred to them that the effects would be different. "
Nevertheless, the reviewer admits that playgoers would buy tickets
to see "Ann Todd in the very seductive flesh. . . . "

Muriel Box's own recollections of reactions to The Seventh
Veil evoke amusement and provide detail usually absent from published reviews.   Critic James Agate, who had called the film "tripe, "
"was seen prowling from circle to stalls . . . his seat not being good
enough. " He was told by an usherette to return the following Monday
when "he could have two of the best seats in the house.   He prompt-
ly replied: "Then you'd better keep four for me.   This is the sort
of damn silly film I happen to like!"14

The Observer critic C. A. Lejeune mentioned the fact that
Eileen Joyce was not given credit for her recording the film.   In a
radio talk, Lejeune "enlarged on the way great soloists doubled for
artists, saying: I don't mind telling you these trade secrets, because I think they reflect great credit on the cinema . . . it would be
courteous to give some recognition to the artist who's actually done
the playing. "

Characterizing The Seventh Veil as "a lovely picture to look
at, " Lejeune declares: "The music itself is magnificent.   But who
plays it?   People are certain to ask and the credit titles don't say. "
Lejeune concludes that the hands on the keyboard belong to Eileen
Joyce, "and personally I think she deserves a mention. . . . "15

The Box team agreed.   Joyce had initially refused credit,
"because she declared it would spoil the illusion for the audience.
Only after Lejeune's comment, were we allowed to add her name at
the end of the film. . . . "16

When Queen Mary wanted to see the film, a private showing was arranged, with Ann Todd present.   The Queen was uncertain which man Francesca went to at the end because she asked Ann Todd, heartily approving of Nicholas as the chosen suitor.

The happiest consequence of the international success of The Seventh Veil was the fact that Sydney Box succeeded Edward Black when Black took a position with Korda, becoming production head at Rank's Gainsborough Studios.   Sydney had earned a reputation for economical movie producing (The Seventh Veil cost only £92,000). Thus, he signed a contract to make at least ten movies annually, each with a budget range of £150,000 to £200,000.

In August 1945 the Box team moved to Gainsborough; Muriel as scenario editor and Betty as a producer at the Islington Studios, Sydney as managing Director.   An understanding of the Anglo-American film industry's predicaments in the mid-forties explains this promotion in the Box team careers.

In June 1947 the British Government imposed a 75 percent tax on the profits earned in Britain by American films.   No new American films were imported in 1948 into Britain, and no duty paid.   The British film business produced too few films for the "4,500 major cinemas in Great Britain" estimated to require "some 450 full-length films a year."[16]   Even though the 75 percent tax was renegotiated, the need for home-made, domestic movies was apparent to Arthur Rank, who sought an answer in Sydney Box.

Sydney Box's reply to the dearth of domestic films was the announcement that he would triple "output at the two studios, that he would keep always three films in production simultaneously, and that he would turn out a new film every month."[17]   The promise was kept; whether or not quality was sacrificed for quantity was debatable.

Patrick Gibbs declared that the speed with which Box films were made was not a factor to be reckoned with.   "Films of the highest class are not, I think, to be expected from Sydney Box." Quoting Sydney Box, Gibbs asserts that "This judgment is confirmed by his own words: 'I believe that a film producer should be a man who combines business ability with artistic taste ... in about equal portions."[18]   But Box emphasized that he would "always think of myself as a writer ... " and that the film industry depends upon writers.   Thus, Gibbs concludes, filmgoers can depend upon one film a month from Mr. Box: "That these films should achieve the highest standard is hardly to be expected; that they are ... satisfactory is indeed a matter for praise of the organisation which turns them out in such efficient fashion."[19]

Gibbs records two traits of the films spewed forth from the Gainsborough Studios: adapting best-selling novels to a star, and screenplays centered on topical incidents or a news headline.   Twice correct, as the Box team films following The Seventh Veil demonstrate.

Muriel and Sydney Box adapted a play by Daphne du Maurier, The Years Between, to the screen in 1946. The film starred Michael Redgrave, Valerie Hobson, and Flora Robeson, in a chronicle of an MP who returns from the war after being presumed dead, finding his wife has been elected in his seat. Halliwell's Film Guide (page 985) dubs it "Stilted variation on the Enoch Arden theme; plot and performance alike unpersuasive. "

Acknowledging it as one of Arthur Rank's Prestige Pictures, the New York Times (March 10, 1947, 25:2) observes that the triangular human relationship it deals with is a muted one "in which the theme and drama are adult and realistic in concept, but one which is strangely passive in deed and ordinary in cinema terms. "

The reviewer explains the intricacies of the plot: the young mother and matron elected to Parliament "falls in love with a neighbor. Some five years later and on the eve of her marriage her husband returns. " An added twist to the situation is the husband's revelation that he "was sworn to secrecy and knew all along that his demise was being arranged ... so that he could work underground ... which his wife deems unnecessarily cruel.... " Sadly, director Compton Bennett sacrifices pace for mood, and the total effect does not match the cast's intense portrayals.

The names of Daphne du Maurier and Michael Redgrave would probably draw customers to the box office, Variety calculated, probably faring best with sophisticated audiences (Vol. 162:18, April 10, 1946). Rating Compton Bennett's direction as "smooth and intelligent" and "Production values ... considerably above average" especially very effective scenes in the House of Commons, Variety places the faults of the film "with scripters Muriel and Sydney Box. Almost half of the film deals with events preceding the start of the stage original, by which time all the interest centers on the love affair between Valerie Hobson and a neighbor farmer, James McKechnie. The presumed dead husband's intrusion into the plot at this juncture is more irritation than intrigue.

"The Cinema" columnist of The Spectator (May 31, 1946) with sympathetic regret analyzes the causes of disappointment in The Years Between. After the exhilarating heights reached by The Seventh Veil--Mr. Box "has come to be regarded in many quarters as something of a film-making magician"--The Years Between touched bottom. Certain critics had faulted The Seventh Veil for a "lack of local roots to the theme"; Mr. Box tried to remedy this criticism and failed.

The British public was already tired of the war. "The scenes of flying-bomb raids and the V-Day celebrations are now curiously boring. " Yet, the film's movement is "ponderous" due to "long static scenes of conversing couples delivering themselves of sentiments as hackneyed as they are sententious. " The largest factor in the film's failure was Michael Redgrave's portrayal of the returned warrior; "his characterisation is quite revolting in its sullen conceit and self-pity. " By using this disagreeable soldier as a central figure, the film does not earn universal interest. "The Years Between is in most ways as bad as The Seventh Veil was good. "

"Story is light, but has many laughs. " Variety (Vol. 162:13, June 5, 1946) informs us that A Girl in a Million was the last picture Sydney Box would make "for outside companies before assuming control for Gainsborough.... Chances not bright for any real returns in U. S. "

The plot "concerns an inventor who after divorcing a nagging wife remarries only to have the second gal pull the same routine as the first. " Specifically, when the divorced man (Hugh Williams) accepts an appointment in an isolated town with few, if any, women in it, he finds that an American colonel moves in, with his niece (Joan Greenwood) whom the hero marries. When this second wife behaves just as the first had--complaining, nagging--the couple separates. When their child is born, a reunion results.

Dramatic echoes of the play Born Yesterday were attributed to A Girl in a Million by the New York Times (July 24, 1950, 15:2) reviewer. It seems that the chemist had promised himself to "cure" his second wife--improve her to his own exactions--of the tendencies exhibited by his first wife--and failed, an impasse self-assured of humor. But the film is "a mite too light to handle. "

"The producing and writing team of Muriel and Sydney Box, a pair of expert hands who have given ample proof that they know how to manipulate a story and dialogue apparently found the situations" in their plot not consistently substantial enough to produce non-stop hilarity. "Several of the scenes are genuinely funny and the principals project the humorous lines casually and effectively. But these sequences are infrequent and badly compensate for a transparent and slowly paced yarn. "

The Box team's next venture, the first under the Arthur Rank banner, was Daybreak (1946). It fared poorly, considering the fact that it starred Ann Todd directed by Compton Bennett for the first time since success in The Seventh Veil. But the film was "endowed with a monotonous script which seems to go out of its way to promote an atmosphere of unrelieved gloom and despondency. "

Halliwell's Film Guide, p. 177 capsules the melancholy tale: "A barber and part-time hangman marries a destitute girl, loses her to a Swedish seaman, and kills himself in such a way as to implicate the other man. Dockside melodrama of extraordinary gloominess; laughable in most respects. A curious follow-up from The Seventh Veil team. "

The British Film Annual (1949) elaborates on the plot with death as its focus. "Eddie keeps a barber's shop. Only his assistant Ron knows that he has another trade ... Eddie is the public hangman. He meets and marries a pretty waif, Frankie. When he inherits his father's barge business, he gives the barber's shop to

Ron and makes a home for Frankie and himself on one of the barges. "
Olaf, a Swedish seaman becomes interested in Frankie who returns
the interest, against her will. When Eddie has to keep "an official
engagement" he leaves, but returns unexpectedly to find Olaf on the
barge. Eddie is knocked overboard by Olaf whom police arrest for
his murder. Then, in despair, Frankie commits suicide. "But
Eddie has dragged himself ashore to take secret shelter with Ron.
Eventually he has the duty of carrying out the death sentence on
Olaf. He relishes the opportunity of avenging Frankie's death. At
the last moment, however, he reveals his identity and returns to the
barber's shop to end his own life. "

In the death-begets-death film, the New York Times (July 4,
1949, 9:2) critic Bosley Crowther found no redeeming qualities.
"There is precious little character or content in this woebegone
study in grief. Neither the barge nor the picture goes anywhere. "

The Man Within (1947) whose American title was The Smugglers, confounded the critics. None of the reviews comes to a
point. This costume story in Technicolor was based on Graham
Greene's novel The Man Within, generating discussion on the issue
of adaptation of novels to screenplays. The Box team adhered to
the plot and characters of the novel: all agree that the acting was
superb. In some undefined way, the ingredients for an excellent
movie were present but not properly implemented.

"An orphan boy discovers that his mysterious new guardian
is a smuggler. Unconvincing period yarn which has managed to
drain every vestige of subtlety from the novel, but at least looks
good. "20

Young Francis Andrews "finds life on board The Good Chance
... the opposite of beer and skittles. Afraid of his new career he
betrays his comrades but when the final test comes proves faithful
to his manhood and wins happiness. This rather flamboyant film
... has its moments.... The whole thing seems rather unreal. "21

James Agee faults the dialogue. "A costume story about a
coward ... out of maybe Stevenson. With more style this might
have been rather good ... I can't remember hearing so many men
so often say, to other men, 'I hate him!'--'I hate you!' "22

The Film Reports consensus agreed that this was a film for
adults, nodding at the musical score composed by Clifton Parker
and played by the London Symphony conducted by Muir Mathieson. 23

> Morbid and terrifying English made film which develops
> around the quotation 'There is another man within me that
> is angry with me. ' Disturbing color photography, the ef-
> fective use of fog to intensify moods and an able cast make
> this tale of smuggling, cruelty, and torture absorbing even
> while it repels. The story, told in flashback, is that of
> a young, poetic lad, influenced by his sordid surroundings

to cowardice, but because of love for the only friend he
ever had he manages to emerge a man of courage. Sex
is portrayed in a frank manner and it is doubtful if American films would be as forthright in treatment of dialogue
and action as in this film. The haunting tune of the
gentleman smuggler, and the symphonic music portray the
conflict in the young man's soul. "

The undecided perplexity of Basil Wright's judgment is found
in The Spectator (April 18, 1947, page 429):

It uses verbal commentary, artificial settings ... and a
great concentration of human relations in close-up. It is
a costume piece concerned with complex psychologies....
A youth (Richard Attenborough) is forced into a smuggling
gang before he has a choice of action or career. He hero-
worships the smugglers' leader (Michael Redgrave), but,
in revenge for an unjustly administered lashing, informs
on the gang, his hero included. Thereafter he is on the
run from the smugglers, the law, and, above all, himself,
for he is a moral and physical coward.... It is a curious
and disturbing film, not easy to analyse, creaking a little
at the joints, yet at moments most engrossing. How much
these contradictory qualities depend on Graham Greene's
original conception, how much on the script by Muriel and
Sydney Box, and how much on Bernard Knowles's direction,
is difficult to determine.... The Man Within ... is a film
I tried to dislike but found impossible to ignore or forget
... it foxed my critical faculties, so you had better see it
for yourselves.

"A dire gap between script and story" caused The Man Within to fail as a film.   The story is told "as evidence given by a boy
under torture ... " granting a major importance to speech in the
film.   Viewing and listening, the movie-goer gets an "uncomfortable
feeling that it is the psychology of the makers we are watching, and
that the characters on the screen are puppets representing something
quite other than the story the makers mean them to tell. "24   Another
flaw is a faltering storyline, especially toward the conclusion of the
picture.

The warmest review was accorded the film by the New York
Times (March 29, 1948, 17:1):

Falls noticeably short of scoring a bull's-eye.   Written
and produced by Muriel and Sydney Box ... the new film
... lacks cohesion both in the screen play and in the direction provided by Bernard Knowles.   As a result 'The
Smugglers' has a distracting tendency to ramble and
doesn't gather sufficient cumulative drive, although some
individual sequences attain forceful proportions. "

Revealing the story and characters, the reviewer T. M. P.

finds the romantic scenes "handled so awkwardly that they are often
unintentionally amusing.... " The action

> does not flow smoothly and there is a profusion of detail
> toward the end that indicates untidy story telling.   Since
> Mr. and Mrs. Box are able craftsmen, and certainly they
> are not sloppy writers, it might well be that "The Smug-
> glers" was subjected to additional editing after leaving its
> producers' hands.   The abrupt transitions of scenes would
> appear to confirm this suspicion.

After two somber films, the Box team turned to another, The
Brothers (1948), based on a novel by L. A. G. Strong.   In it "An
orphan girl comes to a Skye fishing family at the turn of the century,
and causes superstition, sexual jealousy and tragedy.   Wildly melodramatic but good-looking open-air melodrama.... "

The Monthly Film Bulletin 14 (May 31, 1947), page 60 capsules the plot, concluding "This grim story has a beautiful photographic background; but despite its setting, there is no refreshment
to be found in its dealings with sex, hatred, superstition and murder. "

A terse James Agee comments: "Heavy breathing, heavier
dialect, and any number of quaint folk customs on the Island of Skye.
The island and its actual inhabitants are all right; the rest is Mary
Webb with hair on her chest. "[25]

The escapist values of The Brothers are emphasized by Geof-
frey Bell in The Spectator (May 16, 1947) page 557, review.   Appreciative of the indigenous values of this folk tale, Bell considers
them used for their escape, out-of-this-world aspects.

> The story ... concerns a convent-bred girl who works as
> a servant for a father and his two sons in a tiny village
> on Skye.   The girl ... is unwise enough to show interest
> in the scion of a rival clan, and this, coupled with the
> rivalry of the two brothers for her hand, brings her to a
> sad end.   Yes, the "escapism" is there, from the first
> superbly photographed horizon of rock-encrusted sea, to
> the remoteness of folk who pay no heed to "Sassenach
> English laws" against distilling liquor....   Yet the faith-
> fulness to local idiom and atmosphere ... pulls this film
> well into the art class, though not, I fear, into the art
> gallery.   Besides photography, the direction ... and act-
> ing are good.

But, Bell complains, the characters appear as "picturesque
native" persons, only one side of their lives is shown.   "This, to
me, represents escapism at an all-too-adult level. "   Bell finds "the
sterilised quality" of the atmosphere which seems like "Shangri-La"
escapism, too.   And, in the musical background, "Muir Mathieson
has allowed the music to be used sometimes to touch the bottom of
banality, largely through triteness of timing. "

The musical score by Cedric Thorpe Davie utilized three
types of melodic treatment.   The review in Film Music Notes VII:5
(May/June 1948), page 9, defines these three as "folk music of the
region, " then the "music derived and developed from these folk
sources, " and last music "having no particular local character ...
used in the conventional way to increase the punch of tense and/or
violent scenes. " The review describes lapses in this third type of
treatment; the lapses are compensated "by the high quality of the
other bridges and backgrounds. " Reviewer William Hamilton then
describes the best part of the musical score:

> The picture's most intrinsically interesting and compelling
> music is provided by a women's chorus, unidentified in the
> credits, which is heard several times in songs presumably
> indigenous to the island. Their purpose is a scene- and
> mood-setting, and, in combination with some very beauti-
> ful panoramic photography, they impart an integrity to the
> film which would otherwise have been lost in the blind
> alleys of a rather disjointed script.

Variety cautions, "It will not be everybody's entertainment,
and will do best with discriminating audiences.... "[26] Calling it
"Starkly uncompromising" the Variety critic must have read the
novel because he states: "No attempt has been made to win favor
of those who cannot stomach a grim story, and even the contem-
plated happy ending (not in the book) has been discarded in favor of
one more logical. " This refers to the action of the Macrae son
taking the orphan Mary out in his boat.   Neither return. "In the
book he alone comes back. "

The possibility of several endings for the film being photographed enters speculation here.   The New York Times (May 5,
1948, 30:4) review dislikes the ending, and the script as well.

> Unfortunately, the screen play by Muriel and Sydney Box
> ... is a sketchy and choppy affair and quite a consider-
> able truncation of the novel....   Either by nature or by
> cutting, it is full of non sequiturs, and its suddenly happy
> ending is as fake as some indoor studio scenes.   It is
> thoroughly out of character that the younger brother should
> finally kidnap the girl.

Various endings, maladroit editing, bewildering storyline notwith-
standing, the review finds the film "told with a great deal of beauty
but with considerable confusion as to plot ... " and recalling the
Island-set films Man of Aran and The Edge of the World in its natural settings. "More melodramatic than ethnic, more hackneyed than
hewn from the rocks.... "

In Dear Murderer (1947) Peter Rogers joined Muriel and Sydney Box in writing the screenplay, based on a stage play by St.
John Legh Clowes.   Both Boxes produced the film.   The account of
the circumstances threatening a husband's hoped-for perfect murder

of his wife's lover was a successful West End play, but Halliwell's
Film Guide (page 181) considers it "boringly filmed. " The New York
Times critic T. M. P. (May 8, 1948, 12:2) points out that it "could
have generated twice as much excitement had it unfolded at a faster
tempo ... " although "it has so much in its favor in the way of suspense and artful manipulation of circumstance.... "

    In the role of an angry husband who decides to do away with
his wife's lover, only to discover that there is a second man in his
wife's life, "Eric Portman gives a highly attractive performance. "
By arranging appearances to show that the first lover did away with
the second, the husband creates the situation Scotland Yard investi-
gates "in a suspenseful manner and with regard for logic. " All
the picture "needed to be top notch was a director who would have
made more than pedestrian use of the camera. "

    The Spectator (June 13, 1947), page 684, agrees: "The film
is extremely exciting. There are no subtleties of the camera, but
suspense is engendered by the story itself. " While Eric Portman is
identified as the murderer, no review discloses the trap in which he
was caught.

    With murder still in the plot, the Box team's next effort was
a comedy titled Holiday Camp (1947). With Peter Rogers, the
Boxes tossed off this cheery opus, based on a story by Godfrey
Winn, and in production realized they had epitomized Mr. and Mrs.
Average Citizen in their characters of Mr. and Mrs. Huggett who
deserved a series which was destined to be made.

    Halliwell's Film Guide (page 331) describes this innocuous
idyll as "A seminal compendium comedy drama, a bore in itself but
establishing several post-war norms of the British cinema, including
the Huggetts. " More episode than storyline, "A murderer on the
prowl affects people's enjoyment in various ways" at a summer holiday camp.

    Seeing a cross-section of English citizenry at play, The Spec-
tator (August 15, 1947), page 205, effervesces at the vacationers
who are spinsters, runaway lovers, good-time girls, quiet young
men, card-sharpers, and families with children. As the critic
Virginia Graham suggests, seeing the film is probably easier than
experiencing a holiday camp. "It remains a joyful experience to
witness some thousands of not very happy people snatching a brief
week of forgetfulness in a beautifully appointed concentration camp. "

    The Monthly Film Bulletin 14 (August 1947), page 111 details
the plot:

        The Huggett family--Joe, the missus, 16-year-old Harry
        and 21-year-old Joan--go to a holiday camp. Many things
        happen while they are there, the fates entangling them
        with a murder, two confidence tricksters and a number of
        pleasant harmless people.... This is a film built around

the authentic atmosphere of a holiday camp with its regimented gaiety and heartaches. It has humour, sentiment and suspense, with no pretence of offering anything to linger in the memory. . . .

And there is a happy ending, of course. Variety 167 (August 10, 1947), page 15 predicted the film "should have popular appeal" even though "For the U.S. perhaps less might have been left to the imagination, and the abrupt ending visually clarified. "

Against a background of communal recreation, "the problems and histories unfold: the maniac posing as an ex-R.A.F. pilot ... who exudes charm and claims another victim before the law catches up with him; the busman who cleans out the crooks who have robbed his son at cards; the embittered sailor who finds consolation with the war widow, and the youthful pianist who must sacrifice his music to face up to family responsibilities with the young girl he has wronged. " The characters are contrasted nicely, Variety observes, and they look down-to-earth.   "Artistically and technically it is a commendable piece of work. "

The New York Times (Jan. 24, 1948, 11:2) review chimes:

There is nothing about "Holiday Camp" that actually can be called unique or even different, as there is never any doubt about how the various problems are going to be resolved.   But here is an atmosphere of freshness, spontaneity and gaiety about the proceedings that is altogether charming.

With such warm responses to this merry bit of Britannia, the Boxes wrote the script Here Come the Huggetts (1948), aided by Peter Rogers, and Mabel and Denis Constanduros. This appears to be the first feature film involving all three Boxes. Betty E. Box is listed as Producer in the British Film Annual 1949 review of the film.

With tongue in cheek, Muriel differentiates among the duties of the Film Producer, the Director, and the Executive Producer. This last is quite unlike the customary depiction of him (it is a him) in movies and on the stage. He doesn't have to be a middle-aged, overweight, loud-speaking, constant cigar smoker with a low literacy level. Irrespective of personality, this gentleman ably manipulates the pursestrings for many movies simultaneously and referees conflicts between the Director and Producer. Sydney Box was an Executive Producer. Muriel describes the typical Director as looking worried and telling everyone, artists and technicians, what to do and when, while shooting the film. This was Muriel's customary capacity.

The Producer appears more anxiety-stricken than the Director because this person has to explain to all concerned why they really cannot make the film as they wish to but as finances and

circumstances otherwise dictate. This was Betty Box's bailiwick.
The role of Producer, in fact, constituted Betty Box's entire career.

In Odd Woman Out, Muriel Box salutes her sister-in-law's
long list of accomplishments, noting biographical data as well. Sydney had assigned Betty to the production head position at Islington
Studios. The director she worked with most often was Ralph Thomas.
Together they made several films and a number of them were quite
popular. The first in the series, titled Doctor in the House, has
been considered one of her best productions. Betty Box married
Peter Rogers in 1949. For her prowess as a film producer she
was later awarded an OBE (Order of the British Empire).

At the same time, Muriel was building a sound foundation for
her own career. Her scriptwriting expertise and all-round knowledge
of all phases of moviemaking were preparing her for directing films.

Ken Annakin directed Here Come the Huggetts, although he
is not mentioned in any reviews cited. The Huggetts were likeable
and life-like enough to spawn a series of funny films, though not
scripted by the Box team, as successful in the comedy vein as The
Doctor series was for Betty Box.

In a backward look at the Huggett family, Halliwell's Film
Guide (page 322) sighs: "A suburban family has its ups and downs.
Cosy domestic comedy drama, a presage of TV soap operas to come
or Britain's answer to the Hardys, depending how you look at it.
Tolerable at the time. " A note adds this tidbit of trivia: "The
Huggetts had actually originated in Holiday Camp the previous year,
and appeared again in Vote for Huggett and The Huggetts Abroad;
Jack Warner and Kathleen Harrison became an inseparable duo for
many years. "

The Monthly Film Bulletin 16:2 (January, 1949), page 2, considers the story negligible, but

> most of the characters are so natural and human, we seem
> actually to be sharing the lives and emotions of a real,
> typically English family. Kathleen Harrison and Jack
> Warner repeat their Holiday Camp success as the mother
> and father, and are ably supported by the rest of the
> cast. . . . "

The British Film Annual (1949), pages 175-176 illustrates
the storyline with photos from the film. The mishaps and poor judgments of the family members cumulate, evoking amusement and empathy. Daughter Jane cannot decide between two suitors; "Daughter
Pet misjudges the relationship between her father and her flashy
cousin Diana, who is staying with them while Mrs. Huggett is in
the hospital. Seeking to 'save' her parents' marriage Pet cajoles
the boy next door to lay siege to Diana. "

When Mr. Huggett finds a job for Diana in the factory where

he is a foreman, she "loses the firm an important order" thereby jeopardizing Mr. Huggett's job. "Then, in a crowd watching a Royal Wedding, Mr. Huggett collects a black eye in a fight prompted by exasperation at seeing nothing of the spectacle. " The boy next door, Peter,

> borrows Mr. Huggett's car, wraps it round a traffic is-
> land and lands himself, his employer, and Diana in gaol--
> a situation all the more miserable because Peter is due to
> be best man at Jane's wedding next day and also because
> Mr. Huggett cannot find the car when his factory catches
> fire. Both bridegroom and best man are missing on the
> wedding morning, for Jimmy has rushed off to bail out
> Peter. Jane, thinking herself deserted, faints. Diana's
> mother blames Mr. Huggett for her daughter's trouble and
> Mrs. Huggett wages battle with the police. But in the end,
> of course, all is well.

The Spectator reviewer (December 3, 1948), page 729, smiles and frowns, issuing this opinion:

> The Box family propose making a series of films round
> the Huggett family.... The first of the series, Here Come
> the Huggetts, is, frankly, not a bit good. In pursuing the
> affairs, educational or amorous, of Mr. Huggett's girls,
> not to mention the love life of a blonde cousin of unbeliev-
> able minxhood, Miss Diana Dors, the film loses sight of
> both credibility and cohesion. The Huggetts do not feel
> like a family, neither do they look like one, and for all
> Miss Harrison's basic Mum-dom they remain amorphous.
> This film will be a great success.

"Scripting is bad, both in plot and dialog, " says Variety 172 (Dec. 8, 1948) page 11, which is completely negative in its brief three-paragraph article. Predicting that this "ineffective production ... will achieve little in the home market and less abroad ... " Variety found the story one "built around a series of trivial adven-tures which fail to click ... " and expressed sympathy for the Hug-gett parents, Kathleen Harrison and Jack Warner, both of whom are first rate artists" who "don't have a chance here. " The New York Times did not review the film, tacitly agreeing with Variety. The subsequent Huggett movies were not released in the United States, though they continued to captivate cheers and chuckles at home.

With Frank Harvey, the Box team wrote the script for Por-trait from Life (1948) or The Girl in the Painting, its U.S. title. The Illustrated London News cinema column (January 8, 1949), page 60 considered it

> a clumsy and not very probable tale of an English Army
> Major who is so haunted by a portrait he has casually
> seen in London, in a picture-gallery, that he goes in search
> of the model among the concentration camps of Germany.

When he discovers her, she proves to have lost her memory and to have forgotten even the identity of her real
father, whom the Major had met in London. The film
concludes ... with the girl slowly recovering her memory
and being restored to her real parent. ...

Based on a story by David Evans, the film "is chiefly remarkable
for Miss Zetterling's striking ... poignancy as the lost girl. ... "

Rating the film suitable for young people, the Film Reports
consensus was far more impressed by it than the London reviewer.

This absorbing tale combines a melodramatic plot with im-
pressively realistic backgrounds. ... Suspense is sustained
throughout by convincing direction and acting. The authentic scenes of life among the tragic outcasts made home-
less by war heighten the dramatic impact.

"This picture is unexceptional ... " The Spectator (Dec. 24,
1948), page 837, announces. But the acting of Mai Zetterling in
the central role is so good, she "has ... the ability to act everybody else off the screen, which makes for a very unbalanced production. "

Agreeing, the New York Times (August 22, 1949, 13:1) notices that "when she is off the screen ... 'The Girl in the Painting'
sags most noticeably. " The reviewer T. M. P. considers it another near-hit from the Box stable. Most of the strengths of the
film are matched by weaknesses.

It "stems from an intriguing idea, and there are several very
effective sequences ... plus a fine performance by the Swedish actress, Mai Zetterling. ... If the whole ... were as good as its
parts, the posting of this notice would be a much more pleasant
task. "

Analyzing its defects, there is "Too much, rather than too
little, story and plodding direction ... the authors give so much attention to setting each little detail in its proper place that the story
loses its vitality. " Also, "Things which might well have been suggested pictorially are developed at too great narrative length and
the chances are you will guess the outcome of it all long before
the authors are willing to let the secret out. ... "

With a quickened pace and less detail the picture could have
been the adult counterpart to the film The Search, which also had a
background of German concentration camps.

In form, Easy Money (1949) the Box team's next film recalls
Quartet, a four-part film based on short stories by W. Somerset
Maugham. 27 In Easy Money, the "four episodes are based on a single
theme--the enormous change wrought in the lives of ordinary people
by football pool prizes. "28 In Episode One, Philip Stafford "dis-

covers that he has 'scooped the pool.'" Then his family finds out
that they forgot to mail the coupon. Next they discover that "the
coupon they forgot to post was the wrong one--and they win the
money after all."[29] The Grandma in the Stafford family, "on hearing that the family has completed an all-correct pools coupon mur-
murs, 'Well, I think I shall go to bed.'"[30]

In Episode Two, a henpecked City clerk wins a fortune, decides to quit his job, and suffers a heart attack when he tries to
hand in his resignation.

A nightclub singer convinces her man friend to fake a winning
coupon in Episode Three, while the last segment of the film, Episode Four, recounts the revenge of a double-bass player in an orchestra made possible by his winning coupon. Using homegrown subject
material of universal interest, with wish fulfillment, novelty, humor,
insight into human nature, and appropriate music, the Box team
achieved an appealing crowd-pleaser.

The Monthly Film Bulletin 15 (Feb. 29, 1948), page 15, suggests that "the film is quite good propaganda for football pools, but
it is only moderate entertainment." Commenting on the use of music, the review remarks that "For the first two stories, there is
music around the Episodes (i. e. accompanying the commentary, not
in them.) In Episodes 3 and 4, however, there is background music in addition to the necessary featured music--a bad plan, perhaps,
but well carried out."

Critic Harold Brown in Film Music Notes VIII, 4 (March-
April 1949), page 18, reveals the story of Episode Four in the context of his article.

> Music ... is limited mostly to the title, introduction, and
> final episode concerning a harassed double bass player
> who is bored with the colorless oom-pah of bass parts.
> Winning a large sum in a football pool he saves his orches-
> tra from financial disaster by making an anonymous con-
> tribution subject to certain conditions, and the film winds
> up with the entire bass section lined up in the very front
> of the orchestra, playing its inexorable, considerable [sic]
> amplified oom-pah.

Referring to Mr. Brady as responsible for the music in the
film when the film score is correctly attributed to Temple Abady,
Harold Brown goes on to comment: "A fine cooperation between composer and sound engineer is achieved here, for the music forms a
continuous background to the narration, and, without disturbing the
narration in the least, is audible in every note."

Episode Four's music though "is adequate enough, but both
the episode and the music fall short of being fine humor, owing to
the lack of an authentic ring in the behind-the-scenes orchestral
life. But for those even casually conversant with music, the episode
may be quite delightful."

"Episode Four is almost a comic cartoon. It features a dejected musician--a droll double-bass player, who, after sampling high life on the proceeds of his winning coupon, returns to the orchestra he loves and saves it from financial disaster. " This vignette clearly was the best of the quartet, actor Edward Rigby receiving praise even from the New York Times (Feb. 14, 1949, 15:3). In "the film's most adroit and satisfying antic ... Mr. Rigby's flamboyant description of his art, his exit from the orchestra and his subsequent return to the fold, is a beautifully broad, laugh provoking and heart warming lampoon, a cheerfully fitting climax to the collection. " Overall, "the delineations of the little people involved leaves little to be desired. " The second segment is "thin, " while the third is "an undistinguished adventure. "

With one eye on the movie box office and the other on theatre audiences, Variety 169:22 (Feb. 4, 1948) devotes a paragraph of explanation about football pools for American readers who may be unfamiliar with legalized gambling, in silent approval of "such a cast-iron subject and ... formula of 'If I Had a Million'.... " It forecasts that "Pic will draw more on title and theme than marquee names ... " and recommends "drastic clipping" (was the film too long?). And the acting "calls for no particular comment, with the exception of Edward Rigby, who is a standout. "

Not all of the humor of Easy Money was in the film. Muriel Box relates an anecdote about the reception of a scene in Episode Four.

It happened that one scene in the film evoked uproarious and unexpected laughter and merriment when first viewed by the critics and journalists. Several reviewers wondered out loud about the scene being missed by the censors. When word of this scene got to Arthur Rank he asked the Boxes to tell him what scene it was that provoked the laughs. They said they didn't know, and Rank decided to reread the script to identify it.

Muriel reveals that the scene in dispute was written from an encounter between Sir Thomas Beecham and a member of his orchestra who purportedly played a false note several times. Stopping the rehearsal, Beecham expressed his exasperation by picking out the offender and asking him, surprised as he was, to stand up. The musician did. Beecham asked him his name. The musician replied that his last name was Ball, and added, in deference, "Sir. " Beecham just looked at him, then commenced the rehearsal. As Muriel observes, the connotation of the musician's reply was not appreciated by Arthur Rank, because the Boxes did not hear from him on this point, and the film remained intact.

However, most encounters with film censors were sobering and frustrating struggles. Not every film was cut but many were, some of them abridged even in Hollywood. Each censor-ordered change denoted time and money lost, not to mention frayed tempers, loss of artistic intention and integrity, arguments between actors, and directors, and disruption of the scheduled shooting of a film-in-progress.

In most cases, the censor won. Consultative discussion beforehand, as Muriel Box observes, when tried, resulted in dashed hopes. She cites Giles Cooper's Everything in the Garden and J. B. Priestley's The Tober and the Tulpa as instances. The Cooper work was filmed in the United States, but the Priestley work was never made.

Good Time Girl (1949) dealt with female juvenile delinquency and met with a negative review from The New York Times (Sept. 25, 1950, 18:5).

> Hardly new in concept or sparkling in execution, this film commentary on one facet of the post-war London scene has been illustrated before and with better results.... The fact of the matter is that Muriel and Sydney Box and Ted Willis, the scenarists, and David MacDonald, the director, have leaned--awkwardly in most instances--on transparent and largely unconvincing melodramatic devices to spin their doleful tale....

The case history of Gwen Rawlings is told to a young runaway in juvenile court, who, after the film chronicle of Gwen's unfortunate experiences, decides to return home.

The Blind Goddess (1949), representing justice, was the Box team's next project. Strangely, the English reviews were favorable while the U. S. critics reacted coolly. In a majority of Box films, the U. S. critics were kinder, perhaps easier to please, than their British counterparts, in spite of cutting required by censorship rules, title changes, and other upsetting changes.

The Boxes adapted the film from a successful play by Patrick Hastings. In it, "The private secretary to a public figure finds that his idol has feet of clay, and suffers in court for his discovery. Courtroom drama from an old-fashioned stage play: surefire for addicts, but routine as a film."[30]

The Monthly Film Bulletin 15:124 (Sept. 30, 1948) enthuses: "Somewhat tedious in the beginning, it moves to an exciting finish and interest is maintained the whole way through.... This is a very pleasant film which should not be missed."

Punning, the New York Times (June 23, 1949, 33:3) review states that

> justice is not blind ... but merely myopic and rather routine. For this yarn about the trial of a British peer accused of converting moneys for DP rehabilitation to his own use, is dependent on dialogue and court sequences in establishing facts which seem obvious almost from the be-

ginning. And, while that dialogue makes sense, it is no substitute for drama. "

Following a short plot summary, Variety (Sept. 29, 1948), page 18, predicts "reasonably modest results at the boxoffice. " Even though "The Film is very much a carbon copy of the original play, and in consequence suffers from its stagey atmosphere. But lack of movement is not of prime importance in this type of production, which is clearly designed to stress the melodramatic angles brought into full play during the trial scene. "

The next Box production was a fiasco, and a grandscale one, to boot. Muriel and Sydney read the screenplay Christopher Columbus by novelist Rafael Sabatini. They agreed it was historically inexact and poorly written, and said "No" to the project. But they were ordered to do it. By this time, so much money had been spent on it, they had to complete the project to try to gain back its costs. So they tried.

Everything went wrong. Filmed on location, two of three ships met ill-fated ends at the beginning. The Nina was built for the film and was lost. The Santa Maria suffered a faulty rocking apparatus and later caught fire. Only wreckage remained. Models of ships used did not look real when photographed. Actress Florence Eldridge accidentally burned her face when trying to light a cigarette. The cotton wool she wore under her eyeglasses for the Queen Isabella role caught fire instead. When the film was shown to the critics no one had a good word to say for it. As the Boxes had correctly anticipated, Christopher Columbus did not have the required elements for a successful movie.

The reviews detailed all shortcomings, but were not insulting to the film. Halliwell's Film Guide (page 137) complains, "An extraordinarily tediously paced historical account of basically undramatic events.... " It continues,

> A dearth of dramatic incidents makes it move too slowly. The first half of the film, taken up with life at Court, is long and tedious. This is relieved by the voyage and first meeting of explorers and natives, but the tempo slows down again towards the end ... the costumes ... look uncommonly new. Many of these were obviously designed to give full justice to the glorious Technicolor.

The Spectator (June 17, 1949), page 818, attempts politeness by indexing the veracity of the storyline. "If it is by no means an inspired or inspiring picture it gives a reasonable undistorted account of the great explorer's life. " Fredric March "makes a convincing Columbus" and Florence Eldridge "a gracious and sympathetic Queen Isabella. " Only history is to blame if the film is static, Columbus having waited six years in the Court of Spain before being heard.

Two hours long is the length of Christopher Columbus (1949),
the first hour covering Columbus's sojourn at court. "In the second
hour we not only cross the Atlantic and discover the West Indies;
we also make the voyage back, see Columbus's reception in Spain,
and stay with him to his death. ... " Then, The Illustrated London
News (June 25, 1949, page 892, inserts commendation. "This is a
worthy and even a fine film. ... it is bound to thrill America as
well as Europe ... the narration is authoritative, the direction good
if not masterly, and the acting ... first-class. ... "

The basic difficulty is that "The subject ... calls for nothing
short of greatness as distinct from mere high competence. Quite
the nearest thing to the requisite greatness seemed to me to be
Arthur Bliss's musical score." (No review in Film Music Notes of
this film can be located.)

Film Reports generously confers praise on each element in
the film's production, including the music. "Played by the Royal
Philharmonic Orchestra" the score "is a fine composite of medieval
melodies played in many instances on instruments of the period."
Apparently the movie was not overlong for the Film Reports critics.

> This sumptuous and enlightening chronicle combines in-
> spiration, artistry and respect for factual authenticity with
> compelling emotional appeal. ... Long research underlies
> the exquisite beauty of costume and setting. ... Columbus'
> three ships are reproduced in exact detail. Direction sets
> a standard from which there are no lapses. ... The film
> is a valuable contribution to the education of our youth. ...

The film "gives large pictorial illustration to everything but
the man himself." This is the central criticism lodged by Bosley
Crowther in the New York Times (Oct. 13, 1949, 33:3). "The picture of him that is captured is static and flat. ... For the script
that has been concocted by Cyril Roberts and Muriel and Sydney Box
is largely an uninspired succession of legendary but lifeless episode,
of tableaux consecrated by history, with a few fictional fancies
thrown in."

Christopher Columbus "fails to get into top box-office class.
In fact it turns out to be an uncertain piece of entertainment which
likely will be helped along on both sides of the Atlantic by its title
and star." Variety (June 22, 1949), page 6, adds that Hollywood
could probably have done a better job! Noting that the U. S. version
in which the voices of Lincoln and F. D. Roosevelt are heard is
"omitted from the British version," Variety decides that David Mac-
Donald's direction portrays Columbus "as a frustrated character
rather than an inspired mariner."

All agree that the second half of Columbus's life is of greater interest. "Columbus is accused of misruling. A Royal Commis-
sioner who is sent out has him shackled and sent back to Spain. On
his return his property and titles are restored but he is forbidden

to leave the country. " The film ends as "he lies on his deathbed and sees a vision of the mighty nation that is to arise in the New World. "

After the fiasco of Christopher Columbus, Muriel wrote the script for Noel Coward's film The Astonished Heart, adapting it from one of his Tonight at Eight-Thirty plays. Coward read the script and delighted Muriel by saying it was the finest adaptation of any of his own works he'd ever read. He added a number of scenes to it, improving the quality of the script. Although Muriel did not get a credit for contributing to the screenplay, she found the experience of working with Coward, though peppered by embarrassing moments, a rewarding endeavor.

The Box team's next venture inadvertently, and finally, cast Muriel Box into the role of director. In a to-the-rescue spirit, Muriel stepped into film directing because of difficulties encountered in the making of Cockpit. This was based on a play by Bridget Boland. The finished film was of such poor quality that those in charge would not release it. Rather than dismiss Cockpit as a total loss, Sydney and Muriel Box took on the job of trying to revise certain portions of it, photographing them, and then reassembling the movie for distribution so that some money could be made from it.

When the revised script was completed, the question of a director was uppermost. No one wanted the job. By this time, the original film director was long gone. When Muriel volunteered to accept the assignment for no remuneration at all, Sydney approached the film company board for its decision. The Board nodded yes, with some trepidation. Muriel Box, then in her mid-forties, with years of experience in every possible sector of the film industry, began to direct, or re-direct, Cockpit.

First, the film was re-titled The Lost People. Then Muriel had to view and re-view the completed film she was to dissect and restructure. She used a moviola machine to help her. This small-sized projector is usually found in the cutting rooms of film studios where editors use it to look at and place in story order the lengths of film which make up the movie. After viewing and photographing, she discovered that she had redone more than half of the film. Not truly satisfied with what she had had to do, Muriel, nevertheless, knew that The Lost People was quite better than Cockpit.

Her first directing effort garnered poor reviews, but, most importantly, the box-office receipts did pay for the production costs of making it. And that was good enough. To Muriel, this patchwork task which paid for itself meant that she could direct films, handle the personalities of artists and technicians, give instructions and commands with self-confidence. What's more, she liked doing it and now was anxious to direct again.

Halliwell's Film Guide (page 449) capsules the plot: "Displaced persons gather for comfort in a disused German theatre.

Once again a very flat film has been unsuitably made from an effective piece of theatre, with all possible types present and all views represented. "

Muriel Box is given credit for "Additional scenes written and directed" in the Monthly Film Bulletin 16 (Sept. 30, 1949), pages 157-58.   Bernard Knowles is listed as director.   As the MFB review indicates, the pivotal character is a young British officer placed in charge of "a dispersal centre for displaced persons" located in a theatre.   He "struggles to keep order among the various nationalities and political factions, until a rumour of bubonic plague unites Communists and Catholics in fear.   When it turns out to be no more than a rumour, the battles and intrigues begin again. "

The theme has lost its topicality, and the treatment of the theme completely wrong.

> The script is deplorably crude and stilted, but a greater
> disaster comes with the direction.   Technically incom-
> petent, flat and lifeless, it achieves climaxes solely by
> loud, emphatic bursts of background music over clumsily-
> handled crowd movements....   One can only hope, at
> least, that the film will never be shown abroad.

The Spectator (Aug. 26, 1949), page 264, pegs the lesson to be learned from The Lost People in one line: "under a common fear will men live peaceably with one another. "   The New York Times (Oct. 2, 1950, 19:4) remarks, "A lot could and should happen during thirty-six hours in a post-war Berlin theatre crammed with several thousand displaced persons awaiting transportation under the sole supervision of a British officer and his aide.   Not much does, however.... "

Differing, Variety 175 (Sept. 7, 1949), page 18, found the film "competently directed"!   And the reviewer takes some length to disclose the plot and to evaluate the acting roles.   "While lacking some of the poignant moments of the stage version, this story of the melting pot of a dispersal camp ... provides satisfying dramatic entertainment.   But its depressing subject will limit its appeal. "

Muriel's career as film director took a backward step in the film So Long at the Fair, a tale set in the Paris of the Great Exhibition.   Muriel wrote the first draft.   Sydney wrote another. The revision of both scripts coalesced into the final shooting script. Star Jean Simmons liked the script but was noncommittal toward the prospect of a woman director.   But then she consulted her husband-to-be actor Stewart Granger who said No.   Muriel then was given another assignment.   She got acquainted with a new bit of technology called the Independent Frame, while another director, male of course, directed the film.

The Lost People appears to have been Muriel Box's first

and last directing job for Gainsborough. Rank sold the Shepherd's
Bush studios. The caused Muriel's resignation as Script Editor,
presumably before the sale. However, Sydney was still under contract to the Arthur Rank firm as a producer for an additional two
years, so he remained employed.

By 1950, the Box team had made and released almost 40 feature films. Understandably, they were fatigued and ready to vacation.

They decided to make a tour of the United States, in what
turned out to be a working vacation. Muriel shot some exterior
scenes for a Graham Greene story Across the Bridge, which she
hoped to direct. The Boxes visited James and Pamela Mason in
Hollywood, and saw as much of the film industry there as possible.

Muriel Box attests several times in her autobiography to a
surprising fact: the process of filmmaking became more trouble-
some and complex, rather than less, with the passage of time.
Moviemaking got harder, not easier. As cinematic proof, Muriel
cites The Happy Family (1952) which opened in London after good
reviews and especially enthusiastic ones from Chicago and New York.
The film premiered in New York with the title Mr. Lord Says No!
the customary procedure being a London premiere. This was Muriel
Box's first full directing assignment with a script she and Sydney
had adapted from a play by Michael Clayton Hutton.

"The playing is strenuous, but an obvious, repetitive script
and amateurish direction make it increasingly apparent that the materials' comic possibilities have been much more satisfactorily re-
alised before."[31]

The film was centered on the 1951 Festival of Britain (Box
topicality of subject once more). "Shortly before the opening ... the
Lord family are told that an architect's mistake in design has made
it necessary for their home and grocer's shop on the South Bank to
come down to make way for the Festival road. Clinging to their
property in the face of official appeals, offers of a new house, and
threats of eviction, the Lords decide to withstand a siege and barri-
cade themselves in. After a week without water or light they are
on the point of surrender when the Government capitulates. The
road branches round their shop."[32]

Considering that the film was cut because it perturbed one
critic (unnamed) with its lack of "good taste," and that additional
adjustments had to be made before distribution, the movie fared
quite well in the States. The Christian Century 69:295 (Mar. 5,
1952) advises viewers they will find in the picture "Low-pressure
humor in satire on bureaucracy, spiritualism, British shibboleths,
human nature in general.

Bosley Crowther in the New York Times (Feb. 12, 1952)
22:5, disliked it. "The burden in this whimsy ... is a script so

forced and imitative that it makes an intolerable load. Penned by
that usually clever couple, Muriel and Sydney Box ... " Crowther
salutes the theme (Man's home is his castle) but hints that Mr.
Lord and family should not have come to New York. "The farce
collapses painfully upon them long before the end, and what humor
there is sounds so parochial that it belongs in earshot of Waterloo
Road.... "

"Mild comedy entry for the 'art' spots" is Variety's label for
the film, explaining, "Import is a fair bet for art-type operations.
Scripters Muriel and Sydney Box tell about a family of Britons who
refuse to relinquish their home for a government project. " Although
"there are some instances of straining in the portrayals of very,
very British people ... " Variety commends the director. "In directing, Muriel Box gave full attention to the subtleties in the whim-
sical material.... "

While the picture was a profitable one, its financial woes per-
sisted for some time. The Box team did not know that the money
made by The Happy Family was invested by its distributors, without
their cognizance, in the purchase of pictures made in the United
States, which, unhappily, did not do well at the box office. So that
when the Box team tried to collect its share of the profits from The
Happy Family the distributors responded by announcing that they might
liquidate their assets. Luckily, so much time had elapsed that the
Boxes' next film, Street Corner, about policewomen, was premiered--
this was in the Spring of 1953--thereby easing the strain on funds.

In Odd Woman Out, Muriel details her amusing and sobering
impressions of police duties from a female point-of-view. In preparation for Street Corner, she visited police stations, courts, and pris-
ons, gathering incidents, facts, anecdotes, and contending with Scotland Yard authorities about making the film. She records enduring
a series of squabbles with the police long before Street Corner, one
of her best-liked movies, was scheduled to start.

Sydney finished the eighth version of the script while wrangling
with distributors hard to please. Work was to start with photographing outside scenes in late September of 1952, with inside scenes to
be done two weeks later. Such a high state of confusion and frayed
tempers was reached that Muriel's diary records that Sydney drove
off in his car, while she rested quietly at home.

Street Corner was partially inspired by the success of the
film Blue Lamp (1949) a popular picture about the London police
which was filmed with authentic locales. Halliwell's Film Guide
(page 86) describes the film to which Street Corner was compared,
and may have been the model for:

A young man joins London police force. The elderly copper who trains him is killed in a shootout, but the killer
is apprehended. Seminal British police film which spawned
not only a long line of semi-documentary imitations but

also the twenty-year TV series Dixon of Dock Green for
which the shot PC was happily revived. As an entertainment, pacy but dated; more important, it burnished the
image of the British copper for a generation or more.

Halliwell (page 728) then devotes a few words to Street Corner:
"Days in the lives of the women police in Chelsea. Patter-plotted
female Blue Lamp; just about watchable. "

Both direction and script are stereotyped, and the total effect synthetic in spite of use of London locales. The Monthly Film
Bulletin 20:56 (April, 1953) review leads us to believe the action too
predictable and the formula too familiar. "Keeping firmly to the
Blue Lamp formula, the film has the standard ingredients of its type:
crooks operating from a shady and improbable night club; cameo
parts ...; cups of tea in the police canteen, and a final chase across
a bombsite. " The MFB concludes: "the policewomen ... seem to
have the makings of a good hockey team. "

Films in Review V:1 (January, 1954), pages 32-33, purrs
praise on Both Sides of the Law, the U.S. title. "Muriel and Sidney
[sic] Box have scripted a carefully-plotted melodrama involving London's policewomen. " The film is good, and what gives it distinction
is "the way in which Miss Box, who also directed, keeps the film
moving along. Her galaxy of London types is plausibly individualized
and is so utilized that interest does not flag and the ending is not
just clutter, as so often happens in multi-character films. "

Likening it to the U.S. film Detective Story, the review ap-
preciates the fact that "Miss Box was fortunate in getting Jean
Barker, an artist with scissors, to edit her film and give it suspense and pace. Both Sides of the Law is one of the firmly knit
thrillers the English like to lavish care and attention on. "

Philip Hartung in Commonweal (February 26, 1954), page 525,
pens one paragraph of praise:

> Both Sides of the Law tells a story of policewomen in Lon-
> don and the routine cases that have to be handled by the
> Chelsea Police Station. Director Muriel Box, who also
> had a hand in writing the script, does a very good job in
> making all these tags of plots jell into a whole. Anne
> Crawford and Rosamund John are excellent as a couple of
> women of the law. "

"Rack this one up as a top-flight drama from overseas. "
That was the conclusion of Catholic World 178:383 (February 1954)
reviewer Robert Kass. Calling it a blend of The Blue Lamp and Detective Story, Kass relates two of the cases the policewomen deal
with. The first involves "an eighteen-year-old shoplifter who ditches
her truck-driver husband to have a fling with a flashy hoodlum. "
The second focuses on "a young woman, a deserter from the Women's
Army, whose bigamous alliance with two husbands is discovered after

she dives into the Thames to rescue a drowning child. " "Expertly edited" the film "clicks away from start to finish. The acting is exemplary. ... "

In Saturday Review 37 (March 13, 1954), page 28, Arthur Knight calls it "another of those cross-section stories that seem so to intrigue the British. " He points out that "the picture also explores the loves and frustrations of a number of the policewomen. Obviously, none of these characters can be developed sufficiently to matter very much, and the film soon falls into a flat semi-documentary style that even a wildly melodramatic chase finale fails to alter. "

Classifying it as a "British meller about femmes on London's police force; lack of marquee names will hurt in U. S. " Variety 190 (March 25, 1953), page 24, credits Muriel Box's direction as "smooth and efficient. " The story is a series of "cameos which are neatly dove-tailed to give an overall picture of femme coppers. "

Both Sides of the Law "is lucid and informative without being particularly exciting. " This complaint is lodged by the New York Times (Jan. 12, 1954, 19:2). "The skirted police ... are intelligent and feminine ... but only a modicum of incisive characterization is allowed to seep through the complex proceedings. " But, what with an A. W. O. L. WAC, a bigamist, a shoplifter, gangsters, a baby on a roof edge, and a drowning lad, the policewomen are surely busy.

In 1953 Muriel Box directed a short film titled A Prince for Cynthia, in which a secretary dreams she is kidnapped by a foreign prince. Sydney Box appears not to have had a hand in this venture.

Somerset Maugham's story The Beachcomber was tackled next. To minimize expenses, all the locations were shot without the principals in Ceylon. It was too expensive to move the cast, and their stand-ins to Ceylon, plus living expenses during filming. Then, as director, Muriel faced, in each day's shooting, the prospect of keeping the alcoholic star, Robert Newton, in the role of Ginger Ted, a drunk, sober until midday.

Halliwell's Film Guide (page 219), lists it as a "Styleless remake of Vessel of Wrath; the acting just about holds the interest, but all other contributions are flat. " Written by Sydney Box, the script adhered to the original Maugham tale and the first version made in 1938, in which an alcoholic reforms after an unwelcome friendship with a lady missionary.

No mention is made of Muriel Box's directing in The Monthly Film Bulletin 21:127 (Sept. 1954), but all other facets of the production come in for criticism. "The earlier version ... was not particularly good; and this is somewhat worse. The ... story is presented with no imagination and with surprising tastelessness--the utmost fun is extracted from the follies of temperance and ... reading the Bible. " While Robert Newton, Paul Rogers, and Glynis Johns

fare tolerably well, "Francis Chagrin's music is importunate; the locations in colour are disappointing. "

Moira Walsh in America 92:463 (Jan. 29, 1955), identifies the
story as one about the "raffish British remittance man on a South
Seas island who is brought to rectitude and romantic heel by a spin-
ster missionary. To a present-day adult audience it is likelier to
suggest a bargain basement edition of the African Queen. In its new
version it is more melodrama than Maugham envisioned and less
bitter. Still it has a little social satire, a good deal of humor and
charm and excellent location photography in Technicolor.... "

Newsweek 44:83 (Dec. 20, 1954) sums it up as "Good cast,
good Maugham, and pretty good fun. It recalls that actor Robert
Newton was cast in the Resident's role in the 1938 version; in this
Box film Newton plays the hard-drinking remittance man. "

Robert Hatch in Nation 179:470 (November 27, 1954), can't
resist comparing the 1938 film with its remake.

> It is now thoroughly whimsical and succeeds in making
> vice and virtue look equally good fun. The great treat ...
> is to see how the ferociously blasphemous remittance man,
> when at last he foreswears booze and native girls, is re-
> warded with the pure but full-blooded love of as plump a
> missionary (Glynis Johns) as ever brought the doxology to
> the heathen.

Philosophically, Films in Review 6:4 (April, 1955) page 190,
sighs: "It is a pat story, but a pleasant one.... Indeed, The Beachcomber contains the essence of all that Maugham has to say about
his fellow man: There's a little bad in the best of us and a little
good in the worst. "

Time 65:75 (Jan. 24, 1955) is quite taken with Robert Newton's portrayal of Ginger Ted and his "reward. " When marooned on
a desert isle with the missionary lady he ignores her, only to find
himself congratulated by the parson "for sparing her. "

The New York Times (Jan. 17, 1955, 27:5) reminds us that
comparisons are "odious, but sometimes unavoidable. " Of course,
this remake is not as fine as the original film.

> It is merely a pleasant adventure and not the riotous jape
> its predecessor was.... Muriel Box, who directed from
> her husband's script, has kept things moving at a gentle
> pace. But she has infused the proceedings with enough
> tropic charm ... to give an observer the wanderlust. It
> is, in short, a lovely and colorful diversion. Unfortunate-
> ly, this "Beachcomber" does not have the hilarity, in-
> cisiveness and stature of the original.

Variety 195 (Aug. 18, 1954), page 6, predicted it "should do

goodly biz in most countries.   It is well adapted and suitably back-
grounded, with authentic local color and all trappings of native
drums, witch doctors and the ineradicable prejudice against the
white man's medicine. "

　　　Action begins when "the beachcomber gets out of hand and
wrecks the wineshop. "   He is jailed.

> An outbreak of cholera brings a sense of responsibility
> to the drunkard who goes to a neighboring island with the
> Welsh girl as medical assistant and their strange, anta-
> gonistic relationship ends in marriage.   Dramatic high-
> lights are a fight between an elephant and a crocodile and
> escape from death when the girl is bound by the malevolent
> witch doctor to be trodden underfoot by the same elephant.

Variety credits Muriel Box with intelligent direction, while graciously
only mentioning the 1938 film, with no comparisons.

　　　To Dorothy a Son was a successful London play which failed
on Broadway.   It dealt with an American singer who plans to inherit
$2, 000, 000 if her ex-husband fails to become a father by a set dead-
line.   Peter Rogers wrote the screenplay from Roger MacDougall's
play and produced the film which Muriel Box directed.   The Monthly
Film Bulletin 22:12 (Jan. 1955) deems it "A stagey film from a
stagey play. . . .   Direction and playing are rather ponderous. "

　　　Raymond Durgnat expected a different type of film and was
disappointed when he didn't get it.

> Muriel Box's To Dorothy a Son (1954) sets its cap for the
> distaff side of the box-office, apparently on the assumption
> that women relish the spectacle of thoroughly hen-pecked
> mates.   Struggling composer John Gregson, country-
> cottaging it, gets it not only from the tyrannical and preg-
> nant wife (Peggy Cummins) but also from glamourous ex-
> flame Shelley Winters.   This battle of the Amazons, a
> whiningly self-righteous English one versus a sweetly glit-
> tering American one, might have been quite Homeric.
> Alas, a boring plot fobs us off with tittle-tattle about an
> inheritance. [33]

　　　Philip T. Hartung of Commonweal 63:643 (March 23, 1956),
declares angrily: "I could not have cared less about the people involved or what they had to say on any subject. "   The picture isn't
up to the expected English standards.

> This is particularly surprising because it is directed by
> the very capable Muriel Box; but considering the mediocre
> material she had to work with . . . it should not be surpris-
> ing that the film is so flat. . . .   The effect is somewhat like
> that of an early talkie, with much rushing around over noth-
> ing and a great deal of shouted converation about marriage,
> divorce and the coming baby.

The New York Times (Sept. 1, 1956, 19:3) critic was delighted! Using the word delivery--the U.S. title was Cash on De-
livery--often in his review, the film, in his words, is "a bright,
British farce that was fun on delivery...." The clearest explication
of the curlicued plot is delivered next: Uncle Joe started it. In
his will, he designated his niece Myrtle La Mar, a brassy nightclub
singer, as his heiress ($2,000,000 is at stake) "provided her ex-
husband Tony had not become a father on a certain June 30. If
Tony had produced a son by that time, it would be a $2,000,000
baby for Tony. "

> The New York Times continues in high delight:

>> So Myrtle locates him near London. He is happily mar-
>> ried to Dorothy, who is expecting a baby any day. In
>> fact, the stork is overdue. Then it turns out Myrtle and
>> Tony weren't legally divorced. Myrtle tries to woo him
>> back. When Tony, bedecked with lipstick smears, re-
>> turns to the expectant mother, he finds himself in a rather
>> awkward position. Myrtle won't divorce him and Dorothy
>> won't marry him....

The deadline passes with no baby. "But wait. There are more
complications. " Time zone differences are baffling. Then twins
are born, a girl and a boy. Myrtle happily shares--half and half--
her inheritance.

Variety 201 (Feb. 1, 1956), page 18, condenses the appeal
of Cash on Delivery as "Shelley Winters toplining British-lensed
comedy to help domestic market booking chances as program offering. "

Muriel Box's direction goes without comment, but the musical
score by Lambert Williamson "plays its part in the humor having
identifying themes for characters and situations. " However, "'Give
Me a Man,' by Paddy Roberts and 'You're the Only one,' by Jacques
Abram and George Thorn, are a couple of songs heard to no particular advantage. " So that the music may have been too intrusive
and purposeless.

Remembering, Muriel Box relates an anecdote about the tact-
ful management required for Shelley Winters in this film. Winters'
acting style was brilliant but inconsistent. Winters rarely did a
scene the same way twice. If portions of a scene had to be matched
by the editor for a continuous movement or gesture, that portion had
to be repeated endlessly until an exact fitting could be made. Only
Winters' unflagging and robust sense of humor helped everyone
through the deadly repeat scenes.

As Muriel records in Odd Woman Out Winters approached her
at the party-like gathering at the end of the film and thanked for her
patience, and not losing her temper. Winters even suggested that
they do another film together, although this never happened. As

Muriel observes Winters owned the permission to distribute Cash on Delivery (its American title), in the States.   Another musical score was used in the film shown in the United States, and, of course, as Muriel muses sardonically, after the U. S. censors and distributors had re-arranged and altered scenes, the film that has left the director's hands has been mightily sea-changed.

Eyewitness, her next directing assignment, was a thriller infused with humor for comic relief.   Halliwell's Film Guide (page 269), sums up the plot: "A maniacal burglar pursues a witness of his crime into the emergency ward of a local hospital.   Naive but adequate suspenser with too many character cameos getting in the way of the plot. "

The Monthly Film Bulletin 23:104 (August 1956), discloses the story, but faults the funny characters as overdone.

> The theme of Eyewitness, a cat and mouse chase between killer and his intended victim, is a serviceable one; but here the producers have so overladen the story-line with cosy comic characters as to make one wonder if their intention was deliberately to guy their material ... the melodrama is unadventurously developed.

Films and Filming 3:1 (October 1956), page 26, doesn't mention the comic elements at all.   Reviewer P. L. Mannock's verdict: "To me this is a competent but routine programme offering from the Rank stable, uninspired in treatment and suggesting that the cycle of hospital film plots might well be given a rest. "

The storyline, by Janet Green, rather than the acting and directing, appears to be at fault.

> Packed with action, this British crime melodrama is at the same time lifeless, ... the leading players go through the story with no special credit anywhere.   It is not their fault that the narrative has mechanics without ingenuity.... The plot's kick-off, a pair who killed a cinema manager out to kill the girl who witnessed the crime, has good tension, but their skulking in the hospital grounds gets less and less exciting....

The New York Times did not review Eyewitness.   Variety 203 (August 22, 1956), page 18, captions it "Compact, standard thriller of a murderer's attempt to get at an injured witness to prevent identification.... "   And the review is the best the picture got!

> A neatly made, unpretentious thriller that should do well for the home market.   A murderer's attempt to kill a woman who witnessed his crime makes for suspenseful action, although the story is improbable in some of its twists.   Pic is well acted and well served by its director and camera crew.

As Muriel explains it in Odd Woman Out, Eyewitness was the
easiest movie she ever helped to make.   She confides that if a
movie progresses smoothly with no impediments, no emotional alter-
cations, no thorny issues raised that she becomes anxious, simply
because such a state of affairs is so improbable.   Ordinarily, di-
lemmas are plentiful.   She cites Eyewitness as the only film she
recalls having absolutely no conflicts of time or personnel or funds.
Although the picture was deemed merely average by critics and audiences, everyone on the payroll for Eyewitness enjoyed good rapport,
and usually worked in high good spirits to boot.

As a spoof of the British television industry, Simon and Laura
(1955) did well at the box office.   As a stageplay by Alan Melville it
was moderately successful.   With the screenplay by Peter Blackmore,
it was, in Halliwell's Film Guide's annotation, an "Adequate film of
a reasonable sophisticated West End comedy; good lines and performances" (page 793).

The Monthly Film Bulletin 23:9 (January 1956) agrees with
the "sophistication. "   "Handsomely mounted and more sophisticated
than the usual run of British comedies, Simon and Laura provides
a gentle but sometimes telling satire at the expense of the BBC and
the acting profession.   The plot is by no means original, but crisp
treatment, some bright dialogue and practised playing see it enter-
tainingly through. "

Films and Filming 2:4 (January 1956), page 24, reviewer
Robert A. Pollock couldn't agree more.   "The domestic plot may
seem a trifle hackneyed.   Nevertheless, in its present setting with
the witty dialogue, high standard of acting and wonderful sets ... it
makes for extremely good comedy.   Peter Finch and Kay Kendall in
the name parts are excellent.... "

The secret of the film's success "lies in the fact that it is
contemporary. "   A synopsis of the plot reveals that Simon and
Laura's marriage is falling apart, and "Simon is going back to
Mother for the fourth time when his agent ... offers a daily series
on BBC Television depicting the married bliss of two celebrities.
For money's sake" Simon and Laura agree to do the job.   "Their
lives are invaded by the BBC....   As in all good comedies, there
is a happy ending. "

The behind-the-scenes revelations of the television industry
are expertly done, but story, dialogue, photography, and other facets of the movie do not measure up.   This is Moira Walsh's opinion in America 95:412 (July 28, 1956).

> It is apparently virtually impossible to concoct a satire on
> TV that isn't funny.   This one is British and, as a conse-
> quence, its eccentric collection of producers, agents, pre-
> cocious child actors, typical audiences, etc. has a particu-
> lar BBC flavor.   The comic aspects of the industry--its
> serious discussion of fatuous ideas, its patronizing set of

assumptions and taboos, its peculiar jargon and complicated mechanics and its general air of chaos--appear, however, to be the same the world over and the movie captures them with considerable deftness and bite.

However,

The excerpts from the couple's television show ... are
obviously contrived piecemeal for screen purposes and
bear little resemblance to serial TV.... And the bargain-
basement Noel Coward bickering of the principals is soon
tiresome and ultimately tasteless.

John McCarten in the New Yorker 32 (July 21, 1956), page
45, calls it "antic hay" and "a rather thin affair. " He considers
"The joke that is the core of the matter ... hardly warrants the ex-
haustive treatment it is given. "

Newsweek 48 (July 23, 1956), page 76, confuses Betty Box
with Muriel, referring to the latter's prowess with the Doctor in
the House series of movies! Anyhow, "she has lavished her satirical wit on a rather hallowed institution, the BBC. The result, unfortunately, is only a slender little farce. "

Once again, sadly, the word "flat" is applied to a Muriel
Box movie. Bosley Crowther of the New York Times (July 3, 1956,
17:2) suspects that "Peter Blackmore, who wrote the script for this
affair, found the prospect more hilarious than it is made to appear
on the screen. Somehow the farcical confusion around the studio is
pretty forced and flat. "

Under "the busy direction of Muriel Box" the thespian couple,
on the verge of separation, are chosen to play the ideal couple,
Simon and Laura. "They are turned topsy-turvy by the mad demands
made on them in the ... caverns of the B. B. C. studio. They are
made to be saccharine sweethearts when they would like to cut each
other's throats. The suggestion is even made to them that their
rating might rise if they would have a child ... they are saddled
with an adopted son on their show. This leads to further mad confusion. "

But Crowther finds this farce too predictable. "Simon and
Laura takes an idea that is pretty pat at the start and makes it
even patter--or just patter--as it goes along. "

What Muriel Box best recalls about this film is a tense Kay
Kendall. Plagued by anxieties, the actress barely started working
in her role of Laura when she complained to Earl St. John, an
Executive Producer in the Rank organization, that she could not continue because she felt uneasy taking direction from a woman. When
Muriel was told about the actress's reaction to her, she felt injured
and was on the verge of letting someone else direct. But St. John
and Sydney Box urged Kendall to carry on, assuring her that she

would do very well as Laura. And she did. The role of Laura has been considered one of the actress's best film portrayals.

Variety 206 (March 6, 1957), on page 6, points out each aspect of the film that would be sure to please ticket-buyers. The reviewer assured readers: "Slickly adapted, it makes good laugh material, unveiling backstage problems and all the tricks of the trade. There is a good deal of slapstick rough and tumble which will please the kids and enough satirical digs at the infant of the entertainment medium to amuse the more technically minded. " The climax of the film, and probably of the TV series depicted in the movie, was a Christmas party which led to a "general free-for-all. Instead of the anticipated fury of the powers that be, ... it is hailed as the tops. "

As the "silvering matinee idol" Peter Finch is a perfect Simon, while Kay Kendall "is the wildcat with enthusiasm in the 'Taming of Shrew' tradition.... Real life British radio personalities are introduced giving an emphasized authenticity. "

The Box team's next assignment was experimental in numerous ways, but happily so. Scripted by Muriel and Sydney Box, A Novel Affair (1957) was a double-header: it was a story within a story, half black-and-white, half in Technicolor, and the four principals played two roles each. Most reviews were well aware that this was something different, devoting more than usual care to explication of the storyline, and the divergence between intention and execution.

Films & Filming (April, 1957), page 27, expresses the critical consensus: "Muriel and Sydney Box have devised a delightful idea, one that might have been the great British film satire. "

The gist of the film is as follows: "A lady novelist bases a character on her virile chauffeur; he reads the book and thinks she fancies him. Feeble comedy, half of it consisting of a dramatization of the heroine's very dull novel. " In an explanation of the manner by which The Passionate Stranger, the British title, misfires, Films & Filming (April 1957), page 27, offers analysis:

> The central section of the film, which is a reconstruction
> of the novel as read by the chauffeur, Carlo, is in colour.
> After a promising start, it misses its target in almost
> every scene. Instead of being a brittle parody of some of
> the worst aspects of British literature, it settles uncom-
> fortably for a number of cliches, acted more with heart
> in hand than tongue in cheek. They are all too reminiscent
> of some recent British screen romances to be either good
> humour or good drama. When the film returns to actual-
> ity and Carlo (in black and white) sets out to woo the lady,
> the laughs come more easily.... What a disappointment
> that, having found such a good idea, Muriel Box should be
> all for caution instead of passion!

"A slightly over-protracted but still very effective narration, " according to The Illustrated London News (Feb. 23, 1957), page 312. Alan Dent in his "The World of the Cinema" column describes the sandwich form of the film.

> The fun of it is that we see the lady novelist's own story in black-and-white at the beginning and the end of the film, whereas we see her novel enacted in gorgeous colour in the middle, even as the chauffeur reads it. With a shade more of cutting, this--directed by Muriel Box--would be first-rate entertainment. It is, in any case, quite brilliantly acted. It is nearly good.

The distinctions between serious reality in black-and-white and humorous satire in colour are unclear, The Spectator (February 22, 1957), page 252 discerns:

> There is an excellent satirical idea in The Passionate Stranger, but it fails to come off.... What Muriel Box, the director, has failed to make clear, though, is where the satire begins and ends, and what she, we and the actors are meant to take seriously. It is not at all a bad story....

The Spectator favors "the old restful monochrome" to the "in-colour" segments:

> There were dreadful moments when Miss Box, having decided to guy the lending library taste in fiction ("The great house, " I quote from memory, "lay before him, expectant, like a woman waiting to be kissed") seemed to decide that there were likely to be too many of the lending library ladies among her audience for her to dismiss them as merrily as all that; and what began and ended as satire seemed almost, for some excruciating patches in the middle, to be asking us to take it straight.

Films in Review 8:9 (November 1957) 464, reports that "Its plot is little more than a protracted situation.... A Novel Affair is pleasant and gentle satire that is possibly too gentle to be fully appreciated in Britain. " Appearing to prefer the fantasy to fact, in contrast to The Spectator, Films in Review explains its reasons and, lamentably, names the director Betty Box!

> These concluding sequences lack surprise and are too drawn-out. Preston Sturges' handling of a not dissimilar situation in Unfaithfully Yours was much wittier and far superior. The trouble with A Novel Affair is that it attempts two satires: of the so-called passionate novel, and of the British conception of that form of literature. The secondary satire, a kidding of British "restraint, " is so underplayed that one might almost take much of it seriously.... Had director Betty Box been a little less subtle she could have been much funnier.

"Fluff and nonsense, " was the judgment of Newsweek 50:87
(Sept. 2, 1957). But a glowing review comes from Janet Winn of
New Republic (March 10, 1958), pages 22-23. "The film ... doesn't
overwork the object of its derision, but depends for its comic effect
on a beautiful contrivance of its own. " This is the bi-color film.
Margaret Leighton as the lady novelist whose husband Ralph Richardson is confined to a wheel-chair looks for fresh subject material for
a novel.

> The fortuitous arrival of Carlo (Carlo Justini), a handsome
> young Italian hired to act as chauffeur to the incapacitated
> Mr. Richardson, provides the novelist with her donnée ...
> she grinds out a perfectly horrible specimen of the ro-
> mantic novel, in which a lady pianist, her invalid husband,
> and a virile Italian chauffeur named Mario arrange them-
> selves in the customary flaccid triangle. We pursue this
> work in its entirety, in a technicolor dramatization.

Winn reports that this trio acts "as if they almost mean it"
Miss Leighton with heavy breathing, Mr. Richardson with a beard,
as "a cross between Clifford Chatterly and Commander Whitehead"
and Mario in a "baby-blue uniform.... The novel ... ends, with
the husband murdered and the lovers 'inextricably bound' by common guilt. "

When Carlo reads this novel he tries to duplicate its action.
"His attempt to make life conform to fiction soon brings him in for
a number of surprises. " In the novel, an auto breakdown prompts
a night at the inn for the lady and her chauffeur. In reality, when
Carlo adds sugar to the gas tank of the car, and the auto does stall
on the highway, the lady is picked up by a helpful motorist and
Carlo left to wait for the tow truck.

For Janet Winn, the film illustrates the "chief difficulty with
the cheap romance, which is its disinclination to say anything re-
motely resembling the truth. " Her last sentence: "It will take
some doing to match the achievement of A Novel Affair, or that of
the three characters who played the six principal roles. "

Philip Hartung waxes enthusiastically in Commonweal 66:570
(Sept. 6, 1957). "... By no means a great picture, but it is an
amusing one, made especially pleasant by a healthy, real-life relationship between the husband and wife. " He continues, "It holds
one's interest from beginning to end" and "a good cast and unusual
twists keep it running smoothly. " Observing that the novel acted
out in the film "is patterned rather strongly after Lady Chatterly's
Lover, " Hartung relishes the fact that it takes "quite a bit of maneu-
vering on the part of the wife to convince the passionate Italian that
the story was only a story. " And the Box team is praised. "Muriel Box, who directed ... and wrote the screenplay with her husband
Sydney, has given the film style and a slick polish. "

Bosley Crowther of the New York Times (August 28, 1957,

22:1) finds "this little bit of nonsense from Muriel and Sydney Box
is not quite as flimsy and pretentious as it may at first sound."
He defines it further as "neither novel nor much of an affair" in
which "a thin and even tedious bit of kidding is being done...."
With a nod at the "adroit performances" of the three principals,
Crowther's chief criticism is that "the interior story is so ponderous and it so completely outweighs the little black-and-white whim-
sey that surrounds it that it drags down the whole idea."

Variety 206 (March 6, 1957), page 6, seems pleased with the
film.

> There's nothing particularly new about the basic idea of a
> story within a story, but the fresh treatment in The Pas-
> sionate Stranger is good for quite a few laughs and should
> make for fair boxoffice returns ... Muriel and Sydney
> Box have collaborated on a screenplay which exploits a
> well-worn situation for favorable results.

And the "added gimmick" of a two-toned movie helps. But the "obvious failing of the script is that the earlier action is repetitious
although there's a new slant and a new meaning to it." Ditto the
climax. "Miss Box has shown a nice light touch in handling the
plot and the characters, and even in dealing with the corny situations which emerge from the novel."

Muriel Box declares that her aim was to satirize the romantic novel. The two-color technique, rosy versus realistic, she used
did involve technical perplexities that were successfully solved. Unexpectedly, another snag showed up. She knew that a portion of the
chauffeur's dialogue would have to have a fresh sound track synchronized to the actual dialogue spoken by Carlo. But Carlo could not
fit his own lip movements to what appeared on the film, even though
he made the greatest efforts to do so. Another answer to this dilemma had to be found.

Actor Robert Rietti solved it by accomplishing what Carlo
could not: he spoke dialogue with an Italian accent and timed his
lip movements perfectly. He was not credited for this task which
enlarged Carlo's prowess as an actor and the applause for his role.

The next film that Muriel Box made is her favorite. The
Truth About Women was an original script written by Sydney and
Muriel Box, with definite feminist themes humorously presented.
Intentionally, but innocuously, the female situation in various places
in the world is represented from early in the twentieth century up
to present times.

Acknowledging her leanings toward feminism, Muriel Box
salutes her reading of Virginia Woolf's A Room of One's Own as the
start of her own persuasion to become active in the struggle for
equality of the sexes. In The Truth About Women she struck a blow
for equal rights for women. The film's budget was the largest of

any she had directed, to date: £183, 000. Made in color, it
boasted 40 sets, and Cecil Beaton designed clothes for all the stars
featured in it.

Halliwell's Film Guide (page 801) notes: "Tedious charade
with neither wit nor grace. " Failing to be charmed also, was the
reviewer in the Monthly Film Bulletin 25:39 (March 1958). The
flashback storytelling plot is neatly captured:

> In an effort to help his son-in-law understand his daughter
> Diana, Humphrey Tavistock recalls his own early romantic
> and marital adventures. In Yekrut he was sentenced to
> banishment for trying to smuggle the pretty Saida from
> the Sultan's harem. In Paris he was challenged to a duel
> by the outraged husband of lovely Louise.   In America he
> was jilted by an heiress.   In London he married Helen,
> an artist who died in childbirth.   Wounded in the first
> World War, Humphrey fell in love with his nurse, Julie,
> but lost her during a complicated divorce action brought
> by her husband.   Eventually he met again his first love,
> Ambrosine, and married her.

In spite of this multi-locale narrative, the review dismisses
The Truth About Women as "Lacking real wit or polish ... an ex-
travagently upholstered charade ... dull script ... uninspired direction. "

Disagreeing, Derek Conrad in Films & Filming (April 1958),
page 23, calls it "excellently acted, beautifully photographed ... and
well directed (by Muriel Box).   Worth a visit if you want to see
Britain do something as well, if not better, than Hollywood which in
these days is rare indeed. "   Conrad ponders on the quiet release of
the film.   "No West End premiere ... no 'tub-thumping' publicity
has been accorded The Truth About Women, yet it proves to be an
above average British answer to those well made women's magazine
fiction story films that are imported from Hollywood. ... "

The New York Herald Tribune's reviewer Joe Pihodna (August
29, 1958) judges it as "Nonsense presented with a straight face. ...
Doesn't really get to the core of the matter. "

The conclusion of Newsweek 52 (September 8, 1958), page 95,
is "You can live without this one. "   The English don't know much
about love, and this comedy "tends to confirm the reputation. ...
Toothless old Harry delivers himself of that toothless old saw:
'Women--you can't live with them and you can't live without them. ' "

Philip Hartung in Commonweal 68:567 (September 5, 1958) expresses more reservation than commendation. The film, for him,

> is not meant to be taken seriously.   Beautifully produced
> by Sydney Box and nicely directed by Muriel Box (both of
> whom wrote the script) the film is a tour de force, a

series of incidents told in flashbacks by Laurence Harvey
who was a young man in the Diplomatic Corps at the turn
of the century.

However, it

> is a strange hodge-podge of a picture, sometimes quite
> amusing, sometimes cynically satirical ... somehow the
> film's makers got so entranced with Eastman Color and
> sets and costumes and the elaborate roster of stars that
> they forgot where they were going and the finished picture,
> although it is a continual delight to the eye, becomes a
> pompous bore.

In all reviews, including Howard Thompson's in the New York
Times (August 29, 1958, 18:2), the actresses in the five episodes--
Diane Cilento, Julie Harris, Mai Zetterling, Eva Gabor, and Jackie
Laine as Saida--are complimented on their performances. "Visually,
the picture is luscious. The five episodes that carry the well-born
hero from young manhood to the fireside spread out over beautifully
tinted, lavish period and modern settings." The last two segments,
involving Julie Harris and Mai Zetterling, "make the picture matter.
Perhaps the alert Boxes intended this as their aging, disillusioned
hero's reward." The opening portions, though, are "laboriously
arch"; as a whole, it is a "Sophisticated fare thee well in an erratic
but basically good-natured color package."

The caption in Variety 209 (February 12, 1958), page 18,
reads: "Overlong, uneven comedy which is often witty; star cast
should make this a reliable booking." In a warmly affirmative
article, Variety faults the film first for its need to be "written and
directed with a more frivolous and even cynical touch."

In neutral tones, Variety continues,

> Sydney Box has piled a heap of stars and top class fea-
> ture players into this comedy. The result is that 'The
> Truth About Women' should make an attractive booking for
> houses on either side of the Atlantic. It is an overlong
> and rather old-fashioned comedy which effervesces quite
> often, but is then bogged down by flat passages. More
> ruthless cutting and a tighter screenplay by Sydney and
> Muriel Box would have been an advantage. The dialog,
> too, varies from the very witty to the naive.

But, Variety predicts that the film

> will garner a lot of yocks from all types of audiences.
> There are some shrewd observations about the relationship
> between the two sexes. Femme patrons will ... appre-
> ciate the manner in which the distaff side invariably comes
> out the victors in their clashes with the star...."

The surprising response The Truth About Women received when it was first shown to movie distributors is recorded in Odd Woman Out. The undercurrent of humor did not catch their fancies. When Muriel heard that the firm for whom she'd made it, British Lion, wasn't planning to give it a sneak showing or one intended for critics, she was deeply disappointed. Her film was being dealt with unfairly. She had to defend it. She sent a message to David Kingsley, who had made the negative decision. He answered even more gloomily that there was no reason to show the film unless good criticisms were sure to be earned. This signified that the film would be released and shown to audiences without any publicity preceding it. Muriel fully anticipated that The Truth About Women would die an early death.

But this did not happen. Luckily, the film critics who had heard about the film being made got curious and wondered why it was given such unusual treatment. A cluster of critics decided to see it, and they paid for their own tickets! With the result that on the first morning after its showing, The Truth About Women had a cornucopia of first-rate reviews awarded to it.

Leonard Mosely, of the Daily Express, carolled his satisfaction. He couldn't figure out why the movie was treated so poorly by the distributors. Moaning about the need for good comedy, he points to The Truth About Women with glee. He even writes that he had to find out where it was being screened, funny and well-acted as it was, in order to write a review about it. Mosely identifies closely with the hero, who enjoys one passionate adventure with a lovely woman after another, and never appears to tire of them.

In spite of raves such as Mosely's, The Truth About Women did not do as well as Muriel hoped, and she attributes its popularity with distributors and audiences as diminished greatly because of its unjustified initial consideration.

Muriel Box next directed Subway in the Sky (1958) which, from an absence of American reviews, possibly did not cross the Atlantic. Halliwell's Film Guide (page 730) characterizes it as a "Tedious photographed play with precious few points of dramatic interest." Based on a play by Ian Main, and co-produced by Sydney Box, it dealt with a Berlin cabaret star who "finds her landlady's ex-husband, a deserter, hiding in her apartment...." He and she set out "to prove his innocence of drug-smuggling."

Starring Van Johnson and Hildegarde Neff, the film was "served rather better by its sets and photography than the subject merits." To this pronouncement, the Monthly Film Bulletin 26:36 (March 1959) adds, "Although the cast ... perform with admirable seriousness, it remains extremely difficult to accept the highly unlikely characters and events of this smooth slice of romantic melodrama...."

A larger measure of approval is cast toward Subway by Derek

Conrad in Films & Filming (April 1959), page 23: "Subway in the Sky is a British film made to appeal to the international market. It does so without resorting to the familiar catchpenny tricks of the casting of incongruous Americans or the use of American-style (but quite obviously set in England) sets." Derek Conrad disagrees with Monthly Film Bulletin as to the credibility of the principals in the story: "The main characters ... are American and German, and the setting is West Berlin. Not one false note is struck, and in a cat-and-mouse story like Subway ... this is essential." The plot is believable, too.

> American Major Van Johnson is on the run from the military police, accused of peddling Army drugs in his care to his German wife.... Arriving at his wife's flat in West Berlin, he discovers that it has been let to a night club entertainer (Hildegarde Neff). Close on his heels is Military Police Captain Carson ... Mr. Johnson, of course, ends up innocent and in a clinch with his night club chanteur [sic].

However, the settings for the film express economy instead of validity.

> I find it a great pity that the producers of this picture couldn't save up enough German Marks to afford some location shooting in the eminently filmable city of Berlin ... one can sense director Muriel Box's effort to get out of the flat without going out into the streets. However, let us be grateful to Subway ... for its entertainment value and the sheer professionalism of its players....

Derek Conrad is especially appreciative of "the dry martini charm of the delectable Miss Neff...."

The next work that Muriel Box wanted to adapt to the screen was one that invited censorship. Pick-Up Girl was a play that had been produced in London and New York shortly before 1950. The bold and raw truth of its timely story, the chronicle of a delinquent teen-aged girl unable to meet the challenges of poverty, an oppressive environment, and her own needs for nurture and sex, appealed to Muriel as frank and truthful, worthy of a wider audience. Pick-Up Girl had been viewed on television screens but Muriel believed a theatrical film would be palatable and popular with audiences. She debated the issues of venereal diseases, syphilis and gonorrhea, being mentioned in her movie script for two hours with John Trevelyan, the film censor. She finally won the debate by informing him that since both diseases were named on placards posted in public toilets why shouldn't the diseases be mentioned in her film? Trevelyan agreed, in the end.

Emerging victorious after several small skirmishes, Muriel Box directed Too Young to Love, awarded an X certificate, based on Elsa Shelley's play. Scripted by the Box team, the film is la-

beled, by Halliwell's Film Guide (page 790), a "Tepid filming of a
popular exploitation play of the fifties, mysteriously made in England. " The Monthly Film Bulletin 27:26 (February 1960) reports the
plot in detail, focused upon a fifteen-year-old prostitute brought before a Brooklyn juvenile court. "Apart from being pointlessly toned
down, Elsa Shelley's old club theatre success has been adapted to
the screen with depressingly unimaginative fidelity and an almost
total lack of cinema sense. "

    Critic Raymond Durgnat warns discriminating film-goers to
stay away in his review in Films & Filming 6:25 (April 1960).

> Teenagers take another bashing! Elizabeth is only fifteen,
> sweet, loving, but, ... her mum made her do chores ...
> she fell into loose company ... and ... "intimate rela-
> tions, " an abortion, and syphilis. But the understanding
> old Judge sorts her out with a few kind words. This low-
> budget adaptation of an outdated play seems to be slanted
> for American television, and so treats the sexsational in
> a sweetness-and-light style.... It makes almost no at-
> tempt to come to grips with reality....

    "Routine juvenile delinquency drama, with some sensitive
performances; fair prospects. " With that caption, Variety 218
(March 16, 1970), page 6, heralds "A sincere effort, but it never
moves. " It is wordy and slow, too, and Variety predicts it "will
depend largely on its sex theme for success at the boxoffice. And
it may have a struggle. " Thanks to the performance of actor Thomas Mitchell as the understanding judge, interest is maintained in the
plot, which takes the young girl into an adventure with a sailor, an
abortion, an affair with a middle-aged man, and contracting syphilis.
Heeding the advice of the judge, the young girl goes to the hospital
and later to an approved school.

    This Other Eden appears to have been a political comedy di-
rected by Muriel Box in 1959 which was not widely distributed or reviewed. From a play by Louis d'Alton and written for the screen by
Patrick Kirwan and Blanaid Irvine, the movie was hard to follow,
diluting its impact. The notice in the Monthly Film Bulletin 26:140
(October 1959) discerns that "It aims at too many satirical targets
and ... hits none. " In Ireland, a British colonel's bastard is
blamed when a church student destroys a statue on learning that his
father led the I.R.A. This sentence ropes in an otherwise tangled
and twisted narrative acted by the Abbey Players, who were "forced
to oscillate between seriousness and humour. " The "poor script"
introduces several issues but doesn't probe them: "Irish hatred of
the English, anti-Catholicism, newspaper morality; glorification of
the I.R.A...."

    In 1959, at age 52, Sydney Box collapsed. Muriel Box fore-
saw his breakdown, as the notation in her diary dated July 26, 1959,
observes. She writes that she is concerned about the long hours Sydney regularly works, including the evenings dining with business col-

leagues. He is working too intensely without adequate rest, but apparently is happy doing so. Making films is the core of his existence, but not hers. To make movies just for the sake of making movies is not that satisfying a career. Other choices remain.

On Saturday, August 22, 1959, Muriel records that Sydney flew to New York on business. Shortly after his return, he had to fly to Newcastle for a meeting. She cannot comment on or restrain Sydney's hectic pace without irritating him, so she pursues silence as the wisest course. But keeping quiet takes its toll of her, too.

After his breakdown, Sydney Box was ordered to refrain from working for a year, perhaps longer. He assigned his workload to Peter Rogers, his brother-in-law. Then the Box team moved to Spain, and the south of France. While Sydney rested and tried to recover, Muriel directed a film for the Children's Film Foundation, titled The Piper's Tune (1961). It is listed in the British National Film Catalogue as a period film about children "fleeing from Napoleon's army" who are "betrayed by spy posing as doctor. "

The constraints under which Muriel made this film were horrendous. On a budget of £22, 000 she had to direct a very large cast on location in the mountains and finish in five weeks. Filming in North Wales, Muriel gives herself well-deserved self-praise by stating that she spent her fifty-sixth birthday climbing a mountain twice, a very exhausting exercise.

About this fine young people's film, the Monthly Film Bulletin 29 (March 1962), pages 40-41, reports:

> The escape route of refugees from Napoleon's armies lies across mountain country, starting from a farm owned by Martinez. A band of escaping children are held captive by a French platoon while a traitor poses as a doctor to discover the secret route. He joins them on their breakout journey, but is shot by soldiers. Even though the children know he is a spy, they save his life before leading the soldiers into an ambush and rejoining their parents. Invigorating, suspenseful and jumping with action, this is a straightforward contribution to the children's market by A. C. T. Films and director Muriel Box for the C. F. F. Though the thin plot could have done with more carefully rounded characterisation ... the adventure is quite believable, and exciting where the children are concerned....

Rattle of a Simple Man (1964) was the last feature film Muriel Box directed. Halliwell's Film Guide (page 718) does not praise it. "Archetypal farcical situation with sentiment added to string it out to twice its proper length. Production values modest but adequate. " With the screenplay by Charles Dyer, who adapted it from his stage play, the plot is slight but attempts to define conditions of sincerity and integrity in what is a two-character encounter.

The plot is given in the British National Film Catalogue (page 120):

> Percy Winthram comes to London from Manchester for the Cup Final. After the game he and his companions end the evening in a Soho strip club. Percy is innocent, shy and embarrassed. Ginger bets he won't take a blonde home and sleep with her. Percy, after an agonized moment, accepts the blonde, who has overheard the bet, accepts too but when they get home Percy's courage fails him. Cyrenne is sympathetic and tells him of her aristocratic background. Impressed, he boasts of his conquests and their mutual trust and liking grows. The illusions are shattered by the intervention of Cyrenne's family and Percy leaves having lost his bet. Unable to bear losing her he stops the departing coach and hurries back with the excuse of getting his rattle....

The Monthly Film Bulletin 31:151 (October 1964) adds more particulars to the plot, and compares the stage to the screenplay. Returning to Cyrenne's flat, Percy is

> abashed by her matter-of-fact advances.... They have a cup of tea ... open their hearts to each other. Percy begins to overcome his timidity, while Cyrenne is delighted to meet a man who treats her with respect. They make urgent plans to spend a week's holiday together, with a view to marriage if all goes well. A slight hitch occurs when Percy catches a glimpse of Cyrenne's sordid, cafe-owning Italian family....

Percy tries to leave, but can't. "Haunted by the memory of Cyrenne, ... he stops the coach and hurries back to her."

MFB views the merits of the stage play as a "two-hander" in which "the humour almost counterbalanced the sentimentality." But in the film "everything has been conventionally opened out and coarsened." Cyrenne's family members are "pure melodrama; and the whole atmosphere of London sin is fetchingly ludicrous." Diane Cilento, as Cyrenne, "almost achieves the impossible in creating a character out of nothing."

The review in The Tablet (September 12, 1964), page 1035, considers "its major premise is unacceptable, but there is all the same real compassion and understanding in this story...." Deeming the two principals "damaged creatures" the review faults director Muriel Box for a lack of ruthlessness because the film is overextended and the happy end lacks conviction.

John Cutts in Films in Review 11:29 (Nov. 1964) aims cutting observations at the film. Cutts is bored by the cosy chat between a "regional" and a "swish-looking bird ... who play noughts and crosses, feed pigeons, drink endless cups of tea and gradually re-

veal that neither is quite the person the other took them to be.
"What can--or rather, what does one say about a gummy piece of
contrivance like this? ... an indifferently made, laboriously played
and crudely written piece of caricature. Remarkable perhaps only
for its all-round ineptitude. "

Opposed to this view, is the charitable commentary from
Commonweal 81:519 (January 15, 1965). The prostitute as acted by
Diane Cilento "with an air of sophistication, ... is rather incred-
ible.... " The film's close

> suggests that these two quite different people might be
> good for each other and may even be able to help each
> other. Muriel Box has directed her characters well, but
> Rattle, in spite of its occasional poignant moments, has
> to be chalked up as just another fanciful movie about a
> prostitute with a heart of tarnished gold.

Robert Hatch trains his critical eye on Rattle of a Simple
Man in his Films column in Nation 200:67 (January 18, 1965), and
comes up with the film's warmest praise:

> A small British picture, made with modest amounts of wit
> and slapstick, on one of the most indestructible formulas
> of popular entertainment--the slow dance to consummation
> of a virginal bumpkin and a good-hearted whore.... There
> is not a believable moment in it, and it has been roasted
> in the press. But I thought its performance beguiling and
> its absurdities sufficiently ingenious to make a pleasant
> show.

For Time 85:54 (January 8, 1965) the focus of the film is
Harry Corbett, who is

> entirely believable as a Lancashire bloke of almost in-
> vincible rectitude. For 39 years he has been a virgin,
> and that is the crux of this lacklusty comedy.... The
> boob and the bawd ... meet, maunder, ... and slowly un-
> cover their loneliness. Actress Cilento [is] strikingly mis-
> cast.... Worst still, added scenes and nonessential char-
> acters only give the viewers time to think dark thoughts
> ....

In the two years between films The Piper's Tune and Rattle,
the Box team enjoyed a round the world cruise, with stops at Australia, Honolulu, San Francisco, and New York. Sydney continued
recuperating from his collapse. Muriel was in mourning for her
mother. Still, the Box team even while traveling devoted their morn-
ings to writing. In the afternoons they took tours and viewed their
host area's places of interest and significance.

Arriving home, Muriel had the first draft of a novel, The
Big Switch, which was published in 1964. It was hailed with warm

excitement by the Sunday Express reviewer who described it as full of laughs spawned by the comic consideration of the state of the world if ruled primarily by women.

Sadly, the enthusiasms and interests of the Box team began to separate on their return home from their cruise. Sydney returned to work, busier than ever in television, the theatre, and films. He was employed as an agent, he managed a farm, he directed a television firm.

Muriel became active in the Campaign for Nuclear Disarmament. Turning from films, the Box team had written a play titled Stranger in My Bed, which Muriel directed and produced. Confronting this divergence in their activities, Muriel and Sydney discussed divorce. Sydney was not at all concerned about obtaining one, while Muriel hoped a reunion would be possible, and a return to their former sharing of creative and commercial enterprises.

When Sydney departed for Hollywood and Australia, Muriel established Femina Books, a publishing house. She was managing director. Vera Brittain, Anona Winn, and Anne Edwards served as directors immediately faced with the task of getting publishable manuscripts. The Board solved this issue by writing themselves. Vera Brittain began a book on author Radclyffe Hall. And Muriel wrote the first book published by Femina Books, a biography of Marie Stopes, the feminist pioneer whose life Muriel had wanted to portray on film but found impossible to do so.

Subsequent to several years' of singlehood, Muriel Box was issued her final divorce decree from Sydney Box in 1969. On August 28, 1970 she was married to a Lord Chancellor, Sir Gerald Gardiner, becoming Lady Gardiner.

A brief observation tallies the decade of the seventies as regards Muriel and Betty Box. Editor F. Maurice Speed in Film Reviews 1978/79 (London: W. H. Allen, 1978), page 98, ponders: "Although Mrs. Box has proven herself to be one of Britain's top screenwriters and directors, her talents have been ignored in recent years. Her sister-in-law, Betty Box, has not directed anything, but was producer on a number of films."

While the Box team is no longer active in filmmaking they are pursuing related activities. Sydney, residing in Perth, Australia, has had several books published. Among them are Diary of a Drop-Out (1969), Alibi in the Rough (1977), and Second Only to Murder (1978). Muriel continues in her publishing venture, while Betty continues producing movies in England.

Focusing on Sydney and Muriel, what contributions did they make to popular culture? What does their roster of thirty-plus feature films add up to? Can a judgment be made?

The Motion Picture Almanac listed Muriel and Sydney Box un-

til the 1972 annual; their names are no longer listed in it.   Charles
Ford merits Muriel Box for serving many apprenticeships and master-
ing all tasks in cinematic creation.   In his Femmes cinéastes (Paris:
Denoël-Gonthier, 1972, page 97), he comments on the values of the
Box films shown in France (many of them were not).   In his overall
favorable criticisms, he indexes humor in all its guises as a trademark, mentioning the wit in Street Corner, the bright gaiety of The
Beachcomber, the guffaws and underlying tier of forced pretension
in Simon and Laura.   Subway in the Sky, Ford notes, was a film
with no exterior locations, all action being confined to the theatre
serving as a displaced persons center.   Box proved her competence
as a director in handling this film with its wide range of characters.

        The British Film Guide (1979) gives this mildly deprecating
resume of Muriel Box's career:

> One of only two women directors regularly employed in
> British features ... sister-in-law of our only woman pro-
> ducer, Betty Box.   Her own films are for the most part
> "women's pictures"--a mild account of adventures in the
> women's police force, a series of comedies such as The
> Passionate Stranger and The Truth About Women.   They
> are part of the magazine fiction of the screen--and no less
> competently organised than most magazine fiction....

        Not one of Muriel Box's films is mentioned in Ivan Butler's
Cinema in Britain: an illustrated survey (New York: A. S. Barnes,
1973).

        In the first issue of Movie, a periodical that first appeared
in May, 1962, was a chart compiled to summarize the magazine's
board of directors' taste in film directors.   This chart can be read
on an unnumbered front page of Movie Reader, edited by Ian Cameron
(New York: Praeger, 1972).   It places British and American film
directors into these categories: Great; Brilliant; Very Talented;
Talented; Competent or Ambitious, and the rest.   This bottom group
includes Muriel Box, among the rest.

        An unbiased view of the Box team's efforts is now called for.
From 1939 to 1964 Muriel and Sydney collaborated in making films.
Betty Box joined them later and is still working.   If the three Boxes
were not inspired, they were industrious, organized, committed.
Sydney rescued the faltering English film industry in 1945 by putting
it on a productive and profitable basis.   He set up a veritable moviemaking assembly-line, met budget and time limits, introduced novel
methods of financing film production.   With one hand he joined Muriel in plotting film scripts; with the other hand assisting Betty to
implement his techniques and concepts to improve the product while
mass-producing it.   Betty added her own talents to effecting the
efficiencies and technical improvements recommended by Sydney,
producing a roster of good films on her own.   Muriel managed to
write and/or direct at least three dozen movies, assisting in several
for which she got no credit.   All three improvised and improved this

mass production type of film factory, in which a staff of reliables
and quality-conscious technicians and artists labored in what appears
to have been a consistent and committed manner.

Chipping away at this contribution of historical magnitude are
the words of film reviewers discounting the products. Predictable,
flat, imitative, too topical, formularized, banal, derivative, second-
rate, froth, tosh, nonsense.

Lacking originality? True. Most Box movies were adapta-
tions. Imitative? Probably. Box films do remind one of others
similar in the same time frame. Easy Money in four parts recalls
Quartet. The Seventh Veil echoes Spellbound, and other "psychic"
movies after World War II. The family saga of the Huggetts spawn-
ing a series successful at the box office fits the pattern of the Hardy
family series in the United States. If the Boxes chose headline
topics to plot their films--examples are Mr. Lord Says No! and
Too Young to Love--they did so with the knowledge that the filmgoer was familiar with their subject material, and would empathize
with it.

Innovative? Yes. The Boxes learned to use Technicolor,
the Independent Frame technique, the definitive use of classical and
semi-classical music played by symphonic musicians as background
for films. Muriel's feminist considerations were implemented whenever possible. For economy's sake, the Box team worked with
young writers and artists, springboarding successful careers in
abundance.

The Box team excelled at producing mass entertainment movies
at a profit. That was their goal, their achievement. They produced
entertainments. Not great epics, or expensive extravaganzas, exercises in directorial style, or esoteric studies, or quality classics.
The Box team knew everything there was to know about making
movies. They were, for three decades, competent, committed
craftspersons succeeding admirably in reaching their goal: to make
affordable movies to entertain an international audience. A distinctive feat.

In the Monthly Film Bulletin the Box team feature films were
listed as entertainments; the other classes of films being educational
films, shorts, and documentary and interest shorts. The Box
team's entertainments fall neatly into niches labelled nonsense comedies, war-based dramas, historical films, crime pictures, and
melodramas.

The nonsense comedies are Simon and Laura, Mr. Lord Says
No!, Here Come the Huggetts, Facts of Love, To Dorothy a Son,
Holiday Camp, and A Novel Affair. The war-based dramas are
The Girl in the Painting, Subway in the Sky, The Lost People, and
The Years Between. The historical films are Christopher Columbus,
The Piper's Tune, The Smugglers, The Brothers, and This Other
Eden. The crime pictures are Street Corner, Dear Murderer, Day-

break, The Blind Goddess, Too Young to Love, Alibi Inn, Good Time
Girl, and Eyewitness.   The melodramas are Rattle of a Simple Man,
The Truth About Women, Easy Money, A Girl in a Million, The
Beachcomber, and The Seventh Veil.

What was the Box team's best film? Probably the one viewers remember warmly and want to see again, the unforgettable The
Seventh Veil. Although melodramatic, it rises to a niche of its own
above the arch and artful comedy of Simon and Laura, the triumphant
female insights of The Truth About Women, the feminist-oriented
Street Corner, the cozy clichés of Here Come the Huggetts.

More experienced as a screenwriter than as a director, Muriel Box excelled in bringing these conventional movies of several types
to mass audiences. Her films were faulted for overuse of the flashback technique, cliché situations, nonsense for its own sake, excessive length, flatness; they were too topical, too predictable, not
original, too cheaply made and showing it!

But these deficiencies tend to evaporate when a comprehensive
view of her filmography is taken. The number of movies she con-
tributed to plus those she co-wrote, produced and directed is amazing, and probably unmatched by any other woman filmmaker. The
sheer volume of films turned out by the Box team excuses their
deficiencies.

Muriel Box has not written a text on filmmaking techniques
nor her credo on the mystique of making movies. She worked in
films as a practical craftswoman placed under severe restrictions of
time and money. The virtues she brought to her films were her insights into human nature, ironic and tragic, realized visually, her
pervasive senses of humor and justice, her ear for the music needed
as background on the soundtrack, and for the rhythm and voices
needed for appropriate dialogue. With no apology, she made films
to please and amuse, not to edify or preach a message. She built
lagniappe into her plots: something extra--startling or funny or
nice--for the moviegoer to remember, to talk about with a snort or
a smile. There is comic relief in Muriel Box's crime pictures and
somber scenes of revelation in her comedies. Her shrewd judgment
of the public's interests, and her service of those interests in film
form, places her into a position without rivals. Muriel Box was an
entertainer, a prolific maker of movies as entertainments.

FILMOGRAPHY

Screenwriter:

Alibi Inn (1935)

The Facts of Love (1945)

The Seventh Veil (1945)

The Years Between (1947)
Here Come the Huggetts (1948)
Holiday Camp (1948)
The Smugglers (1948)
The Brothers (1948)
Dear Murderer (1948)
Easy Money (1949)
The Blind Goddess (1949)
Daybreak (1949)
The Girl in the Painting (1949)
Christopher Columbus (1949)
A Girl in a Million (1950)
Good Time Girl (1950)
The Lost People (1950)
Mr. Lord Says No! (1952)
Both Sides of the Law (1954)
A Novel Affair (1957)
The Truth About Women (1958)

Producer:

The Smugglers (1948)
Dear Murderer (1948)
The Brothers (1948)
A Girl in a Million (1950)
The Truth About Women (1958)

Director:

Mr. Lord Says No! (1952)
A Prince for Cynthia (1953)
Both Sides of the Law (1954)
The Beachcomber (1955)
Simon and Laura (1956)
Cash on Delivery (1956)
Eyewitness (1956)
A Novel Affair (1957)

The Truth About Women (1958)

This Other Eden (1959)

Subway in the Sky (1959)

Too Young to Love (1960)

The Piper's Tune (1962)

Rattle of a Simple Man (1964)

NOTES

1. Muriel Box, Odd Woman Out.   London: Leslie Frewin, 1974,
    p. 162.
2. Ibid., p. 47.
3. Ibid., p. 80.
4. Ibid., p. 187.
5. Ibid.
6. Ibid., p. 171.
7. Ibid., p. 174.
8. James Agate, Around Cinemas (second series).   London:
    Home & Van Thral, Ltd., 1948, pp. 267-269.
9. Time, 46:27 (Dec. 31, 1945), p. 90.
10. Ibid.
11. Box, p. 74.
12. Ibid.
13. The Seventh Veil [play].   Boston: Baker, 1952.
14. Box, pp. 182-183.
15. Ibid.
16. Roy Arnes, A Critical History of British Cinema.   New York:
    Oxford University Press, 1978, p. 170.
17. Patrick Gibbs, "Sydney Box and the Problem of Production,"
    World Review (January 1948), p. 56.
18. Ibid.
19. Ibid., p. 59.
20. Leslie Halliwell, Halliwell's Film Guide (second edition).
    New York: Scribner's, 1979, p. 478.
21. Monthly Film Bulletin 15:72 (June 1948), p. 73.
22. James Agee, Agee on Film.   New York: McDowell & Obolen-
    sky, 1958, p. 302.
23. No date cited.
24. Robert Herring, "Reflections on the Post-War British Cinema,"
    Life & Letters 53 (April-June 1947), p. 217 and 219.
25. Agee, p. 306.
26. Variety 166 (May 14, 1947), p. 15.
27. The British Film Annual (1949), p. 40.
28. Ibid.
29. Ibid.
30. Halliwell, p. 82.
31. Monthly Film Bulletin 19 (May 1952), p. 65.
32. Ibid.
33. Raymond Durgnat, A Mirror for England.   London: Faber &
    Faber, 1970, pp. 181-182.

7. MAYA DEREN: DELICATE MAGICIAN OF FILM

Born: 1917, Kiev, Russia
Died: October 13, 1961, New York City

> "The form proper of film is, for me, accomplished only
> when the elements, whatever their original context, are
> related according to the special character of the instru-
> ment of film itself--the camera and the editing--so that
> the reality that emerges is a new one--one which only film
> can achieve and which could not be accomplished by the
> exercise of any other instrument. " [Jeanne Betancourt
> Women in Focus. Dayton, Ohio: Pflaum, 1974, page 114.]

A most lucid introduction to the films of Maya Deren is Parker
Tyler's "Experimental Film: A New Growth, " in Kenyon Review
11:1 (1949). "The films of the newest and best American experimenter, Maya Deren, maintain an original orthodoxy of soundlessness, puristically lacking even musical background and without subtitles. ... " Tyler explains that films such as Deren's were shown
by "a new film society, Cinema 16, at 59 Park Avenue, New York,
with enrollment open by subscription. " The purpose of Cinema 16
was "to further the appreciation of the motion picture as an art and
as a social force by the exhibition, promotion, and production of
documentary and experimental film. "

On page 143, Tyler expands his evaluation of this "newest
and best American experimenter. "

> Creatively outstanding are the visual poems of Maya Deren,
> very personal and subjective--symbolic in scope but with
> a lively sense of film vision; she thinks in the cinematic
> medium. Her work is imperfect but in the best sense
> "experimental, " showing least trace of the inept and de-
> graded borrowings of other creative experimenters from
> the classic Surrealist films. Yet it is instructive to con-
> sider that even her work betrays the presence of the ex-
> perimental film "cliche, " originally situated in the visions
> of Cocteau and Dali.

Tested by time, Tyler's capsule of criticism retains the truth
of Deren's monumental achievement. Her numerous speaking en-
gagements on campuses and with fraternal and art organizations took
her all over the United States. She published two books and more
than two hundred articles explicating her theories of the nature and

grammar of film.   She established a nutritive climate and a national audience for the personal poetic statement type of movie she espoused, primarily by initiating a distribution network for exhibiting the type of films she made herself.

Sheldon Renan called her the Mother of the Underground Film. Regina Cornwell's appellative term, shared with filmmaker Germaine Dulac, is "activist of the avant-garde. "[1]   To Anaïs Nin, Deren's friend, she was a "symbolist. "   In Nin's judgment, Deren was certainly influenced by Cocteau, although Deren rejected the interpretation of her films via symbols.   To subtract Deren's films and related contributions to the grammar of film would be to erase huge chunks of the history and attainments of the independent American film.

Deren was the daughter, and one guesses the only child, of a Russian psychiatrist who emigrated in 1922 from Kiev, Russia, Deren's birth city, to Syracuse, New York.   Her father, Solomon Deren, was employed by the State Institute for the Feeble Minded, in Syracuse, and later became its director.   Deren was schooled first in Switzerland, at the League of Nations School in Geneva, then attended the University of Syracuse to study journalism.   She married and moved to New York City.   After obtaining a B. A. from New York University, she was divorced.   Later, she earned an M. A. from Smith College, writing her thesis on French symbolist poetry.   From the time that she moved to New York, she had written poetry.   Once her formal education was completed, she became intrigued with modern dance and wanted to write a book about it. In want of a practitioner and collaborator, Deren approached Katharine Dunham and outlined her proposal.   Dunham became interested to the degree that Deren toured with Dunham's Dance Group in the period 1940-41, somewhat in the capacity of a secretary.   The plan to co-author the book was abandoned.

Deren's integration with the Dunham group, which performed to music of the Caribbean islands, prompted her to study Haitian voodoo and to record Haitian music.   The song, dance, and ritual of Haiti coalesced into Deren's book The Divine Horsemen; the living gods of Haiti (New York: Longmans, 1953), a study of voodooism. Deren's obituary in The New York Times 23:4 (October 14, 1961) records that she studied in Haiti upon being awarded a Guggenheim Fellowship for creative work in motion pictures in 1946.

The juncture at which Deren became interested in film is not documented.   She may have turned from poetry and prose to film before or at the time Katharine Dunham introduced Deren to Alexander Hackenschmied when the Dance Group was in Los Angeles.   They were married in 1942.

Hackenschmied was an experienced filmmaker.   With him as mentor and guide, Deren discovered the art form most congenial to her abilities and temperament.   Her own poetic efforts left her dissatisfied.   Her forays into modern dance detoured into her study of

Haitian voodoo. "Maya was frustrated because her mind worked in images, which she ~~would then translate into words. Once she took up the camera there was no more need to translate. The medium was direct.~~ It was through her relationship with Alexander Hammid that she recognized how suitable film was to her artistic and moral intentions...."[2]

Hackenschmied changed his name, spurred by his wife, to Hammid at the close of World War II. He was working on an assignment in Hollywood when he met Deren and was considered a highly reputable filmmaker associated with the U.S. Office of War Information. Deren's senior by ten years, he had been born in Prague, Czechoslovakia, where he was known for his films The Earth Sings (1933), Crisis (1938), Lights Out in Europe (1939), and Forgotten Village (1941). He made two films in the war years that were widely distributed and praised: Valley of the Tennessee (1944), and Toscanini: Hymn of the Nations (1945).

In 1943, apparently without her husband's assistance, Deren tried to make a movie titled Witch's Candle with Surrealist painters Matta and Duchamp. The trio intended to adapt "the Surrealist aesthetic into a film promoting open defiance of normal time and space relationships...."[3] The project was never completed.

With Hammid, in that year of 1943, Deren reached the goal she had set for the abandoned Witch's Candle, achieving it with distinction in Meshes of the Afternoon. "Deren's philosophy of film emphasized 'film poetry' rather than 'film prose,' which was to her analagous [sic] to a stage play and developed horizontally." Consequently, says Parker Tyler, "we see that there is the magical ... built in the vertical dimensions of dream to become complicated metaphors ... an ideogram, or word structured by an aggregate of images ... literally ... picture language...."[4]

Meshes was completed in eighteen days at the Hammid-Deren home in Los Angeles. They used their own 16mm equipment, outlining the action and deciding techniques for filming as they progressed with no script and no actors but themselves. From its premiere to the present time, Meshes (1943) remains a milestone in the chronology of the independent film in the United States.

David Curtis, in Experimental Cinema (New York: Universe Books, 1971, page 135), summarizes Deren's acting in Meshes: "In it she plays a girl who is finally driven to suicide by her obsessive subconscious reaction to a number of half-dreamed incidents. A knife, first seen lying on a table, repeatedly confronts her until she allows herself to 'submit' and be killed by it." Curtis contrasts the severing of the time-space unity while maintaining action continuity in Meshes with the effect of Surrealism:

> The film is close to the French Surrealist genre, but Deren replaces the deliberately arbitrary treatment of time and location ... with a ... calculated technique.

She likes, for example, to show the true proportions of
a room, then to stretch a person's movement across it
by the use of slow motion and repeat shots subtly disguised
in the editing. By establishing a continuity of camera
movement she achieves a double shock from an unexpected
move between one location and another. . . .

For Sharon Smith, Meshes portrays two realities: ". . . contrasts imaginative and objective reality. At the beginning of the film
the division between the two seems clear enough. A woman is sitting
in a chair, walking upstairs, listening to a record player. But since
ordinary and extraordinary events are intercut dispassionately, imagination has become reality by the end of the film. . . . "5 Apparently,
then, not only are the co-ordinates of time-space-action upset but
exterior and interior are mingled, fragmenting, uniting.

As listed in Bonnie Dawson's Women's Films in Print (p. 30),
the black and white, silent Meshes is ". . . Noted for its imagery
and symbolism, preoccupation with the unconscious, and shifting
transitions between dream, nightmare, and reality. . . . "

Deren's own conception of Meshes is quoted in Sadoul's Dictionary of Films (Berkeley: University of California Press, 1972, p.
217):

"This first film is concerned with the relationship between
the imaginative and objective reality. The film begins in
actuality and, eventually, ends there. But in the meantime
the imagination, here given as a dream, intervenes. It
seizes upon a casual incident and, elaborating it into
critical proportions, thrusts back into reality the product
of its convolutions. The protagonist does not suffer some
subjective delusion of which the world outside remains independent, if not obvious; on the contrary, she is, in
actuality, destroyed by an imaginative action. "

In Sadoul's own perception, ". . . this is one of the seminal
films of the American experimental cinema. . . . " He couples Meshes
with At Land, Deren's next film. The technique by which Deren-
Hammid annihilated space and time and captured a chaotic, order-
less dream-trance topography is outlined by Betancourt:

Among the qualities of dreams recognized by all of us is
lack of coherent, continuous space. Through editing, the
movie camera can follow a step that originates in one
locus by its fall in a completely different geography.
When the persona of the film is walking, knife in hand, to
murder herself, she starts on the beach; her foot falls in
the grass; again it falls in a different grassy area; then
onto a sidewalk; and finally, onto a carpet. This rendering of dream space, through cinema, is quickly recognized.
But to Maya it is more than that. It also indicates the aspect of universal ritual that is inherent in all her works
. . . . 6

This ritual establishes continuity and the expected in a limbo-like land of the unknown and sudden change without transition. In this <u>Meshes</u> landscape,

> running gets you nowhere. . . . Maya approaches the stair-
> case within the house. She climbs in slow motion, as we
> watch in close-up from below. Then, from middle stair-
> case, we see her climb farther, coming up in slow motion.
> Earlier she was running. . . . She gained no distance . . .
> even though she ran. . . . The stairs also serve to demon-
> strate the dream-fall, where you catch yourself just in
> time. Here Maya starts to fall back, back, backward
> through the window only to catch herself on an interior
> stair. . . . 7

Betancourt indicates how closely Deren's film devices are re-lated to her intentions. The combining of realities is done by fusing a human eye (Deren's) and a mechanical eye (camera's).

> . . . there is a close-up of her eye. The eye starts to
> close. Cut to a long-shot view that she sees out the win-
> dow from the chair. This scene darkens as though a filter
> or mesh curtain is falling over it. Now we see the eye
> closed. Then back to the filtered view which zooms out
> to include a cylinder that leads as a tunnel, the tunnel of
> a telescopic lens. The draped figure enters from the
> right into the long-irised shot. The cylinder, so clearly
> a camera part, relates directly to the fact that this in-
> terior vision, this view of her dream, is possible only
> through the strategies of the movie camera. This eye-
> camera metaphor is later elaborated. . . . 8

An analysis of the camerawork in this extraordinary portion of <u>Meshes</u> details further.

> . . . the camera withdraws through a cylindrical tube, as
> if entering through the woman's pupil into the recesses of
> her mind. In the dream the space becomes quite differ-
> ent and so, too, do the woman's movements and the move-
> ments of the camera. Space is no longer continuous; ac-
> tions begun in the interior continue in the exterior. At
> one point, when the woman smashes the mirror, exterior
> and interior appear simultaneously. The compositions
> within the frame become unstable, the patterns fragmented
> and jagged. The camera repeatedly adopts odd angles of
> vision and sometimes tilts abruptly and rocks from side
> to side. There are no more long, continuous pans. The
> woman's movements are stylized, while normal speed and
> continuity are abandoned and gravity is ignored. . . . 9

A reading of the discursive and analytical articles about <u>Meshes</u> renders the impression that as eye-engaging as the film must be in the viewing, that four portions of it emerge for the film stu-

dent.   These are the camera-eye metaphor, Deren ascending and
descending the stair, the feet traversing diverse terrains in a fluid
unbroken gait, and a fourth, which is most memorable of the four:
Deren herself

> ... looking through the window ..., suddenly appearing,
> almost immediately vanishing, is one of the most haunting and
> most frequently reproduced images in the film, not so
> much, one suspects, because of its significance to the film
> as a whole, but because its sensuous appeal endows it with
> a separate existence, as if it were a still photograph in-
> serted to provide a moment of clear and crystalline plea-
> sure in a context of mystery and horror. Of course, the
> film as a whole is remarkable for its involvement with the
> senses, and this shot, which juxtaposes the unreality of
> reflection with the reality of flesh and allows the eye to
> search while the body is confined, might well serve as a
> symbol for some of the basic themes of the film, a photo-
> graphic icon meant to imply more than it states. ... [10]

This extensive study of Meshes in Lincoln F. Johnson's Film:
Space, Time, Light, and Sound (New York: Holt, Rinehart and Winston, 1974), extends to the use of the swish-pan camera movement
and the soundtrack.   The camera is used adroitly to "describe" the
house interior.

> ... The long, slow pan across the living room to the din-
> ing room stresses continuity of space, a pushoff to black
> serving to mask the splice necessitated by a shift in cam-
> era position as the pan reaches the dining room.   A
> swish pan from the knife to the telephone accomplishes
> the same purpose as the camera reverses its direction
> and quickens the pace to conform to the stride of the wom-
> an approaching the stairs.   Each space ... is thus linked
> to the next by the movement of the camera. ... [11]

In the soundtrack for Meshes, Johnson finds an aural parallel
supremely well suited to the mood of the film.   As he defines it,
"... parallel sound imitates, reinforces, or intensifies the visual or
dramatic content and the formal rhythms of a film. ... "[12] Composed
by Teiji Ito (who was to become Deren's second (according to Sharon
Smith) or third (according to The New York Times) husband, "... its
reedy half-tones and its wooden percussion, parallels the mood of
eerie mystery and reinforces the climactic moments.   Though its
long-drawn-out notes and sharp rappings often contrast with the
rhythm of action and cutting, they augment the sense of disorienta-
tion. ... "[13]

While Meshes was imitated widely, none of its prototypes
could equal or surpass its intricately woven structure and the depth
of its mood, Johnson states.   The manipulation of space and movement to shape a visually perceived dream and to elicit feelings of
anxiety and uncertainty is superbly done, the film as an entity mark-

ing a significant stride forward in the personal, small-scale documentary film.

Although Deren persistently claimed she was not influenced by any school of artistic thought and that her films were self-inspired and without mentor or model, a challenging diptych is drawn between Meshes and a little-known film 1 A. M. by Charlie Chaplin. "... Meshes finds its most immediate formal affinities with the European cinema of the 1920's, and, more specifically--as P. Adams Sitney determines in 'The Idea of Morphology' (Film Culture, Spring 1972)--with Dali's and Buñuel's surrealist film Un Chien Andalou...."[14] Sitney finds the design and mood of the Buñuel film very like Deren's Meshes: both are steeped in sexual turbulence subtly masked, both are amalgams of poetic self-analysis, the absurd and the sorrowful; with technical improvisation creating swift changes and cautious continuities. Meshes, Sitney discerns, stems from a European film type known as the trance which is "characterized by 'a somnambulistic character, a somnambulistic hero wandering through an imposing landscape....' "

While admitting that Meshes is derived from, or is itself, a trance film, Ronald Tuch in "Chaplin and the American Avant Garde" in Film Library Quarterly 7:2 (1974), on page 18 aligns "formal affinities" in the Chaplin and Deren films. The Chaplin film 1 A. M. "contains a wide range of formal characteristics which influence Meshes...." Tuch considers Dadaism and surrealism both the ancestral grounds from which Chaplin, Buñuel and Deren derived 1 A. M., Un Chien Andalou, and Meshes, respectively. Tuch lists five similarities between the Chaplin and Deren films. The titles suggest a specific time. In both, the trance state motivates the characters. Chaplin and Deren "choreographed" their films. Both films are one-person performances, containing no straightforward flow of action. Tuch ponders: "It is possible to read 1 A. M. as a primitive film upon which Deren imposes the more involved motifs of ellipses and erotic symbols...." A broader correspondence in the two films lies in the realization that in them Chaplin and Deren confront an environment which they have set up for themselves.

P. Adams Sitney brings the profoundest and most detailed examination of Deren's films to the reader in his Visionary Film; the American avant-garde, 2nd edition (New York: Oxford University Press, 1979). Sitney aligns the Deren-Hammid alliance producing Meshes in 1943 very like the team of Salvador Dali and Luis Buñuel making Un Chien Andalou in 1928. Numerous additional similarities exist in the two films. In Un Chien, images were merged that held no logical connection, hence no story continuity resulted. Instead, a dream-like reality with irrational changes and sudden alterations without cause was achieved--exactly the effect Dali-Buñuel sought. In Buñuel's own reflections on Un Chien, he wrote: "NOTHING, in the film, SYMBOLIZES ANYTHING. "[15]

In its famous opening sequence, Un Chien shows Buñuel, as actor, slicing a girl's eye with a straight razor. While sharpening

the razor, he looks up to see a frill of cloud about to cross the
moon. As he starts to slice, the cloud frill cuts across the circular moon. In this metaphor of horror, the camera next views the
razor completing the cut, and the contents of the eyeball spilling out.

Sitney compares this sliced eyeball sequence in Un Chien to
one of Deren's eye and a window. The fundamental action in Meshes,
Sitney asserts, happens when Deren is seated in an armchair and
"slowly caresses herself as a shot of her eye and the window are
intercut until they are both clouded over. " In this first portion of
Meshes, Sitney discerns that the audience sees exactly what the protagonist (Deren) herself sees. No full-figure shots are used. In
the entire start of Meshes, Sitney sees a clear-cut formula for the
idea of first person in cinema. Later, third person is used.

In the second sequence of Meshes, a dark figure with a mirror face, walks in the same direction the young woman had walked
in the first sequence. The young woman runs after it, but cannot
reach it. Defeated, she enters the house without a key. We see
her face for the first time. She sees a knife where the phone had
been, on the stairs. She ascends the stairs in slow motion.
Gradually she falls through a drapery of black gauze into the bedroom. Pulling aside the bedcovers, she sees the knife there. She
leaves, stepping backward through the gauze. Downstairs, the woman sees herself sleeping in the chair. She turns off the record-
player, approaching the window again through which she sees a third
Maya Deren pursuing the dark figure outside. The third Maya takes
a key from her mouth, enters the house. Inside, she sees the dark
figure going upstairs where it vanishes after placing the flower on
the bed, where the knife is visible. Next we see the girl, still
sleeping in the chair.

The camera then looks out the window without the girl present. Again, the scene of the pursuit of the dark figure is seen.
The Maya Deren figure takes a key from her mouth, but now it
turns into the knife. Entering the house, Deren finds two Maya
Derens sitting at the dining room table. She sits, too, putting the
key on the table. After several repeated gestures of touching
throats, the third Maya Deren stands, wearing goggles, holding the
knife in a menacing manner. Next, we see the famous stepping
from beach to grass to mud to pavement to a rug. Deren interpreted this: "What I meant when I planned that four-stride sequence
was that you have to come a long way--from the very beginning of
time--to kill yourself, like life first emerging from primitive waters. "16

The woman is about to stab her other self asleep in the chair,
when her eyes open to the man awakening her. They go up to the
bedroom. He places the flower on the bed and she lies next to it.
When the man caresses her, the flower becomes the knife, which
she grasps. She stabs the man's face, but it is now a mirror that
is broken glass falling to a sandy beach of ocean waves. Then,
with no transition, the man walks on the road, enters the house

where he finds the woman her throat slit, with shards of glass
around her.   The end.

Deren recorded her own insights into Meshes:

> It reproduces the way in which the sub-conscious of an in-
> dividual will develop, interpret and elaborate an apparently
> simple and casual incident into a critical emotional experi-
> ence. . . . Part of the achievement of this film consists in
> the manner in which cinematic techniques are employed to
> give a malevolent vitality to inanimate objects.   The film
> is culminated by a double-ending in which it would seem
> that the imagined achieved, for her, such force that it be-
> came reality. 17

Sitney indexes the likenesses shared by Meshes and Un Chien
Andalou.   Meshes may not have been intrinsically a Freudian or Surrealist film, but the beliefs of both support the structure of the film,
while Un Chien most assuredly expressed a blend of the fragmented,
irrational, and amorphous qualities associated with the ideas of
Freud and André Breton.   Both films, according to Sitney, use a
framework and a double ending.   Un Chien presents a wobbly world
ruled by absurdity.   Meshes portrays a mind poised between a firm
reality and subconscious disorder.   In both films there is cutting on
action across disjunctive spaces, with unexpected changes in locale.
Both films use the theme of the double individual.

However, Meshes employs no metaphors, while Un Chien
constantly uses them.   The visualization of space in Meshes is
linear, yet curved; Un Chien uses the four directional co-ordinates.
Sitney concludes here that Meshes is a type of psychodrama, while
Un Chien is not.

The relevant question here is whether or not Deren-Hammid
saw the Dali-Buñuel film, and were influenced by it.   Did they read
Dali's book in which he discusses the film?   No one knows.   Sitney
guesses that Deren-Hammid were probably more aware of Orson
Welles' stunning feat in Citizen Kane rather than the Dali-Buñuel
film.

An equally engrossing case is made by Thomas E. Volosek
attributing the technical excellence of Meshes to Hammid, a fact occasionally overlooked by documented sources.   Also, Meshes resembles Hammid's early film Aimless Walk, and Volosek contends,
Hammid influenced Deren's films in specific ways.   Deren was the
first to credit her husband's collaborative efforts.   She wrote in a
letter: "My debt to him for teaching me the mechanics of film expression, and, more than that, the principle of infinite pains, is
enormous.   I wish that all young filmmakers would have the luck
for a similar apprenticeship. "18   Hammid photographed all of Meshes,
except for the two scenes in which he acted, when Deren pushed the
camera button.   He created the special effects and edited the film.
Hammid credits himself.   " 'In Meshes it was completely my concept

of shooting ... because at that time Maya had no film training, only interest. ' "19 And he recognizes that Meshes is like his Aimless Walk: both deal with multiple selves. It was Hammid who achieved three Maya Derens in Meshes, who used gauzes for an other-worldly atmosphere, who employed slow-motion photography so stunningly, who achieved a liquid flow in transitions, and had an unusual manner of using a handheld camera. However, Volosek observes that this array of special effects would suffer without expertise guiding the nearly 200 shots in the film. Hammid was responsible for the excellent lighting, exact positions for the camera, neat matching of "shot-countershot series, "20 point-of-view shots extremely well done, as well as editing that was flawless. But none of Hammid's films, including Aimless Walk, reaches the emotional zeniths attained in Meshes. Hammid's contributions to Meshes then were technical and intellectual, whereas Deren keyed the moods and tensions in it.

Specific facets of Hammid's filmmaking technique are recognized by Volosek appearing in Aimless Walk and reappearing in the context of Meshes. Both films have an ambiguous ending that revises the significance of all previous actions. And in both, an individual late-occurring scene modulates the whole narrative in a compelling way: in Meshes this scene is the entirely realistic segment in which the man first appears, waking the woman with a kiss, and ending when she falls asleep a second time. Volosek compares this segment to the train appearing late in Aimless Walk.

Hammid's finest talent in filmmaking is probably his ability to combine film space with film action. Volosek perceives this infiltration of space with action and action with space in all of Hammid's own films and those he made with Deren. Hammid's training as an architect, and his studies in music and photography support this achievement especially apparent, in Volosek's eyes, in his use of shadows to identify and relate space to the woman (Deren) in Meshes.

Released the following year, At Land (1944) with Deren's name only, captures the same mood as Meshes and deals with facsimile images of an individual (Deren) woman. Hammid's masterly use of panning in At Land is discerned by Volosek; Hammid's technique of "distancing" with the camera is similar in Aimless Walk and At Land. Telescoping of time is achieved by this "distancing" and Volosek examples it in the final shot of At Land. When the woman runs along the beach leaving her footprints behind, the camera stays focused on them. An invisible cut comes next, followed by the camera panning slowly after the footprints. Her arms held high in the air, the woman is seen still running far away on the beach. She is much farther away than it would have been possible for her to run in the time that the camera stopped to focus on her footprints. This clever collapse of time is Hammid's eloquent expertise.

At Land is the earliest of what P. Adams Sitney calls pure American trance films. In a classic trance film the central character mingles with others until it meets its own past. At Land's open form lends itself to this form of exploration, a confrontation with the self, occurring in all of Deren's films. Hammid recalls that the idea for At Land stemmed from the famous four-stride sequence in Meshes. Deren records that this sequence "rang a bell ... in my head ... I kept saying to myself 'There's a door there leading to something. ... ' "21 It led to At Land, for which Deren set up the scenes. Hella Heyman photographed and Hammid helped and advised.

Each scene in At Land blends with the next in an unbroken continuous line. These smooth fusions call for editing planned far in advance of photographing. The climax of At Land illustrates this fusion: it is seen as one shot sweeping over a series of sand dunes as Deren walks away from the camera over them. At each dune, she reaches its peak, and disappears down the farther side. This up, over and down walking was captured in a succession of meticulously joined shots that coalesce into one unity. We get the visual effect of a long time in one moment because the walk between dunes was omitted. We experience the clever collapse of time once again. The soundlessness of this fifteen-minute work enhances the mingling of action with environment, underscoring the theme of the film--a quest for identity.

Deren recorded her intentions for At Land in her essay, "Cinematography: The Creative Use of Reality":

> ... In my At Land, it has been the technique by which the dynamic of the Odyssey is reversed and the protagonist, instead of undertaking the long voyage of search for adventure, finds instead that the universe itself has usurped the dynamic action which was once the prerogative of human will, and confronts her with a volatile and relentless metamorphosis in which her personal identity is the sole constancy. ... 22

Betancourt views At Land an individual's quest for domination of its own destiny, and she suggests that the film's theme premises a paramount concept of the feminist movement, namely, that each woman should decide for herself her own affairs, unimpeded by her sexuality.

At Land includes several shots of astounding virtuosity--a few unsurpassed in Deren's body of films. Close-ups are excitingly juxtaposed with extreme long shots, while the locales fluctuate from shore to forest to a hut, indoors, to a rock, then a cliff.

The opening shot is of Deren herself being washed up from sea to shore. "She rises to climb up driftwood onto the dining room table of a formal room. While everyone ignores her, she crawls on her belly to the head of the table. ... "23 A chess game (the game of life?) is a recurring element in Deren's movements in a nonsensical landscape, and maybe it contains the key to identity which

Deren, the protagonist, is seeking. "... the chess game going on there continues without anyone, except perhaps Maya's will, controlling it. A pawn falls off the table through a hole in the driftwood and into the sea.... "24 Later, Deren comes upon a game of chess on the shore. "... She distracts the women playing, grabs the pawn and runs. As she runs there are brilliant cuts to shots of herself in various other poses of the film. So you get the image of the persona of the film watching her own life. The last shot is of Maya running--arms up in the air, pawn in hand--down to the beach.... "25

Betancourt gleans several sexual themes in At Land, most markedly in the scene in which Deren strokes the hair of the women chess players. But, as Betancourt interprets this action and its subsequences, "... This, too, she passes by ... leaving the women (lesbianism) and running down the beach with the controls of her own life ... she is rejecting sex as the ruling dynamic of her existence.... "26

Anaïs Nin saw the beginning of the film being photographed (presumably by Hammid, although Hella Heyman later became her camerawoman) and recorded it in her diary for August 1945, as happening during a stroll with friends in Amagansett.

> ... From afar, we observed what seemed to be a body being rolled by the waves toward the shore. Two men were watching it. When it rolled at their feet the body would stand up and soon after run into the waves and begin again. As we came nearer we were puzzled. It was a woman. She had abundant long hair which floated as she let herself be rolled by the waves. She had to do this several times for the young man who was filming. We watched for a while, exchanged smiles, and walked on. Later we found out this was Maya Deren and her husband.... She was making another surrealist film. We became friends. Maya invited us to come and see the film when it was finished.... The film was original. It was a dream. It had many strange effects which reminded me of Cocteau. Friends had acted in it whom I recognized. And we recognized the scene by the seashore.... 27

Nin describes Deren as a Russian Jewess with a fascinating face. This was the face in the window most often used to illustrate Deren's films in dictionaries and film company brochures.

> Under the wealth of curly, wild hair, which she allowed to frame her face in a halo, she had pale-blue eyes, and a primitive face. The mouth was wide and fleshy, the nose with a touch of South Sea-islander fullness. When Sasha, Alexander Hammid, Deren's husband filmed her ... he caught a moment when Maya appeared at a glass window, and, softened by the glass, she created a truly Botticelli effect.... 28

The Hammids moved from Los Angeles to New York after making Meshes. Anaïs Nin visited their Greenwich Village apartment to see Meshes with a group of friends. Nin was impressed by the Hammids' apartment decorated with exotic masks, statuettes, drums and musical instruments, unique art objects. Even more was Nin and the group enthused by their hostess and her filmmaking plans. Nin relates that she disagreed with Deren's cinematic theories. Deren disavowed any relationship or dependence on surrealists. She said she was not influenced by Cocteau. Her films could and should not be analyzed in psychological terms, her screen images could not be interpreted for coherent meaning. Deren confided she was planning another film. She looked at her guests with the speculative eye of a film director. 29

Film critic James Agee was not mesmerized by Deren or her films as his commentary affirms: "Meshes ... and At Land, can be roughly classified as 'dream' films and also approach, as Parker Tyler has said, 'a type of personal expression in cinema analogous to the lyric poem.' Their quality seems to me to be impaired by Miss Deren's performance in the central roles...."

While finding "many satisfactions of mood and implication" in the films, Agee determines that he

> cannot feel there is anything really original about them--
> that they do anything important, for instance, which was
> not done, and done to an ill-deserved death, by some of
> the European avant-gardists, and especially by the sur-
> realists, of the 1920's. At worst, in fact, they are
> solemnly, arrogantly, distressingly pretentious and arty.
> Nevertheless, I think they are to be seen, and that there
> is a good deal in them to be liked, enjoyed, and respected
> 30

Agee then pointedly observes that his "reality" and Deren's "reality, " "in its conventional camera sense..." are vastly different concepts.

Intrigued as Deren was by the capabilities of the camera to begin and hold a continuity of human movement, she returned to her earlier art form, the dance, in her third film. In A Study in Choreography for Camera (1945) she "concentrates entirely upon the continuity of camera movement which becomes the main subject of the film...." A human step which changes location, as in Meshes, is employed once more.

"Talley Beatty, the dancer, begins a step--the lowering of his extended leg--in an open wood space, and completes it, apparently in the same shot, in an enclosed room. His dance takes him through as many changes of location as of movement.... "31

Parker Tyler gives the film studious scrutiny in a chapter titled "Ciné-Dance, " solemnly applauding Deren's stunning achievement.

Deren established by direct illustration the fact that the shift from one viewpoint to another in film shots is a fundamental matter of rhythm, one might say a pulsation of space that significantly, pointedly qualifies the original dance movement. In this now famous work, done in slow motion, a solo dancer begins a figure in the woods, continues it without apparent interruption in a studio, then in a vast hall in a museum, to reach its climax on a cliff overlooking a river. The space about the dancer has also moved and in a given rhythm; this has been effected by total changes in the camera's viewpoint implying wide spatial shifts. With this method of altering environment and isolating parts of the dancer's body as he enters the new scene, a greatly condensed space gathers behind the dancer, heaps up under him, so that his dance acquires a new mysterious force (particularly in aerial suspension) while the choreographic pattern remains quite intact and he himself exerts no extra effort.... 32

The camera itself must dance with the dancer in ciné-dance, Tyler declares, and only the most gifted of creators of films recognizes this aesthetic truism and can implement this collaboration of mobile human and mechanical instruments. In Tyler's judgment, Deren succeeded admirably in this co-operative linkage of movements.

The eminence of Choreography for P. Adams Sitney lies in the fact that Deren made two fresh observations on the nature of dance and film and successfully implemented them. She realized that space and time in film are created space and time. And she realized that the camera can be used to record and preserve dances, but its optimal use is as a dancer itself taking part in the filmed dancing.

Choreography was subtitled Pas de Deux: the couple dancing is Talley Beatty and the camera. In three minutes, the length of the film, Choreography compresses space and expands time. The tension and cohesion of the film is rooted in the camera dancing with the dancer, in compressed space and expanded time. This use of one dance movement as a unified film resembles imagism in poetry, in P. Adams Sitney's opinion. It starts with the camera panning round an open space in a forest. In completing the circle, the camera "sees" the dancer several times. Each time, the dancer progresses in a movement of slow stretching. When the panning ends, he places his foot beyond the frame, and steps down into a room. Then he dances through rooms, woods, and a courtyard, pirouetting first in a very slow, then to a very fast, speed. Beatty finishes with an extended floating leap, captured in many ascending and descending shots, settling back into the forest where he began to dance.

The film "forecasts the shift from narrative to imagistic structures within the avant-garde film movement. "33

Anaïs Nin did act in Deren's next venture, Ritual in Transfigured Time (1945-1946). She records the entire enterprise in her
Diary, dated March 1946. Maya asked Gore Vidal, Rita, a black
woman, Nin and others to take parts in the film. They agreed.
This group volunteered to enact a party scene. Deren instructed
her cast to be natural. She would not direct the scene in the customary manner; actors would create their own words and movements,
and Deren would film it. 34

Deren defines the theme of Ritual as "about the nature and
process of change...." Ritual examines the qualities of time, in
Betancourt's words, "Time as it influences change. Time is contracted, expanded, stopped.... "35

What is the impact of time upon a party? This seems to be
the question Deren wanted her camera to reply to in the unrehearsed
party scenes described by Nin, detailing the difficulties Deren encountered, and the participants' reactions to their assignment. The
undirected attempts of the amateur actors to act as themselves displeased Deren. Shooting time lengthened under hot lights, as all
tried to achieve an undeliberate festive effect without suggestions or
prompting from Deren. The frustrated actors danced, dined, drank,
conversed, laughed. For Nin, the party scene failed. She wanted to
volunteer a script of sorts, appropriate dialogue at the very least,
but didn't dare. The entire party episode was meaningless although
Deren, perched on a high stool, appeared to be satisfied when it
was done. 36

Deren's preparations for filming--drawings, musings, self-
reminders--are found in Film Culture, 39 (Winter 1965), an issue
dedicated to her, including her book Anagram, all proof of her dili-
gence before filming.

Betancourt elaborates the incidents in Ritual in the party
scene Nin described. A widow, Rita Christiani, is dream-walking
and assuming her other self, Maya Deren. She attends a party
acted out as a ritual dance. Party members move in slow motion,
then freeze. Movements are repeated. Each one greets, dances,
talks, gestures, departs. Then Rita meets Frank Westbrook. They
dance in slow motion. Suddenly they are transported to a sculpture
garden. As Rita dances, Frank does "two jumps like a rooster. "
One by one, women, Anaïs Nin among them, come dance with him.
Frank jumps like a rooster after dancing with each one. "As Rita
flees from him, she turns to the camera with the face of Maya.
Frank jumps and turns in a third-position pose. When he lands he
is not on the ground, but in another part of the garden as a statue
on a pedestal.... "37 He pursues Rita, who runs, with leaping, as
Maya, into the ocean. Then she turns and drops through the lower
edge of the frame. Then, "... Through the upper edge, a white
form drops twice in close-up, each time falling, falling, until the
full form has passed through the screen. Her widow's garb is white
in negative. A close-up of her face ends the film as she lifts her
veil and opens her eyes.... "38

Once again, Betancourt plumbs this action line for meaning and her gloss favors the woman-seeking-love (Frank Westbrook) and-freedom theme. Nin reports the actors' reactions to scenes filmed in a variety of locations, and how she and other volunteers felt when they saw the completed film. 39

One day the cast was dancing amid Greek-looking columns and statuary in Yonkers. On another day in May 1946, Deren phoned Nin, asking her to be in Grand Street or Central Park at 7 a. m. to start shooting. An incident occurred in the Park which negatively altered the cast's estimate of Deren's character. For one scene, Deren asked ballet dancer Frank Westbrook to jump from one rocky area to another. Nin and the others objected to Deren's direction because of the obvious hazards to Westbrook's career. His professional career was at stake, he could easily injure himself, cast members pointed out. Deren remained adamant. She insisted that Westbrook do as she said, or she would not let him be in the film. Westbrook complied. Nin reports that she and all others in this film venture discovered that their feelings for Deren had dramatically changed. She seemed to be unfeeling, too autocratic. Although they respected her filmmaking abilities, they liked her less. 40

Once completed, Ritual was viewed by all participants in its making. All of them, including Nin, were stunned and speechless. All had had misgivings about acting in the film, Nin confides, anticipating that their defects and faults would be exposed and visible, and worse, probably magnified and intensified by Deren's camera. Sadly, their fears were confirmed. Nin was afraid of close-ups and Westbrook was worried that his skin would not photograph well. 41

Editing and good camera angles would prevent this feared exposure of blemishes. So Maya and Alex had assured them. But, Nin observes, all the actors found their flaws in the film and augmented as well. Deren soothed her co-workers by saying that theirs was the customary response; everyone is astounded at first sight of his or her image on screen. Deren explained that she obtained their signatures on release forms prior to filming for just this reason. She urged them not to be concerned. Alex Hammid impressed the actors as considering his wife's film far more important than the cast's reactions to their screen images.

Nin considered Ritual a failure as a film and she enumerates reasons why. 42 Compared to Meshes, in which Deren wrought a poeticized miraculous vision, Ritual lacks poetry, and fails to render believable characters. The concept of characters who are interchangeable is confusing and unsatisfactory. The party scene is the poorest part of the film; the early scenes involving statues is most appealing.

Nin found Deren too inflexible in her direction of Ritual. Deren's lack of human concern for her volunteer actors is reflected in Ritual, Nin states, and her lack of compassion subverted the essence and effect of the film. 43

Confining his consideration of Ritual to its dance aspects, Parker Tyler views it as a positive step into the difficult terrain of dance-on-film. "The title ... perfectly suggests the universal limits of the possibilities of ciné-dance.... " The film itself

> is a chase and a matter of life-and-death; by telescoping certain dance sequences in slow motion and with "freezes, " she produces a tension technically related to Griffith's while being much closer to actual dance. Ciné-dance is a twin plastique participating in film and in dance as film itself participates in time and in space.... 44

Tyler here refers to a suspenseful sequence in the film The Two Orphans in which, by speedy editing, a quickened heartbeat rhythm is obtained.

P. Adams Sitney honors Ritual with its most detailed and perceptive analysis. As Deren's most complex work it holds her attainments and failures of theoretical thought on film. Ritual involves two central figures (a pure trance film has only one) and several supporting figures in a tripartite film: opening, a party, and a dance. These support figures represent mythological forms (the Fates and the Graces) assisting at a rite, a process Deren called "widow into bride. " Sitney categorizes Ritual as an extreme form of trance film, leaning toward ceremonious ritual and myth.

At the film's opening, Deren appears in a double doorway, wearing black. She walks to another room, bringing a scarf and a length of yarn with her. She beckons to a woman, "the widow, " who sleepwalks, enters and makes a ball of the yarn. Deren, as "the invoker" sings and chants, manipulating the wool in her hands. The widow, looking mesmerized, continues rolling yarn into a ball.

A third woman, "the guide, " joins them. At a signal from her, the widow is released from her spell after the invoker raises her arms and drops the yarn.

The party scene commences. A group choreomania develops. All dance in patterns which are repeated. Then, all stop, "suspended in a frozen frame. "45 Deren arrived at this accurate depiction of dance movement by printing many copies of a few of the most intricate steps, repeating these identical shots at exact intervals, punctuating them with the freeze shots.

During the dance, a young man tries to approach the widow. When they meet, the scene changes to a meadow where the dancers are posed just as they were at the party. A triad of women, dressed like the Graces, dance; one of them is recognized as the guide woman. The widow and young man are fleeing and pursuing each other, the widow becoming the invoker and back again as widow, with a corresponding change of scarves, from widow's black to bride's white.

Next, the widow discovers her pursuer has become a statue. But in a series of freeze frames he comes alive, leaps to the grass, running after the widow in ballet-like jumps. They pass the guide woman. Just as the man reaches the widow she becomes the invoker again, running into the ocean, sinking into it, her black dress now white. She is a bride ready for her pursuer who does not follow her into the water. She has "married" the sea.

Drawing upon dance and myth, Deren created a psychodramatic ritual using the cinematic techniques she by now had assimilated: not only freeze frames, and repeat shots, but shifting identities, body movements, and locales.

In fact, Ritual was to be the first of a series of studies of cinematic ritual. Deren applied for a Guggenheim Foundation Grant proposing a film dealing with elements of ritual in children's games corresponding to historical rites in Bali and Haiti. She approached Margaret Mead and Gregory Bateson, anthropologists, for assistance in her proposal, and got it. She received the grant money in 1946, journeyed to Haiti (she made three trips in all) but authored the book The Divine Horsemen instead. The ceremonial act, the pattern of movement, skilled gestures, any type of step-like body motion appealed to Deren as cinematic material. As late as 1954, Deren was planning a movie based on circus acts.

In 1946, Deren published her monograph on the film aesthetic: An Anagram of Ideas on Art, Form and the Film (New York: Alicat Book Shop Press, 1946).

The first paragraph of a review of Anagram by Arthur Rosenheimer, Jr. in Theatre Arts 31 (January 1947), pages 68-9, appears to substantiate the opinions of Anaïs Nin.

> ... This book is a tight, closely reasoned investigation
> into the nature of art and of film which tends to prove
> that the four pictures made by the author are the only true
> films, whereas all pictures that have gone before have
> been but wretched profanations of film technique. Miss
> Deren is not one to do things by halves--either in her pic-
> tures or in her writings. Included in her condemnation is
> even Eisenstein's Potemkin; she objects to its "literary"
> derivations.

Anagram projects two major premises: the rejection of symbolism in film and an analysis of independent and industrial filmmaking, with a strong option for the former. By rejecting all literary, artistic, and psychological connotations, the filmmaker frees the medium to find itself, to do what cannot be done in any other art form. Objects and actions in film must have the right to be comprehended as representing only themselves and nothing more, nothing else. Deren's concept of "what you see is what it is" antedates and foreshadows the "against interpretation" thesis of Susan Sontag by several decades.

Deren called her works "chamber films," small efforts by
an amateur, burdened with obligations only to self and the medium.
Such amateurs are most likely to explore and discover the true nature of film. For her, film revealed itself as tantalizingly tempting
territory ripe for revelation.

In her tally of the characteristics of the independent versus
the industrial film, the latter comes under attack for its customary
circumscription of artistic aims. In the making of an independent
film, the participants are not paid or the salaries are nominal; the
working time is sporadic and extended; the film's distribution is un-
organized and "accidental"; the quality of the film must be sustained
throughout the film so that the film can be enjoyed again and again.
Films made within the industry enlist actors on a payroll; the filming is done as quickly as possible, "on schedule"; distribution is
planned with an eye for profits which are sometimes guaranteed,
and the film is geared to a one-time viewing. This type of movie
does not anticipate revival; its plot activity, not its moods or
themes, must be maintained throughout the length of the film.

While the scope of Anagram includes Deren's meditations on
art in general, scoring valid points of observation and experience
and extending discussion from the anagram she composed as a topic
center, it is her formulative thinking on the nature of film that com-
prises the memorable core of the book. As Rosenheimer concludes
his review "... her pamphlet, whose original, anagrammatic form
is itself an evidence of her original thinking on the problems of her
art offers a valuable insight into the philosophy and aesthetic that
shapes the film outside of Hollywood...."

Anagram reflects Deren's experiences as an amateur filmmaker desiring the attendance of larger audiences and the promotion
of this type of documentary filmmaking for independent individuals
like herself. With four films finished, Deren looked for and could
not find an established film distributor who would agree to promote
and publicize them. She was forced to act as her own agent, using
her apartment as home and business address, mailing brochures to
and calling upon educational institutions in her immediate area.
Then, as Curtis best summarizes her next step,

> ... Early in 1946 she rented the Provincetown Playhouse
> on MacDougal Street, New York, for a one-night show of
> her first three films (this story has become almost
> apocryphal). They generated such an interest that repeat
> screenings were arranged at once. This sudden success
> led to a whole series of performances all over the States,
> a highspot being their showing at the Film as Art series in
> San Francisco.... [46]

It was in 1947 that Deren was awarded the First International
Prize at the 16mm Film Festival at Cannes, and, with Amos Vogel,
formed the Cinema 16 society. In 1954, Vogel and Deren set up
the Creative Film Foundation as an aid to experimental filmmakers.
(Its first awards were given to Shirley Clarke and Stan Brakhage.)

In 1948 Deren explored, from a dance aspect, Woo (or Wu)
Tang boxing. Her film Meditation on Violence (1948) places the
camera first as a spectator watching a boxer exercising. Then the
camera itself becomes the boxer's sparring partner, dodging, ward-
ing off, trying to return, the boxer's blows. The adjustments, pans,
and zooms of the camera simulate a human response. This dance
poem (what Parker Tyler dubs ciné-dance) is contoured to express
the movements and the meaning of those movements in this form of
boxing.

> ... Deren explains (in Film Culture 29) that an essential
> part of Woo Tang boxing is that "it never extends boxing
> to the extreme--but always rounds it about.... No move-
> ment is ever concluded, it merely leads again. That
> makes it metaphoric, dynamic, the very principle of life
> itself. " The film's form is deliberately without climax--
> the whole of the last part runs backwards--but so well
> balanced are the movements, so well "rounded about, "
> that this reversal is accepted as quite natural; again--
> "the basic principle of life is that the dynamic was the
> functional flow of negative and positive, repeated. "47

Parker Tyler found it "... A challenging commentary on all
violence ... " although most film source dictionaries describe it as
a poetic dance film, a category that nicely encloses Deren's last
four films, most especially The Very Eye of Night (1959) completed
only two years before Deren's death in 1961. Specifically designed
to be shown in its negative state, Deren employed members of the
Metropolitan Opera Ballet School to create this "... celestial ciné-
ballet of night.... The dancers become cosmic and four-dimensional,
advancing, as if planets in the night sky, by the blind incalculable
accuracies of sleepwalkers.... "48

> ... If, as I have done in my recent film The Very Eye of
> Night, one eliminates the horizon line and any background
> which would reveal the movement of the total field, then
> the eye accepts the frame as stable and ascribes all move-
> ment to the figure within it. The hand-held camera, mov-
> ing and revolving over the white figures on a totally black
> ground, produces images in which their movement is as
> gravity-free and as three-dimensional as that of birds in
> air or fish in water. In the absence of any absolute ori-
> entation, the push and pull of their interrelationships be-
> comes the major dialogue.... 49

The majority of dance films made subsequent to The Very
Eye use this terminal film of Deren's as a starting point. Its influence has been so penetrating and profound that it has "set standards for every dance film that followed ... " according to Curtis
(page 136). Indeed, if Deren's last four films are viewed consecu-
tively, one would see in them a gathering of specific difficulties in
the nature of dance movement matched by decidedly differing complexities of camerawork resulting in a coincidence of both with the

parallel perplexities resolved with grace and vitality. In this ciné-dance quartet, Deren evolved a viable form of ciné-choreography which could adapt and adjust itself to the commercial feature film, most meritoriously in West Side Story (1961). As Shirley Clarke, filmmaker of dance films, when interviewed by Gretchen Berg in Dance Perspectives (Summer 1967), pp. 20-23, admitted: "... I had not known something that Maya Deren knew instinctively: That in making a dance film you had to destroy one art in order to be true to the other...."

Jonas Mekas engages in a defensive interpretation of The Very Eye without any mention of dance, while relating it to her first film Meshes.

> ... to me, The Very Eye of Night is a very thought-out film, clear and crystalline. Maya Deren differs from most of the other experimentalists through her clarity of purpose, clarity of images, universality of symbols ... the area in which Maya Deren digs is not so much her own personal subconscious as a universal subconscious.... The Very Eye ... is best understood in the context of Miss Deren's whole work, as we trace her inner journey through the space-time breakings, through the modern myths [sic] imagery, black-white rituals. The movements and tensions of her films seem to be predestined. The unfolding, growth, and climax of Meshes ..., now reinforced by Teiji Ito's score, have something of the tragic predestination of Greek tragedy, while the suspense is trembling on that blade of a knife. Although The Very Eye ... is less tense, it has the same tragic predestination of the stars ... we are caught, first, not by the intellect of her films, but by the intensity of her visual rhythms, since she is an artist using cinema in its purest sense.... [50]

Mekas describes a theatre bursting with an audience sitting and standing apart from the seated spectators during Deren's film showings. With the dateline March 15, 1962, he comments on Alain Resnais' film Last Year at Marienbad: "... This shows how little our critics know about what is going on in modern cinema. Had they known Maya Deren's Ritual in Transfigured Time or Meshes in [sic] the Afternoon--both made fifteen years ago--they would have found little that is revolutionary in Marienbad...." [51]

In The Very Eye, P. Adams Sitney declares that Deren uses cinematic terms which she had deplored in Anagram. He explains:

> Although ... Deren ... disassociates herself from the non-objective painters of the 1940s and attacks them in her Anagram, her polemic is infused with a rhetoric they shared, and one sees in her last film, The Very Eye ..., a drift toward late Cubist space--a loss of depth, the breakdown of horizontal and vertical centrality ... and the affirmation of the screen's surface.... [52]

In fact, both Meditation and The Very Eye show "excessive styliza-
tion, both intellectual and graphical." 53   But Sitney pronounces
Deren's endeavors to imitate the processes of the human mind on
film as lofty, and he traces her films as developing from dream
(Meshes), to ritual (Ritual in Transfigured Time), to myth (The
Very Eye of Night).   If Deren had lived a longer life, the genesis
of her filmic themes would be easier to understand.

Deren traces the essence and evolution of her six short
films in a letter to her friend, James Card, dated April 19, 1955.
In it she mentions emergency surgery she had undergone a year
earlier.   She emerged from a condition near death to a heightened
exuberance for living life.   In filmmaking, she progressed from how
things felt to the way things were.   She called Meshes her "point of
departure," and "almost expressionist."   At Land portrayed the dor-
mant energy in ever-changing nature, while Choreography concentrated on the essence of this natural change.   In Ritual, she defined
the process of alteration.   Meditation is an extension of this study
of metamorphosis.   In The Very Eye she expressed her intensified
appreciation for life and its living derived from her swift and affirmative recovery from surgery.   On this film, Deren mused, "I think
it's taken me out in space about as far as I can go ... there truly
seems no place to go from here."   She adds, "Each film was built
as a chamber and became a corridor, like a chain reaction." 54

Because Choreography is an extension and abstraction of At
Land, and because Meditation is an extension and abstraction of
Ritual, this quartet appears to be the core of her work, with Meshes
as a parenthetical opening and The Very Eye as a parenthetical closing.   Too neat recapitulations of any filmmaker's catalogue of works
are to be avoided; they best serve as starting lines for discussion
and appreciation.   Assurance that Deren's films assist in identifying
the grammar of film exists in the continuing interest and study of
her life, in the hundreds of articles she wrote in film, and the films
themselves.

A retrospective of her six films in New York was reviewed
by Janet Maslin in The New York Times Film Reviews 1977-1978
(May 4, C 16:1).   The effect of seeing the films, plus out-takes (15
minutes of extra and unused footage from Choreography) back-to-back
in 90 minutes was an exercise in exhaustion.   Maslin reports that
Deren's films require and should be attended with nothing less than
total undistracted concentration.   Because of the dense symbolic significances in the films, none of them longer than fifteen minutes,
Maslin recommends taking Deren films in minute portions due to
their "relentless intensity."   And, because Deren "tended to repeat
herself somewhat, in both her extreme attentiveness to the voluptu-
ous possibilities of the human body and in her predilection for shifting characters back and forth between natural, primitive-looking locales and abstract, 'socialized' settings."

Deren's films and theories of films have gained an appreciative audience in Western Europe.   Two articles appeared in Frauen

und Film, 10 (December 1976) discussing her work and her stature in the archives of filmmakers. [55] Presently regarded as a ground-breaker in the art of experimental film, Deren appears to have had her detractors and her defenders in her own time.

A review of her first four films by Manny Farber in New Republic 115 (October 28, 1946), on pages 555 and 556, reveals his well-intentioned opaque attempt to apply Hollywood standards of criticism to Deren's puzzling productions. Noting that they had already been screened for arts groups and college clubs, Farber labeled them "lesbianish, freezing, arty, eclectic, conventional and safe." In his judgment, Deren's films "show people who look mesmerized ... moving through situations that have been contrived to have some Freudian meaning." Farber takes measure of Deren's "touch" as "totally lacking in sensuousness, humor, and love, and she seems to petrify the subject until it takes on the character of a museum piece." Meshes is "cluttered with corny, amateurishly arranged symbols and mainly concerned with sex...."

"The waves operate in reverse" in At Land, somehow propelling a dead Deren in a sarong to the beach. Deren's acting "reminds you of tough leather." When she looks at "the stand of beachwood you are reminded of arty beach photographs and annoyed by the pansyish composing and lighting." To finish his bleak experience in viewing Meshes, Farber complains that "it is hard to believe that there is not one exciting detail in the whole episode."

An incensed Deren responded to Farber's review in New Republic 115 (Nov. 11, 1946), on page 630. "My objection is not that Mr. Farber does not like the films and/or me, but that he does not explain or justify his appraisal of them." Deren objects to his assertion that her films are imbued with sex; she objects to his terms "lesbianish" and "pansyish." Farber's failure to mention the films Choreography and Ritual in his review was unjust. Deren closes her complaint by listing the names of notables who had seen and appreciated her films, among them Le Corbusier, George Amberg of the Museum of Modern Art, and Walter Terry of The New York Herald Tribune, adding that these same films had been purchased by universities and museums all over the United States.

Three years later, Anthony Bower in Nation 168 (January 1, 1949), pages 25-26, perceived the "wonderful sense of the relation between the dance and the camera" in Choreography. The Chinese shadow-boxing-like movements in Meditation while subtle are static and do not "allow the maximum play to Miss Deren's invention." Bower finds Deren "a bold and provocative experimenter, and her films deserve interest and support."

Although Deren's pioneering efforts and her films were admired and discussed, the filmmaker's sharply self-focused proclamations of her theories were misunderstood, not fully comprehended, or disagreed with, by her peers in the same and related disciplines. An example of Deren's voiced expression of her credos on the poetic film is found in an exchange which took place in October 1953 sponsored by the Cinema 16 Club. Organized by Amos Vogel, it was a symposium chaired by Willard Maas on the topic "Poetry and the Film. " Its participants were playwright Arthur Miller, poet Dylan Thomas, film critic Parker Tyler, and Deren.

Deren began to define "poetry" in her reply to the challenge issued to outline ". .. some of the basic esthetic principles of the poetic film. .. . "56 For Deren,

> ... The distinction of poetry is its construction ... and
> the poetic construct arises from the fact, if you will, that
> it is a "vertical" investigation of a situation ... you have
> poetry concerned ... not with what is occurring but with
> what it feels like or what it means. ... 57

She contrasts this verticality of the poem with the longitudinal development of the drama, then expands on the compounds of the two up-and-across art forms. Then, ". .. the short films to my mind, ... are comparable to lyric poems, and they are completely a 'vertical, ' or what I would call a poetic construct, and they are complete as such. ... "58 She closes her remarks by using examples of recent films in which a horizontal story line is fused with a vertical poetic commentary.

The symposium did not react directly to Deren's definitive exposition, but progressed in terms of visual and verbal images in film. In reply to a question from the audience, Arthur Miller said, "To hell with that 'vertical' and 'horizontal. ' It doesn't mean anything. (Applause.) I understand perfectly what it means, but the point is, if an action is worth anything emotionally, it proceeds to get deeper into its meaning as it progresses, as it reveals. ... "59

Another symposium account describes Deren as confronting "Dylan Thomas's shameless hot-dogging and Arthur Miller's windy pontifications. " When Gay Talese "wrote Deren up, he mentioned her interest in voodoo, her Japanese husband, her cats--everything but her film work. "60 The symposium appears to have cast Deren into the role of an earnest explainer of a thesis reluctantly received and at a tepid temperature, too.

Jonas Mekas gestures with his thumb down on Deren's film work in Experimental Film in America (New York: Macmillan, 1972, pages 24-25). The caption under which his flagellations are thrust is "The Lack of Creative Inspiration, Technical Crudity and Thematic Narrowness. " A film critic and filmmaker himself, Mekas states his negations: "The supposed depth of Maya Deren is artificial, without the ingenious spontaneity which we find, for instance, in Brakhage's or Anger's work. ... " Mekas finds the moral void of the films made by "these film poets" reprehensible.

> If we look into these films for moral values, we would find
> ... that, if the struggle of the new film poets to make a

dramatic affirmation of value could be plotted on a graph,
the result would be a parabolic curve extending from the
absolute zero of Maya Deren to the absolute zero of Stanley Brakhage. . . .

For the year 1955, Mekas called avant-garde film "a conspiracy of homosexuality" in Film Culture (May-June 1955). Deren reacted angrily to this accusation, which included her, because she felt
that it might jeopardize her limited income as a lecturer. Deren's
expressed reaction altered Mekas' total stance on avant-garde films
apparently.

Deren's friend Stan Brakhage, also a filmmaker, recalls that
Deren lived in Greenwich Village as he did in extremely harsh circumstances. Deren confided to Brakhage that she wanted them both
to sue the Mekas brothers (Jonas and his brother Adolfas). They
were publishers, therefore they had to be rich! This myth evaporated when Deren phoned Brakhage to come at once to her apartment.
She told him the Mekas brothers were poor. They could not sue
them. Brakhage found Deren raging at the apologetic-looking brothers in her apartment, audible from the moment Brakhage entered
the building. Brakhage testifies to Deren's moneyless debt-plagued
life-style in 1959. "Maya could never believe this society was going
to do this to her. "61

By 1978, 17 years after Deren's death, her films were seen
as provocative as ever, her contributions to the cinematic art in
clear focus, beyond debate. She had invented two types of films:
the psychodrama and the ciné-dance. Meshes remains "probably the
most widely-seen avant-garde film ever made. " Many of its effects
"have yet to be bettered. "62

In At Land Deren's genius devised a style of editing that
shaped a "'creative geography, ' a continuous, impossible landscape
out of a number of different locations. "63 Although her dance films
are less inspired and The Very Eye her weakest work, Choreography was the first true-to-life dance film. Deren's overload of "cultural baggage, " her extended explanations and considerations of the
nature of film can be understood now as expressing the exuberance
Deren brought to her role of film marketing, in the screening, distributing, and selling of her own films. "The best of her work has
yet to be exhausted, but it was primarily for the chances that she
took with her life that every independent filmmaker in America remains in her debt. "64

With the passage of time, Deren accumulated scores of personal and professional admirers convinced of the enduring values of
her work. Her untimely death in 1961 from a cerebral hemorrhage
at age 44 became a rallying point for independent filmmakers and
film critics.

Rudolf Arnheim wrote a eulogy to Maya Deren:

This miracle of photography ... is essentially materialistic.
There is another, quieter, but more magical, one, which
is that of the transformation of reality accomplished by the
medium itself. ... This transformation is the true miracle
of the photographic image; and Maya Deren was one of its
most delicate magicians. ... 65

Curtis hails Deren as a leader who "pioneered a dynamic approach to the screening of films by the filmmakers themselves that
led to a complete restructuring of non-theatrical distribution in the
United States."66

In a film dictionary, Deren is cited as

Perhaps the most important figure in the postwar development of the personal, independent film in the USA. ... Her
first films ... strikingly individual, injected a new vitality
into the independent American cinema. Her later films,
less symbolic, but equally personal, are experiments in
space and time, explorations of movement, rhythm, and
form. ... 67

A biography of Deren was announced in PMLA (May 1977),
page 512: "Four women preparing a three-volume biography of
writer, film maker, and authority on Haitian vodoun request letters
by, to, or about Maya Deren (1917-1961). ... " The four authors are
Millicent Hodson (dance), VéVé Clark (Caribbean studies), Catrina
Neiman (folklore and mythology), and Francine Bailey (portrait photography). The authors are advised and assisted by Jonas Mekas,
Teiji Ito (Deren's widower), and her mother, Mrs. Mary Deren.
Volume I was projected for publication by Film Culture magazine in
1977. The Legend of Maya Deren continues.

Deren's legacy opened a corridor in the cinematic art largely
unapproached until her incursions. All epigones are advised to heed
the word in which Deren defined her own threshold to making films:
"... The great art expressions will come later, as they always have,
and they will be dedicated, again, to the agony and the experience
rather than the incident."68

FILMOGRAPHY

Meshes of the Afternoon (1943) with A. Hammid

The Witch's Candle (1943) Unfinished

At Land (1944)

A Study in Choreography for Camera (1945)

Ritual in Transfigured Time (1946)

Meditation on Violence (1948)

The Very Eye of Night (1959)

Note: Deren's Haitian film footage remains unedited and untitled.

NOTES

1. Regina Cornwell, "Maya Deren and Germaine Dulac: Activists of the Avant-Garde," Film Library Quarterly 5 (Winter 1971/72), p. 30.
2. Joanne Betancourt, Women in Focus. Dayton, Ohio: Pflaum, 1974, p. 17.
3. J. Pyros, "Notes on Women Directors," Take One 3:2 (1972), p. 9.
4. Parker Tyler, "Experimental Film: A New Growth," Kenyon Review 11:1 (1949), p. 143.
5. Women Who Make Movies. New York: Hopkinson, Blake, 1976, p. 34.
6. Betancourt, p. 102.
7. Ibid., pp. 102-103.
8. Ibid., p. 103.
9. Ibid.
10. Lincoln F. Johnson, Film: Space, Time, Light, and Sound. New York: Holt, Rinehart and Winston, 1974, p. 136.
11. Ibid., p. 56.
12. Ibid., p. 53.
13. Ibid., p. 177.
14. Ronald Tuch, "Chaplin and the American Avant Garde," Film Library Quarterly 7:2 (1974), p. 17.
15. P. Adams Sitney, Visionary Film (second edition). New York: Oxford University Press, 1979, p. 4.
16. Ibid., p. 23.
17. Ibid., p. 9.
18. Thomas E. Volosek, Alexander Hammid: A Survey of His Film-Making Career. New York: Ungar, 1977, p. 283.
19. Ibid.
20. Ibid., p. 284.
21. Sitney, p. 23.
22. Betancourt, p. 169.
23. Ibid., p. 15.
24. Ibid.
25. Ibid.
26. Ibid.
27. The Diary of Anaïs Nin (1944-1947). Volume IV. New York: Harcourt Brace Jovanovich, 1971, pp. 75-76.
28. Ibid., p. 76.
29. Ibid.
30. James Agee, Agee on Film: Reviews and Comments. Volume I. New York: Grosset and Dunlap, 1958, pp. 190-191.
31. David Curtis, Experimental Cinema. New York: Universe Books, 1971, p. 11.
32. Parker Tyler, Sex, Psyche, Etcetera in the Film. New York: Horizon Press, 1969, p. 181.

33.   Sitney, p. 195.
34.   Anaïs Nin, Volume IV, p. 135.
35.   Betancourt, p. 115.
36.   Anaïs Nin, Volume IV, pp. 135-136.
37.   Betancourt, p. 114.
38.   Ibid., p. 115.
39.   Anaïs Nin, Volume IV, p. 145.
40.   Ibid., pp. 146-147.
41.   Ibid., p. 156.
42.   Ibid., p. 149.
43.   Ibid.
44.   Tyler, Sex, Psyche, Etcetera in the Film, pp. 183-184.
45.   Sitney, p. 32.
46.   Curtis, p. 59.
47.   "The Cleveland Lecture, " Film Culture 29 (Summer 1963), p.
      70.
48.   Bonnie Dawson, comp. Womens Films in Print: An Annotated
      Guide to 800 16mm Films by Women. San Francisco: Book-
      legger Press, 1975, p. 31.
49.   Curtis, p. 59.
50.   Jonas Mekas, Movie Journal: The Rise of the New American
      Cinema, 1959-1971. New York: Macmillan, 1972, p. 2.
51.   Ibid., p. 54.
52.   Sitney, p. 195.
53.   Ibid., p. 28.
54.   Maya Deren, "A Letter to James Card, " in Women and the
      Cinema: A Critical Anthology, ed. by Karyn Kay and Gerald
      Peary. New York: E. P. Dutton, 1977, pp. 229-230.
55.   M. Bronstein and S. Grossman, "Zu Maya Derens Filmarbeit, "
      Frauen und Film 10 (Dec. 1976), pp. 11-35; and Maya Deren,
      "Film-in-Progress-Thematisches Statement, " pp. 36-43.
56.   Amos Vogel, "Poetry and the Film: A Symposium, " Film Cul-
      ture 29 (Summer 1963), p. 171.
57.   Ibid., p. 174.
58.   Ibid.
59.   Ibid., p. 184.
60.   J. Hoberman, "The Maya Mystique, " Village Voice 23 (20),
      May 15, 1978, p. 54.
61.   M. Tuchman, "The Mekas Brothers: Brakhage & Baillie
      Traveling Circus, " Film Comment 14 (March-April 1978), p.
      12.
62.   J. Hoberman, "The Maya Mystique, " Village Voice 23 (20)
      May 15, 1978, p. 54.
63.   Ibid.
64.   Ibid.
65.   Film Culture 39 (Winter 1965), p. 3-4.
66.   Curtis, p. 15.
67.   Georges Sadoul, A Dictionary of Filmmakers, ed. and updated
      by Peter Morris. Berkeley: University of California Press,
      1972, p. 61.
68.   Ibid.

8. IDA LUPINO: DARING THE FAMILY TRADITION

Born: February 4, 1918, London, England

"I never planned to become a director. The fates and a combination of luck--good and bad--were responsible."[1]

Newsweek declared in 1940: "Every so often Hollywood 'discovers' Ida Lupino. This time she will undoubtedly stay discovered!"[2] The versatile Lupino is destined for recurring reassessments of the merits she has racked up as a multi-faceted Muse exercising her innumerable talents in a lengthy, too sparsely, applauded career. Her work has embraced so many forms of endeavor that a new Lupino could be "discovered" in each of them.

As the living antithesis of single-mindedness, the word for Lupino is daring:

> Daring to sacrifice security to realize a vision, rather than playing it safe for comfort; daring to be inventive in concept and different in technique; daring to do "A" movies on "Z" budgets long before it was fashionable, risking unknown faces, gambling on untried subjects; daring to shoot big while shooting fast; daring to direct at a time terrifyingly tough for women; daring to be daring. She has been playwright, screenwriter, author, dancer, singer, artist, designer, musician, song-writer, composer (The Aladdin Suite, her composition, was played by the Los Angeles Philharmonic), as well as actress, television and motion-picture producer-director, and all-around film maker.[3]

Lupino was the first, and probably only, woman filmmaker in a Hollywood studio in the fifties. Placing all the products of her cinematic and television camera into critical perspective, the film historian discovers Lupino once again as--to use Parker's phrase--

> the truly Compleat Film Maker [who] was born under a dining table during a Zeppelin raid on London at the end of World War L. Her mother was actress Connie Emerald; her father, actor-author Stanley Lupino. Ida was the first female in the Lupino line, one of Britain's oldest families, to achieve international fame. The Lupinos, a lusty genealogical tree sprouting actors, singers, writers, mimes, jugglers, acrobats, comics, and puppeteers, date all the way back 400 years to the Italian Renaissance clown, Grimaldi.[4]

It is safe to state that Lupino's extraordinarily stunning hereditary heritage accounts for her attainments in the performing arts as much as her purposeful pursuit of excellence in several of them. She became an actress because the family tradition made it obligatory. Pleasing the family and living with the constant expectation of having to perform have prodded Lupino to explore all avenues of her seemingly inexhaustible compass of talents. She was the grand-niece of Harry and Mark, niece of Barry, and second cousin of Lupino Lane, all performing artists. Her maternal forebears were a theatrical family, too, and her mother, Connie, a child actress.

Not surprisingly, then, the seven-year-old Ida at school "wrote and produced a play for her schoolmates called Mademoiselle. When she was ten her father built a little theatre for her and her younger sister Rita, complete with lights, and seats for a hundred spectators. "5

At age twelve, she enrolled in the Royal Academy of Dramatic Art. There she was "involved in as many as eight student rehearsals and performances simultaneously. "6 She obtained occasional work in films and toured the British provinces with a stage company.

American film producer Allan Dwan gave Lupino her first noteworthy role in films: an ingenue character in Her First Affair (1933). That same year she was imported to Hollywood, accompanied by her mother, for the title role in Alice in Wonderland, a Paramount production. She was judged not suitable and was not cast for that role. She waited six months, with a salary of $600 each week, until she began work in The Search for Beauty, embarking upon seven years of busy, if not artistically fulfilling, acting. In 1939, she succeeded in winning the role of Bessie in The Light That Failed and reached stardom.

As Lupino tells it, she was weary of the vacuous blond roles assigned to her and worked in radio when studios fired her or did not pick up her option. After critical raves for her performance as Bessie she was out of film work for a year and returned to radio acting.

Having been under contract to Paramount from 1934 to 1939, Lupino reached star status: "after years of undifferentiated parts as bleached blond ingenues in countless Paramount flicks, Lupino moved heaven and earth to get her all-important role in The Light That Failed.... "7 She signed a contract with Warner Bros., but was immediately borrowed by Columbia to play the lead in Ladies in Retirement, her all-time favorite role.

In the subsequent eight years, she acted in a full galaxy of film roles, refusing to be typecast. Neurotic wives may have been her specialty, but Lupino was just as credible as a dancer (Thank Your Lucky Stars, 1943), as Emily Brontë (Devotion, 1946), and a nightclub singer (The Man I Love, 1947). Even with this startling diversity and depth in her roster of screen credits, Lupino has never won an Academy Award and had to wait until 1972 to be nominated for an acting award as Best Supporting Actress in Junior Bonner by the New York Film Critics and The National Society of Film Critics.

After a decade of acting, Lupino once again dared to try a new role, that of scripting, directing, and producing films. Why did she form a film production company in 1949? For reply, here is Francine Parker:

> Restive and dissatisfied as an actress, finding the glamour side of the acting life totally distressing, Ida Lupino always yearned for something more. It became increasingly urgent for her to make statements about herself and the world around her. She learned directing while keeping busy at Warner Brothers where, "you were either between pictures or on suspension. "8

Parker describes viewing all of the Lupino feature films made between 1949 and 1954, at one sitting, back to back, with two director friends. "We were speechless--surprisingly overcome with the breathtaking power and decidedly female yet universal sensibility of the Lupino work. Afterwards, we realized we had seen a glimpse of ourselves. " For Parker, the "split aspect of the female person is the recurring theme running through all of Lupino's films. "9 The exception being, of course, The Hitchhiker, Lupino's own favorite, with its all-male cast. Parker continues: "This ... double-woman, subliminal though she may be, symbolizes and embodies the essential schizophrenia of woman's world. "10

This twinned vision of the female sphere, a diplopic dimension of Lupino's woman protagonists and character roles, was rarely discerned and mentioned by film critics in the fifties. Certainly Lupino herself did not explicate her overt or subliminal feministic messages in her boldly stated filmmaking mission. The goal of Filmmakers, her company, was "To do high quality, low budget, independent films on provocative subject matter, to tell 'how America lives, ' and to be commercially successful at it. "11

Parker quotes another Lupino declaration in 1950: "If Hollywood is to remain on top of the film world, I know one thing for sure--there must be more experimentation with out-of-the-way film subjects. "12 And Lupino dared to do what she declared.

Sharon Smith describes Lupino's achievement: "She eschewed gloss for down-to-earth but provocative stories that were shot fast in practical locations, with little-known performers. She made it work. "13

The credit for directing Not Wanted (1949) is attributed to Elmer Clifton who suffered a heart attack after the first three days of filming. As co-writer and producer, Lupino stepped into his role and completed the film.

Newsweek (Aug. 1, 1949), p. 64, applauded the acting and the expertise which disarmed the censors while exploring the unpleasantries of the pregnant young woman.

> Taking the Johnson office by the horns, Ida Lupino has chosen for her first venture as a producer the story of a rash young teen-ager who discovers that men picked up in bars can sometimes lead a girl to unwished-for motherhood. The plot ... goes on to pay tribute to the havens that care for unwed mothers and their offspring.... Despite the fact that Sally's progress from indiscretion to the haven, where she goes through the agony of giving up her baby, is paced much too slowly for comfort, the story is told with compelling naturalness and lack of moral indignation.... Miss Lupino ... at least rates the proverbial "E" for commonsensical effort for handling a subject that ordinarily sits poorly on the Hollywood stomach.

Time (Aug. 8, 1949), pp. 68-69, bestows guarded praise in its review:

> It emerges as an earnest and unadorned account of a tragic problem. Much of the picture's force comes from its flat--and often flat footed--insistence on telling the story straight. Its dirty children, dilapidated porches and stuffy hall bedrooms are authentically grimy; its dialogue often catches the nagging overtones of everyday frustration and defeat. But its brightest achievement is the fresh, engaging and often stirring performances of its two young principals.... For a movie produced on a paltry budget ($154,000), Not Wanted is an impressive job.

The issue of morality, however, was evaded in the film for reviewer Philip T. Hartung in The Commonweal (Aug. 12, 1949), p. 438. The film's "greatest asset is in its honesty in facing facts at the home for girls who are pregnant and not married." Hartung approves of the sincerity and idealism of Not Wanted, especially "in the scenes ... at the Haven, a refuge for unwed mothers." In flashback narration, Sally "steals" her baby from its adoptive parents and is apprehended by police for her "crime." Hartung continues:

> Although Director Elmer Clifton has rather successfully avoided sensationalism in this story that could have been merely a hot number, he dwells at too great length on the events leading up to the girl's fall. It is not until the scenes at The Haven that the picture takes on real interest.

Hartung concludes: "The picture's greatest fault is in its avoidance of any discussion of the immorality of the girl's behavior with the pianist.... 'Not Wanted' deserves serious consideration."

"Dramatically limp when it is not downright dull, " was the
reviewer's judgment, signed T. M. P. , in The New York Times
Film Reviews (July 25, 1949, 11:4). "The causes of this unhappy
situation are sufficiently broad to be shared in almost equal measure
by the script writer, the director, and the performers. . . .   'Not
Wanted' may be classed as a solemn, good-intentioned object lesson
which falls short of making the grade as satisfactory entertainment. "

And "the emotional turmoil of the girl smacks of too much
contrivance, despite the earnestness of the authors to give the narrative substance as a case history drama. "   Although the casting of
the little-known actors was "a good bid for realism" the reviewer
faults Sally Forrest as the girl for playing "in one key, " while se-
ducer Leo Penn's portrayal "adds up to nothing more than sulkiness. "
Only Keefe Brasselle's characterization of a wounded war veteran
was a "bright performance. "

Contemporary critics view Not Wanted from the vantage point
of a quarter century's perspective.   In contrast to the consumerist
vocabulary used in 1949 reviews is the precise and piercing discourse
of Claire Johnston's article on the sexist ideology in films made by
women titled "Women's Cinema as Counter Cinema, " in Bill Nichols'
textbook Movies and Methods: An Anthology (Berkeley: University
of California Press, 1976, p. 216).   Johnston elects Not Wanted for
examination.

> An analysis of Not Wanted ... gives some idea of the dis-
> turbing ambiguity of her films and their relationship to the
> sexist ideology. . . .   Lupino is not concerned with employ-
> ing purely formal means to obtain her objective; in fact,
> it is doubtful whether she operated at a conscious level at
> all in subverting the sexist ideology.   The film tells the
> story of a young girl, Sally Kelton, and is told from her
> subjective viewpoint and filtered through her imagination.
> She has an illegitimate child which is eventually adopted;
> unable to come to terms with losing the child, she snatches
> one from a pram and ends up in the hands of the author-
> ities.   Finally, she finds a substitute for the child in the
> person of a crippled young man, who, through a process
> of symbolic castration--in which he is forced to chase her
> until he can no longer stand, whereupon she takes him up
> in her arms as he performs childlike gestures, --provides
> the "happy ending. "   Though Lupino's films in no way ex-
> plicitly attack or expose the workings of the sexist ideol-
> ogy, reverberations within the narrative, produced by the
> convergence of two irreconcilable strands--Hollywood myths
> of woman v. the female perspective--cause a series of
> distortions within the very structure of the narrative; the
> mark of disablement puts the film under the sign of dis-
> ease and frustration.   An example of this process is, for
> instance, the inverted "happy ending" of the film.

As Ronnie Scheib indicates, the essential passivity "of ready-

made lives" in Lupino's films induces feminists to argue that all
her films, beginning with Not Wanted, are anti-feminist. "Certainly
most of Lupino's films are about women and all are about passivity.
Lupino makes films about the inability to act.... "14

Tagging Lupino as an "auteuress, " Scheib, in his richly detailed and studiously challenging style, proceeds to explicate the
values he has discovered in her feature films. For Scheib, Not
Wanted "resembles its publicity very little. " The film is free of
"the head-shaking compassion for the 'poor unfortunate'" ... and
"tawdry sensationalism" as well. "Its heroine Sally ... is a pretty
young girl waitressing in a cafe, frustrated by the narrow unchanging
colorlessness of small-town lower-class respectability. Her romantic dreams crystallize around the spot-lit figure of a not-so-up-and-
coming piano player Steve ... in town for a short gig. "15

Scheib likens the story elements in Not Wanted to those in
Raoul Walsh's masterpiece The Man I Love, starring Lupino, especially a waitress named Sally and a piano player who can't settle
down. "But where Lupino is the dynamic center of The Man I Love,
holding the film and the family together, Sally Forrest leaves pieces
of her life scattered across the map. "16

The meaningful use of space as an "emotional entity" in a
Lupino film is analyzed by Scheib. "It's not that the space ex-
pressionistically reflects the character's emotional state, but that
his way of inhabiting it, of sharing or defending it against intrusion,
defines his relationship to the world. "17

Scheib examples this in Steve's reluctance to share his private anxieties with Sally, while readily sharing his piano bench with
her. Later, Drew, Sally's man friend, easily shares any environment with her and is "at home" in it. Drew can even joke about
losing a leg in the war. Having nearly accepted Drew's marriage
proposal, Sally discovers she is pregnant by Steve. She runs away.
Then, "Sally's life takes on a nomad purposelessness, marked by
suitcases, bus stations, rooming-houses, odd jobs. Sally is the
first in a long line of Lupino wanderers.... Lupino's characters
are shell-shocked veterans who wonder if they can ever go home
again.... "18

In temporary refuge in the home for unwed mothers, "Sally's
baby happens to her in total passivity. She is lifted unyielding, almost inert, from the bed to the stretcher, her face beaded with
moisture, the walls going by above her head as in sharp-edged hallucination.... There are many such 'spacey' moments in Lupino's
films, moments of extreme emotional stress causing visual distortion, or moments of total obliviousness to the world. "19

In economic exigency, Sally realizes that she cannot work
and care for her baby. She is forced to place her infant in an adoption agency. Scheib credits Lupino with a "strong social sense,
heritage of her Warners days, "20 an essential component of her au-

teur abilities. Sally sits in a jail cell because she has kidnapped a baby "to replace the one she has lost. "21

On the run once again, Sally's "final instinctive headlong flight--with Drew in painful pursuit ... compresses, with extraordinary physical immediacy, the cumulative pain, desperation, and striving of the entire film into ten unrelenting minutes. When Drew finally falls forward ... Sally stops running.... "22

Scheib credits Lupino with an "almost 'documentary' sense of locale" which creates a "very special tension. "23 He compares her auteur qualities to those of Fuller, Ray, and Aldrich. Like these directors, Lupino's characters' consciousnesses fill the screen but not the world, according to Scheib, thereby questioning "the subjective heroic consciousness structures of traditional Hollywood film. "24

In Never Fear (1950) the central character is a polio victim. Still rampant and its etiology undiagnosed, poliomyelitis was a dreaded disease and a newsworthy topic. Lupino had recovered from an onslaught of polio in 1934; thus probably implemented her own experiences into the script. The rehabilitation scenes were filmed at the Kabat-Kaiser Institute in Santa Monica, reinforcing the documentary facets of the film.

Meager notices heralded this saga of a dance pair disabled because the young woman sustains an attack of polio, undergoing therapy to regain the use of her legs. The Commonweal gives it a mere mention. The Christian Century 67 (April 5, 1950), p. 447, grudgingly tenders a few lines: "Unpretentious, making documentary use of current rehabilitation progress. Commendable in its picture of triumph over disaster.... "

Two brief paragraphs are found in The Rotarian 76 (May 1950), p. 41.

Produced and directed by Ida Lupino. Drama. Disheartened and embittered when struck down by polio, girl dancer eventually learns that her usefulness is not necessarily at an end, triumphs over her misfortune. A simple, unassuming story that makes use of considerable documentary footage, is inspiring in its demonstration of what determination and subjection of selfish concern can do. "

Scheib agrees that this is Lupino's most autobiographical film. "But, like all Lupino's films, it is a road-not-taken autobiography, the story of a dancer who couldn't become a choreographer.... "25

The starting scenes establish the personal and professional engagement of Carol (Sally Forrest) and Guy (Keefe Brasselle) her partner-choreographer-fiancé. The pair have successfully produced a new nightclub act. Once Carol is afflicted with polio, the couple's happy equilibrium is destroyed. The mutations in the couple's relationship are graphically depicted.

> The camera dollies in and holds on Guy, working on a new routine at the piano, off-handedly throwing enthusiastic remarks over his shoulder, only to unexpectedly cut to Carol behind him, literally hanging on the ropes of the stage in slowly dawning awareness of her illness, exploring the silent disaster, the invisible process of change within her. The inwardness of Carol's experience is intensified by a few out-of-focus, sound distorted point-of-view shots of Guy, at the piano, unconscious of what is happening behind him.... For the next several scenes Carol is never seen in closeup. She recedes from the camera. The camera only regains its position of intimacy to record her self-willed isolation.... 26

Carol undergoes many weeks of concentrated exercises. Then, encouraged by her progress, "Talismanically mantled in Guy's faith-restoring nightgown-gift, caught up in a light-spilled epiphany, she wills herself to walk and fails--falling forward and pounding the floor with her fists. "27

For Scheib, one of the most fascinating facets of Lupino's films is the interrelationship "Of a claustrophobic 'woman's picture' emotionalism and a full-frame documentary realism ... neither pole of which subsumes the other. "28 In Never Fear, this facet is found in a wheelchair square-dance date, an "uneasy mirror of Carol's past partnership with Guy. "

> In the precision coordination of the chrome-flashing wheelchairs, and the shifting patterned formations and reformations of the couples, the "insert" shots of Carol's flushed eager face appear as colorful details in the long-shot fresco of the dance--until Carol looks up to see Guy standing against a giant-gardenia-papered wall holding a gardenia (signature throughout of his constancy), like some dreamdoubled specter of her past life. 29

In time, Carol and Guy detach from each other. Carol enjoys the companionship of another patient; Guy befriends a secretary in the real-estate office where he now works. How does the film end? The film is preceded by the statement that Never Fear is a true story. How did the real-life Carol resolve her situation? The film is not explicit. Whether or not Carol will again resume her career, or settle for less, is "never resolved, or, for that matter, denied. " In Scheib's view, the strength and weakness of Lupino's films is "never to completely avoid or resolve. " The audience does not know if Carol continues her career with or without Guy, but she does "salvage her personality, "30 she becomes, through healing, a whole person once more.

The plot of Outrage (1950), which Lupino co-scripted and directed, is the converse of Not Wanted. In Not Wanted a teen-ager throws herself into the arms of a brooding piano player. In Outrage a young "office worker in a Midwestern city ... is brutally assaulted

late one night on her way home from work. "[31] Both women experience an unexpected and fearful mutation with subsequent despair and
renewal. The cardinal dissimilarity in plot is that the rape victim,
acted by Mala Powers, in Outrage, does not become pregnant. She
takes refuge at an orange ranch where a minister attempts to restore her trust in herself and others.

Newsweek (Oct. 30, 1950), p. 50, merits the producers, including Lupino, for their discreet approach to, but questions the absence of remedies for, the crime of rape.

> Under Miss Lupino's direction, "Outrage" achieves a
> plausible picture of shock and the girl's terrified reaction
> to her family, neighbors, and sympathetic fiancé. ... But
> after that ... the film turns irrevocably sententious and
> tedious. Even under these circumstances, Mala Powers
> manages to give a surprisingly effective performance.

Similarly, The New York Times Film Reviews (Oct. 16, 1950),
30:5, praises Lupino and her associates

> for restraint and a modicum of courage in jousting with
> another social problem in "Outrage. " ... But the drama
> ... is an indictment which loses a great deal of its effect
> by lapsing into run-of-the-mill plot lines. Its preachment
> is indeed honorable, but its execution lacks punch and con-
> viction. ...

Faulting Outrage as trite and obvious, the critic closes with "Miss
Lupino and company, ... are pointing--in good taste--to a social
blight. But they are merely doing that and nothing more. "

The Monthly Film Bulletin[32] dismisses Outrage as "An unconvincing mixture of sensationalism, sentiment, and half-baked sociology. "

Opening with the happy news that Ann (Mala Powers) has a
fiancé, the outrage of Ann's rape instantly changes her social situation, Scheib observes. Ann has worked overtime. Finished, she
starts to go home. Finding herself pursued and alone, Ann runs.
Her rapist-to-be runs faster. The camera follows her frantic flight,
then returns to the man, then forward to Ann in a mounting back-
and-forth, cat-and-mouse game until Ann, in a truck yard, stumbles
and falls onto a platform. As the man emerges from shadows to attack her, "the camera pulls up and away from two figures soon lost
to sight, pausing ... where a man at an upstairs window peers out
and, seeing nothing, closes the window on the rape scene. ... "[33]

At home, Ann's rape results in "an instant male-female
polarization. "[34] Ann's father consults with a police officer downstairs. Ann's mother and a policewoman sit near Ann in bed. When
Ann re-enters the world outside her home, she finds avid interest,
averted eyes, too helpful empathy. In a line-up of suspects in the

police station, Ann is forced to decide which, if any, could be her assailant.

Scheib asserts that the crime of rape affects not only the attacker and victim but the entire community and the families involved, and that Lupino's direction of this film expresses this psychological impact. "Rape opens up the whole carefully-wrapped sexual can of worms: the 'activity' of feminine passivity; man as violent aggressor [sic]; woman as guilty-innocent invitation to original sin vs. male exploitation...."[35]

Outrage divides itself into halves, with the second half of the film quiet, almost dull in contrast to the violence and kinetic plotturns of the first half. Scheib calls this a "radical city-country split." The latter half of the film, encompassing Ann's rehabilitation at a ranch is an "organic panorama where nothing seems separate."[36] In opposition, the start of the film is citybound, boxed in, segmented.

At the ranch, Doc Ferguson becomes Ann's mentor and therapeutist. Due to his fervent pleas, Ann is absolved of her crime (striking and injuring a man who teases her for a kiss, recalling her rapist) at a formal hearing. Although Doc and Ann enjoy a warm, nearly falling-in-love closeness, their relationship remains unresolved. Scheib comments: "The finally unresolved sexual and social tension within the film (an undercurrent in all Lupino's work, often through the somewhat ambivalent father-figures) reflect perhaps equally Lupino's own uncertainties about male-female sexual identity ...."[37] And, perhaps, the viewers' own uncertain attitudes toward rape as the grossest of violations of male and female identities. Not a happy or unhappy ending, but one which Lupino leaves to the viewers' discretion, in which Ann will work toward a re-admittance to the cityscape where parents, fiancé, and her job may or may not welcome her.

In his probing analysis of Outrage, Scheib considers the shift of interest from Ann to Doc in the second half of the film very significant in that this "prefigures a gradual change of focus in Lupino's films; a multiple, alternating point of view which, although structured around one character, nevertheless separates and localizes the social and familial forces that shape, develop or limit his consciousness of the world and of his place in it."[38] This plural, back-and-forth viewpoint is extensively used in Lupino's Hard, Fast and Beautiful (1951), The Hitchhiker (1953), The Bigamist (1953), and Private Hell 36 (1954).

Lupino received a Holiday award for her accomplishments in the first three of her films. As documented in Holiday 9 (January 1951), pp. 79-86, the Award reads: "To the woman in the motion-picture industry who has done most to improve standards and to honestly present American life, ideals and people to the rest of the world." The citation states that she helped produce and direct

   low-budget films of honesty and significance. Without ex-

cessive sentimentality and equally without blatant sensationalism, Not Wanted surprised the cliché set not only by
winning critical acclaim but by making a decent showing at
the box office. Since she has touched upon the problem
of polio (Never Fear), has given us a non-sensational and
moving film on the distasteful subject of rape (Outrage)
and is working on a sports movie about tennis which is
happily distant from the Rover Boy approach (Mother of a
Champion).... For pioneering, for good picture-making,
for integrity, Miss Lupino has helped Hollywood in the
eyes of the world.

Adapted by Margaret Wilkerson from the John R. Tunis story,
Mother of a Champion was retitled Hard, Fast and Beautiful (1951).
Reviewing for The New York Times (July 2, 1951, 16:6), Bosley
Crowther didn't think much of it. "A trite and foolish thing. It
simply recounts the quick parabola that a girl tennis player describes
in becoming a tennis champion and then chucking it all for love. "
The artistic level of the acting, Crowther observes, is soporific.
Sally Forrest as the daughter is a "silly, callow child" and Claire
Trevor as her mother "is equally fatuous ... with a sly and greedy
eye. " For Crowther, the sole appeal of the film is in the scenes of
women playing tennis, tournament tennis, at that, and "some of it
played at Forest Hills. " But, "the shots are abominably matched--
as badly matched (to pun a wee bit) as the agile Miss Forrest is. "

The film fared slightly better in the judgment of the critic of
Time 57 (June 25, 1951), p. 93. He finds the film's title mislead-
ing! A viewer does not expect a serious tale of a teen-aged tennis
star whose talents are exploited by her ambitious mother who schemes
to obtain a life of luxury and glamor for herself.

> While exposing the mother's schemes the picture also pur-
> ports to expose the corruption of amateur tennis.... The
> script overplays Sally's rebellion and her mother's come-
> uppance as much as it exaggerates her spoils of tennis
> over-commercialism. Actress Trevor holds out best ...
> against the abrupt, overwrought style that Director Ida Lu-
> pino, staging her fourth movie, seems to have carried over
> intact from her own jittery screen personality. "

The Commonweal commends Trevor's performance as noteworthy in a mediocre movie.

> Mom seems to be in for a beating in Hollywood these days.
> The villain, if any ... is played by Claire Trevor, who
> gives one of those frightening performances that made Bette
> Davis so popular.... Since the story is pretty much on
> the soap-opera side, it has to have a happy ending and
> this comes about when Sally sees what's going on and gets
> smart enough to give Mom the gate. "39

Yet another terse commentary was "Unusual but not very effective
melodrama. "40

Opposed to these declamations of mediocrity and overacting is Scheib's psychologically oriented discussion of characters true-to-life in a storyline structured upon an actual series of incidents in the life of a tennis-player, the film itself not outdated, not trite, but convincingly contemporary. Scheib discovers far more than a manipulative mother, an unconcerned athlete daughter, bland boy-friend, and compassionate father involved in an elite sport. He identi-fies the confusion of Florence's mother, Millie, as the core from which the story unfolds. This confusion is related to the audience in Claire Trevor's voice-over narration starting the film. Millie has projected her own unrealized ambitions and dreams of glory from herself, and from her ineffectual husband, a Mr. Average American, to Florence who displays a remarkable talent in tennis. The triangle of active and dominant mother / passive daughter / passive father reverses to defeated, passive mother / decisive daughter / active father through the storyline, and, in this, Scheib finds the articulation of Lupino's mystique as director.

Millie's voice-over is both apology and explanation, addressed to Florence and about Florence: "'I always wanted something better for you and I made up my mind to get it, no matter what I had to do' ... the mid-film disappearance of the voice-over when she can no longer read what is happening to her or to Florence, eloquently attests to an alienation and near-schizophrenia which render her as much victim as victimizer. "[41] When Millie's dominance over Flor-ence falters, then fails, and when Florence directs her own destiny, on and off the tennis court, then the voice-over ends.

The credibility of Florence's story depends on her own ado-lescent unawareness, an uninformed good-intentioned passivity. She does not know that her parents sleep in separate beds, nor that the regulations for amateur and professional tennis greatly differ. In Scheib's words,

> The entire film revolves around the contrast between the coordinated meshing of will and action, mind and body on the tennis court and the total inability to relate (indeed the total unconsciousness of any need to relate) this to the world outside which she perceives as an unproblematic whole--while all those around her concur through misguided love or calculation, to make it appear so. [42]

In Millie's colleague, a shrewd sports promoter, Florence finds a hard-driving tennis coach. "Florence accepts $50 to make a rich kid look good, and cannot understand her fiancé's disgust. "[43] Florence has no grasp of financial matters, so that her awareness of her mother and promoter as exploiters of her tennis talent arrives when three quarters of the film has been seen.

However, the action of the characters is dominated by the film's "brilliantly edited tennis sequences ... the cross-cut conver-gence of the hopes and fears of others hang suspended on her force-ful drives and hard-line serves. " Contrast this statement with Bosley Crowther's observation that "the shots are abominably matched.... "

Although Florence appears to be playing the game for its own sake, she may be learning to play the game of life concurrently. "For the matches are not merely pretexts, semi-documentary recreations or loose fields of victory and defeat, but rich, many-stranded, intensely dramatic events. "[44] Slowly Florence feels the stress of the game, identifies the stakes of the game, uncovers the fact of her own exploitation for money by her mother and the promoter.

As Scheib points out, Florence reacts as do most of Lupino's heroines with an articulated reversal from passive to active. Florence and Millie angrily argue face-to-face, exchanging caustic realities, themselves exchanging personalities: Millie becomes as her daughter has been, cowed, docile, obedient, while Florence becomes a controlled and authoritative figure.

Submerged in bitter realities, Florence is consoled and stabilized by her father in his hospital bed. "He reaffirms the value of love while banishing the forces of ambition, dismissing his lifetime spouse with a weary 'Get lost, Millie.' "[45] Thus fortified, Florence returns to defend her tennis championship successfully, only to announce that she is giving up the game. She will play tennis on Sundays with her husband.

Francine Parker and Ronnie Scheib agree that "Claire Trevor and Sally Forrest portray two aspects of the same woman. "[46] This pairing, Scheib asserts, comes from "socially imposed feminine role models." Lupino shows what a fusion of the mother and daughter into one vital individual could be during the tennis tour in which an enlightened Florence takes charge of her own affairs. But this Florence triumphs only to retreat into the nice-woman nonentity at the film's end, just as Ann in Outrage did, Scheib declares.

"Hard, Fast and Beautiful is a pivotal film in Lupino's work, mid-point between the more subjectively charged single-focus early films and the colder, more detached, multiple-viewpoint late films."[47] Lupino switched from young girl passivity to the inertia of a middle-aged male or, as Scheib explicates it, "A helpless entrapment between two modes of life, of action. "[48]

The film was The Hitchhiker (1952) now considered Lupino's best feature film, and her own personal favorite. The script was based "on the real life case of William Cook, the 21-year-old kidnapper and hitch-hiking slayer of six. "[49] In its 71 minutes, this taut thriller builds terror and tension to a maddeningly exciting finish. Edmond O'Brien and Frank Lovejoy portray two men preparing to enjoy a long-wished-for fishing trip in Mexico when their car, their lives, are overtaken by a psychopathic killer (William Tallman).

Here again the reviews received when initially shown differ glaringly from the judgments rendered on The Hitchhiker now. The reviewers' reactions cluster upon the factual basis of the story and the means by which the suspense is sustained.

Philip T. Hartung in The Commonweal 58 (May 29, 1953),
p. 201, complains that the film "piles terror on terror without relief until, without meaning to, it almost becomes a parody of itself. "

The New Yorker 29 (May 9, 1953) p. 29, implies the opposite: "a movie based on an actual occurrence, but it doesn't hold
up for its distance. "

Arthur Knight in the Saturday Review 36 (Mar. 21, 1953), p.
29, believes that the film "resorts to one of the most ingenuous
script devices in history.... Collier Young and Ida Lupino, who
wrote the screenplay, explain this rather glaring weakness in their
script quite simply: The man's crazy!"

Parker Tyler wrote in his "Movies" column in Theatre Arts
37 (April 1953), p. 37, that "The excuse for the bareness of its
bromidic plot is that it is said really to have happened to a couple
of fellows who gave a ride to a hitch-hiker ... everyone responsible
... including its director, Ida Lupino, seems to have done his job
with disarming seriousness. "

Classifying the film as "a straightforward, scary sermon, "
Newsweek 41 (May 11, 1953), p. 106, gives "Thanks to Ida Lupino's
direction, and the conviction imparted to their roles by the three
men, the film manages to have a good deal of suspense and shock
value without benefit of notably ingenious situations. "

In the same vein, Time 61 (April 6, 1953), p. 107, calls it

> a crisp little thriller.... It ends with the Mexican police
> closing in on the killer and his intended victims.... The
> picture's outcome is fairly predictable, and the drama con-
> fined to one basic situation ... works up a good deal of
> sweaty suspense without using false theatrics. As co-
> scripted by Actress Ida Lupino, The Hitchhiker is a know-
> ing job, as harsh and unrelieved as the barren Mexican
> settings against which it is played....

Predictably, The New York Times (April 30, 1953, 39:3) reviewer, initialed A. W. , offers a balanced view of the film's merits
and demerits.

> An unrelenting but superficial study of abnormal psychology
> coupled with standard chase melodrama, it moves swiftly
> to an obvious conclusion ... builds its tension slowly and
> carefully but is incapable of maintaining it throughout....
> However, Miss Lupino's brisk direction and the solid por-
> trayals by the three principals overcome, to a large de-
> gree, the film's cops-versus-killer format.

Scheib reserves his highest praise for this "classic ... tour-
de-force thriller.... The technical brilliance Lupino displays in
every one of her films seems to have been more visible to all when

no longer in the service of her own very original and perhaps dis-
orientingly 'odd' perspective. "[50] With examples, Scheib notes Lupino's "striking compositions, " "the on-pulse kinetic editing, " and
the "full utilization of contrasts between night and day, inside and
outside, " and more. Scheib persuades us that "these are elements
very hard at work in all of Lupino's films, and very much responsible
for the mysterious 'feelings' critics are willing to ascribe to her
films while denying to her the means of creating it. "[51]

The manner in which two middle-class men endure captivity
by a crazy killer is not only the plot of The Hitchhiker, but also
the nucleus of Lupino's auteurism. White-collar worker Frank Lovejoy is used to taking orders. He fares better with the commands of
the criminal while Edmond O'Brien, accustomed to his boss-role in
running an auto service and repair station, is easily and quickly annoyed at the killer's dominance, and he shows it.

Lupino followed this "man's picture" with another, The Bigamist (1953), "about a man who is married to two women and tormented by guilt. Joan Fontaine plays his career-minded wife, who
is anxious to adopt a baby, while Ida Lupino enacts the other woman. "[52]

In an interview, Lupino was asked why she acted in addition
to directing The Bigamist. "I was forced to do that. Joan Fontaine
wanted me as the director but said I must also play the other woman because having another name added value. "[53] As for directing
and acting simultaneously, Lupino admitted it was doubly hard to direct and then to act her role, unable to watch her own performance
as a director would. She solved this conflict by using her cameraman to monitor her acting, signaling her when she emoted too much.
However, Lupino adds, producing and directing tasks mesh nicely,
usually posing no problems.

The tone of the criticism in Films in Review 5 (Feb. 1954),
pp. 96-97, is sexist and condescending.

> Ida Lupino is developing into a capable director of minor
> pictures, and in this trifle about a traveling salesman
> whose good intentions land him in bigamy, her directorial
> skill saves a sudsy tale from some of its lack of substance.
> Miss Lupino also acts the part of the Los Angeles waitress
> with whom the lonely salesman (Edmond O'Brien) consoles
> himself while absent from his childless, business-executive
> wife in San Francisco. When Lupino becomes pregnant
> O'Brien ... takes to bigamy. This is discovered by an
> investigator for California's adoption service ... when Fon-
> taine applies for a child. The film ends with O'Brien
> awaiting sentence, being smiled at by both wives.... The
> touches of directorial skill which hide some of the implausi-
> bilities in the script occur at the ... outset.... Perhaps
> the most surprising thing about Miss Lupino's direction is
> that she did not try to queer or curtail the scenes in which
> Miss Fontaine had opportunities for being glamorous.

The critic of Time 59 (Jan. 4, 1954), p. 61, cast the film into the soap opera category. The storyline is "heavy with laborious emotions, rather too pat to be lifelike. It suggests a moralistic diagram, with overtones of sermon...." However, "the narrative has the ... purpose of making it clear how ... a thoroughly goodhearted man might ... land in a bigamous situation."

The Monthly Film Bulletin sighs: "The film seems to have summoned all its energy to shout defiantly that bigamous marriages exist and, finding no one to defy, retires defeated."54

Another plot summary informs us: "Minor melodrama which took its subject seriously but failed to make absorbing drama of it. Very much a family affair, starring the producer's present and past wives, the latter also directing."55 Yes, Collier Young had been married to Joan Fontaine and was married to Lupino when the film was made.

The critic of The New York Times (Dec. 26, 1953, 10:4), initialed H. H. T., agreed with the Time Reviewer. "We have, in short, the perfect format for soap opera." But the movie was made with skill and gentility. "Notable on two counts, primarily for the singular perception and skillful compactness, extending from Mr. Young's script down to the least significant bit player. It also ascertains ... that a low-budget in adult hands can outstrip the most spectacular commercial tonnage." But the basic premise is unacceptable. "It's hard to believe why a realistic road salesman ... should annex secret martyrdom by legalizing his pregnant mistress. This rather naive nobility also applies, latently, to both ladies, and the incidents of deadlock and discovery are calmly devoid of any sound and fury." Here, perhaps, is the passivity which keys Lupino's films.

The criticism closes with praise for Lupino:

> But "The Bigamist" belongs to Miss Lupino, and in more ways than one. This fragile director keels the action with such mounting tension, muted compassion and sharklike alacrity for behavior detail that the average spectator may feel he is eavesdropping on the excellent dialogue. And as the decent, wistful waitress, Edmond's Other Wife, her performance glowingly underscores the real text of her picture, to wit, an insidious point of no return for the lonely.

Scheib penetrates the psychological depths of The Bigamist, ascribing its excellence to the interaction of its three principals. "Films structured around a self-reflective hero" are unusual, Scheib asserts, but even more so "is the depiction of passivity not as a state but as a process of consciousness."56 The bigamist himself feels utter no-solution perplexity to his own situation, reacting with no-action. "It is the bigamist's deepening awareness of the complexities, values, ironies, and contradictions inherent in his situation--

the literal coexistence of so many possible yet impossible alterna-
tives--that the film traces far more than his reaction to the situation itself. "[57]

The bigamist's wife and mistress are not cast into rigidly
polarized roles, but the gulf between their personalities and potentialities is evidenced not merely in the acting, but in Lupino's camerawork. She used two different cameramen for herself in the role
of the waitress, and for Joan Fontaine as the sterile wife from an
upper-class family. "Fontaine is seen in multi-room, large, open,
light-filled spaces; Lupino in much smaller, darkly intimate, and
somewhat shabby surroundings. "[58]

Is The Bigamist a pro-feminist film or not? Equivocation
replies. "Lupino's films may seem decidedly non-feminist (and
The Bigamist provides a classic example, with its career as alienating substitute for a more 'natural' desire for children) but they are
far less endorsements of the status quo than thoroughgoing analyses
of it. "[59]

Scheib concludes firmly, however, that it is O'Brien's passivity as the bigamist that "dominates the film, the two women representing his former driving, future-oriented ambition vs. the relaxed,
unassuming, take-it-as-it-comes intimacy that tempts him in middle-
age. "[60]

There is a decided lack of subjectivity in Lupino's later films,
starting with The Hitchhiker and looming larger in The Bigamist.
No excitement, no emotional energy is generated in these, nor in
Lupino's Private Hell 36, "Lupino's late films, although technically
very accomplished, lack the intense emotional vibrancy of her earlier work. "[61]

Private Hell 36, co-scripted by Young and Lupino, was considered a B picture, a melodrama about an honest cop. It is memorable now more for the appearance of Howard Duff, Lupino's third
husband, in it, than for its non-controversial storyline. Lupino appeared in it briefly, as a nightclub entertainer.

The New York Times (Sept. 4, 1954, 6:1) gives it a brief
notice. "An honest policeman is the best policeman ... the manner
of illustrating this non-controversial point is not a great deal more
original than the point itself.... Just an average melodrama about
cops. "

The Filmmakers group distributed this film as it did The
Bigamist in a less-than-satisfactory manner, which resulted in too
few bookings for both films. For this reason, Filmmakers wanted
to enter the film distribution and booking facet of moviemaking.
Lupino was against it.

She describes her four Filmmakers years as the happiest of
her life. It was a group of friendly peers. Everyone offered ideas

and story concepts and discussed them. Her partners' decision to begin film distribution ended these warm relationships and the business itself. "I'm very sorry that my partners chose to go into film distribution. If they hadn't, I think we still would be going today."[62] Lupino wanted Filmmakers to continue making films, assigning distribution to outside sources. She was voted down. Filmmakers failed shortly afterward; the firm dissolved.

This pivotal hinge of fate opened the door to television directing for Lupino, a new career for which her Filmmakers experiences provided firm support.

The seven feature films Lupino completed in the period 1949-1954, taken as an entity, exhibit certain traits. Collectively viewed, Lupino's films do bear the mark of their maker. If film critics (Ronnie Scheib as example) wish to use "auteuress" as a descriptive noun for Lupino, then the term underscores a singular signature for her as director.

From 1949 to 1954, reviewers found her films too reportorial in their documentary delineation, with too-decided doctrines embedded in the unknotting of their plots. Perhaps Lupino's approach was more ad hoc than aspiring, her works more crafted than created, more implemented than inspired, with sparse symbolism and absent imagery. But Lupino never reached for rainbows. She has told Francine Parker that she is pleased with her films.

In 1980, Ronnie Scheib looks at these same films and identifies in them Lupino's technical brilliance and fresh and sensible treatment of socioeconomic crises: abortion, adoption, bigamy, rape, crimes of several sorts. She dealt with significant subjects not overtly and frankly considered in Hollywood films up to that time period and did so in a distinctive style.

The range of subject materials and type of television show Lupino directed proved to be even broader than her movie stories. As Lupino tells it, "The producer who started me began me in Westerns."[63] She laughs at the irony of her situation. The producer had seen The Hitchhiker and was favorably impressed. He hired Lupino to direct cowboy and action-adventures shows. She directed Richard Boone in Have Gun--Will Travel, Robert Taylor in Hong Kong, and David Janssen in The Fugitive. Here she was directing Manhunt and The Untouchables, male-oriented films, after working in vehicles appealing to women.

Lupino's transition to television directing was initiated by actor Richard Boone, "'Here I am, a little old ex-limey broad,' she told him, 'who can't get a job.'" Boone assigned her to direct a Have Gun--Will Travel script, "which included a rape, eight murders, and a sandstorm. 'Doll,' Boone told her--he called her Doll or Ides or Loopy, 'I don't care what you do. Just don't ask me to rehearse.'"[64]

Another version regarding Lupino's entry into TV making is
Lupino's reply to a question posed by Debra Weiner in an interview:
"How did you become a director for television after Filmmakers went
out of business?"[65] Lupino recalls that she directed a television
series about Mary Seurat, who was accused of complicity in the
assassination of Abraham Lincoln. Lupino researched this incident
for three days, completing the film On Trial, with Joseph Cotten, in
three days more.

The hardest work she's ever done, Lupino assures her interviewer, has been television directing. After On Trial, TV directing
jobs flocked to her. She was so busy she didn't direct a movie until The Trouble with Angels in 1966.

Lupino's own name for herself as TV director was "Mother. "
She did such a superb job of enlisting the cooperation of cast and
crew, following orders herself faithfully, that she swiftly became
typecast as an "action director.... Producers saw, marveled, and
began hiring her to take care of their worst mayhem. "[66]

Lupino's "worst mayhem" appeared in episodes she directed
for Sam Benedict and The Untouchables, whose plots were propelled
by the black emotions of fear and terror, jealousy, revenge and
hate. Lupino soon became known as

> the female Hitchcock ... The Untouchables' Bob Stack
> (Eliot Ness) attributes her success to the fact that as an
> actress "she knows when something would feel uncomfort-
> able on a performer. " She is also famed for her "glue, "
> her ability to link scenes smoothly, as when the distorted
> image of a gangster in a funhouse mirror gives way in an
> eyeblink to a beautiful girl looking in a mirror at a new
> fur wrap.... To the cast of The Untouchables, she is an
> A-plus director. ["Mother Lupino, " 81 Time (Feb. 8,
> 1963), page 42.]

From the mid-fifties well into the sixties, Lupino directed
more than one hundred television shows. Of these, she believes her
best was the Mary Seurat show, which she wrote and directed. Of
this film, and of Lupino's technique, writer Jack Edmund Nolan comments:

> She's especially fond of the slow ease-in shot, and of
> sweeping views of a set or an exterior (a rarity in U. S.
> TV films). She almost never uses odd-ball framing or
> other gimmicks merely for virtuosity's sake. They say
> she stays within the budget and finishes on time.... Here
> are her most distinctively directed TV-movies (all except
> the "Twilight Zone" and "Gilligan's Island" segments are
> 60 or 90 minute films): What Beckoning Ghost? ('61), in
> which a woman discovers a room filled with props for her
> own funeral and the title character grabs at her from a
> mirror. Low-key and soft-focus all the way. Guillotine

('61) consists of three 20-minute films--a costume item
about a fortune-hunting couple, a Dostoievskian exposition
of the gambling vice, and a superbly directed wax museum
chestnut.... La Strega ('62), a non-frightening, naturalistic and believable account of witchcraft on the south Italian
coast. The Man in the Cooler ('62) had the bit about an
undercover cop joining bootleggers to expose them, but
with Murnau-ish touches.... Heart of Marble, Body of
Stone ('63), in which a drunken and supposedly pregnant
model wreaks havoc in a hospital. To Walk in Grace ('64)
was a "Dr. Kildare" segment. Gena Rowlands played a
novelist whose inadequacy as a writer is the show's well-
made point.... The Masks ('64) is a vividly directed Rod
Serling yarn about a millionaire who invites his unworthy
heirs in for a final confrontation. Day in the Year ('64)
used a quasi-documentary approach for a yarn about a
high school girl who can no longer function because of an
overdose of narcotics. And several untitled segments of
"Gilligan's Island, " the funniest of which had an antiquated
pilot (Hans Conreid) marooned on an island, too frightened
to fly off. [67]

In Films in Review XII (March 1961), p. 166, Don Miller
praises the TV series of Hong Kong shows: "Someone in the production end is to be congratulated for a wise choice of directors
... including ... Ida Lupino.... "

Does Lupino enjoy directing films? "Well, no, I'd rather
write a song (she has written 28 of them) or a short story.... My
old boy and I have gotta eat, don't we?"[68] Lupino's expertise runs
on a very wide track. Frank Price, executive producer of The
Virginian, says he hired Lupino for her ability to handle sentimental
stories "'with great taste ... You use Ida when you have a story
about a woman with some dimension, and you really want it hard-
hitting. ' "[69]

On the set, crew members like her.

> "I don't believe in wearing the pants, " Mother says. "You
> don't tell a man, actors, crews. You suggest to them.
> Let's try something crazy here. That is, if it's comfort-
> able for you, love. And they wind up making Mother look
> good.... Still, directing keeps you in a constant state of
> first-night nerves.... You may be terrified but you
> mustn't show it on the set. Nothing goes according to
> Hoyle.... Reshuffle your schedule.... Keep your sense
> of humor, don't panic. I sometimes wonder how anything
> gets on film. And yet, if I don't work, it's Panic Man-
> or.... [70]

How and from whom did Lupino learn directing? On movie
sets, watching directors of the so-called "Tough Guy" school, among
them Lupino's own favorites: Wild Bill Wellman, Raoul Walsh, Fritz

Lang, and Michael Curtiz.   "'There was none of this nonsense,'
she recalls.   'I mean you got your backside in there, baby, and
you did it.'"71

Lupino's best-known and most popular acting assignment during
her TV tenuredom was initiated by her ex-husband Collier Young.
She was the Eve in Mr. Adams and Eve, a situation comedy scripted
by Sol Saks about a married couple who are film stars striving to
maintain a normal domestic life amid the antics and artificialities
of their super careerdoms.   The production premiered in December
1956, was nominated for the Emmy Awards, and completed 68 episodes.

Lupino's television assignments encompassed every genre.
The inescapable conclusion is that the small TV screen provided her
with more challenging materials to direct than the large movie
screen ever did, in addition to the opportunity to express a personal
viewpoint.

"Since 1958 she's directed many ... western series such as
'The Virginian,' 'Daniel Boone,' 'Gunsmoke,' and 'The Road West.'
Though these shows, involving much violence and occasionally a military talent for handling masses of cattle, established her salty but
reliable reputation with TV producers, they don't really represent
her best work.   Her TV dramas ... do."

Jack Edmund Nolan in "Ida Lupino: Director," Film Fan
Monthly 89 (Nov. 1968), pp. 9-10, supports his statement with a
provocative supposition: Lupino's best TV dramas and movies deal
with certain types of subject material.   With examples, Nolan indexes
these as (1) "girlhood and its fears" in movies Hard, Fast and Beautiful and The Trouble with Angels, and TV dramas Day in the Year
and Holloway's Daughters;   (2) a disabled woman, in movies Never
Fear and TV drama The Last of the Somervilles; (3) "the female at
bay," in TV dramas Mr. George and The Closed Cabinet; (4) a character's work gone unrewarded in A Fist of Five and To Walk in
Grace; (5) witches, in TV dramas La Strega and an untitled segment
in the Bewitched series, and (6) "a female revenging herself on
some poor male" as in What Beckoning Ghost?, Guillotine, The
Threatening Eye, Bow to a Master and others, all TV dramas.

These are Lupino's best directorial efforts, Nolan posits.
"She digs into action, drama and mystery series easily once they're
underway.   Love stories have not been her long suit; some of the
love affairs in her TV films have been a bit abnormal (La Strega,
Heart of Marble, Body of Stone, etc.).   But in her private bag, horror, mystery, action--many believe her to be the best woman director in history."

Lupino is always employed, as Nolan reports, because "Her
'no-nonsense' approach, documentary eye and ability to handle players of both sexes (she acted herself and that helps) endear her to
producers, who also enjoy her coming in within budget."   In spite

of perennial employment Lupino acted concurrently with directing,
sometimes in the same series, plus others, because of her low
salary. "At $2000-$3000 per filmed hour" as a director averaging
"eight televised hours a year" Lupino worked as an actress to supplement her income, being on record as "the main source of income
in her own marriage."

With more than one hundred TV series films to her credit,
Lupino's talents and techniques have surely scored more brightly
as a director in the television tube, and more frequently, than on
the movie screen.

In 1966, Lupino directed a feature film with less than happy
reactions from the critics. Variety (March 30, 1966) cited in Filmfacts IV (June 15, 1966), pp. 99-100, considered The Trouble with
Angels (1966) "oriented to convenient future televising." The film
was too sickeningly sweet to swallow. "An appealing story idea
has lost impact via repetitive plotting and pacing, plus routine direction.... Director Ida Lupino ... maintained too leisurely a pace,
even within the individual vignettes. A visual same-ness also tends
in time to pale the charm of certain sequences...."

The sugary story line dealt with a pair of reluctant arrivals
at a convent school who caper and blunder wildly until one of them
decides to join the Order, while the other pauses to reflect upon her
future. Much of the film's humor and sentiments were gratuitous
for Bosley Crowther in The New York Times (4/7/66). "It has the
quality of hit-or-miss contrivance rather than homely, schoolgirl
truth.... There is so much that is icky in this picture...."

Rex Reed's comment in Big Screen, Little Screen (New York:
Macmillan, 1971, p. 349), complains that The Trouble with Angels
"is an Ida Lupino-directed series of vacuous little vignettes mixing
up some pious (and unconvincing) nuns like Rosalind Russell with
some nauseating little brats like Hayley Mills. The result is harm-
less, but about as indigestible as cold tea at a wedding breakfast."

Moira Walsh in America 114 (April 16, 1966), p. 568, doesn't
mention Lupino, but reveals a fact unnoted by others: the movie
deals with convent life as it was thirty years ago, not as it was in
1966. "The film is supposed to be about the present day, and here
it comes to grief ... portrays uncritically--and as though they were
a matter of present fact--many of the rigid and ill-considered practices of convent schools that have long since been softened or elim-
inated...." Sadly, this inaccurate time frame hinders any insight into the character or the nature of the religious vocation, for Walsh.

But Philip T. Hartung in The Commonweal 84 (April 15, 1966),
p. 118, has kind words. "Can stand on its own feet, or wings.
Maybe what nun pictures need is a woman director. Miss Lupino
has the right touch."

Once more, thirty years later, Ronnie Scheib finds more than

a candied confection of a nun picture in The Trouble with Angels.
"Angels is a study of a young girl's sexual awakening but this time
in a purely feminine context. ...   Few films have so umproblematical-
ly and so unsensationally depicted love between women as a natural
stage in a woman's life, or confounded the physical and metaphysical
so completely in the emotional experience of that love. "72   But,
Scheib admits the film fails as a totality.

> Few films have had so fatally innoucuous [sic] a frame.
> Despite Lupino's fine directorial control of the near-
> screwball comic timing and tone ... she can do little to
> relate the true subject of her film to its fake script-bound
> opposition between mischievous prankishness as "comic"
> adolescent rebellion and Mother-Superior-Knows-Best
> quaintness as moral profundity. 73

In the decade of the seventies Lupino returned to acting in
films, meshing these assignments with TV work.   In 1971 she appeared in Woman in Chains.   Next, in a New York Times interview
(Oct. 10, 1972, 50:1) she announced her acceptance of the role of
Steve McQueen's mother in Junior Bonner (1972) a film chronicling
the adventures of a rodeo performer.   Although she was nominated
for Best Supporting Actress by the New York Film Critics and the
National Society of Film Critics, critic Stanley Kauffmann felt she
was miscast in her role of the Arizona mother.   In Living Images
(New York: Harper & Row, 1975, p. 129), he remarks that "she
looks and sounds wrong from beginning to end.   (And of course she
is hailed with critical rapture; she is English and an old-timer,
therefore, this must be good acting.).... "

In 1973, Lupino appeared as Mrs. Forrester in The Letters.
In 1975, she was Mrs. Preston in The Devil's Rain, and in 1976
she had a leading role in The Food of the Gods, based on a portion
of an H. G. Wells novel.

The petite Lupino, with light blue eyes and smokey voice cannot tolerate seeing herself on the screen.   She states that she is not
a Method actress and does not believe in women's liberation efforts.

> Any woman who wishes to smash into the world of men
> isn't very feminine ... Baby, we can't go smashing.   I
> believe women should be struck regularly--like a gong.
> Or is it bong? If a woman has a man who loves her, she
> better stick close to home.   I've turned down jobs in
> Europe because I'd have to leave my husband and my daugh-
> ter and my cats.   I couldn't accept those jobs unless I
> was a guy. 74

Lupino has had scores of job offers in Spain, Yugoslavia,
England, and Greece to direct, but she prefers to stay close to her
home in Mandeville Canyon near Los Angeles.   "I have my old boy
and my daughter and I love them and life is too short for me to leave
them and go flipping off for five or six or seven months.   I just
won't go. "75

However, a brief note in The New York Times (Sept. 28, 1973, 27:2) reported that Lupino would seek a divorce from her husband Howard Duff, who moved from their Brentwood residence, where Lupino continues to live with their daughter Bridget.

Is Lupino, film director, unique? A recent census of film directors nods Yes. In June 1980 "a committee of women members of the Directors Guild of America invited executives of all the major studios and television networks ... to a meeting.... The producers were presented with a package of statistics that pointed out that of the 7332 feature films ... released by major distributors during the last thirty years, only 14, or two-tenths of 1 per cent, were directed by women. And that out of 65, 500 hours of national network, prime-time dramatic television for the same period, only 115 hours ..., or two-tenths of 1 per cent, were directed by women...."76 And 35 of those 115 hours were directed by Ida Lupino. No other woman has accomplished this stunning feat. Yet, Lupino is the first to point out that it would have been hard for her to become a director, too--except that she worked within her own company, Filmmakers. Surprisingly, she "does not regard her successful directing career as gratifying and insists that it has all been simple economic necessity. If one includes the numerous television features she has directed, the total is sufficiently large so that 'I've lost count,' but she explains, 'I would like to be quietly, happily married and be able to stay home and write.'"77

She disagrees with the concept that her films show

> a special feminine sensibility. "They were not only about women's problems, they were definitely about men's too. I certainly wasn't about to crash the man's world because I had no idea of wanting to be a director. I had to take over my first picture; with the second, we couldn't afford anybody else. I think men are the greatest thing since coffee, Seven Up, tea! Nobody can get me to say anything about our opposite sex."78

Marjorie Rosen finds it "ironic that Lupino's comprehension of woman's social-economic role corresponds with Hollywood's most traditional conservative attitudes."79 It's okay if a woman has to work. It's not okay if a woman is bored and doesn't want to stay at home. And Rosen speculates on the possibility that Lupino may have been hired as director because her salary was less than what would have been paid to a male director.

What would she like to do next?

> What I'd really like to do is pick up in 1967 where we left off some ten or so years ago, with an independent company, discovering new talent, writing our own scripts and making good provocative pictures.... I am now polishing an original screenplay called "Murders and Minuets," a suspense story.... When I'm satisfied with the script I'd like to direct it. 80

She has replied to this question with a totally different answer. "Really, my dream is that some dear old man would see my old movies on television and leave me an oil well in his will . . . ."81

In the early eighties, Lupino lives alone, a near-recluse, caring for her three cats. Her artistic ardors apparently rest quiescently, perhaps temporarily. Only time will tell if she will dare more in the years to come. As she has so often affirmed, all of her endeavors have been, to differing degrees, for the sake of "doing what I can to justify my ancestors' faith in the ultimate destiny of the theatre."82 Her family traditions will eventually spur her on to explore fresh skeins, and to re-enter well-used ones, in the spectrum of the Nine Muses. And then, Ida Lupino, the "poor man's Bette Davis," the "Mother Directress," the "Auteuress," will dare again, and be discovered, one more time.

FILMOGRAPHY

Theatrical Films

Not Wanted (1949). Producer, co-screenwriter, director. Note: Elmer Clifton directed the initial days of filming. He was unable to continue because of a heart attack; Lupino completed the film, but declined taking credit for it. Also in 1949, Jack Edmund Nolan (Film Fan Monthly 89 [Nov. 1968], p. 11) claims Lupino produced a TV film but he does not name it.

Never Fear (1950). Co-screenwriter, director. Note: The film was retitled The Young Lovers and probably shown with this name.

Outrage (1950). Co-screenwriter, director.

On Dangerous Ground (1951). Director (?), actress. Note: Lupino is credited with directing this film and Beware, My Lovely (1951) by Charles A. Aaronson, et al. (editors) in the 1953-54 Motion Picture and Television Almanac (New York: Quigley Publications, 1953), on page 183. Reviews of On Dangerous Ground in New Republic 126:22 (January 22, 1952) and in Newsweek 39:103 (February 18, 1952) reveal that Lupino acted the role of a blind woman in the film. No mention is made of her directing it.

Beware, My Lovely (1951). Director (?), producer (?), actress.

On the Loose (1951). Producer (?). Note: Patricia Erens, in Sexual Stratagems: The World of Women in Film (New York: Horizon Press, 1979), states on page 298 that Lupino produced On the Loose and Beware, My Lovely in 1951. No other documented source confirms these credits. Lupino acted the role of a deaf mute housewife in Beware, My Lovely in a Theatre Arts 36:88 (July 1952) review. She is not cited director.

Hard, Fast and Beautiful (1951).   Director.

The Hitchhiker (1953).   Co-screenwriter, director.

The Bigamist (1953).   Co-producer, director, actress.

Private Hell 36 (1954).   Co-screenwriter, actress.

The Trouble with Angels (1966).   Director.

Television Films

Four Star Playhouse series
   several segments (1959)

On Trial series
   Mary Seurat (1959)

Alfred Hitchcock Presents series
   Sybilla (1960)
   A Crime for Mothers (1960)

Have Gun--Will Travel series
   The Trial (1960)
   Lady with a Gun (1960)
   The Gold Bar (1961)

Dick Powell Theatre series
   several segments (1961)

Thriller series
   all segments (1961)
   three segments (1962)
   Mr. George
   What Beckoning Ghost?
   Guillotine
   Trio for Terror
   The Closed Cabinet
   Dialogs with Death
   The Last of the Somervilles
   The Bride Who Died Twice
   The Lethal Ladies
   La Strega (1962)

Hong Kong series
   untitled segments (1962)

The Untouchables series
   A Fist of Five (1962)
   The Man in the Cooler (1963)

Mr. Novak series
   Love in the Wrong Season (1963)

"Breaking Point" series
    Heart of Marble, Body of Stone (1963)

Dr. Kildare series
    To Walk in Grace (1964)

Kraft Suspense Theatre series
    The Threatening Eye (1964)

Twilight Zone series
    The Masks (1964)

Mr. Novak series
    Day in the Year (1964)

Gilligan's Island series
    untitled segments, Oct. 17, 1964; Oct. 24, 1964

Bewitched series
    "A" Is for Aardvark (1964)
    untitled segment, Jan. 10, 1965

The Fugitive series
    Glass Tightrope (1964)
    Garden House (1964)

The Rogues series
    Hugger-Mugger by the Sea (1965)
    Bow to a Master (1965)

Dundee and the Culhane series
    Thy Brother's Keeper Brief (1965)

Mr. Novak series
    May Day, May Day (1965)

The Virginian series
    Deadeye Dick (1966)

The Big Valley series
    several untitled segments (1966)

Chrysler Theater series
    Holloway's Daughters (1966)

Gilligan's Island series
    untitled segment Oct. 3, 1966

I Love a Mystery (TV pilot film) (1966). Note: According to Jack
    Edmund Nolan this was a Universal film with Don Knotts, Jack
    Weston, and Les Crane, directed by Lupino.

Daniel Boone series
    The King's Shilling (1967)

NOTES

1. Francine Parker, "Discovering Ida Lupino, " Action, v. 2, n. 3, (May/June 1967), p. 14.
2. Ibid., p. 19.
3. Ibid.
4. Ibid., p. 20.
5. Jerry Vermilye, "Ida Lupino, " Films in Review X (May 1959), p. 266.
6. Parker, p. 21.
7. Ibid., p. 23.
8. Ibid., p. 21.
9. Ibid., p. 23.
10. Ibid.
11. Ibid., p. 21.
12. Ibid.
13. Sharon Smith, Women Who Make Movies. New York: Hopkinson and Blake, 1975, pp. 38-39.
14. Ronnie Scheib, "Ida Lupino: Auteuress, " Film Comment 16 (Jan. 1980), p. 54.
15. Ibid.
16. Ibid., p. 57.
17. Ibid.
18. Ibid.
19. Ibid., p. 58.
20. Ibid.
21. Ibid.
22. Ibid.
23. Ibid., p. 59.
24. Ibid., p. 58.
25. Ibid.
26. Ibid.
27. Ibid.
28. Ibid., p. 59.
29. Ibid., p. 58.
30. Ibid., p. 59.
31. Newsweek, Oct. 30, 1950, p. 50.
32. Leslie Halliwell, Halliwell's Film Guide (second edition; first American edition). New York: Scribner's, 1980, p. 663.
33. Scheib, p. 59.
34. Ibid.
35. Ibid.
36. Ibid.
37. Ibid., p. 61.
38. Ibid.
39. The Commonweal 54 (July 27, 1951), p. 380.
40. Halliwell, p. 37.
41. Scheib, p. 61.
42. Ibid., p. 62.
43. Ibid.
44. Ibid., p. 62.
45. Ibid.
46. Ibid.

47. Ibid., p. 63.
48. Ibid.
49. Vermilye, p. 279.
50. Scheib, p. 63.
51. Ibid.
52. Helen Rippier Wheeler, Womanhood Media Supplement: Additional Current Resources About Women. Metuchen, N. J.: The Scarecrow Press, 1975, p. 156.
53. Debra Weiner, "Interview with Ida Lupino," in Karyn Kay and Gerald Peary, Women and the Cinema. New York: Dutton, 1977, p. 175.
54. Halliwell, p. 86.
55. Ibid.
56. Scheib, p. 64.
57. Ibid.
58. Ibid.
59. Ibid.
60. Ibid.
61. Ibid.
62. Weiner, pp. 175-76.
63. Ibid., p. 177.
64. Dwight Whitney, "Follow Mother, here we go kiddies," TV Guide v. 14, no. 41 (October 8, 1966), p. 15.
65. Weiner, p. 176.
66. Whitney, p. 15.
67. Jack Edmund Nolan, "Ida Lupino," Films in Review XVI, pp. 61-62.
68. Whitney, p. 16.
69. Ibid.
70. Ibid., p. 18.
71. Ibid.
72. Scheib, p. 64.
73. Ibid.
74. Ida Lupino, "Me, Mother Directress," Action, v. 2, no. 3 (June 1967), p. 15.
75. Ibid.
76. Sally Ogle Davis, "7332 Major Films--'14 Directed by Women,'" San Francisco Chronicle (Datebook), January 25, 1981, pp. 17 and 22.
77. Marjorie Rosen, Popcorn Venus. New York: Coward, McCann & Geoghegan, 1973, p. 379.
78. Ibid.
79. Ibid., p. 380.
80. Lupino, p. 16.
81. Weiner, p. 178.
82. Whitney, p. 18.

9. MAI ZETTERLING: THE UNCOMPROMISER

Born: May 24, 1925 Vasteras, Sweden (Mai Elisabet Zetterling
Hughes)

> "I want very strongly to do things I believe in. I can't
> do jobs for the money, I just can't do it. I can only do
> things in my own way and on my own terms. "[1]

Zetterling's attempts to produce films evolved from the disappoint-
ments she experienced as an actress. "I began to have a declining
interest in performing some years ago. I'd started acting in Stockholm when I was fourteen and had left school. Since I came from
a working-class background, it was absolutely necessary for me to
to work, and acting was an instinctive move away from a shopgirl
existence. "[2]

She was educated in Stockholm. Then, the Zetterling family
lived abroad for many years, in Australia or South Africa (the documentation is inconclusive), returning to Sweden, where, interestingly
enough, Mai made her debut on stage and screen in the same year,
1941. She attended the school of the Royal Dramatic Theatre in
Stockholm for three years, married ballet-dancer and ice-hockey
player Tutte Lemkow, and bore two children, a son, Louis, and a
daughter, Etienne.

Zetterling acted on stage and screen, most prominently in
the film Torment (1947) written by Ingmar Bergman and directed by
Alf Sjoeberg. Zetterling considers it--the American title was Frenzy
--her best acting achievement. A contract with the J. Arthur Rank
organization followed. Zetterling then appeared in English films
Quartet and Only Two Can Play with Peter Sellers after her performance in Frieda (1947), her first English-speaking role. On the
British stage, she acted in plays by Chekhov, Anouilh, and Ibsen.

In her autobiography, filmmaker Muriel Box describes the difficulties she encountered with Mai Zetterling's coiffure in her film
Cockpit, later renamed The Lost People. Zetterling initially performed her role with short, curly hair. When she was called back
to do added scenes she returned with long hair for the role of the
child she was acting in the Ibsen play The Wild Duck. Since she
could not cut her hair, Zetterling wore a wig, enlarging the size of
her head markedly. "When the film came to be shown, one critic,
unaware of having to contend with two 'crowning glories' instead of
one, justifiably remarked that we had transformed Mai into a 'female
Harpo Marx'!"[3]

In March of 1953, Lemkow divorced Zetterling, who then married David Hughes, English novelist, on April 23 of that year. Hollywood films beckoned. In the fall of 1953 Zetterling was on her way to film <u>Knock on Wood</u> with Danny Kaye. There she appraised her prospects in the United States as an Imported European Actress. Her decision was negative. "I made the picture and went straight back to a London theatre to do Ibsen's <u>A Doll's House,</u> leaving behind several contract offers, and what people kept calling 'good money. '... I can't say I've ever regretted it. "[4]

Her rejection of Hollywood's promises of stellar roles and generous salaries intensified her disillusionment with acting. "As an actress, I had been horrified many times by directors who weren't careful with their jobs, people with vast reputations who never even bothered to do their homework.... Little by little I began to realize that making films was what I wanted to do. "[5]

Derek Elley describes Zetterling's transition from actress to director:

> During the late '50's she underwent greater and greater disillusionment with acting as a sole outlet for expression. Its limitations and lack of total creative control make her hanker after direction as a means of achieving her desires, and, apparently on impulse, she proposed the idea of a film on Lapland to her husband. [6]

Zetterling confides her own feelings about the changeover from acting to directing.

> It takes a lot of strength to break up a life you've been pursuing and start something else from scratch, but I said let's try to make films and David was very much with me. He agreed it's worth everything to do what you really want to do. Also, I had come to a point in my life where I said no more compromise, thank you, and this makes you feel very strong as well. [7]

The wife-actress and husband-novelist formulated a five-year plan for making films, starting with documentaries. Zetterling approached BBC's Roger Moorfoot with her idea for a film about "Sweden's genteel infusion into Lapland. " Moorfoot advanced a portion of the funds used to film <u>The Polite Invasion</u> in Jookmook, Lapland, in January 1960. With one cameraman, Zetterling and Hughes undertook to teach themselves all the component tasks involved in filmmaking. This thirty-minute short work so pleased BBC that three more documentaries were completed in similar style while Zetterling continued to accept acting assignments.

Each documentary they made evinced a progressively maturing efficiency in film techniques which Elley designates as the keystone of Zetterling's film work. The completed documentaries were <u>Lords of Little Egypt</u> (1961), about the gypsies at Saintes-Maries-de-la-Mer;

The Prosperity Race (1962), an incisive view of Swedish affluence
which was not appreciated in Stockholm; and Do-It-Yourself Democra-
cy (1963), on Iceland.   The Zetterling-Hughes team's first independent effort was a fifteen-minute anti-war short The War Game (1963),
"not to be confused with the controversial BBC documentary about a
hypothetical atomic attack, "[8] also released in 1963 with the same
title.

Zetterling explains: "I'm very anti-war.   Civilization has
grown enough so man should no longer kill. "[9]   Peter Cowie capsules
the content of this first-prize winner at the Venice Film Festival in
1963 as "an alarming little allegory on the latent dangers of the arms
race, as two young boys pursue each other to the top of a block of
flats, struggling for the possession of a toy gun. "[10]   The War Game
was praised at the Leipzig and London 1963 Film Festivals when
shown.

The British National Film Catalog for 1964, volume 2, (The
British National Film Catalogue Ltd., London, 1965), on page 124,
conveys the conflict and its resolution in three sentences: "Two
small boys on a modern city housing estate quarrel over a toy gun.
They chase each other on to the flat roof of the tower block until on
the brink of a sheer fall the quarrel ends.   Then one of the boys
drops the gun. "

Derek Elley reveals how the metaphor of the munitions race
is conveyed by Zetterling in the film.   Actors Joseph Robinson and
Ian Ellis as the boys playing on a building site, become more and
more involved, step by step, in their game, unaware and unheeding
of what the consequences could be.   A sense of enlarging evil derives, Elley explains, from Zetterling's concise editing and her capture of startling shots of the two actors in playful contention which
evolves into earnest antagonism.   The accumulation of events, planned
and happenstance, which emerge innocently enough but evolve toward
malevolent accident, is represented here in suspenseful, not-too-
obvious style.

Zetterling and Hughes made their first feature film in Sweden for the Sandrews Company.   Titled Loving Couples (1964), Zetterling borrowed its name from a novel by Swedish author Agnes
von Krusenstjerna: a very lengthy, seven volume work, The Misses
von Pahlen.   Zetterling chose as a basis for her film only volume
five of the novel, titled Alskande par.   She worked for a year to
condense it into a viable script, accompanied by sketches she made
of each shot, with camera position and other technical details.   The
script considers three expectant mothers in a Stockholm hospital
who recall their lives in the moment of, and then beyond, the births
of their babies.

Derek Elley developed a guide of his own for analysis and
criticism of Zetterling's canon of films based on his study and
evaluation of Loving Couples.   His guide posits that Zetterling constructed a credo, a theory of filmmaking, which she adhered to in

Loving Couples and all her later films with rare deviations from its tenets. Zetterling loves flashbacks; Elley asserts that she uses them often and well. She enjoys working with intricate time structures as in Night Games and Doctor Glas. The emotional peaks of her films tend to take place at parties or social gatherings. The picture as an artistic composition is a goal Zetterling consistently strives for. She savors the stark contrasts possible with black and white film, and the range of grays intervening. And all of these, Elley says, are used in Loving Couples.

American film critics liked it. "The Swedish actress-turned-moviemaker has made an auspicious directorial debut indeed with Loving Couples, ... a study of three women and their society in bold and beautiful terms ... commercial though her premises may be, they are never cheap. " This is Judith Crist's judgment in the New York World Journal Tribune (Filmfacts 1966).

The New York Times critic A. H. Weiler dubbed it "a woman's vale of tears ... starkly, often erotically revealed. " Weiler points out that her "initial effort behind the camera is bold, if complicated, in presenting facets of amour, illicit and otherwise, at too great length. The points her couples illustrate seem varied, but become obvious long before the film's conclusion. " He likens the film to Ingmar Bergman's Brink of Life which also linked the experiences of several pregnant women. The theses of the two films differ, however. Zetterling's "... is a reflection of moral decay in the middle and upper classes of Sweden in 1915. " She is interested in portrayal not of the physiology of her principal characters, but the antecedent events in their lives, "revealed in a series of convoluted, sometimes overlapping flashbacks.... " Weiler finds "The photography, especially in sylvan surroundings, is a decided attribute ... " and believes "Zetterling has come up with an arresting, serious drama that proves she knows the directorial craft and is a welcome addition to it. "11

Time's opinion: "Though Director Zetterling often seems overzealous in deploring the dilemma of women, she times her surprises so effectively that movie-goers of all sexes, married or single, will have no trouble staying awake. "12 Variety's comment was negative: "... the inability to give this tale of intertwined female lives some cohesion and form hurts. "13

Raymond Durgnat savors the irony of the Edwardian era pervading the film, traces similarities to Ingmar Bergman's work, and details its flaws and merits.

> ... the Edwardian era has acquired the reputation of being the halcyon days of elegant leisure.... Now Mai Zetterling ... joins Max Ophuls in denouncing that myth.... The title, Loving Couples, is ironic, since the upper-middle-class cult of "the family" concealed a consistent war against the heart, and against woman, natural custodian of its truths.... The film indicts a spiritual climate which,

though on the retreat, is still powerfully with us, and in
a sense, it constitutes a materialist, feminine riposte to
all that is reactionary, misogynist and mystic in Bergman.
Unfortunately, the story, and the personalities through
whom it is told amount to little more than a reshuffling
of the Bergman pack. . . . Perhaps the echoes are deliberate; the film is taking the "Bergman world, " trying
to offer a more materialist, earthy analysis of it. [14]

Durgnat finds the use of flashbacks within flashbacks confusing.
The scenes are "gummed together. " The "compositions awkward. "
"The film is spirited enough, . . . often gives the effect of being a
'rough sketch' for a Bergman film, before the nuances and the overt
ones have made themselves felt. " As assets, Durgnat declares the
photography "beautifully textured" and several themes in the film
"strike the imagination"; he hopes that Zetterling will "try a simpler,
newer subject next time" she makes a film. [15]

Peter Cowie agrees with Durgnat on Zetterling's unwieldy
timeframe, finding it, at the same time, conventional in "adhering
to the rambling series of novels on which it is based. "[16] For
Cowie, the several-skeined plot is burdensome; "too many characters . . . seem expendable and the first half of the film fails to match
later developments. "[17] Agreeing with Durgnat, Cowie praises Zetterling's excellent evocation of the "Edwardian hypocrisy" of the
European upper classes before World War I. Hence the men in
Loving Couples either "seek their sexual gratification without a
thought for the consequences" or "stay at home 'lapping cream like
castrated tomcats. ' "[18]

"A woman is formed emotionally by men and never quite
breaks free of them, even if she would like to, " claims director
Zetterling. [19] Hence Angela observes "Marriage--it's like falling
asleep for the rest of your life. " Adele erupts with, "There isn't
any love--it's just beds, dirt and slime!" Resigned Petra sighs,
"It's so easy to be feminine and feeble, but I simply can't be. "[20]

Cowie observes, "It is this struggle to achieve freedom while
retaining an essential femininity that balances the film's elaborate
frolics. "[21] He concludes:

> The individual scenes are sometimes impeccable, and the
> memories are dovetailed into one another with an admirable
> fluidity of movement and sound. The stiff gatherings, the
> music of the brass band or the melancholy piano, and the
> love sequences are manoeuvred most impressively, and
> the dialogue often sparkles with that wit and irony at which
> Bergman excels. [22]

In her description of Loving Couples, Jeanne Betancourt casts
a decidedly feminist interpretation upon the film's characters and
themes. [23] For Betancourt it is an "angry" film in which "Men are
treated with little or no sympathy. Zetterling seems to be settling

some old accounts. The innuendoes of male chauvinism in Hollywood-style movies are blatantly blown up ... cigars and driving as symbols of the phallic ego are played up as two gynecologists leave the hospital. "24 The film arrests the viewer with several scenes from commonplace experiences of women never before filmed. For example, the female views of a gynecological exam and the hospital corridor ceilings from a rolling stretcher.

Betancourt concurs with the critics in her assessment of Zetterling's use of the interwoven flashbacks: "as a major device it often gives ... either a banal or contrived tone.... The satiric, angry tone of the film, however, counterbalances the sentimental, contrived flashback form. "25

She expresses the fusion of feminist viewpoint and camera craft which she sees in this scene:

> When Angela speaks of her unborn child during her early pregnancy she says, "My artist, my explorer, my girl. " In the closing shots of the film Angela's child is born. The camera closes in on the newborn with a narrowing rectangular frame, reflecting limitations the real world places on our young girls. 26

Betancourt's penultimate sentence: "Loving Couples is entertaining and fun at the same time that it is blatantly feminist and dramatically serious. "27

Cynthia Grenier summarizes the pictorial impact of Loving Couples in The New York Herald Tribune, May 30, 1965:

> An unsentimental examination of the search for woman's independence, the film coolly, graphically, but quite unsensationally reports in the course of its action the fornication of two dogs, disposal of a three-month fetus, lesbianism, homosexual play in a church, attempted rape of a thirteen-year-old, nudity, and the emergence of a child from its mother's womb. 28

The genesis of Zetterling's second feature film, Night Games, shares several characteristics with her first. The foremost is its derivation from a novel, her own this time. When Zetterling tried to write it, as Derek Elley informs us, "it was only when she was half-way through that she decided to switch mediums. With David Hughes she formed a 50 page synopsis from which the film was developed; only later did she sit down and finish the novel ... "29 with the same title.

What was the storyline of this novel-film that caused a furor before and after its banning from the Venice Film Festival in 1966? A sexually inhibited middle-aged man returns to his family home before his marriage. He realizes that he must destroy his home to destroy the memories of his childhood spent there. He hosts a party, announcing that he intends to blow up the house. As guests run out, the man and his fiancée watch the house burn to the ground.

A majority of the critics and reviewers remarked upon the Freudian doctrines expressed in Night Games. Several mentioned the Marxian elements manifest in the film. But only one observer, Derek Elley, identified the film's theme as loneliness, and the desperation rooted in that state of being. Zetterling brought to Night Games a rare fusion of hard-nosed resolve enriched but not weakened by comicality. Her humor enters and extends into scenes and subject areas ordinarily not graced by smile or guffaw.

Further, Elley discerns that Zetterling does not probe or explicate the roots of character Jan's Oedipal proclivities. On this count, she's been criticized for her trivialization of sex and its full spectrum of perversions and aberrations. Questioned about the unconventional sexual behaviors of her film characters, Zetterling somberly states her conviction that human nature arrives at an affirmative view of life usually by encountering and experiencing a series of depressant and negative attitudes.

Elley mentions a reference to Bergman's film The Silence in Night Games. This occurs when a character asks for music to end the stillness, in Night Games, a direct reference to the earlier film. This may be Zetterling's salute to Bergman's accomplishments. Or, it may be her effort to link artistically the two films. The close of Night Games is too easy, Elley continues, but it works well within its allegorical dimensions. He compliments Zetterling on her depiction of Jan's childhood and her transitions from past to present skillfully managed by alterations in focus and light, while her imagery is always compelling, if occasionally obscure.

Elley's studious explication of Night Games, objectively academic, offers a somber contrast to the tongue-in-cheek, shocked-but-still-spectating American critics who consistently devoted equal, if not more, appraisal to the erotic and physical action in the film than to formulations of themes and idealogues in the film, and directorial and photographic techniques used.

Rex Reed's thumbs-down-but-fascinated review is an amusing specimen of an oblique selling job embossed with a debasement of the director:

> Too sexy to show in public, cried the festival officials ... and after a first glimpse there's reason to consider the banned Italians pretty lucky critters.... Zetterling seems hell-bent on directing her own projects to show a woman's independence in transferring to the screen subjects no man would dream of photographing. 30

For Reed, the film is mad, mad, mad: angry, insane, chaotic. He indexes the pungency of the scenes in a rising crescendo which centers on the male protagonist's memories:

slobbering, lecherous old men shoot holes through his
school-boy maps with rifles.... His mother gives birth
to a stillborn child at a costume party while guests look
on ... a saxophonist plays progressive jazz over the bed.
Then the dead fetus is christened with champagne and destroyed.   (Sell that to the Legion of Decency.) ...
the hero vomits on the screen three times ... plays with
cockatoos and wears his mother's earrings, lipstick, and
false eyelashes.   The mother ... forces him to mastur-
bate while she looks on.   All of this madness for the sake
of madness has a kind of queer fascination, but it becomes
tiresome as the camera tricks get trickier and the dialogue
pretentious.... 31

Reed finally takes aim at the director of this outrageous opus:

a scandale that has the taste of persimmons, but it is
filled with such incredibly juvenile Freudian pap that audiences are more likely to giggle than gasp.   She simply
has nothing to say.... If Miss Zetterling is suggesting
that impotence and pseudohomosexuality brought on by a
lifetime of sexual anxiety can be cured by a keg of dyna-
mite, her naiveté is too embarrassing to provoke further
discussion.... 32

For Pauline Kael

Night Games is a Gothic tale about decadence and impotence combining the worst of Fellini with the worst of
Bergman ... beats even the most baroque castrations and
... excesses in Tennessee Williams's plays.... It seems
like a huge joke--part Freudian, part Marxist--but it isn't
played for comedy.   Mai Zetterling directs in the grand
manner, with elaborate shifts between past and present, and
the kind of visual style that is usually described as "stark, "
and she is more than competent.   The movie isn't dead,
but it's ludicrous ... I've never seen a movie with such
sophisticated technique joined to such bizarrely naive content.   But there are good moments.... 33

Vernon Young's commentary is akin in spirit and substance
to Rex Reed's.

Mai Zetterling makes it clear in Night Games that she is
never going to forgive God for having made her a woman
and for not supplying her with a rotting upper-class family.
To repair the latter deficiency she has invented one--very
poorly.   Her sexually impotent hero is a country gentleman ... very nasty to women, who discovers ... that the
real source of his affliction (now, you won't tell anyone
who hasn't seen the movie, will you?) is that he is sexually fixated on his mother!   The ending is in the classic
mode, too--that of the pyromanic ritual... I overlooked

Miss Zetterling's two conspicuous contributions to fearless
film-making: a publicly conducted accouchement and a
steady glimpse of a naked boy with an erection. To a
New York Times interviewer Miss Zetterling complained,
"Some people seem to have thought this film was erotic
... !"34

Bosley Crowther's New York Times review, though reiterating
the sex-without-meaning-scenes, does refrain from sexist statements
about the director, while aiming for insight into the goals and intentions of the director in the film.

Night Games is loaded with material of the most explicit
and licentious sort ... awfully raw on the screen. Indeed
... so deliberately overdrawn--and sometimes so ponderous and clumsy in their Freudian symbolism--that one
might guess Miss Zetterling is either out to shock us ...
or she is mischievously putting us on. I would rather suspect the latter.... Miss Zetterling has skill and eye for
color in creating visual images. But she takes us through
a chamber of horrors without shedding any real light.... 35

Crowther, with Crist, suggest that comic ridicule, even sting-
ing satire, may be Zetterling's artistic intention and cinematic goal
in Night Games.

Like Crowther, Ernest Callenbach is affected by the Freudian
relationships, the psychological naiveté, and the horror generated by
their linkage. Callenbach connects Torment (1946) in which Zetterling acted the role of a cigar-stand girl to Night Games: both are
in the same tradition. He explains that the shocking scenes are
necessary to the film: "Depravities which are not shocking, or
which are presented in a way to lessen their shock ... would not interest Zetterling, or an audience."

Callenback enjoys the flashbacks used: "flashbacks introduced,
in the great old castle's halls and rooms, with a kind of sleight-of-
time like Bergman's in Wild Strawberries."36 He declares that Zetterling deserves to be taken seriously. "She operates with an imagery that is something like earlier Bergman, something like Fellini;
and her invention, though it is not so rich and strange as theirs, is
stronger than that of most contemporary directors--Night Games has
an obsessive visual quality to match the psychology of its hero."37

In his brief, wholly negative review, Rene Jordan dubs Zetterling a "would-be directress," and objects to the imagery that
Callenbach finds striking, and to the pecuniary potential of the film.

There is a plethora of cliché symbols in Night Games.
Snow is purity; caged birds are release; the mother's fake
coffin turns out to be empty. And there are symbols within symbols--even a pornographic movie within this pornographic movie. Night Games would be merely ludicrous

were it not for the fact that a claque of amoral intellectuals
has combined with money-grubbing distributors to promote
it. 38

Variety observes:

> as a lure to the prurient and sensation seekers, it has no
> peer ... this film is made with intelligence and determina-
> tion.... Zetterling's ... intent was not to excite but to
> shock, to show many negatives ... a film of much interest
> and some importance.... Technically, it's in the best
> Swedish tradition, with crisp photography, suitable music,
> etc.... 39

The critic of Time magazine can be credited with the most
negative judgment of all quoted. "Zetterling's style reveals her as
a cinemagpie. Her symbols are bad Bergman, her decor is awful
Ophuls, her decadence is phony Fellini ... the frames add up to
nothing more than an album of porny photographs. "40

Francis Koval reported upon the Venice Film Festival in
1966, commenting in weary veteran style upon the reporters-only
audience viewing the picture.

> September 2. The Palazzo del cinema was surrounded by
> police this morning and press cards were checked at three
> different points as the 500 journalists accredited ... filed
> into the non-public screening of Night Games.... The
> Swedish delegation is elated by the hub-bub, which will
> help to sell Miss Zetterling's picture all over the world,
> whether it's good, bad or indifferent. Aside from its sex-
> ploiting bits, it's an indifferent film.... 41

Not as good as Loving Couples, Koval snorts, offended by the
orgies in Night Games: "it is overloaded with the Swedish symbolism
that went out of fashion 20 years ago. However, the black-&-white
photography is magnificent, and Ingrid Thulin's performance as the
degenerate mother is remarkable. "42

Peter Cowie appears to agree with Koval on the excess of
extravaganza-style behavior. "Without the orgies there would not
be much left of Night Games. The very evils that Miss Zetterling
attacks provide the ballast for her own film. "43 Cowie asserts,
orgies aside, that the film is

> Zetterling's most complex formal achievement. Past and
> present are blended subtly and continually ... but by the
> second half of the film the divertissements at the manor
> have assumed too dominant a role.... The cruelty, the
> masochism, the elegance: all these ingredients are exag-
> gerated to a point beyond their dramatic relevance. 44

Cowie quotes Zetterling's statements on her artistic intentions:

"I tried to film a story of modern Europe ... I try to be honest,
so it shows signs of decadence.   Perverted sex is one of these
signs.... "45

Derek Elley provides a smooth transition from Night Games
to Zetterling's third film, Doctor Glas.   "Night Games went on to
take a key place in the development of sexual licence in the cinema
during the Sixties.   Zetterling's third feature, Doktor Glas ... created not half the fuss of its predecessor, chiefly through its lack of
exploitable material. "46

Based on a novel by Hjalmar Soderberg, published in 1905,
it "charts the obsession of a young practitioner for the wife of a
pastor.   The story is again told in flashback (a single, uninterrupted
episode) and is Zetterling's harshest examination of loneliness. "
The film is a far cry from Night Games, Elley concludes.   It is
the most pessimistic of her films, has been criticized for its slow
pace, contains an undefined quality and place in her career ladder,
and has not been widely screened.   But, thematically, Elley claims,
Doktor Glas is in line with Zetterling's other films.

Filmfacts (1969) synopsizes the film, then summarizes several
reviews from other sources.   From these extracts, the publication
adds up the critical arithmetic: "3 favorable, 1 mixed, 3 negative. "47

The very old protagonist recalls his youthful lust for the wife
of a pastor whose proclivity for sexual coitus became abhorrent to
her.   Though the wife doesn't respond to the physician's erotic desires for her, even when her lover abandons her, the doctor breaks
his professional code of ethics and administers a lethal poison to
the pastor.

Critical reactions to this somber study of an unpunished
crime and the killer's conscience, according to Filmfacts (1969)
were sharply divided between those who found it "a superb and sensitive film" ... and those who found it a "grim and neurotic study that
is depressing to watch. "48   Without exception, the critics agreed
that actor Per Oscarsson's performance was topnotch, and several
mention Zetterling's excellent high-contrast photography.

Stanley Kauffmann's judgment is unemotional.   "The film's
texture gets thin because its irony is familiar and its final impact
small ... the picture lacks the weight to give it any bite.   Still
Miss Zetterling must be congratulated on her refinements.   There
are some pleasures in the way the film is made.... "   He notes
that the film takes place inside of Doctor Glas's mind.   Although
the direction is "quite unoriginal, " Kauffmann finds that the director

has used some taste and imagination in her borrowings.
The time-lapses in the 1905 story are nicely covered by
out-of-focus episodes in the present, in which the sounds
of the modern world and the old man's voice link the epi-

sodes of the past ... the bulk of the film ... is drama-
tized in quick flashes of memory, dream, and daydream,
usually in high-contrast photography. (Heavy blacks, va-
cant whites.) She has a good feeling for the turn of the
century. ... she conveys that Glas lives in a figurative
glass bell. (The word-play may even have been in Soderberg's mind)....49

Joseph Gelmis confides that he expected the film to be about
a physician's bedside manner. Instead,

the film turned out to be something of a revelation ... a
first-rate thematic equivalent of a Dostoevskian novel like
Crime and Punishment, an offbeat psychological thriller
about obsession, loneliness, murder and conscience....
It is much too oblique and personal a film to achieve wide-
spread popularity, I suspect. In technique the film has
the look and feel of a 1930s or 1940s picture--with very
little razzle-dazzle camera work and most of the effects
... achieved by varying the contrast of the black and white
print and making it overexposed and burnt out at times
and blurred at other times.... The film works as beautifully as it does because of the absolutely stunning performance by Per Oscarsson as Doctor Glas. The character is similar to the physician in ... Wild Strawberries
who can't filter out the dreams from his conscious life
and whose memories coexist in time for him with the present...."50

Least laudatory is Vincent Canby:

Mai Zetterling, the Swedish actress who now directs
movies, seems to see herself as a tour guide of the soul
... Doctor Glas is technically good, handsomely photographed ... and totally devoid of passion, either on the
part of the characters within the movie or on the part of
the moviemaker herself. Miss Zetterling is such a stolid,
literal director that even scenes of sexual hallucination
look like road maps for a subconscious as flat as Iowa
....51

The most detailed and appreciative analysis of Doctor Glas
appears in Take One. The description of the death scene recreates
the character and camera movements for the reader, wholly keyed
to phallic destruction.

The climactic scene is ... a model of controlled construction. Seated with the doctor in an outdoor cafe, the minister receives his order of Vichy water, while the doctor
pretends to take a pill, letting it fall to the ground. Watching the people surrounding ... he offers a pill to the accepting reverend, eyes his surroundings again (as before,
but this time closer) counts the seconds for the pill to take

effect, crushes his own into the gravel beneath his foot, drops his pocket-watch, in close-up, ambiguously between his legs. The camera cuts back to show the one slumped over dead, the other dazed and distracted. The image goes out of focus and the camera begins to pan as we hear the voices of the excited surrounding crowd. Cut imperceptibly to the out-of-focus present; the event is at once as remembered. The doctor, in freeing the woman he desires from the man she hates, has enslaved his conscience forever. The result is true, even tantalizing, in the Hitchcockian sense ..., suspense has arisen from the careful ordering of seemingly ordinary images. Zetterling retains some of the good-natured vulgarity of her first two films...."52

And, of course, Take One mentions the excellence of Oscarsson as the doctor.

In The Girls (Flickorna) released in 1968, Zetterling returned to a feminist theme with female principals as in Loving Couples. Viewed at the First International Festival of Women's Films in September 1972, The Girls fails to affirm its feminist themes according to Elenore Lester. She attributes this failure partially to the fact that "Women feature filmmakers who have chosen to step outside of the conventional treatments in dealing with women are working on as yet unprocessed psychic material, and they tend to flounder and fudge."53

As in Loving Couples, there are three women in leading roles of equal weight. In The Girls they are actresses performing in Lysistrata, on tour. As Lester explains,

> They become seriously affected by the feminist message in the play and start acting out in life some of the rebellious impulses that have been stirred up. At this point Zetterling's hands seem to fall off the steering wheel.... The women cannot change the fact that in the core of their being they are committed to their lives as wives, mothers, and mistresses. They keep fantasizing on abortive rebellions ... they mouth limp rhetoric ... Zetterling's chief cinematic failure--the overreliance on these fantasies--is a direct correlation of the women's essential unwillingness to alter their lives.... 54

Roger Greenspun, The New York Times critic, concurs in this lack of a feminist message in his assessment (June 7, 1972, 51:1): "never formulates a feminist manifesto, and its heroines seem only to divide themselves between Greek comedy and soap opera...."

Greenspun's verdict is negative, and apologetically so,

> Miss Zetterling's technique is endlessly elaborate, full of

staged fantasy sequences, heavy symbolism, and tricks of
exposure; and as the women move more deeply inside themselves they seem less and less in touch with ordinary
reality--not more radical but more unstable.   The men,
colleagues, husbands, chance acquaintances, essentially
have no inner lives; they merely have dull or ugly surfaces.
However, the women have their souls and their glamorous
beauty too--a beauty that is more slavishly revered by
Miss Zetterling than it is, say, in many of the films of
Ingmar Bergman.   Of course no movie starring Bibi Anderson, Harriet Andersson, and Gunnel Lindblom can be all
bad. ...   Such observations are perhaps two parts sexism
to one part film criticism, but they are a function of how
movies live for me; I think for most people.   That Mai
Zetterling working with so much has arrived at so little
is less an indication of new directions than of directorial
failure.

Betancourt's description of the film adds to our understanding
of the parallel Zetterling designed between ancient and modern woman's statuses and stratagems, while admitting the failure of twentieth-
century epigones in their approaches to the timeless female issues.

Betancourt observes the audiences in the film, and the com-
mingling of conscious reality and subconscious event in the minds of
the three women.

The more the actresses get involved in the play, the more
they become aware that their audiences aren't relating to it
the way they do.   Yet The Girls doesn't resolve the issues of the actresses' oppression, for they are unsuccessful in applying the lesson of the Aristophanes play to their
own lives.   The film repeats the confrontation that occurs
in the middle of the play when Lysistrata asks her audience
to remain and talk about the play.   "I thought that you'd
like to talk about what we've seen. ...   Is it possible to
change the world?..."   No one responds, and so too the
actresses don't ... respond to the moral of the play....
The further you get into the film, the more difficult it is
to tell what is fantasy and what is real ... when Lysistrata
announces to her husband and the crowd at a cast party
that she is getting a divorce, one doesn't know if she really said it, if she imagines it, or if she said it as an
empty, ironic gesture. 55

Betancourt's article includes two women critics' views.   Molly
Haskell states in Village Voice, June 29, 1972, p. 67: "It is ruefully comic, like a majorette marching bravely down the street with
a banner saying 'we the people' while turning to see if anyone is following. ... "56   Marjorie Rosen expresses ambivalence in the Saturday
Review, August 12, 1972, p. 32: "The Girls is self-conscious and
self-indulgent in its repeated use of flashbacks, fantasies, and rhetoric; too often these tools distract and confuse.   Yet it is rich, ex-

citing political work that just may be trying to say too much too
vehemently. "57

Linda Gross, in the Los Angeles Times, September 25, 1975
(the film previewed in that city three years later), agrees with Rosen:
"Tries to embrace too many issues. Her methods, at times, are
stagey and ponderous. The film desperately needs cutting. Yet in
its intensity The Girls forcefully carries a personal vision of the
lack of communication that can exist not only between men and wom-
en but also between women and women and women and themselves. "
Exampling this is Liz, enacted by Bibi Andersson, who, Gross
states, "identifies more and more with her role as Lysistrata and
becomes increasingly isolated from her husband and the other wom-
en. ... "58

In a provincial village, Liz tries to inform her dinner hosts
of her feminist convictions and fails, just as she had earlier appealed
to a restless theatre audience to consider the importance of feminist
views and failed. As in Night Games, Derek Elley points out in
Liz's two speeches a stunning fusion of desperation with a dark comicality, an applaudable example of Zetterling's talent for using a
union of opposed qualities ably.

Liz becomes the dominant character as the film progresses,
Elley asserts, confirming not only the absence of exchanges with human beings, but additionally the lack of communication between the
play and its theatre audience. When Liz attempts to arouse her own
sex to female liberation actions, she fails, reaching a final peak of
frustration and humiliation. When her own husband jokes, "This
means war!" in a jovial manner, she gives up, defeated. After her
failed emotional striptease Liz finishes her plea by baring her
breasts and thrusting them at the males closest to her. She has, at
last, secured their attention in this powerful scene.

For Elley, The Girls is Zetterling's most intensive and extensive film. He ticks off its merits: Various brands of humor
abound. Reality and fantasy mesh neatly. Zetterling's technical expertise is uniformly operative. And her imagery is at its most arresting here. He stresses that the film's entertainment values may
lead to a misunderstanding of Zetterling's objectives. These are,
he asserts, not to record the rationale for women's liberation, not
to propagandize within a candied capsule, but to explore the effects
of emotional isolation.

In her detailed review, Thérèse Giraud outlines the plot
chronologically, with the timeless universalities of woman's situation
significantly expressed in twentieth-century terms. Giraud takes
note of the anti-war and pro-suffragette stance in the film, admires
it, and agrees with the true life conclusion declared by Erland
Josephson "This means War!"59

The Girls is Zetterling's "most effective contribution to
Swedish cinema, " Peter Cowie asserts, and the director's truest

talent may be for crackling cutting-edge comedy.   Affirming that
"woman owes her emancipation, in the Swedish cinema, to Ingmar
Bergman" Cowie hypothesizes:

> Yet perhaps only Mai Zetterling has reproduced the ig-
> nominy implicit in Strindberg's summing up of all love,
> "the highest and the finest, that must sink to the lowest
> and the foulest. " Her style may be too pretentious, her
> dialogue too declamatory, but the sincerity of her attack
> on male hegemony is unquestionable. [60]

In 1971, Zetterling made a threefold departure from black-
and-white feature films located in Scandinavia.   She replaced cameraman Rune Ericson with John Bulmer, and filmed a documentary for
television, in color, in southern France.   Shown on American and
British television, this film about Vincent Van Gogh was titled Vincent the Dutchman.   Zetterling depicts the renowned artist's life
situation "in sunny Arles thirty months before dying at the age of
thirty-five. "[61]

Actor Michael Gough (no relation to the artist, according to
Derek Elley) goes to Arles to portray Van Gogh.   Slowly, he meta-
morphoses into the painter, a psychic transfer like Zetterling's own
transformation from actress to director-screenwriter.   Vincent's
loneliness, his sense of alienation, and consuming lethargy and despair is rendered all the more pungent in flamboyantly lush fields of
red poppies as he strolls through them, the air of the countryside
aswarm with sounds of crickets and sheep.

Here is one journalist's list of characteristics shared, in his
judgment, by Van Gogh and Zetterling, after a viewing of Vincent:
"Tenacity, stripping away of possessions, lack of reward, no compromise.   It sounds familiar.   Van Gogh?"[62]

In an American Cinematographer (November 1972), 53:11, interview, Zetterling explains what happened after she completed the
Van Gogh film: David Wolper called her and said, "You can choose
any phase of the Olympics that you like.   Feel absolutely free. "
She chose to film the weightlifting sequence.   "It's so far out and
it seemed so remote that it fascinated me. "

Penelope Gilliatt describes the resultant film in her review of
Visions of Eight: "an eight-fragment film about the 1972 Olympics in
Munich as seen by, in alphabetical order, Milos Forman, Kon Ichi-
kawa, Claude Lelouch, Juri Ozerov, Arthur Penn, Michael Pfleghar,
John Schlesinger, and Mai Zetterling. "[63]   After describing the sports
involved, Gilliatt observes that it laces together eight sketches

> that often seem mostly to stress the truth of truisms about
> differences in the national outlook of their directors.   Mai
> Zetterling, for instance, who is not interested in sports,
> says at the start of her piece that she is fascinated by ob-
> sessions, which only underlines a cliché about Swedish-
> ness. [64]

The whole film doesn't cumulate--most reviewers mention this trait--
so one is left with images and spoken lines as viewer, and with
sparse analysis of what each filmmaker of the double-four roster
could and did accomplish, the merest recital of director, sport, and
athlete occupying the available page space. In Media Review Digest,
Part I (1973/74), twenty-two reviews of Visions of Eight are accorded a plus, minus, or both (mixed review). Also recorded is
the fact that the film won a Gold Medal at the Atlanta International
Film Festival.

In the American Cinematographer interview mentioned, Zetterling's replies to questions provide us with a minuscule case study of
preparation for a film, and her working relationship with her cameraman, Rune Ericson. When asked if she had "any sort of stylized
visual approach" to her subject before beginning, she replied: "I
had two headings in my notes. One of them said 'ISOLATION' and
the other said 'OBSESSION'. " She said she wanted to emphasize the
individual facet of the sport. "They feel very, very alone all the
time.... That lone-wolf stuff is very interesting and that's what
I've been trying to get. "65 As for obsession, she said that any
sportsman had to be obsessed, or fanatical to a certain degree. As
for Ericson, "The Strongest" segment in Visions of Eight, is their
fourth joint effort. They are different sorts of people, they bully
each other, but understand each other. "He's a very technical man,
and I like that.... " He is "very open to trying new things. On our
other films we've made lots of tests and tried to do unusual things
like using different types of lighting that hadn't been tried before in
Sweden. "

Zetterling found it easy to establish rapport with the weight-
lifters: "... it hasn't been that difficult.... They've generally been
very helpful. " If they were surprised by a woman director they
didn't show it. "66

The National Review found the segments of Visions of Eight by
Arthur Penn and John Schlesinger "finest. " And, "Zetterling's
weight-lifters ... much engaged in an outlandishly vain, truly silly
endeavor. Still, in the context of the Games, they are somehow
beautiful too. "67

Ken Gay in his review agrees with the National Review judgment: Schlesinger's segment was best, and Penn's one of the best.
"Mai Zetterling ... records those physically immense men who lift
weights, and gives us a macabre film essay, full of human frustration and passion, as these solid looking men fight their emotions. "68

Penelope Houston cites "Mai Zetterling's filming of the weight-
lifters, including one marvellous competitor solemnly frog-jumping
up a flight of steps, takes what honours there are. "69 Her praise
includes the segments of Forman, Penn, and Schlesinger, too.

From New Statesman: "Elsewhere in this disappointment were
nice bits: Miss Zetterling astutely settling on the conveyorbelt feeding

of weight-lifters.... "70   In his review, Benny Green of Punch
doesn't mention Zetterling at all.

Richard Schickel's review was titled "Non-Olympian. "   He
is wholly negative about the film, therefore worth quoting.

> A more accurate title might have been "Cheap Shots of
> Eight. "   These impressions of the 1972 Olympic Games
> have almost nothing of value to say either about the Munich
> spectacle or about athletics in general.   What the film does
> do is bring together in one handy package most of the reign-
> ing clichés of contemporary film making.   As such, it
> should be must viewing at every film school in the world;
> elsewhere it may be enjoyably and profitably avoided. "
> Schickel has harsh words for Zetterling.   "The most
> abused device is ironic cross-cutting.   Mai Zetterling has
> her somber Swedish fun jumping from over-muscled weight
> lifters to shots of mass-food preparation in the Olympic
> Village.   But since these athletes are not overweight, con-
> sidering their specialty, her juxtaposition of images is
> superficial and the idea behind it banal. "71

Derek Elley's analysis of "The Strongest" episode is as warm
with praise as Schickel's is dark with disgust.   Elley finds the
themes of loneliness and obsession superbly expressed in the film
segment.

"Zetterling shows her subjects at work, driving themselves
deep into masochistic regions every bit as lonely as those inhabited
by Doktor Glas, Jan in Night Games or Liz in The Girls. "   The
weight lifters are comfortable only with their own kind, akin to the
actresses in The Girls, or the society in Night Games, Elley affirms.   The director's own reactions to the weight lifters are captured
by the camera to good effect.   "There is a genuine sympathy to be
found in her obvious amazement at these sportsmen which makes her
episode in Visions of Eight so successful; allied with her definite approach and technical virtuosity (a feature of all her works, and best
seen here in the visually-incisive band-playing sequence), "The
Strongest" has a depth and sense of sustained argument which es-
capes every other of the seven segments.   The final image is a
memorable example of achieving one's ends by the simplest means,
and shows Zetterling (for once, satisfactorily) solving the problem of
her endings: after a sustained coda showing the competitors depart-
ing (like giants to the hills) and the equipment and paraphernalia of
the contest being slowly dismantled, she holds on to a banner showing the weightlifting logo as, finally and inexorably, it falls into a
crumpled heap on the floor. "72

As "the best of an uneven bunch, " Elley rated Forman's,
Pfleghar's, and Zetterling's Olympic contributions.   Unsurprising
recalling that Zetterling began her apprenticeship as a director

doing documentaries for the BBC in London ... Everybody

said: "oh, you'll find it very difficult, my dear. " But I
decided I would learn it the hard way by making very
small things to begin with. ... I was lucky enough to have
an idea that appealed to them. Also, the head of the documentary section at the time was very much a woman's
champion and he felt that women should have more chance
to direct on TV. So I came to the right man at the right
time with the right idea ... at one point, there was only
my husband David and myself and one cameraman ...
which meant that we each had five or six different jobs to
do. I even shot the camera and the sound at times and I
sat in the cutting room with it for about a year, I think.
But I'm really glad I learned it the hard way. The picture
was very successful, so I did four more documentaries.
I love doing documentaries because my own personality is
such that I like being plunged into new worlds. ... "73

Two projected feature films failed to materialize for Zetterling in that fateful year, 1972. One of these dealt with methylated
spirits drinkers in London, tentatively titled Bury Me in My Boots.
She was asked to make this film with a star. And even though Zetterling had the right of final cut in her contract, she didn't make
the picture. This rejection of terms counter to her ethical and
artistic intentions is partially responsible for the hiatus in her filmmaking career. In the 1972 interview, Zetterling wondered if she
would ever do something good, vowing that she would continue trying.

In twenty years' of collaborative effort, the Zetterling-Hughes
team has racked up four feature and several documentary films,
with plans for more to come. Declaring her favorite film directors
as Buñuel and Paolini, Zetterling intends to make more films, on
her own terms, and to venture into fresh areas of creative endeavor.

In the early sixties, Zetterling and her husband moved from
the unfashionable side of the Thames (London) to a house in Hamp-
shire, and then to a farm near Nimes, in southern France, where
they presently live in a back-to-nature style, cultivating herbs and
vegetables, growing almond trees and lavender bushes. "My next
book is going to be a herbal book. I make my own tonics, astrin-
gents for the face.... I start making soap next.... I'm having
bees too.... I find a tremendous serenity in living this kind of
life. "74

Since Night Games was published in 1966, Zetterling has had
three books in print: Black Sun (1974), Bird of Passage (1977),
and Shadow of the Sun (1979).

How does she feel about being a woman and a film director?
"A woman as a director is more gullible, questions her instincts.... "
It is like ruling a country for three months, she says, and "Most
women are not used to that. "

Zetterling is a petite size, "with the kind of open, wondering face we associate with children. Her coloring is pure Scandinavian --wheat-colored hair, luminous, peachy tan skin, eyes the medium blue of the Swedish flag. "75

Interviewed after Visions of Eight, Zetterling is described as "squat, frumpy, likable, with a sagging, fleshy face and serious Scandinavian eyes.... "76 Her acting roles in 18 films bequeath a presence and intuitive understanding of the nature of the actor as artist. "Directing an actor is a very complex and difficult thing.... You have to be fantastically delicate [with them] not to hurt anything ... being a director is very tough, it makes one very cross. "77

She admits she is devoted to the cause of women's liberation and hates the manners men have when reacting to female aggressiveness (hers). Zetterling pooh-poohs the notion that a woman loses her sensuality because she is in command.

She has been working on a documentary on tennis champion Stan Smith. She has been asked "'to do the World Cup, to do something about the really big boys in football next year. ' She smiles. 'Now I've become a sort of leading sports director which is very funny, very comic. ' "78

The Zetterling-Hughes team is preparing a script for a documentary film on Iceland. But she doesn't plan to channel her creativity strictly into films. "The change is still within me. But whatever it is, I won't compromise.... It will be something I believe in. "79

FILMOGRAPHY

Feature

Loving Couples (1965)

Night Games (1966)

Doctor Glas (1968)

The Girls (1968)

Documentary

The Polite Invasion (1960)

Lords of Little Egypt (1961)

The Prosperity Race (1962)

Do-It-Yourself-Democracy (1963)

The War Game (1963)

Vincent the Dutchman (1971)

"The Strongest" in Visions of Eight (1972 Munich Olympiade film)

Mayerling (undated) *

Idiot's Delight (undated) *

NOTES

1. Craig McGregor, "Mai is behind the camera now, " New York Times Biography Edition (April 30, 1972), p. 899.
2. Joanne Stang, "In Sweden it's easier to play 'Night Games,'" New York Times (Oct. 9, 1966), page uncited.
3. Muriel Box, Odd Woman Out. London: Leslie Frewin, 1974, p. 200.
4. Stang, n. p.
5. Ibid.
6. Derek Elley, "Hiding it under a bushel: Mai Zetterling. Free Fall...." Films and Filming, XX (April 1974), p. 29.
7. Stang, n. p.
8. William Wolf, "Mai Zetterling censures the censor, " Cue (October 8, 1966), no page cited.
9. Ibid.
10. Peter Cowie, Sweden 2. New York: A. S. Barnes, 1970, p. 238.
11. A. H. Weiler, The New York Times, Sept. 20, 1966, 38:1.
12. Filmfacts, 1966. Ed. Ernest Parmentier, American Film Institute.
13. Ibid.
14. Raymond Durgnat, "Loving Couples, " Films & Filming, II (Sept. 1965), pp. 26-27.
15. Ibid. , p. 27.
16. Cowie, p. 238.
17. Ibid. , p. 241.
18. Ibid. , p. 239.
19. Ibid.
20. Ibid.
21. Ibid.
22. Ibid. , p. 241.
23. Jeanne Betancourt, Women in Focus. Dayton, Ohio: Pflaum, 1974, pp. 90-93.
24. Ibid. , p. 93.
25. Ibid.
26. Ibid.
27. Ibid.
28. Ibid. , p. 91.
29. Elley, p. 31.
30. Rex Reed, Big Screen/Little Screen. New York: Macmillan, 1971, p. 361.

*Cited in the 1980 International Motion Picture Almanac as TV documentaries.

31. Ibid.
32. Ibid., p. 362.
33. Pauline Kael, Kiss Kiss, Bang Bang. Boston: Little Brown, 1968, pp. 103-104.
34. Vernon Young, On Film. Chicago: Quadrangle Books, 1972, p. 296.
35. Bosley Crowther, The New York Times, December 20, 1966, 58:1.
36. Film Quarterly, 20:2 (Winter 1966-67), pp. 37-38.
37. Ibid., p. 38.
38. Films in Review, XVIII:1 (January 1967), p. 53.
39. Filmfacts, 1966.
40. Ibid.
41. Films in Review, XVII:8 (October 1966), p. 468.
42. Ibid.
43. Cowie, p. 241.
44. Ibid.
45. Ibid.
46. Filmfacts, 1969. Ed. Ernest Parmentier, American Film Institute.
47. Ibid.
48. Filmfacts, 1966.
49. Ibid.
50. Ibid.
51. Ibid.
52. Take One 2 (Nov.-Dec. 1968), pp. 22-23.
53. "At Last: A Festival of Women's Films," Ms. 1 (Oct. 1972), p. 26.
54. Ibid.
55. Betancourt, p. 63.
56. Ibid., p. 62.
57. Ibid., p. 63.
58. Film Review Digest 1, 2 (1975), p. 150.
59. "Les filles de Mai Zetterling," Cahiers du Cinéma v. 262-263 (Jan. 1976), pp. 24 and 26.
60. Cowie, p. 243.
61. Elley, p. 32.
62. McGregor, p. 902.
63. New Yorker, August 20, 1969, p. 69.
64. Ibid.
65. "Mai Zetterling at the Olympic Games," American Cinematographer (November 1972), p. 1277.
66. Ibid., p. 1321.
67. David Brudnoy, "Obsessions 3," National Review 25 (Oct. 12, 1973), p. 1127.
68. Films and Filming 19:12 (September 1973), p. 55.
69. "Festivals 73: Cannes," Sight and Sound 42 (Summer 1973), p. 143.
70. John Coleman, "Game Pie," New Statesman 86 (Sept. 7, 1972), p. 324.
71. Time 102 (Sept. 17, 1972), p. 96.
72. Elley, p. 29.
73. "Mai Zetterling at the Olympic Games," p. 1321.
74. Louise Sweeney, "Mai Zetterling," The Christian Science Monitor, (Dec. 14, 1973) Second Section, p. 16.

75. Ibid., p. 16.
76. McGregor, p. 899.
77. Sweeney, p. 16.
78. Ibid., p. 17.
79. McGregor, p. 899.

10. SHIRLEY CLARKE: REALITY RENDERED

Born: October 2, 1925, Manhattan, New York

> "I used to feel that I could never do a film about myself
> because my life wasn't interesting enough to waste anyone's
> time--including my own--looking at it. My life is just one
> long bore. The most interesting thing about me is my
> work--since I have less and less life, social life and hu-
> man relationships. Pretty much everything I do is related
> to my work or 'image,' which is why I do the work. I
> do the work to make me happy--not because I've got any
> burning message to get out. "[1]

If anyone personifies the struggles and satisfactions of the independent filmmaker in the United States that individual is Shirley Clarke.
She is the quintessential representative of the independent American
filmmaking movement in its near half century evolution. Being female has served to strengthen her position as an exemplar.

    In An Introduction to the American Underground Film (New
York: Dutton, 1967), Sheldon Renan dates and describes the emer-
gence of individuals making films outside the corporate structure of
the film industry prior to World War II. Preceded by what Renan
labels "The First Avant Garde in Europe" a smaller wave of activity
developed in the United States in the twenties. But, "As in Europe,
the avant-garde in America essentially disappeared in 1931" (page
79). A few avant-garde films were completed in the Depression
decade, notably those of Mary Ellen Bute and her husband, Ted Ne-
meth. When the Depression ended in 1939-1940, the Second Film
Avant-garde took root, waxing in the eleven-year period 1943-1954.
"The work that set the dominant style in live action for that period
was Maya Deren and Alexander Hammid's Meshes of the Afternoon
(1943)" (page 84).

    A West Coast Revival of independent filmmaking matched a
similar flourishing in films in the New York Area. Two definite
types of films surfaced in both places: a stylized type of psychodrama, and a dance and pattern film.

    As Renan states on page 91: "Allied to the psychodramas
were the dance films. Deren set the style with A Study in Choreography for Camera, which showed dance, but with the element of cinematic control added to poetic effect. "

275

Clarke's dance film Bridges-Go-Round (1958) is a tardy entry in Renan's list of dance films made a decade earlier: Sarah Arledge's Introspection (1947) and Sidney Peterson's Horror Dream (1947), as instances. Renan describes Clarke's work as "a superimpositional 'dance' of New York bridges" (page 91).

Although a West Coast Abstract School in film was active during the forties and fifties, no such counterpart existed on the East Coast. By 1954, the Second Film Avant-Garde disappeared. As Renan summarizes, on page 97:

> Films produced in the Second Avant-Garde differed from those produced in the first in that they were more personal and less commercial. The film-makers worked on 16 mm, not 35 mm, and they financed their films themselves. Yet while the experimental films were made with integrity, many of them lacked vitality. Their emphasis was on other arts, and they tended to be, ... as literary, as static, and as limited as the commercial films from which they had set themselves apart. Their initial premises and their resulting forms were not so very new, and in the end, many film-makers, their interests, energy, and finances exhausted, found themselves in a cul-de-sac. The Second Avant-Garde as a movement ended around 1954.

But, as Renan hastens to qualify, then talented film artists all over the United States continued to make films through the sixties and seventies, forming the Third Film Avant-Garde. Major distinctions in subject, style, and technique divide the Second from the Third Avant-Gardes. While the Second Avant-Garde films tended to derive from drama, poetry, or related arts, they took form as visual essays, personal documentations of experience, and genre-less portraits. Third Avant-Garde films, according to Renan (page 101) were "all primarily personal, personal expression, personal works of art." They were complex, too, Renan observes, "With much rapid cutting, disparate continuity, and mobile handheld photography." These filmmakers wanted to "manipulate reality with camera and editing and to produce ... a film reality that had a sense of being film."

The subsequent Fourth Avant-Garde in film is dubbed Expanded Cinema by Renan, and it includes the applications of optical experiment, holography, laser beams, and similar electronic wizardries to the creation of motion pictures.

How does Shirley Clarke fit into this historical sketch? She made her first film in 1953 and her last film in 1967. Her initial short films were Second Avant-Garde in type, made post-1954 when this movement was dying. Her later feature films more appropriately fit into the Third Avant-Garde slot. This disjunction in time can be traced to Clarke's unusual succession of occupations: dancer first, filmmaker second, and videotape artist third. Clarke's second phase as a filmmaker has earned her an international reputation

as a topnotch artist, warranting extended critical attention and an examination of all her films.

Clarke was born rich and Jewish in New York City, October
2, 1925. As Marjorie Rosen quaintly words it, "This smallish, dark-
ish woman with a Dutch-boy cap placed rakishly on her salt-and-
pepper hair ... has a conventional poor-little-rich-girl story to call
her own. Only in Shirley Clarke's case the silver spoon was kosher;
Grand-daddy was a famous inventor; Mommy spoke seven languages;
and Daddy made and lost millions. "2

Clarke concedes that a Park Avenue address did not exclude
her from the emotional stresses of adolescence. Clarke was the
eldest of three sisters, "fiercely competitive, " and she had a learning disability.

> "It was fifth grade before I learned to read, seventh grade
> before I wrote. All this later turned out to have physical
> roots, a right-brain-right-handed thing whose name I for-
> got. So for the longest time, until I discovered dance at
> fourteen, suddenly became the class dancer, and popular,
> I was the outsider. But the child that observes has many
> advantages; eventually she identifies with 'out' people. "3

Clarke's Park Avenue address was a peculiar embarrassment during her dance studies with dollarless devotees. She never
had to work to live, but she wanted independence--to forsake the
Park Avenue home of her parents.

"So Shirley married to buy freedom. The romance was short-
lived; but the relationship lasted 12 years. "4 Bert Clarke helped
Shirley with her first dance films. The birth of their daughter
Wendy triggered surgery and hospital stays. After a lengthy bout
with hyperthyroidism, Clarke began to dance again and to continue
learning filmmaking.

After her dancing school and university studies, Clarke studied
and performed with the Martha Graham, Hanya Holm, and Doris
Humphrey dance companies. In 1942, Clarke's choreographed work
was performed at the 92nd Street Y. M. C. A. In 1946 she was elected
president of the National Dance Association which sent ballet companies and films abroad. In 1953 she began making dance films of
Daniel Nagrin, Anna Sokolow, and Paul Sanasardo.

Why did she switch careers? Why did Clarke abandon dancing
for filming dances? To Sharon Smith in Women Who Make Movies
(New York: Hopkinson & Blake, 1976) Clarke replied that working
up from the bottom was not her style. She had to start at the top.
With a gift of $1500 she decided she could make several dance
films, and become a great filmmaker in the process. Beginning
the project, she discovered she had spent all her money for film
stock for a single film!

Another reply from Clarke is found in Jay Leyda's Voices of Film Experience--1894 to the Present (New York: Macmillan, 1977, page 77): "I started in films by doing everything myself. I was writer, director, cameraman, editor, sound engineer, and lab messenger. I enjoyed it and learned a great deal about the craft."

It was the relationship between dance and film, and the combined two, that tantalized Clarke. In a conversation with Storm De-Hirsch, Clarke answers the query a third time:

> I had seen a bunch of dance films and I thought they were just awful, and it occurred to me that you really had to be an idiot not to be able to make a good dance film-- what was so tough about it? And I went into it thinking ... that, since I knew about dance, I would learn about this rather simple thing called film and do it.... The fact that I never realized was that one art destroyed another.... I think that if you're going to think of doing a dance film and taking already existing dance and transferring it onto film--you will destroy that dance. That does not mean though that you cannot make a dance for film and it was this that I finally learned and that this was the mistake that had been made till then. 5

Her feeling for film "became much more intriguing and exciting than just dance, in terms of action and passivity. Dance for me started to be too limited. There were too many other things that danced. "6

As Karen Cooper comments: "Only Maya Deren's Choreography for Camera preceeded [sic] Clarke's experimental work in ciné-dance. "7 Clarke's film Dance in the Sun (1953) "cut back and forth between a man dancing in the natural environment (the beach) and the artificial (the stage). "8 Clarke's film Bullfight (1954) apparently was unreviewed.

Clarke relates the circumstances that led to her making a third film, In Paris Parks (1955). She'd gone to France to make a dance film. While there, she took her daughter to the park each day. So she made a film of children playing, not dancing, in the park in 1955. The movements of the children as edited by Clarke and supported by a musical score result in a choreographed work which Clarke calls kinetic.

In 1957 she made an eight-minute film called A Moment in Love. In it, "A boy and a girl meet in a romantic wooded glen and with a leap into space take off into a dance. Multiple images and controlled color turn the lovers into blossoming flowers. "9

Clarke credits her film In Paris Parks for bringing her next assignment to her, Loops. Her assignment came from "Willard Van Dyke to make fifteen $2\frac{1}{2}$ minute films for the Brussels World's Fair. That's how I got to know Willard, Donn Pennebaker, and Richard Leacock--and we all shared this interest in film. "10

As Clarke explains, this type of filmmaking was known as the cinéma-vérité movement to the French and Europeans. Americans called it the hand-held-camera-with-sound movement. Moviemakers all knew one another, visiting frequently. Clarke recalls that Godard would visit, inquiring about the types of equipment the Americans were using.

J. Pyros in "Notes on Women Film Directors" in Take One 3:2 (Nov. /Dec. 1970), on page 7, credits Clarke with making Brussells [sic] Loops in 1958, describing it as 12 films each $2\frac{1}{2}$ minutes long, "destroyed by the United States State Department. "

In Bridges-Go-Round (1958) Clarke filmed "Manhattan Island as a maypole. The bridges around it, detached from their moorings, execute a bewitching, beguiling dance. "[11] Released in two versions, electronic sound or music, one cannot be sure which version critics viewed and heard.

Henry Breitrose in Film Quarterly XIII, No. 4, (Summer 1960), on page 57, categorizes Clarke as an "Instinctual film-maker, whose feeling for movement generally seems to have carried over into her feelings for the camera. " If the film has a theme, Breitrose ponders, it is linkage, the live linkages of the bridges themselves, connecting Manhattan to

> Brooklyn, Queens, the Bronx, and the New Jersey shore. In actuality, the bridges become plastic materials for a highly abstract subjective study in structures and movements. The images were printed "bi-packed"--running sandwiched together through the printer--in order to give them equal intensity. They are manipulated in a complex but extremely arresting way: the great steel girders, the taut cables, the towers and railings and roadways and abutments seem almost to dance. An exciting sense of color works with Mrs. Clarke's lively rhythmic sense.

As photographed by Bert and Shirley Clarke, the bridges not only go round but come alive as self-initiated, expanding and contracting in immobile space, entities. A viewer's customary concept of a bridge is radically altered by viewing Bridges-Go-Round. Breitrose examples this alteration:

> One particularly striking shot in Bridges is a zoom backward from an automobile moving forward--so that the bridge pillars remain in place but light poles on the periphery of the screen whizz past. The shot effectively confuses one's ordinary sense of depth perception, and creates a new kind of dynamic and realist equivalent of the stage designer's forced perspective.

Andrew Sarris reviewed all the films shown May 4-11, 1976, in a program called "American Avant-Garde Cinema at the Museum of Modern Art in New York City. " The title of his review article

reveals his joyless reception of such films as Kenneth Anger's Fire-
works (1947), Willard Maas' Geography of the Body (1943), and
Clarke's Bridges-Go-Round (1958): "Avant-Garde Films Are More
Boring Than Ever," in Politics and Cinema (New York: Columbia
University Press, 1978). On page 204, Sarris confides that he finds
Clarke's entry in this program "peculiar. Not only has Clarke
leaped into the commercial mainstream, at least by the side creek
standards of the avant-garde; she also displays for urban edifices an
enthusiasm and optimism completely at variance with the traditional
welt-schmertz [sic] of the avant-garde."

Although Sarris is not excited about Bridges, both his observations are correct. Clarke did not remain an independently
financed maker of short films for long, as did other filmmakers
whose films were screened in the program. As for her enthusiasm
for "urban edifices," her next film was about one. This was Skyscraper (1958).

Once again, it was Willard Van Dyke who offered her a job:
co-directing Skyscraper. Clarke explains that Willard wanted to do a
film about construction of a building. When he asked her to do it
she said yes. She would be paid, and she'd be working in 35mm.
She asked for $3500 as payment, thinking this was big money. She
got it. She worked for a year to finish Skyscraper. Then it was
nominated for an Academy Award and got a prize in Venice. Because of Skyscraper, Clarke says, she was able to make The Connection because she had earned a reputation as a successful filmmaker by that time.

Marjorie Rosen likens Skyscraper to a small humorous musical, recording the building of a massive highrise in New York.
Henry Breitrose agrees with Rosen. "Like jazz, Skyscraper simply
'swings.'"[12] He explicates the film.

> Skyscraper is the chronicle of a building, 666 Fifth Avenue,
> from the time its site is cleared (in New York one must
> tear down a used building to build a new one) to its ulti-
> mate employment as a forty-odd-floor stack of offices.
> But this film is also a comment on the contrast between
> the nobility and unconscious heroism of the actual construc-
> tion workers and the shallow, highly polished routinism for
> which their labor provides a home. The construction
> scenes are shot in black and white, but the use sequences
> go to a kind of neon-red argon-blue Eastmancolor.[13]
> Even when dealing with mechanical processes there is
> an astonishing lyric quality.... Not only are the shots
> edited dynamically (there is almost no matched-action pho-
> tography in the film) but the changes in tempo, the pauses,
> accelerations, retards, and even visual glissandos--such as
> a shot looking up an elevator shaft as the elevator ascends
> --work with a remarkably complex correctness and grace.[14]

Early in the year 1959, Clarke joined forces with filmmakers

Donn Alan Pennebaker, Willard Van Dyke, and Ricky Leacock to
start "'Filmakers,' a sort of co-operative arrangement designed to
share space and equipment and even occasionally film."15

Clarke taught filmmaking at Northwestern University in 1959,
at Columbia University in 1960, and at New York University in the
winter of 1965. In an article by Clarke, "Teaching Film Making
Creatively" which appeared in The Journal of the University Film
Producers Association (JUFPA) 17:3 (1965), pages 6-14, she summarizes the values of an academic environment for filmmaking: It
allows time enough to experiment, it provides an atmosphere in
which films are seriously considered, and provides a place where
new films may be viewed and appreciated.

In a conversation with Sharon Smith, Clarke tried to describe
the impediments to her career as a filmmaker, the first one being
her gender. Too, Clarke realizes that her choice of subjects for
films do not appeal to producers and financiers. She selects extremely controversial subject materials. Drug addiction--and not
condemning it--is a topic she names. A film about blacks in Harlem is not guaranteed to be a safe, pleasing, or profitable enterprise either, Clarke declares. And the film she made for the United
Nations about the plight of children in the developing nations was
banned when completed. This was A Scary Time (1960). Her gender and her choice of subject materials are obstacles enough, Clarke
admits. There are more.

Writing in the summer of 1960, Henry Breitrose reviewed
A Scary Time, observing that it was "unreleased," that Clarke made
it with "Robert Hughes of the UN Film Unit," and that it "was made
for theatrical distribution, with the purpose of predisposing the un-
committed to support government contributions to UNICEF or to give
individual donations."

In a vivid comparison of the for-fun horror of American children at Halloween and true-life horrors of children's lives in certain foreign nations, the film's "Dynamic photography and editing are
here combined with a kind of movement of ideas." A Scary Time
closes with a not-to-be-forgotten "shot of a baby, its face covered
with flies, held on the screen for a very long time...."16

The focus of the film, as Clarke describes it, is children,
those who are skin and bones, living skeleton children who exist.
The film starts with an American child in a skeleton costume going
out on Halloween to collect donations for UNICEF. Later, the child
is in bed. The audience hears a cry, followed by a photo of a
Moroccan infant held in its mother's arms. This is a giant close-
up. Flies are crawling all over the baby. Then the child in bed
hollers out to stop it, make it stop!

UN authorities were not pleased with Clarke's film. They
wanted a film showing the good works performed by the UN for children all over the world: photos of youngsters playing and smiling

in impoverished nations because the UN had given them food and
clothing.   Instead, Clarke sighs, the organization considered A Scary
Time an honest-to-goodness horror film capable of shocking audiences,
which was not the effect it desired.   UN officials voted not to exhibit it.   The film would have been destroyed, Clarke says, if filmmaker Roberto Rossellini had not come to her assistance, protesting
the planned "killing" of her work.

These eight short films made in six years form Clarke's
apprenticeship achievements.   In 1960, Clarke was ready for a more
strenuous challenge.   "By then I felt I knew enough about filmmaking to tackle a feature!"   She left the world of the dance behind
her, and directed The Connection, "based on Jack Gelber's play-
within-a-play about drug addicts, ghetto outsiders, and the morose
underbelly of a putrefying society. "17

The continuing concerns of Clarke for the negative filming
conditions, obtrusive censorship, lack of reliable funding sources,
the absence of a distributive network for screening independently
made films, unjust union demands and zero opportunities for foreign
film exhibition were shared on a grand scale by independent filmmakers.   Protest against these concerns culminated in the establishment of The New American Cinema Group on September 28, 1960.
Twenty-three independent filmmakers "met at 165 West 46th Street"
in New York and "by unanimous vote bound themselves into a free
and open organization. ...   A temporary executive board was elected,
consisting of Shirley Clarke, Emile de Antonio, Edward Bland, Jonas
Mekas, and Lewis Allen. "18

The First Statement of this Group, with the material quoted
above, is found in Film Culture, no. 22-23 (Summer 1961) on pages
130-133.   Dated September 30, 1960, this Statement holds nine resolutions focusing upon the concerns listed above.   Positive plans for
action are included.

> We plan to establish our own cooperative distribution cen-
> ter. ...   It's about time the East Coast had its own film
> festival, one that would serve as a meeting place for the
> New Cinema from all over the world. ...   We shall meet
> with the unions to work out more reasonable methods. ...
> We are not joining together to make money.   We are join-
> ing together to make films.

Most important is the first resolution: "We believe that cinema is indivisibly a personal expression.   We therefore reject the
interference of producers, distributors and investors until our work
is ready to be projected on the screen. "   On a more pragmatic
plane is the ninth resolution: "We pledge to put aside a certain per-
centage of our film profits so as to build up a fund that would be
used to help our members finish films or stand as a guarantor for
the laboratories. "19

This Statement is followed on pp. 124-50, in Film Culture, no.

22-23 (Summer 1961), by a lengthy discussion-type article, "Film Unions and the Low-Budget Independent Film Production--An Exploratory Discussion." No moderator is named. The discussants are "Willard Van Dyke, President of the Screen Directors International Guild; Lew Clyde Stoumen, writer and director; Shirley Clarke, director; James Degangi, producer and former president of the Assistant Director's and Script Clerk's Local 161; Jonas Mekas, writer and director; Adolfas Mekas, writer and director; Gideon Bachmann, radio commentator on the WBAI Radio program, 'Film Art'" (page 134).

Clarke comes off as a feisty, ready-to-fight, anti-union film-maker, with arguments and answers clearly expressed. She speaks from experience early in the debate: "When a low-budget independent film-maker wants to talk to the unions, he can never really get to talk to them. He is merely told that such and such are the rules and he has to obey them." She asks Degangi: "Could you tell what is the minimum crew in New York City on a feature theatrical film?" Degangi replies "there is no such thing...."[20]

Stoumen outlines his negative involvements with craft unions: "Throughout my whole professional career the unions have been interfering with my work."[21]

That "Unions prevent film-makers from working" was accepted as fact and illustrated with examples in the discussion. Because "Hollywood and New York film craft unions are closed shops. They are closed by the unions themselves."[22] This from Stoumen. Clarke refines his observation: "You can never get a picture made, like you do in Italy, with a mixed, union and non-union, crew."[23]

Union evils were exampled then: Featherbedding and the bribery for or outright sale of a union seal, required before a film can be exhibited in the United States.

Clarke relates two instances of her conflict with union procedures while making The Connection.

> On the set of The Connection, we had at least three people that sat there most of the time and really had nothing to do. I don't know them.... There was one person who was called set painter. Now, because of the style of my film, this would be the last thing that I would do, to paint the set. It should be made possible that if I need, I can call the union and get a man for one day or one hour to do some painting, if needed. But there is no reason for him to sit there all the time and play cards. There was the whole mess in the cameraman's union, too. We got really messed up in the still photography, because we could not get the man we wanted, and they insisted that we take another man who was just no good.[24]

Clarke had 20 or 22 union people on the set, and she claims,

"At least five of them were unnecessary. It makes a big difference
on a low budget film. "[25] Clarke apparently did not get the still
photographer of her choice for The Connection.

> I went to the representative of local 624, Jay Rasher, to
> talk about a still photographer. Now it so happened that
> in the cameraman's union there are only six still pho-
> tographers. Rasher, he personally understood exactly
> what I wanted and needed, that we couldn't take a union
> left-over third-rate photographer, etc. Rasher had to go
> to his board, and his board is made of a lot of old time
> guys sitting around, who are involved in protecting their
> jobs. Even if the union representative understood our situa-
> tion and wanted to help us, he could not. His board met
> and his board said NO.... We didn't get a single conces-
> sion on a film costing $150,000 compared to the films
> that cost $3,000,000. They expected from us exactly the
> same. [26]

Where did independent filmmakers get money to make their
films? Their productions, among them Clarke's The Connection,
Jonas Mekas' Guns of the Trees, and Pull My Daisy by Robert Frank
and Alfred Leslie, were financed "on a limited partnership basis, as
it has been used for Broadway plays. "[27]

"The Skyscraper Experiment" (Films & Filming, April 1961,
pp. 12 and 30), affirms that The New American Cinema (NAC) was
not a solitary action. Groups similar in purpose and means were
emerging simultaneously abroad: the Free Cinema in Great Britain,
the Nouvelle Vague in France, and related groups in Poland, Russia,
and Italy. The NAC retained a role of leadership in fulfilling and
acting upon its resolutions. Its most enterprising venture was an
International Exposition escorted around the world by P. Adams Sitney in 1964.

The Connection appears to have encountered and resolved
each one of the difficulties included in the nine resolutions of The
First Statement of the NAC, a plenteous case history for student
filmmakers. When Clarke saw Jack Gelber's play she optioned for
for filming. Most New York critics disapproved of it. The New York
Times called it nothing but a barrage of dirt. Critics such as Henry Hewes of the Saturday Review differed, enabling the play to continue its run at The Living Theater. Funding a film based on a
play which dealt with drug addiction could expect impediments. Nonetheless, The Connection did garner more than two hundred backers,
each one a limited partnership.

Two forms of freedom inhere this type of financing, and Clarke
liked them both.

> First, the artistic freedom.... Usually distributors pre-
> judge an audience and often underestimate it. They need
> someone to tell them what's good. I'm not restricted by

any pre-release commitments to a distributor.... And
... just as wonderful is having enough money to enjoy the
personal freedom of working with a professional crew.   I
started in films the same way as many film-makers, by
doing everything myself ... I enjoyed it.... Yet having
real pro's helping me was an amazingly happy experience
.... 28

Dorothy Oshlag in Sight and Sound 30 (Spring 1961), page 69,
discovers three levels of perception in Jack Gelber's screenplay con-
verging on "... the beat realism of the junkies' world ... undoubtedly never before ... so truthfully explored. "29   The first level deals
with a bunch of addicts waiting for their "connection" of heroin.   The
second level is the entrance of the documentary filmmaker who wants
to photograph this event.   And the third level derives from the camera's poking into the waiting group's reactions, the lens of the camera bringing with it the eyes of the audience watching, responding.

Oshlag visited the set of The Connection on the tenth day of
the shooting schedule (twenty days).   She found that a curious circumstance shaped the set.

> The entire action takes place in one room, the apartment
> or "pad" of a character called Leach.... The room was
> designed with a stairway leading into it so that the entire
> set had to be raised on stilts about five feet off the floor.
> Plotting of camera movements required that the set have
> four walls; so it became, literally, closed.   This, together
> with Miss Clarke's decision to shoot the film in sequence,
> resulted in curious tension and excitement within the four
> walls.   "It was like being in a tree-house, " Shirley Clarke
> observed.   "We felt absolutely remote from everything
> happening around us.... "30

Oshlag reflects on the levels of reality attained in the film:
"We end by seeing a complete film-within-a-film.   We see it while
it is happening, not while an off-screen voice tells us it is happening.
The sensation is unique and will surely point the way to new considerations of film and reality. "31

The clearest explication of the plot of The Connection appears
in the Monthly Film Bulletin 28:163 (December 1961).

> Eight drug addicts are gathered in a Manhattan loft apart-
> ment belonging to Leach.   In order to pay their "connec-
> tion" when he arrives with heroin, the men have agreed
> for a fee to allow Jim Dunn, a would-be documentary film-
> maker, and his cameraman J. J. Burden, to photograph
> them .... four of the men play jazz....   Eventually the
> "connection, " a black named Cowboy, arrives.   He is ac-
> companied by a street salvationist; he has brought her
> along to distract the police.   As the addicts file into the
> bathroom one by one for their shots, the bewildered old

woman begins to suspect that they are drinking. She so
accuses them and is politely but firmly ushered from the
loft.   The men then persuade Dunn to try some heroin so
that he will have a deeper understanding of his film.   After
taking the drug, he becomes violently ill and tells J. J.
to take over.   While Dunn is sleeping, Leach gives himself an overdose of heroin and goes into a coma.   After
Cowboy has given physical aid, Dunn awakens.   Realizing
his experiment is a failure, he tells J. J. to keep the
footage.

Jay Jacobs titles his review of The Connection "Song Without
Words" in The Reporter, 50 (November 8, 1962), page 50.   Complimenting Clarke for "absolutely no compromises with the truth"
Jacobs finds "the result is not so much a movie as an experience
from which it is next to impossible to disengage oneself. "   Clarke
has managed, Jacobs discerns, "without employing any illusionistic
gadgetry, to extend the depth of her playing area, to project the
action outward beyond what a painter would call 'the picture plane, '
and, seemingly at least beyond the audience itself. "   "Complete immersion" is the effect on the audience.

"The Connection appears to be one of those legendary 'firsts'
like Citizen Kane or Breathless, which not only excel filmically, but
also set standards for other film work.   In short, The Connection
is important. "   Colin Young and Gideon Bachmann in "New Wave--
or Gesture?"   (Film Quarterly, Spring 1961, pages 13-14) index the
standard-setting and standard-breaking qualities of the film but do
not criticize it for reasons they best explain:

> The Connection cannot really be subjected to standard criti-
> cism, which tends toward the establishment of objective
> judgments on the perception level alone; rather, its final
> impact will actually depend on the degree to which each
> viewer is able to give to it of his own substance and his
> own life.

"The camera represents the viewer, " Young and Bachmann
point out.   And the actors, "from the original cast of the play" act
for the camera.   Because some of the technical achievements had
not been tried before and Clarke herself had to take camera in hand
at one juncture and shoot a scene herself, there were delays in the
shooting schedule of 19 days.   The Connection is important "primarily
because it was made. "   The authors link it with the work of Godard
in France, Kurasawa in Japan, and Wajda in Poland.   "All the films
made by these people, and The Connection perhaps most of all, are
antifilmic in the sense that they do not explain but present.... "

Penelope Gilliatt (Sight and Sound 30, Summer 1961, pages 145-
146) remarks that The Connection "is one of the rare stage pieces
that is improved in its screen version. "   Tagging no demerits to the
film, Gilliatt compares the film to the play and finds the former has
"more creative flair than any (film) that has come out of America

for years. " She attributes the vast difference in quality to the level of perception; Clarke "has altered the relation of the audience to what is going on. . . . The play hangs on the Pirandellian device of an 'author' who is planted in the audience, complaining intermittently that his work is being ruined by junkie actors. " This "author" inflicts self-consciousness upon the audience. In the film this "author" role is taken over by the director Jim Dunn. "In the cinema the correct, discomfiting question becomes one about our own motives in wanting to spy on drug addicts. In the theatre the audience often felt embarrassed; in the cinema it feels accused ... the camera is the instrument of our own curiosity. "

Not only is The Connection without action, Gilliatt observes, "but it is also very nearly without interaction. . . . " The waiting men are anti-social, talk to themselves. Clarke is praised for her direction of a film with "an impeccable ear for the hipster's patois, and a black, abrupt humour. "

Arthur Knight commends Clarke for "an extraordinary job of cinematizing the original material" in The Connection ("Kicking a Habit, " Saturday Review, April 7, 1962, page 20 and 54). He continues: "I found it fascinating as an exhibit of bravura filmmaking, which it is, but more especially because ... Clarke has dared to venture into territory specifically forbidden to motion pictures. "

As for the level of perception, Knight reports that "As in Antonioni's films, the camera insists that we look ... through sheer virtuosity, the director transforms what is admittedly a distasteful subject into an absorbing experience. "

When The Connection premiered in a suburban Phoenix, Arizona theatre, it played without incident. And the film, which Knight presumably saw in New York, "does not compromise or sensationalize" or try to be popular "(as the Los Angeles version did) by spicing up the proceedings with four letter words. The words are there when they have to be. " This is an equivocal view: Clarke is unflinchingly honest but her film, which she edited, was seen in several versions with censors counting the number of times profane language was used.

As a matter of record The Connection was completed early in 1961; was shown at the Cannes Film Festival where it won a prize, and gained international audiences plus notoriety for a censorship court battle which Variety faithfully reported on from May 10, 1961, until November 14, 1962, in eleven articles. The word in question was "shit, " which Clarke refused to delete or substitute for, since in drug addict jargon it means the drug or dope injected. Anticipating censorship difficulties, Clarke and her co-producer Lewis Allen arrived at their own artistic decisions.

No mention of language problems is made in Newsweek, September 17, 1962, page 60. The film "has an authenticity of which the real director, Shirley Clarke, may be justly proud. " The movie is "tighter, more depressing and more powerful" than the play.

Brendan Gill wrote a negative one-paragraph review of the
film in the New Yorker, November 17, 1962, page 210. "Jack Gelber's play struck me as a stunt that worked, and the movie strikes
me as a stunt that doesn't work. " Gill explains that the improvisation in the play was fascinating. Because there can be no improvisation in a film, there is no fascination.

In a punny, put-down derogation, the Time critic in a review
dated October 5, 1962, on page 98, calls The Connection a "ham-
and-existentialist Zenwich. " Further, "Opium is the religion of the
people in the picture.... They are waiting. Waiting to make the
connection, waiting for the Cowboy to gallop in on a white horse. "
Of course, Cowboy does arrive as a Negro dressed in white, "a
Redeemer. " And, "One by one he injects them with an elixir that
washes away the wretchedness. "

The critic's analytical argument is this: "What was fundamentally wrong with the play remains fundamentally wrong in the
film. It is not life, it is not art, it is not interesting.... Philosophically it is an uninspired restatement of Waiting for Godot;
esthetically, it is just a drop in the Beckett. "

In his "Movie Journal" column, in the Village Voice, Jonas
Mekas records the reception The Connection received from the New
York press. On October 4, 1962, page 17, Mekas philosophically
explicates the "nothing happens" structure of the film as a metaphor
for the predicament of contemporary man. "That is where the meaning ... is: in that nothingness, in that unimportance. It shows
something of the essence of our life today only because it is about
nothing. It doesn't point at truth--it sets truth in motion, it suggests it. "

How is this truth moved, and suggested? "Beneath the supposed meaninglessness of 'The Connection, ' beneath all walking, talking, and jazzing, a sort of spiritual autopsy of contemporary man is
performed, his wounds opened. "

The ambiguous nature of any truths arrived at is recognized
by Mekas: "Not everybody's ready to hear or to feel what 'The
Connection' is saying, to experience what it really is--nor do we
know exactly what it is really about. "

Mekas's own empathy for the film is clear; his column attempts to ready viewers for an extraordinary filmviewing experience.
That he was disappointed and outraged by the published reviews by
New York critics is evidenced by shouting sentences in his October
11, 1962, page 13, column. He begins his invective, in capital letters: "OPEN LETTER TO THE NEW YORK DAILY MOVIE CRITICS. "
He does not name the critics he addresses as "you": "Last week
you butchered what may be the best film--and certainly is one of
the best films--made in this country this year, 'The Connection. '
You have completely misled the American audiences with your bloody
columns. You have made no effort to understand a work of art the

beauty of which could make you cry. " These critics had "dismissed" the film because of "its content ... its techniques, style, and form... " Mekas claims that The Connection is superior to films Cleo from 5 to 7, The Longest Day, and Convicts Four. "... I tell you, I don't even want to read what you have to say: to describe your criteria I could use the same word 'The Connection' uses for heroin. "

With no author cited, an article appeared in the next issue of the Village Voice, October 18, 1962, on page 1, captioned: "'Connection' Film at Judson Church. " The first paragraph reads, "A film that the New York State Board of Regents has ruled unacceptable for public movie houses has been found by a Baptist minister to be positively desirable for showing in his church. While the Regents still refuse to allow theatres to show ... 'The Connection, ' the Reverend Howard Moody has announced that it will be shown twice tomorrow night (Friday, October 19) at Judson Memorial Baptist-Congregationalist Church. "

Reverend Moody gave two reasons for his decision to show the film: Narcotics addiction was a constant concern of his church while censorship had to be opposed. Of the two, the latter was paramount. "... We believe that this film is an honest and forthright work of art on an adult theme. By showing it we are not judging the quality of the film or recommending that everyone see it, but we do believe that it ought not be banned.... " There was no admission charged, but admittance was by ticket only to two showings at 7:30 and 10 p. m. Friday evening.

Stanley Kauffmann sees The Connection as "simply the play as flexed by Gelber. " "Gelber trades on assumptions" thus Gelber's play in film form is "just a sophomore's disillusion. " In Kauffmann's Movie Column in New Republic, October 27, 1962, pages 29-30, he credits the music as an affirmative force. "Four of the eight are jazz musicians who play from time to time, and the jazz does much more than is generally recognized to provide organic free-form feeling, to create mood, and, in a sense, to advance the play. "

The film tries to "blur the dividing line between life and art" for an enveloping effect of immediacy. Kauffmann denounces the artificiality of Clarke's reach for nowness. "The fakery of this 'real' reality reaches its high point when, near the end, the camera moves slowly over the walls of the squalid rooms, showing cracks and dirt.... The climax of the sequence is a close-up of a cockroach crawling.... "

The Connection "has two main aspects: it is an exercise in naturalism and it is a blow at our society ... through ... the Theater of Revolt. " Gelber's fault is that he does not use "even the most sordid details as symbols. " This absence of symbolism condemns Gelber to the status of a "pest. " Kauffmann defines a pest as "the writer who is capable of little more than the reproduction of surfaces, " which in The Connection are "surface details--the taboo language, the bursting boil, the vomit, the nose-picking. If this really is the nature of truth ... why do he and Miss Clarke chicken out of taking us into the toilet...?" The film is not in the same class with Beckett's Waiting for Godot, or Camus' Caligula, or Genet's The Blacks. Kauffmann does commend Clarke's directing as "imaginative and probing."

Bosley Crowther's reaction to The Connection was "monotonous, in addition to being sordid and disagreeable." In his review (The New York Times Film Reviews, October 4, 1962, 44:1) he finds "little about it to warrant the clamorous interest of the average movie-goer or to distinguish it as a significant piece of cinematic art."

Crowther reports that the film was shown twice at the D. W. Griffith Theatre in Manhattan "before being withdrawn on an order of the court." For one hour and forty minutes, Crowther complains, nothing happens. Actors mumble so that they are hard to understand. The camera "does sweep about a good bit to generate a certain nervous tension under Shirley Clarke's bold direction...." And, "As for that controversial language, it scarcely seems out of place, or, indeed, any more offensive than anything else in this drab film."

Clarke's abilities as editor, director, and photographer are described by Lincoln F. Johnson in his book Film: Space, Time, Light, and Sound (New York: Holt, Rinehart and Winston, 1974). In The Connection, Johnson believes "the significance of the play really resides in the words, as the characters analyze themselves and each other and speculate about their lives and life in general. All this is fit material for theatrical production but--viewed superficially at least--unprepossessing material for film." Yet,

> Like Hitchcock, Clarke maintains the unities and the mobility of the camera, but she also exploits the potentialities of editing. With an uncanny awareness of the play's filmic possibilities, she transforms the theater into film perceiving not only how to use the film to reinforce the actors' performances, but also how to use the material environment to extend the action of the play and how to develop rhythms that invest the work with an additional, purely filmic, energy. 32

Next, Johnson comments on the cockroach that critic Stanley Kauffmann objected to: "While one of the characters is speaking ... she moves her lens slowly away from him to follow a cockroach as it aimlessly wanders about a wall, creating a symbolic dimension the theatrical producer could not."33 And, "In one of the musical interludes, she simultaneously develops four contrapuntal rhythms, the rhythm of action, of sound, of moving camera, and of cutting, creating a tension among them that maintains the tension of the drama through the music."34 Clarke's admirable use of a closed environment is appreciated by Johnson in these words: "... Clarke

has recognized that a small space is as adaptable to cinematic observation and exploration as a large one, and that part of the play's
strength and the personality of the characters is to be found in the
almost unreal claustrophobic isolation from the external world.... "35

The reception of The Connection at the Cannes Film Festival
is reported with a sardonic smile in "Cannes 1961, " in Films in
Review, XII, 6 (June-July 1961), on page 327. The film

> has been shown out of competition, and has been welcomed
> by the Left, which is delighted to see a picture about dope
> addicts under capitalism, delighted to have Western Avant-
> garde filmmakers waste themselves on such themes and de-
> lighted to have Western audiences debilitated by such sub-
> ject matter. Cinematically, the film is pretty much a
> photograph of the Jack Gelber off-Broadway play. Socio-
> logically, it treats dope addiction as though it were mere-
> ly a minor vice.... Some of the performances are re-
> pulsively convincing. "

A balanced approach to The Connection was taken by Film
Quarterly 15 (Summer 1962), page 41. Two reviews for and against,
appeared; the "pro" article by Basil Wright, the "con" by Arlene
Croce. Wright pinpoints the success of the film to the fact that
"the audience is now inside the camera itself, and sees everything
through the lens.... " The point of the film, for Wright, is Dunn,
the director, trying a fix himself and getting sick.

> ... Very brilliantly Shirley Clarke and her cast have
> brought it off. It is the anticlimactic moment after the
> Black Mass, something which no one I know of (except
> perhaps de Sade) has ever managed to elaborate. And
> Black Mass there certainly is, with the arrival of Cowboy
> (clad in white samite, etc.) and a Virgin long in the tooth
> called Sister Salvation. (Out of an almost impeccable cast
> these two, played by Carl Lee and Barbara Winchester,
> are really outstanding.)"36

Wright's highest portion of praise is this: "It is the measure
of Shirley Clarke's surety of touch that the film doesn't run down
into nothingness after this moment of revelation, when the fixes are
at last available and the zombies troop one by one to the john.... "37
"The technique of The Connection is superb.... " Wright declares.
"All that is missing is poetry. "38

For Arlene Croce the film isn't real. It, "unfortunately,
doesn't fool you as a living record. "39 The success of the film
at Cannes "was at least partly spurious. "40 Croce reports that
French and British audiences thought they were seeing real American junkies. (British censors closed the play.) The film "is less
effective than the play, less immediate.... "41

"Of Mrs. Clarke's contribution it must be said at once and

with admiration that I have seen what she has attempted to do with the full length of Gelber's play succeed only once, and that briefly, in one or two shots from Welles's 'March of Time' newsreel in Citizen Kane. "42 However, The Connection is a non-movie, like Pull My Daisy and Shadows. "... These films are uncreated. They do not occupy space in time. "43 Croce closes with "the terrible suggestion that Mr. Gelber and Mrs. Clarke, if they are really serious about experimenting with the way it 'really' is, should have come into the film themselves. "44

It took six years for The Connection to be distributed in Canada. Even so, it retained its striking originality, according to Joe Medjuck in Take One (April 1967), page 22. The film is still "extremely theatrical. Each character is given a set piece in which he is interviewed by the director and responds with a long speech about himself. " The major failing of the film is William Redfield's unconvincing performance as Jim Dunn, the film director. Medjuck pronounces the censorship issues raised by the use of the word "shit" "now seem absurd. "

The debates, in and out of court, were real enough, as the continuing series of articles in Variety regarding one four-letter word prove. The attendant publicity could not but assist in bringing The Connection to the attention of audiences everywhere.

The initial mention occurs in Variety May 10, 1961. In the second paragraph of the critical review we read: "It uses some off-color words, but they are part of the scene and never utilized for shock. Subject is treated objectively, and, though censor problems seem certain, it should have no trouble in some enlightened spots. "

"There is no story, " the critic continues, "but it is a successful, living experience ... Miss Clarke shows a definite filmic flair in keeping this one room pic constantly revealing and absorbing. Tensions grow and ebb, revelations are made, and then the climax of a near-death leads to a rout of most of them to end it all on a muted note. "

The critic points out that the film was invited to an "out-of-competition spot at the present Cannes Fest. It is in the running for the International Film Critic's Award. " Clarke is praised for her "virile handling" of the characters in her film, which is "a tour de force. "

Additional aspects of The Connection presented themselves as censorable. Variety reports June 14, 1961, page 3, that the film "prominently features one scene explicitly detailing how a guy gives himself a shot of heroin, while the soundtrack repeatedly carries a word, never before heard on the commercial screen. (The French translation for the word is merde....)"

The reactions of London audiences and critics are reported two weeks later in Variety, June 28, 1961, page 4 and 17. A London paper is quoted:

> "Miss Shirley Clarke ... has refused to cut a single shot
> beyond the brief glimpse of a hypodermic syringe hanging
> from an addict's arm.... The drug is rarely called
> heroin ... repeatedly referred to by the Anglo-Saxon word
> for excrement. Miss Clarke refuses to withdraw that,
> too.... Nor will she cut sequences in which a boil is
> squeezed, a nose is picked and an addict vomits audibly
> though not ... visibly. "

The London paper claims that the several technical imper-
fections, loose ends, and blank film footage achieve an illusion of
authenticity. "The Times raises the curious point that 'The Connection might be more effective if less brilliant. 'The impeccable lighting and artful composition' mars realism and illusion. The Daily
Telegraph speaks of the film as 'a minor triumph for its young director, Shirley Clarke. ' "

Variety, November 1, 1961, reports on page 5 that language
standards of books rather than the press were invoked against the
offensive word in The Connection. "The director of state's film
licensing division in Albany ... upholds his action by charging that
the Shirley Clarke picture is 'obscene' as originally ruled.... "
The dirty word was used 28 times and "offends community standards. "

The impact of this dirty word battle was felt abroad. On
November 22, 1961, Variety reports on page 1 that The Connection
was passed by British censors without cuts, with an X rating. However, this decision to pass the picture without cuts hurt United King-
dom importers. "At Cannes, the film was offered to prominent
British distributors for a nominal guarantee in the region of
$14, 000. " It was understood that if the film was rejected by the
censor, the distributor would lose $3, 000 in expenses. Most dis-
tributors did not choose to exhibit the film. One who did, Charles
Cooper, said it paid off.

"The film at the Academy Cinema, one of the original first
run arties, has been acclaimed by most of the critics and is now
reckoned to return its guarantee on its first run engagement alone.
The remainder of the country should be gravy. "

The dirty word battle report in Variety, February 28, 1962,
continues on page 2 and 60. The Connection's distributor, Irvin
Shapiro of Films Around the World, was denied a license and initiated a lawsuit. "Anglo-Saxondom's second-most tabu word, which
is on the soundtrack of 'The Connection' exactly 11 times will go to
trial during the week of May 7.... " This because "'The Connection'
auspices have flatly refused to consent to an elimination of the
word.... The word is apparently deemed the all-vital commercial
raison d'etre of the production and its best chance of creating a box
office sensation.... "

Victory was the verdict reported July 4, 1962, in Variety,
on page 4, the caption reading: "'Connection wins 4-letter word

from censors: 'Okay'. " The New York Supreme Court, Monday,
July 2, ruled that the film version of the 'junkie' play ... is not
'obscene, ' and thus cannot be denied exhibition in this state because
of the use of an unmentionable word on the soundtrack.... "

From Amsterdam, Hans Saaltink reported in Variety, July 11,
1962, on page 5, that Hafbo Films had bought the rights to the film.
The Connection was released in Amsterdam in the Kriterion Theatre,
"without running into trouble with the Dutch censors. The film received a certificate so that it can be seen by adults of 18 years and
older. No scene was cut and 'The Connection' was shown in its
original version, including the four-letter word. "

Saaltink continues by explaining that Dutch sub-titles were
used with the original soundtrack. "... Four-letter words were
subdued in translation. No attempt was made to capture in Dutch
the nuances of the slang used by the hooked people. " As for audience reception: " The film did not raise any scandal, although
some spectators were revolted and left the theatre. Most of the
audience could stomach the realistic scenes. Most people, however,
were puzzled whether the figures were really junkies or 'only' actors. "

Shirley Clarke and the attorney who fought and won the dirty
word battle Ephraim London appeared on Hugh Downs' Today TV
show. The September 26, 1962, edition of Variety states on pages
5 and 17 that excerpts from The Connection were shown, but not
those containing the offensive word. On the show London was quizzed
about the definition of obscenity and his views regarding voluntary
censorship organizations. Clarke was asked about the need for the
objectionable word. She replied that "I can't believe that the film's
reality rests on a word, but what is involved is to expose life as
it actually is lived, and to have a word which does affect the reality
of the people you are dealing with. "

She did expect difficulties with the use of the word. She expected a court battle. "They (the censors) cut the word, because it
is the only place left where they can censor. All other aspects of
censorship have been overruled in the courts, and this is the last
stand.... "

A lengthy article detailing attorney Ephraim London's appearance before judges in court appears in Variety for October 31, 1962,
on page 20. And two weeks later, November 14 Variety headlines
on page 3 "Connection at White House" and in smaller case letters,
"But Kennedys Happily Absent. " It seems Arthur Schlesinger Jr.
"one of JFK's special assistants" had arranged to show The Connection "as part of the White House's regular Sunday night film showings. " Although Jack Gelber and Shirley were present, the Kennedys
were attending a Madison Square Garden Medicare rally and did not
see the picture. This comedy of mistiming, getting lost, and awkward misunderstanding, as described in Variety, would make an acceptable Hollywood situation comedy film all by itself.

The critical acumen of Raymond Durgnat probes to the essence of The Connection, beyond the use of unpleasant gestures and
words. In Films & Filming 8:4 (January 1962), on page 31, he reflects on the reality of the film.

> At first I thought the film was pretending to watch its
> own gestation so that we should feel like we're in the
> actual pad, man. But this pseudo-Pirandellism is self-
> defeating. . . . This film's unusually pedantic pretence of
> "actuality" only focuses our attention on the quality of pre-
> tence--the long takes, the beautiful composition in-depth,
> the clever stage management (all unhip virtues) and too
> many clangers, e. g. the jazzmen go straight from absolute
> silent to really groovy stuff. . . .

Durgnat reasons, then, that maybe the picture is about "the
disconnection between 'them' and 'us'. . . . But the film cheapens
this issue of non-communication because Dunn is a hopelessly petu-
lant 'stooge'. . . . As all the non-junkies are as eccentric as the
junkies one guesses this is really a farce, that is, a compassionate
anti-tragedy about both the addicts and the others. "

Durgnat concludes that the film "is really about drugs as
suicide rather than drugs as ecstasy" and that the film "needles
but we don't get high. Still, it usefully widens the loopholes in
our ignorance, and so is worth seeing. . . . "

The influence of ethnographer Oscar Lewis upon The Connection is discussed by William Nestrick in his article "Primitivism
and Film, " in University Publishing (Winter 1979). A proponent
of the case study approach, Lewis liked and used what he called
the "Rashomon-like" technique of seeing the family through the eyes
of each of its members. This style of observation lends itself to
"'camera-like view of the movements, conversations and interactions
that occurred. . . . ' "

For Nestrick, "The Connection comes closest to the kind of
cinematic effort that marks the convergence of anthropological and
cinematic concerns; ironically she (Clarke) bravely chooses a genre
despised by film theorists--the filmed play. "

Observes Nestrick: "When the film opened, Stanley Kauffmann was outraged ... he loathed what he thought was a pretense of
'real' reality as against artistic reality ... " and Nestrick continues
with the inevitable cockroach crawling on the wall which Kauffmann
and others vehemently objected to. Nestrick allows that "The plot
does follow a contemptible naturalistic tradition: The Iceman Cometh
syndrome where various individuals succumb to a behavior-changing
drug. . . . " Add to this situation a white film director allowed by addicts to film their fixes for a fee, with a black cameraman. "The
connection becomes a self-creation, involvement at one's own risk. "

In spite of these flaws, Nestrick applauds Clarke's "film construction. " How the two cameras shooting the film are used comes to involve the viewer and rationally explains the tracking of the cockroach crawling on the wall.

> When the cameraman is directed to shift to hand-held camera, we learn how to recognize that kind of shot ... we are shown the placement of microphones for synch sound.... The shots Kauffmann described as cheap naturalism actually come from a formalist's desire for visual interest. Even the cockroach is to be explained as ... a moment when we see the camera refocus: it has tilted from a man performing a monologue to catch the detail of the cockroach.

Nestrick compliments Clarke on her "documentary" and "ethnographic" inclinations. These, he states, are related to her ciné-dance film themes. "Like Maya Deren, Clarke has a sense that the finally edited film is a patterned articulation of motion; the kind of truth that she has envisioned for herself recognizes the significances that are attributed to patterns of movement. " In Nestrick's opinion, this is an approach to a Utopian-like film, a perfect cinematic work.

Clarke describes the time between her international success with The Connection and her next film, The Cool World, as being on the inside track. At this juncture, it was easy for her to get film work. She reports that John F. Kennedy and others urged her to make a film about poet Robert Frost. The assignment was offered to her. She took it. For a moment, she was on the inside track.

During this "in" period, Clarke was employed to direct a feature length documentary on poet Robert Frost. Early in 1962 she began her assignment. As Newsweek (January 29, 1962, in "Frost Bit, " page 81) muses cheerfully: "These unalikes were hitting it off as famously as archy and mehitabel. "

The 87-year-old Frost airily dismissed the prospect of a woman director: "Women have always run my life. " Clarke came through with her customary candor on working with the legendary poet: "When I made Skyscraper, ... I didn't give a damn about skyscrapers, but by the end I was mad about them. I'm sure I'll be made for Frostie. You fall in love with your subject, and then you can make it. Watching that man is beautiful. "

Producer Ed Foote, Clarke and Frost were luncheon guests on President Kennedy's yacht when Foote approached Clarke with the idea for the Frost film. Clarke's first reaction was "Impossible. It wasn't my kind of film.... But speaking with Frost, knowing him, interested me in him as a human being. He knows how to make out. He's had to take plenty and he's never copped out. "

Although Clarke is credited as director, Robert Hughes, who

worked with her on A Scary Time, directed as well as wrote and produced the film.   Terence McCartney-Filgate co-directed an autumn
sequence with Clarke.   And Charlotte Zwerin was Hughes' associate
producer and editor. [45]   No reason is stated for the divisional nature of the directing job.

> Structurally, Robert Frost: A Lover's Quarrel with the
> World is a confrontation of two views of Frost--his public
> performance and his private thoughts, each observed by
> the film-makers and commented on.   About half the pic-
> ture's 52 minutes is reportage of the two public per-
> formances--the one at Sarah Lawrence with a large appre-
> ciate crowd, the one at Amherst a seminar, a more awk-
> ward, intimate group.   The film weaves in and out of
> them, using the sound track as a trigger for the other se-
> quences and sometimes just settling down to watch Frost
> in action. ... [46]

Clarke directed the Ripton, Vermont, scenes on one weekend
with McCartney-Filgate, the Amherst and Sarah Lawrence scenes
plus a few others.   The film follows the seasons of the year.

> We first see Frost as he goes back to open up the cottage
> in Ripton in the spring, to see what survived the winter.
> (For the last 25 years of his life his headquarters was in
> Cambridge.)   The film ends with a fusion of the two
> threads--on the track he says farewell to his Sarah Law-
> rence "crowd, " but we are watching him leave the Ripton
> cottage in the fall.   It was the last time he was to see it.
> He died before they finished shooting. [47]

The film won an Academy Award in the Documentary Division.

In the film, Frost reflects: "A poem can't be worried into
existence.   If it's to give people pleasure, it has to give me pleasure in writing. "[48]

Clarke felt that the film was "Frost's movie, not hers. "
Completing it, she reflected aloud, "Someday I want to do something
that is mine from the start. ...   Now I feel technically secure.   The
next step is finding what I want to say. ... "[49] Warren Miller's
novel The Cool World became Clarke's "next step. "

Harriet Polt interviewed Clarke in the summer of 1963, after
The Cool World was completed.   This interview was published in
Film Comment 2:2 (Spring 1964), pages 31-32.   Polt asked: "If it's
not being too personal, how did you eat during that year, or at other slack times?"   Clarke's answer: "Most film makers have to accept commissions or films, or do other little jobs.   I'm lucky--I
have a husband who has a regular job. "

Polt's next query was about financing The Cool World.   Clarke
explained that she raised money from people who wanted to be "an-

gels, " pointing out that only low-budget films can be financed by
"angels'" money. "The Cool World cost $250,000, which is about
a fourth of what it would have cost to make in Hollywood." How
did Clarke get interested in the "Negro problem"? Clarke observed
that "For the past four or five years I have felt that this is America's key problem. Without a solution to it, we will never have a
free country. After all, we whites are in the minority--two thirds
of the world is colored."

In Clarke's description of the materials and methods used to
prepare for filming lies the secret to the low budget of The Cool
World.

> The exteriors were all shot on location in Harlem. For
> the interiors, the New York Housing Authority gave us the
> use of a whole tenement building which was about to be
> demolished. For each set, we used a different floor of
> the building ... we just used what was there. Our in-
> teriors were all pre-lit ... the camera was hand-held ...
> we used radiomicrophones, so we didn't need a boom.

Carl Lee, who enacts the "Priest" role in the film, did the
casting. Although he applied to settlement houses and other organizations where star pupils were brought to him, the cast was made
up of young men whom Lee happened to meet. A group of them
gathered in a loft and began to improvise scenes from the story.
Because these children had difficulty reading, a mixture of memori-
zation and improvisation was used to help them act their roles.
"These were all kids who had police records, " Clarke explained,
and were good to work with, not complaining about a schedule of
18-hour days and seven days a week. When completed, Clarke
brought The Cool World to Venice's Film Festival.

A portion of this information appears in Polt's review of
The Cool World in the Film Quarterly, 17 (Winter 1963-64), pages
33-35. The major focus of the film is a rumble between two teen-
age rival groups, the Royal Pythons and the Wolves, in Harlem.
Young "Duke" Custis, a Royal Python member, wants to get a gun--
"a piece" as it's called in the film--because he can then become the
leader of his group. The techniques of the documentary filmmaker
are used well to persuade viewers of the authenticity of the film's
locale. (No filmmaker had ever filmed a film in Harlem before:
how could Polt judge?) However, Polt finds The Cool World authentic in locale and characterization, noting that adults in the film were
professional actors, whereas the children were non-professionals.
But, she observes, "sometimes the film tries to be too definitive in
its portrayal of the Negro's situation...."

Occasionally, Polt decides, sensationalism and sentimentality
surface. But only peripherally. She finds one question repeatedly
by Luanne "You mean there's really an ocean at the end of the subway?" ... kept off the shoals of affectation by the terrifying coolness with which Yolanda Rodriguez plays the part.

Jazz music is used effectively in The Cool World just as it was in The Connection. Polt credits the jazz score to "Mal Waldron, played by Dizzy Gillespie, Yuscf Latccf, Arthur Taylor, and Aaron Bell, seemed to me totally in keeping with the action of the film. It is not one of those scores that you don't notice."

The fusion of voices and music on the soundtrack of The Cool World is analyzed by Tony Rayns in Monthly Film Bulletin 4:480 (March 1974), pages 44-45. With young Duke as

> central character, both the turns of the plot and the gen-
> eralities are filtered through his growing self-consciousness
> of his position, explored in a series of introspective voice-
> overs. But these interior monologues ... are only one
> element in an exceptionally well-thought soundtrack--the
> method might best be described as an extension of Kerouac's
> narration for Pull My Daisy--which "orchestrates" Duke's
> voice and Mal Waldron's mournful jazz score with direct
> and post-synched sound into consistently rich, fluid aural
> textures.

Rayns faults the film as "not especially well photographed" and for "redundant social comment...." These are compensated for by "Clarke's knowing understatement of the more extreme scenes.... With the film's good and bad qualities thus in miraculous balance, the element that registers most powerfully is the sheer energy of the characters, their capacities for delicacy and anger alike."

Critic Dorothy Oshlag worked as Production Manager for The Cool World. Her article in Sight and Sound (Summer 1963), pages 121-122, gives us an insider's recollection of what the job was, and what the whole filming crew had to do. Filming was a unique experience, because, as Oshlag reflects: "the story was not only being acted for the camera but was going on around us on the streets...."

The title signifies Negro Harlem, and Oshlag recounts what it was like to film day and night, always drawing a curious crowd who commented, often wittily, on the mixed crew, with gang fights, drunkenness, and dope-peddling happening nearby. Simply not alarming the neighborhood by the camera crew's presence was a chore. "As in any tightly-knit ... city slum, there is [an] underground resistance movement with its own intelligence network spreading over a large area." Once the news was beamed along this network that a movie was being filmed, a new crop of situations had to be dealt with. Oshlag had to explain that "we were ... not in the refrigeration business."

Interiors in the condemned building were no sooner arranged and left in readiness than "vandals would break in to steal anything movable...." The major concern was to finish filming before the bulldozers arrived to demolish the structure. Oshlag reports The Cool World was finished with a week to spare.

In its Spring 1964 issue, Film Comment offered a tripart review of The Cool World, pages 51-53.   Jesse Walker, City Editor of
the New York Amsterdam News admits that the reality of the film
shocked him.   An initial sequence in the film shows Duke with his
classmates on a school bus trip to the New York Stock Exchange
"where they hear a lecture from their Jewish teacher on 'How to
Own a Share of America.' "

Duke and his friends are unimpressed.   They know their gang
is

> their only ticket to owning something.   To Duke, this
> means taking over the control of the gang from Blood, the
> current leader whose addiction to heroin causes him to
> lose the respect of the Pythons.   Duke eventually becomes
> the leader ..., and inevitably ... he winds up being
> dragged away and beaten by cops after he has killed an-
> other youngster in a park rumble....   A sharp turn is in
> the final scene when Duke, a prisoner in the police squad
> car, rides by his mother who is on her way with her new-
> est lover to the nearest bar for a drink.

Walker accords Carl Lee, son of "great Negro actor, Canada
Lee" the highest praise in the role of a Harlem gangster.   "But
the real acting honors go to the kids...." National Director of The
Congress for Racial Equality, James Farmer, also found the film
shocking because "It is the truth. " Farmer recommends that all
Americans see it.

A less glowing look at the film is taken by Gordon Hichens.
The dialogue of the film he finds poor.   Recognizing that the film
evolved from a novel published in 1959, then cast in stage play form
by Warren Miller, the author, with Robert Rossen, who also directed
it, Hichens indexes a few speeches which "show a strong literary
hand. " The non-professionals are "incoherent, " not understood easily.
To this criticism, Clarke reasons that the required improvisatory
methods used might lend a blank manner, a lameness, in the spoken
dialogue.   The youngsters-as-actors were asked if this was something they would do, or not do, if they believed in it.   "If they said
'No, we didn't do it ... From all this comes their attitude, not
mine.... " Hichens finds the spoken lines formulated by non-
professionals inept.   He objects to the amorphous method of composing dialogue and its delivery: the young actors do not directly
express what their "cool world" is, what their place in it is.
Hichens observes:

> The film offers no socially productive externalization of
> these boys' inner-directed resentment ... even the civil
> rights struggle is sensed ... as a naive palliative.   This
> occurs in a sequence where a button-down clean-cut young
> Negro emerges from a library, identifies himself as a
> freedom rider, and proceeds vainly to harangue his addict
> brother about self-reform.

The virtues and flaws of The Cool World are Clarke's own:
"Hers is the coldness, the story-line of half-events, half-happenings,
and the stroboscopic blur and shaky pans masquerading as technical
virtuosity ... the film soon breaks down exactly where she hopes to
succeed, i. e. in making us care about characters as people.... "
Further, Hichens states that the 1962 film didn't need updating from
the 1959 novel: situations and scenes in The Cool World remained
basically the same in the three-year period.

Clarke differed, of course, because Harlem's incidence of
crimes in most categories had increased. Most interestingly, she
explicates the meaning of "cool world, " the world of Harlem: "For
the young boy or girl trying to grow up in this ghetto, his only
answer is to 'play it cool. ' If you're 'cool' you take nothing from
no one and get what you can. Your heroes are the coolest of all. "
Clarke adds: "The whites must learn what it is to be a Negro.... "

Clarke wrote an article "The Cool World" published in Films
and Filming 10:3 (December 1963), on page 7. She claims her film
is dedicated to brotherhood, "right now, not in the future. " Her
impetus for making The Cool World, in part, rests in the fact that
no feature film in America has attempted to deal realistically with
the Negro. Clarke describes the work of her cameraman Baird
Bryant as central to her whole concept of the film. As an instance,
in the bus ride taken to the Wall Street area, Bryant and Clarke decided that the schoolteacher should be the focal point, and that the
camera would stay with him. The children on the bus improvised
and Bryant shot the whole ride.

"For all its brusque cutting, disjointed narrative, and frustrating half-glances at its characters, this is the most important
film document about Negro life in Harlem to have been made so
far. " Albert Johnson begins his examination of The Cool World with
this statement in his article "The Negro in American Films: Some
Recent Works" in Film Quarterly 18 (Summer 1965), pages 26-28.
There is "little humor in the film" but Johnson considers the total
film "a work of visual poetry, and, in sound, a tone poem of the
slums. " Each "character in the film is so vivid that each one
struggles ... to have his story told. " In a comparison with the
novel, Johnson identifies themes of rejection, disillusionment and
despair. Overall, "the desperation of the dark, of being black and
ignored" is so compelling that the central character, Duke, comes
off as "the least interesting person in the story. "

Johnson marvels at Clarke's ability to compress so much into her film. "It is fairly bursting with questions to unresolved
problems and unresolved people. " Because Harlem's "dependence
upon the white world around it is not explored" Johnson feels the
film is incomplete. Most striking is "the undercurrent of anti-white
anger" in the film. "The 'coolness' that must be maintained is an
emotional control, repressed in turmoil, camouflaging the Negro's
realization that the white world, no matter how 'uncool, ' is one in
which he needs a place; a desirable world with which he is not yet
able to cope. "

The cast of characters and a clear plot summary of The Cool
World appear in The American Film Institute Catalog of Motion Pictures: Feature Films 1961-1970.

> Duke, a black adolescent and member of the Royal Py-
> thons, lives in Harlem with his mother and grandmother.
> Following the departure of their friend Littleman's father,
> the Pythons appropriate the apartment, installing Luanne
> as resident prostitute. Despite the fact that Luanne is
> Python president Blood's girl friend, she and Duke fall
> in love. Discovering that Blood is a heroin addict, Duke
> assumes leadership of the gang. During an idyll at Coney
> Island, however, Luanne vanishes, and Duke returns to
> Harlem. During a halfhearted battle with the Wolves, a
> rival gang, Duke stabs an antagonist. Seeking refuge, he
> rushes to Python headquarters, where he discovers the
> corpse of a friend. At home he is apprehended by police.

Andrew Sarris salutes Clarke and her associates for their
efforts "to penetrate the superficial objectivity of the documentary
method.... Clarke flings wet-mop close-ups of eloquently questioning black faces at her white audiences as if these audiences had
never really seen a Negro before--and, in a sense, they never have,
we never have. " But

> Clarke has repeated all the artistic mistakes that defeated
> her first feature. Her camera still sweeps and swoops
> excessively.... She never quite meshes the materials of
> stylized melodrama into the network of realistic cross-
> references.... The end result is that a gang rumble be-
> comes a painless ballet involving graceful animals ... "
> (Confessions of a Cultist, pp. 135-136).

In kinder tones, Stanley Kauffmann recalls that he judged
The Connection to be "sophomoric and spurious, " but that "her direction had skill and intensity. This second film is in some technical aspects less finished, but the intensity has been intensified.
The picture takes us as much by fierce fundamental concern as by
its art. "50

The lack of acting ability is painfully apparent: "Clarke has
not been able to make many of their scenes knit internally and grow. "
An incomprehensible soundtrack, jagged editing, and occasional lofty
language flaw "a work of notable power. " The "impact of the factual ... compensates for many of the drama's inadequacies" Kauffmann declares. The "dramatization of the environment by means
of the plot, instead of vice versa, is the film's chief and fine
achievement. "51

Judith Crist contrasts The Cool World as novel and film and
finds the latter wanting.

> All the humor and breadth of Mr. Miller's work, which

was a touchingly universal story of a slum-ghetto child,
has been deleted for a single-track indictment of the white
world and a grimly bitter tale of tragedy ... the focus of
Miss Clarke's film has somehow shifted from the boy who
must touch our emotions to the passing faces of the crowds
and to the garbage pails.... What would be a personal
story and a potential work of art ultimately becomes a
polemic. 52

Dwight Macdonald expresses the most negative view of The
Cool World in those published reviews considered here. He calls
The Cool World "a disaster in every way.... 53 It is confused,
overstated, chaotically edited, and ... a conventional sob story. "54
Documentary and melodrama are poorly fused. Macdonald feels that
the movie "was directing the director. "55 And the whole film
"elaborately plotted and highly artificial. "56 In defiant tones, Macdonald insists, "I cannot believe that Harlem, or even its teen-age
gangs, are like this. "57 Macdonald concludes: "The ironic point
about The Cool World ... is that this racial libel was made with
the best of intentions. "58 He postscripts that he enjoyed The Connection because the junkies in it were "rendered as individuals"
while The Cool World residents "blur into an oppressed mass.... "59

The New York Times' Bosley Crowther affirms in his review
(April 21, 1964, 42:1) that Clarke's role as director is as a reporter who "uses her camera to assemble facts ... to establish the
nature of the environment and chase after the characters who interest her. " She is an "outsider looking in" recording what she sees.
"Thus the dynamism of this picture ... flows from the brilliant,
brutal picturing of the community as it is.... " The impact of The
Cool World is tremendous. "It blisters the eyes and claws the
senses with its vicious and hideous visual truths ... it gives the
shattering details of an excellent newspaper exposé and binds it with
the conviction of staggering imagery. "

But it is "not a tight and direct film. " Crowther sees a
"certain looseness and vagrancy in the style" of the film. And it
is "marred a little by a too-free use of four-letter words. "

A review of The Cool World from the Venice Festival was
published September 11, 1963. Tagged "Both timely and timeless"
the Variety critic found the film "probably one of the least patron-
izing films ever made of Negro life in New York. " Clarke's directing is commended as "virile, " a style that "keeps this long film
engrossing and revealing most of the way. " She has "a firm hold
on her characters and story. " No preachiness emerges: "The
problems of segregation and civil rights are implicit" in the lives
of the characters. Especially moving were those scenes showing
Duke's blossoming attachment to a 15-year-old prostitute (Luanne)
and his showing her the sea for the first time at Coney Island. "

More than a year later, Variety reviewed the film in San
Francisco, opening with a question: Was The Cool World "an art

film with boxoffice staying power, or is it just an action pic for
quick grind release?"60

A list of cities showing and not showing it follows. It played
Washington, Philadelphia, and Baltimore. But Boston wouldn't touch
it. Successful art house runs, as in New York and San Francisco,
have prevailed. Variety details how the long run in San Francisco
was achieved. The Cool World opened "with minimum advance promotion, " getting primarily a Negro audience. By its fourth week,
though, box-office revenues were sinking. "Then KSFO disk jockey
Don Sherwood began plugging pic on his morning radio show. Attendance picked up and exhib Irving Levin increased promotion.
Fifth week figures shot back up...." Whites as well as Negroes
bought tickets. As of November 10, the film was in its eighth week
and Levin expected a long run.

In Boston, producer Fred Wiseman extended appreciation to
Mr. Levin.

> I think Irving Levin with the help of Don Sherwood has
> provided us with the breakthrough for which we've been
> waiting. At first I had the same fantasies that the theatre
> owners have. They think if they show a movie about
> Negroes, they'll have a riot on their hands.... Levin has
> proved that with proper handling "The Cool World" can
> successfully bring its ... message to a far wider audi-
> ence.... "

Bluntly, and with bitterness, Clarke assesses her relationship with Fred Wiseman, producer of The Cool World, in Susan
Rice's interview article in Take One 3:2 (1972), on page 21. Clarke
declares Wiseman cheated her. And he did a good job of it. She
never saw a financial statement while the film was made or afterward. Then he wouldn't let her have a copy of the film because he
was afraid she would show it for free. Clarke feels that Wiseman
wanted to become a filmmaker, made the film for that reason, and
very effectively excluded her from the profits and the prestige the
film earned.

To Rice's questions about independent filmmaking she tenders
grim facts based on her personal experiences. No one really knows
how to distribute the independent film. And no matter what you are
assured you will make on the film you won't earn a cent. Clarke
reveals that she never made a dollar on any of her films until
Jason. Because she owned Portrait of Jason (1967), her third feature film, she did earn money from it.

The national weekly and biweekly magazine reviews of The
Cool World appeared in 1964, three years after it was finished.
Why the delay? Ebony, in its July 1965 article on page 43, replies,

> It barely missed the jury's prize at last year's Venice
> Film Festival. Yet American distributors steered clear

because of its harsh depiction of Harlem life.   Only recently has the film enjoyed national exposure.   "It went
over big in France and Japan, " says Wiseman, "and is
scheduled to be shown in England, Germany, Belgium and
Ghana.   But distributors here didn't think it too commercial. "

The Ebony article is illustrated with scenes from the film,
a plot summary with acting credits, and an interest in the "group
of underprivileged youngsters who were acting out in real life many
of the events the film depicts.   "'They weren't all problem kids, '
says Wiseman, 'but a couple were on probation even during filming.
One was given a smaller part after he was involved in a stabbing. ' "

The most glowing praise Clarke has received for any of her
work is probably the unsigned review appearing in Newsweek (April
20, 1964), on page 114:

Shirley Clarke is one of the most brilliant documentarists
since Robert Flaherty....   The power of the film is in
Miss Clarke's vision of Harlem, and the manner in which
she uses that vision is the purest kind of moviemaking.
[The Cool World is] a work of art informed by knowing
compassion....   Clarke moves her camera ... showing
us Harlem.   Sometimes she merely lets her lens rubber-
neck, picking up a fancy hat, a fishmonger, an electric
sign.   Often she invents visual rhythms, cutting from a
cigar smoker to a fat man smoking a ceramic pipe, to a
man with a cigarette, or from a little girl skipping, to a
man doing a trick dance on a manhole cover, to a group
of young women twisting outside a record shop.

On page 114 B, the reviewer comments on the authenticity of the
conversations.   The "great virtue of the Warren Miller novel" was
the dialogue; however, "its effect in a film is vastly more powerful....   This is probably the first film in which the word 'faggot'
is used.... "

Stunningly memorable is the close of the film, the rumble of
the Pythons and Wolves in a playground.   "Clarke ... is marvelously balletic about it, without any sacrifice of realism....   One com-
batant scrambles up the Parks Department's climbing arches only to
be knifed in the belly from below.   There is no musical accompaniment.   It is silent and deadly and real. "

The Cinema column in Time on page 123 in the April 17, 1964,
issue dubs the film "an effective sociological shocker. " Observing
that Fifth Avenue dead-ends at 110th Street where Harlem begins,
"the black hole of Manhattan, " the reviewer explains what's wrong
with the film: "It so furiously resents the race prejudice of the
whites that it unconsciously adopts the race prejudice of the Negroes. "
The cinematography is "inexcusably sloppy" and "... the moviemakers too often splice sociology with sensation, documentary with melodrama. "

Brendan Gill in the New Yorker for April 25, 1964, delivers his customary skepticism on pages 171-172:

> The shots of street life in Harlem are extremely fine, but in a surprisingly short time we begin to feel a certain skepticism about the use to which they're being put. ... Miss Clarke indulges the documentary side of her footage irresistibly vivid and compelling but not very relevant, and leaves the plot ... to proceed by awkward fits and starts. And the difficulty Miss Clarke creates for herself is this: The more we recognize the setting as true, the more we perceive that the story is but verisimilitude....

In a comparison with Black Like Me directed by Carl Lerner and The Cool World, Hollis Alpert in Saturday Review, April 25, 1964, page 25, finds Clarke's film the better one. Clarke is

> a young woman whose talent is combined with an uncompromising sense of reality.... While after truth with her camera, and catching a good deal of it, too, Miss Clarke has nevertheless emphasized matters to bring out tones of violence and has only hinted at other forces in the Negro communities.

The Cool World, Alpert claims, "is ... best in its documentary aspects, and occasionally weak in its drama, which is perhaps as it should be." But Clarke's use of profanity is protested. "She has not learned her lesson, because the same word is heard occasionally in The Cool World. But it is hardly the use of any particular word that shocks here; it is rather her use of the camera to portray Negro desperation and violence.... "

Philip T. Hartung compares the two films also, in a Commonweal review dated May 15, 1964, page 237. He asserts that the financial returns and critical receptions accorded them will determine the feasibility of more interracial films being made. "Neither 'Black Like Me' nor 'The Cool World' is a particularly good or appealing movie; but both were made inexpensively, as films go, and other producers will watch their box-office returns with interest. "

Hartung finds Black Like Me "more sensational and surface-skimming than a treatise like this should be." He reasons that visualization of author John Howard Griffin's book, from which Carl and Gerda Lerner wrote the screenplay, may have been frustrating. "And perhaps the whole experiment (which Griffin actually experienced) is futile." As acted by James Whitmore, Hartung criticizes him for not appearing honest-to-goodness Negro in his role of Horton, a white man who makes his face black and travels the South as a Negro. Even though the degrading and frightening experiences Horton endures are engrossing, "in a mixture of documentary ... and hopped-up melodrama [the film] reaches no conclusion other than despair.... "

The Cool World generated even more despair than Black Like
Me.   Hartung credits Clarke for making the non-professional young
people "convincing in their roles, especially Hampton Clanton
whose portrait of Duke is so realistic it hurts.   What Miss Clarke
has not done, however, is allow us to project ourselves into the
story.   In fact, she often wanders far from the plot to give us
vivid, documentary scenes that show Harlem at its worst. "   For
Hartung, the film is "one-sided":

> Dramatically the picture would have done better to explore
> Duke in greater depth and Harlem less.... Only occa-
> sionally do we become involved in Duke's emotional prob-
> lems. No doubt Miss Clarke, for all her brilliant film-
> making, means to say this is a world Duke never made--
> and what chance has he in it? She gives no answers, but
> she succeeds in making us cringe....

The Cool World review in Life by Richard Oulahan, is titled
"Low-Budget Realism, Warts and All, " dated April 24, 1964, page
15.   Oulahan finds nothing new in the subject matter, the lot of
deprived Negroes and ghetto life having been filmed many times.
The film "is ... an excellent example of a new wave--or perhaps it
is just a new ripple--in U. S. filmmaking.   It began several years
ago when the advent of inexpensive and mobile cameras, lights, and
other equipment made it possible for almost anyone to make a shoe-
string picture. "

"The best and the worst in the current wavelet" is found in
The Cool World, being "filmed with considerable sensitivity and ingenuity. "   Clarke flaws her film when she

> slams home her message a mite too insistently.   All is
> stark horror, shame and fear.   That is not the whole
> truth about Harlem, but the whole truth is not the goal in
> films such as this.   Their shoestring producers strive for
> a jarring encounter with reality.   Almost all their efforts
> are message films which view some wart on the U. S. hide
> through a lens darkly.   They are seldom pleasant, but the
> best of them--and The Cool World qualifies as one of the
> best--can overcome their technical shortcomings by stabbing
> at the conscience and tearing at the mind.

Clarke's own satisfaction with the film is voiced in her revelation to Marjorie Rosen: "Do you know, The Cool World played to
lines in Times Square, which was one of the great honors, in fact,
a goal of my life. "[61]

Clarke disliked the "time lapse factor" in making films.   In
her words: "'I spent a brief time making films and a large time
hustling them....'"[62]   The "time lapse" between The Cool World
and Portrait of Jason (1967) was three years.   And "Despite ... impressive initial contributions and despite her great respect in the film
community, Shirley found time hanging heavy between projects. "[63]

With Jonas Mekas and Louis Brigante, Clarke set up the Film-makers Distribution Center in 1966.   Then she worked on a project for the Montreal Expo Show of 1967:   a 12-screen carousel film titled Man in the Polar Regions was the result.

In the "time lapse" Clarke directed a film which has not been released.   Inspired, perhaps, by the Award-winning Frost film, Clarke undertook to portray the Russian poet Vosnesensky. [64]   An architect by training, Andrei Andreevich Vosnesensky abandoned his profession when he met and submitted poems to poet Boris Pasternak. The two men became inseparable friends.

Vosnesensky had graduated from the Moscow Architectural Institute in 1957, and began publishing his poems the following year. In 1959 his book The Craftsman appeared.   The poet toured the United States on a poetry reading circuit.   Another tour to the United States was granted and cancelled three times by authorities in the U. S. S. R.

According to Facts on File (Dec. 28-31, 1967), the poet de-nounced the U. S. S. R. Writers Union for preventing his appearance at a Lincoln Center (New York) Summer Festival.   Vosnesensky wrote a letter of protest to Pravda, which was not published.

The poet did appear July 2 at Moscow's Taganka Theatre, his first public appearance since the cancellation of his American tour. He was applauded and given flowers.   The circumstances fostering Clarke's interest--did she meet him?--in Vosnesensky as a subject for film portrayal remain unknown.   Clarke herself is silent on the subject.

The impetus for filming Jason quite possibly was Clarke's meeting Aaron Paine, the sole character in her dramatic monologue-type film.   The citation in The American Film Institute Catalog of Feature Films, 1961-1970 describes it on page 859:

> This cinéma vérité portrait of Jason Holliday, a 33-year-old black male prostitute who dreams of a career as a nightclub entertainer, is drawn from 12 consecutive hours of filming in a New York City apartment.   As Jason reminisces about his past and speculates about his future, all the while smoking marijuana and drinking, the film-maker and some friends prod him with questions and taunt from off camera.   Jason ... describes ... his traumatic confrontations with his family, the orgies he has attended and the hustling that has formed the pattern of his life....
> His "performance" includes brief impersonations of Mae West, Butterfly McQueen, and Pearl Bailey.   He recalls that he was a college dropout, worked as a bar hustler and as a servile houseboy in San Francisco, has been a heroin addict, and has spent time in jail, on the Bowery, and in a hospital mental ward....

Jonas Mekas sounds a trumpet-like blast of triumph for Jason in his Village Voice 12:45 (August 24, 1967) column on page 23: "The news is out: Shirley Clarke's new film, 'Portrait of Jason,' has been chosen to play at the Lincoln Center's Film Festival this September." Mekas states he has seen the film: "It is one of the important, very important contemporary films. I had the following conversation with Shirley Clarke."

In his first query to Clarke, Mekas asks her how Jason differs from her previous two feature films. Clarke replies that "the shooting experience itself" made the movie different:

> This was the first time the shooting was both exciting and relaxing.... I planned a very simple camera procedure ... I had only one action to follow. For the first time, I was able to give up my intense control and allow Jason and the camera to react to each other. Suddenly it was as if a great weight was lifted, and I could relax and, more important, respond to the emotions spinning round the room.

As for why Clarke chose to do Jason, she cites the reason as people being the most interesting subject of any film. "We have rarely allowed anyone to really speak for himself for more than a few minutes at a time. Just imagine what might happen if someone was given his head and allowed to let go for many consecutive hours. I was curious, and WOW did I find out." And she explains why she considers Aaron Paine an ideal subject to film: Paine did not know enough about filmmaking "to control his own image of himself, unlike my experience filming Robert Frost-- Frost was always playing a mirror image of himself."

Mekas matched the Clarke interview with one of Jason in Village Voice 12:50 (September 28, 1967), page 31. The initial query dealt with the actor's concern about whether the audience would mix up the real person with the filmed Jason.

Jason replies: "I am a great enough actor that one will know where the truth stops and the lie begins. I felt it was such a gas to put the world on.... When I first saw the flick I said, Oh, my God. I'm hurting myself. Then I thought--so what!... " What was his reaction to Clarke's proposal to do Jason? "I am ready to take anything that comes." He did worry if viewers would think he was "homosexual, bisexual, or heterosexual. I wondered if I was great enough to convince them I am all three. The three-sided figure makes a triangular--trisexual. I said: try, anything as long as there is money in it, dig it?"

Mekas then objects to the advertising blurb used to publicize Jason: "Interview with a male prostitute." Not at all, Mekas asserts. Jason is "a very complex human being, as complex as many a Dostoyevsky character." And the film "is one of the most genuine, most outstanding narratives of the decade, in any art form."

In his review of the avant-garde films shown at the New York
Film Festival, Mekas accords praise to three films: Godard's Les
Carabiniers, and Clarke's Portrait of Jason, which he evaluates as
"probably great films." Rossellini's film The Rise of Louis XIV is
a "great film" and Mekas devotes his column to an interview of the
Italian filmmaker.

Quentin Guerlain accords the warmest praise to Jason in
Cinema 4 (Spring 1958), page 48. Its excellence stems from its
director's unerring intuition and good judgment, Guerlain discerns.

> One is tempted to minimize director Shirley Clarke's con-
> tribution to this highly-charged documentary--and for obvi-
> ous reasons. Her subject ... happens to be his own di-
> rector, scriptwriter and choreographer.... All you have
> to do, ostensibly, is give him twelve hours or so of your
> undivided time, a little something ... to help him unwind,
> point your camera--and, presto, you have the nicest slice
> of gritty black Americana to ever find its way into a movie
> can.

But Guerlain knows that making a film is not that easy.
Clarke "had the good horse sense to remain on the fringe of the
show, to employ simple techniques and unobtrusive direction, in
addition to moving with--and anticipating--her subject. It is because
of this discretion that 'Portrait of Jason' is as good as it is. And
that is very good indeed: documentary filmmaking, the 'American
Underground' and cinéma-vérité at their best. "

"Like Lear" Guerlain observes, Jason "is pathetic in a grand
way, telling us more about heartbreak and hard times and the need
for personal identity than any of our Great American Tragedies. "
Jason is a "Ginger Man ... for real ... a true demon for all seasons, and particularly, for the Sixties. "

Honesty is "the most salient feature of Portrait of Jason for
John Hofsess in Take One, 1:7 (1967), page 24. "It is the new
mark of honesty in cinema, and a film by which all others will here-
after be judged. "

> At a time when Hollywood offers us Sidney Poitier as token
> representation of the negro in films ... Miss Clarke cooly
> [sic] gives us Jason ... no greater honesty on film is imagin-
> able.... Miss Clarke shows us how Jason relates to us,
> and how he differs, and one must admit of Jason's per-
> formance as himself that a life which would otherwise have
> been scorned or ignored has been given meaning and im-
> perishability through Miss Clarke's work.

Where Guerlain complimented Clarke on her tact in filming
Jason, the reviewer in Sight and Sound 37 (Winter 1967-1968), page
10, finds "a serious and damaging failure in tact here. " The "high
seriousness of ... Clarke's ... Jason is the one unarguable quality

it has, and the one quality capable of redeeming the arrogance of the conception and the boredom of having to sit through it. "

It's too much to expect of any audience that it should "submit" to it. Clarke made the film as a "commitment ... to the real world around her, and the viewing of the film ought to be in the nature of a commitment by the audience to the real world around it.... " Audiences feel alienated rather than empathic with Jason: first he reveals himself and then he makes us feel guilty. "Jason's imitations aren't very good, nor are his jokes, and the dutiful invisible snickering which follows them is alienating. Similar troubles arise from the questions which are put to Jason towards the end. They are sycophantic in tone, and, worse, they are obviously aimed at whipping the wretched man into a final orgasm of self-confession. There is a serious and damaging failure in tact here. "

The verdict in Film 50 (Winter 1967), pages 32-33, is "An altogether extraordinary and human document. " Jason is "an astounding experience; full of initial shocks, adroit punchlines, and a series of personal revelations replete with humour and bitterness.... Made in one huge session between nine at night and nine the next morning with a camera that had to be loaded every ten minutes and a sound recording that was made non-stop, Jason was primed with pep-pills, marijuana and constant alcohol. He is prompted by voices offscreen suggesting a particular anecdote or point of view.... "

The "shock-climax" comes when "Shirley Clarke's voice asks: 'You lonely?' and Jason answers with utmost vehemence: 'I'm desperate!' "

Charles Hartman, in his review article "The New and Independent Film Maker, " which appeared in the Film Society Review (November 1967), on page 27, prologues his praise of Jason with a sad acknowledgment of

> the problems that have prevented many excellent feature
> ideas from reaching fruition and have kept many finished
> films from being properly exhibited to the public.... It
> is common knowledge in the film business that the cen-
> tralizing force of Hollywood is so pervasive and deadening
> that even quite brilliant American film-makers have been
> blocked in their efforts to by-pass the Hollywood apparatus
> and instead directly reach the public.

Clarke has by-passed Hollywood, Hartman notes. "The Film-makers Distribution Center at 175 Lexington Ave. , New York, plans to tour the film with its director to universities and theaters throughout the country. "

"Clarke ... has re-emerged as a giant figure of American independent film with ... Jason. " ... Perhaps the closest the cinema has yet approached the province of Genet, Jason is an incredible peeling away of a man's soul layer by layer.... "

In a study of homosexuality represented in film, Screening
the Sexes (New York: Holt, Rinehart and Winston, 1972), film
critic Parker Tyler, on pages 155-56, classifies Jason as a homosexual "superannuated or outdated. " With only a few static lapses
in it, Jason "was made entirely in Miss Clarke's living room at the
Chelsea Hotel, New York ... is literally a one-man show, assisted
only by two offstage voices: Miss Clarke's and that of a white male
friend of the subject's. " More a "this is my life' routine" than a
movie, "Jason is one of those 'happy accidents' where, thanks to
Miss Clarke, the right medium was found at the right moment for
the right subject. " Jason was a "startling success with the audience
at the New York Film Festival, 1967, " but "It is not a great film,
no--but it is grandly authentic. ... "

Critic John Simon capsules his criticism in a negative nut-
shell: "100-minute outpourings of a drug-and-drink-sodden, goaded
and taunted Negro male whore strike me not as cinéma-vérité (itself banal enough) but as egregious lack of cinéma-charité. "

Variety's reviewer (October 4, 1967, page 12) captions a
thumbs-down reaction: "Feature-length interview with Negro male
prostitute is more sociology than art, and pretty superficial at that.
Could score in offbeat houses. "

Jason is "undeniably funny" at the start. But then, "as the
evening wears on" he turns somber, recalling his "unhappy childhood
and his degrading adulthood ... it is hard to see these moments as
more than the exuberant excesses of an emotional exhibitionist. "
Besides, the reviewer points out, "Jason's experiences have already
been recounted, with considerably more passion and art in the mush-
rooming litterature [sic] of the 'outcast'. "

Especially objectionable is Clarke, who, in her "off-camera
remarks ... comes across like a Freudian lion tamer. She im-
passionately eggs him on ... lacerates him, attacks him ...
Clarke has ... been exploiting Jason, but to his credit her efforts
don't succeed. " As for "technical achievements" the film doesn't
have any. The reviewer suggests that if Jason "were 45 minutes
shorter, it might be a tolerably perverse record of a nightclub
act. ... "

Reversing Variety's comment on the lack of technical achievements, the Monthly Film Bulletin XLV/530 (March 1968), page 51,
review by Vera Glaessner explicates Clarke's method of filming
Jason as a "reply to the cinéma vérité techniques of Leacock and
Pennebaker. Where their practice is to edit 'revealing' highlights
from an extensive mass of footage, Clarke has here allowed Jason's
monologue to reach the screen intact and in real time. " However,
this "tactic of presenting Jason's monologue in 'real time' only points
up the limitations of film-as-document, revealing the film-making
process to be manipulating the reality it records. " Glaessner concludes, "... the viewer is left floundering in an attempt to place the
objective reality of the subject's verbal confessions against the visual
reality of his presence. ... "

Vincent Canby in The New York Times (September 30, 1967, 26:1), pronounced Jason "extremely funny" and "a curious and fascinating example of cinéma vérité...." And "the film is a good deal more than an unusually frank interview...."

Revelation of a hunger and need for personal identity remarked on by several critics are noted here. Canby finds it in Jason's memories of his parents in Alabama. His mother "had a black soul with white attitudes" and "his father ..." felt disgust for "a son who liked to skip rope." Jason is "an extraordinary recognition and, perhaps, even a kind of reward for having survived."

Andrew Sarris' response to Jason appears in Confessions of a Cultist (New York: Simon and Schuster, 1970), on page 317:

> I enjoyed listening to Jason until Shirley Clarke made the mistake of trying to find the 'real' Jason. I much prefer Jason's con to his conscience ... the man's style does not so much conceal as constitute his substance. Why pick at Jason's tattered soul when it is only his surface charm that keeps him from screaming out of his skull? There should have been more songs and fewer tears. Don't cry, Jason. Just try to entertain us.

The form and flux of Jason impel Leo Braudy in Film Quarterly 22 (Fall 1968), pages 74-77, to theorize on "Bazin's question, What is Cinema?" And "We find ourselves ... still further from an answer...."

The film is "intensely interesting.... The camera tracks Jason around from couch to chair, to hearth, from a fixed position; it zooms in and out on Jason's face; sometimes, it goes out of focus.... Otherwise ... we are made to stare, in real camera time, at a real event."

Jason "may not be a film in the sense usually attached to the term, but it is certainly an immensely curious psychological and social document."

In Judith Crist's opinion,

> A film that demonstrates the difference between an artist (i. e. Miss Clarke) and a commercialist (i. e. Andy Warhol ...) Jason talks and does his "act" and his "bit"; and through the completely frank and therefore shocking exposure of a desperate human we get a throbbing and horrifying and compassionate understanding of what society can make of a man. 65

The best aspect of Jason is that Jason "enjoys himself enormously, getting high on his repeated 'I'." Jason "is no bore," in Brendan Gill's judgment (New Yorker, October 10, 1967) page 159:

He is fascinated by the person he supposes himself to
be.... So determined is he to remain alive and in the
world ... that our prefatory gloom is transformed into
something approaching exhilaration.... This suave phony
... may seem a rubbishy sort of hero, but a hero he un-
questionably is. "

The aspect of laying bare a man's soul to attain truth, and
probably not reaching it, is the core of Jason for Arthur Knight in
Saturday Review, September 9, 1967. After two hours of questions
and answers, musings and rantings, "one feels that no significant
shred of the man's past and personality has been left uncovered or
uncommented upon.... Occasionally, the camera goes slowly out of
focus, sometimes to effect a transition, sometimes quite arbitrarily
to emphasize the ritualistic, oddly impersonal nature of the true con-
fession. "

Like Brendan Gill, Arthur Knight feels intrusion first, revelation last and "the final shocking recognition that even Jason is not
certain that he has told the whole truth. "

Knight contrasts the honesty of Jason with the total objectivity
of Frederic Wiseman's film Titicut Follies, in which "concealed
cameras are pointed ... (there is no commentary) at the guards and
inmates of an unnamed institution in Massachusetts. " Wiseman's
film is "more horrible" in the truths it uncovers than Jason's self-
undress.

From Clarke's three features--Jason, The Cool World, and
The Connection--similarities of subject, locale, and technique surface. All three consider the situation of blacks in a New York locale, the central characters are black males, and crime is a
primary force in the narrative. In each, Clarke "invented" novel
treatments of dialogue, photography, and geography. Each film
earned acclaim and publicity of the box-office bonus type; still, with
these attention-getting, controversial works behind her, Clarke could
not find the financial backing and creative independence that she
needed and deserved.

In 1969, Hollywood beckoned Clarke "in the unlikely person
of Shelley Winters, who'd written a script she wanted Shirley to direct her in. "66 Clarke's reaction to the Hollywood establishment
was incredulity. Producers were delighted at the realness of her
films, then suggested using fake locations for filming. "'So all
the things I'd done they were tossing out the window. Obviously,
the finished film would not have been mine.... To tell the truth,
if I had the talent or the particular abilities to make Hollywood
movies, I guess I'd be making them....' "67

While in Hollywood, Clarke's friend Agnes Varda invited her
to play a role in Lions Love. In it, Clarke was to depict a filmmaker who attempts suicide when Hollywood funding for a proposed
film cannot be found.

In Documentary Explorations (Garden City, N. Y.: Doubleday, 1971) editor G. Roy Levin, on page 287, tries to define the type of film, such as Lions Love, that Varda was making, by exampling Clarke's role in the film. Lions Love presents several kinds of realities. Which one (or all?) is the viewer to place credence in? This type of film mixes

> a direct-cinema method and a fictional element, and, at times ... it gets very confusing as to what is straight up and what isn't. Like there's a scene with Varda getting Shirley Clarke to play a suicide scene; Varda walks into camera range and says, "Play the scene like this," etc., and Shirley Clarke doesn't want to but finally does. Now, I've heard that Shirley Clarke actually did try to commit suicide while making that film, though I'm not sure it's true, and this was then incorporated into the film.

Clarke gives her judgment on this issue of confused realities in the Susan Rice interview article in Take One 3:2 (1972), on page 21. She states flatly that there is no documentary reality as such. She sees no difference between a so-called fiction movie and a so-called documentary film. She says she has never made a documentary film. Simply put, there's no such animal.

In Lions Love, Clarke could not complete the scene as planned. Tony Rayns perceives Clarke's inability to do the scene as directed as "increasingly symbolic of her position" experiencing real enough conflicts with Hollywoodian moviemaking mandates. 68

The Shelley Winters film project evaporated. A very depressed Clarke returned to New York and went to bed. "By 1970 I was lying on my back staring out the window, saying things like, 'If it weren't for my daughter, I wouldn't bother to stay alive.' "69 Clarke's relationship with her daughter Wendy is a warm one. They are friends, sharing several interests, including filmmaking.

While in her slough of despondency, Clarke was the subject of a French TV program made by Andre S. Labarthe and Noel Burch.

Matter-of-factly, Clarke states that she had to stop making films because

> I couldn't find a producer who would accept my films as I wrote them. I didn't have any means of getting money. It may have to do with the fact that people with money do not talk about money to women. That's one of the things that showed up in my Hollywood dealings ... when I got out there, they had a man who was going to be my producer. And he was also going to tell me how I should make my film ... men just don't like to talk to women about money--that's all. 70

Clarke instantly fell in love with videotape and began working with it in January 1971. "She bought two decks and two cameras which a friend helped her set up. From the moment she saw the image in the monitor she never looked in the camera again." She admits her Hollywood trauma was cured when "by an absolute fluke I got a video grant and I've been delightfully high and excited ever since."71

Karen Cooper surmises that videotape was a logical development of Clarke's talents. As a dancer, a maker of dance films, and a proponent of independent filmmaking, Videotape offered Clarke instantaneousness, portability, improvisation, and multiplication of the image on the VT monitor. "This process of feeding material back and forth by focusing the camera on the monitor (is called) 'enfolding.'"72 The half-inch tapes are easily handled and carried. Above all, VT's "playback capability"--no waiting for film to be processed to see what you've done--is what enchants Clarke.

Taping is the core of her life. She loves doing it, and does it every day. Nothing intervenes. Anything that happens, it gets taped. Clarke sees her taping existence as one never-ending electrical line. With filmmaking, Clarke explains, you had to wait three or four years to make one. "'Now I dance with my fingers.'"73 Video is a never ending process, not a product. She emphasizes its use as a means of immediate artistic response rather than its cassette capabilities, "a theme with variations, a sort of fugue which is never finished."74

Early in 1972, Clarke held a video-ball during a Syracuse, New York, art show by John Lennon and Yoko Ono, offering participants views of themselves. And when New York held its Eighth Annual Avant Garde Festival in the winter of 1971-72, Clarke brought to it a large "carnival-size ferris wheel with a VT monitor attached to every sitting compartment."75

Daughter Wendy shares this working enthusiasm for videotape. Wendy has produced and directed a video show of her own, earning approbation from Village Voice's critic, Jonas Mekas. Shirley Clarke is pleased and proud, even envious, of her daughter's achievements. Both women work independently and cooperatively. Clarke is artistic director of the TP Videospace Troupe which tours the United States doing teaching workshops and performing shows. The Troupe uses cable access wherever it happens to be in the community and on campuses. Upcoming potentialities in videotape branch out into a cascade of not-yet-tried and novel art forms. Clarke knows what all of these are. "Right now we could have phone-in disc-jockey shows on cable television.... We should be exploring multiple-monitor setups, team and audience feedback, and developing a new set of perceptions...."76 Clarke views the nature of videotape "like an amorphous and ever-evolving cubist toy or system of game-playing with horizontal as well as vertical possibilities."77

Videotape offers Clarke spontaneity, an implementation of impulse which she thoroughly enjoys. In video, she cautions, you have to be prepared. She has trained herself to set up her equipment so as to be error-free. Working in video, she confides, is the closest she's got to dancing--the high elation felt.

What about videotape's future? Clarke predicts it will travel a twin path. One relates to novel writing or painting, because in video she can create images unlike those in motion pictures. The other is therapeutic in effect, bringing people and their concerns together. But, once again, videotape artists must seek sponsors, worry about audiences. Clarke considers working in cable is probably worse than working for a commercial network. In fact, she concludes, she'd probably prefer working in a network if given a choice.

Clarke's headquarters has been a rooftop apartment in New York's Chelsea Hotel. There she teaches a group of videotapists who are trained as architects, actors, and artists of all genres. The group is halved so that each can respond to the other with camera and monitor. VT aficionados are multiplying and forming a subterranean enclave all their own. Because each participant is a beginner, the atmosphere is open, congenial, and cooperative, similar to the circumstances in which independent filmmakers worked and shared.

Early in 1975, Women in Film held a retrospective show of Clarke's films at the Theatre Vanguard in Los Angeles. There she once again had the chance to negotiate for a film and a television special show too. She lives with the everpresent self queries: Why couldn't she continue to make feature films? Did she lack an important element required for greatness? Why didn't the big money and the big chances come to her as they had for Stanley Kubrick? Clarke replies ruefully that Kubrick began film work about four years before she did. But his destiny, his success as a filmmaker could and should have been hers if she were a man. A simple fact, Clarke affirms.

Trying to define her deficiency, if, indeed there was a lack, Clarke has assessed herself in these words: "I was an experimental filmmaker only in the sense that when I finally felt I had control of the medium, I didn't really have anything burning I wanted to say. My personal 'women's' experiences seemed unimportant. Yet by refusing to go deep into my soul, I feel that my work is not really significant.... "[78]

Regarding the women's liberation movement, Clarke is on record as being for it--with reservations.

> Now everything they say I totally agree with. But their style and manner is boring and unattractive.... They're simply not attractive as people. (Like the Communist Party. There's nothing wrong with the Party, it's just that everybody in it is so goddam unattractive.)... I

cringe to identify with them.... Women have been fan-
tastic for a long time--they act like they invented it. [79]

Because the filmmaking equipment is now portable, women
are equals with men in making films today.   Cameras are no longer
hard-to-move elephantine machines on the shooting set.

Clarke finds the concept and the reality of a Women's Film
Festival beyond endurance.   "Here are all these poor chicks.
They're not going to make it because they're not really recognizing
the women who have made films ... Storm De Hirsch, Mary Ellen
Bute ... God knows my films aren't being shown.   I really don't
know what they expect to accomplish.... "[80]

Early in 1980, Wendy Clarke obtained a grant to make "Love
Tapes. "   She invited individuals to talk for three minutes or less
about love and loving on videotape, and then the opportunity to destroy it if desired.   With photos of a few participants and their
lead statements, the Village Voice 25 (April 28, 1980), pages 64-65,
captions them: "Love Tapes: Embarrassment, unease, romantic
cliché, soap opera torment, and catharsis are revealed by participants in Wendy Clarke's Love Tapes.   A project gives you three
minutes to talk on tape about love....   To make a tape for the
series call 924-4796.   It's your chance to be famous for at least
three minutes.... "

At this moment, Shirley Clarke is probably working with videotape in her apartment, an elfin-sized perpetual motion person wearing a cap on her head.   For her, the headgear she dons works magic
for her.   She has sported derbies and caps.   Her most recent magic
cap is a top hat.

Clarke's hat frames her dark bangs, with a white patch in
the center, drawing attention to her large dark eyes.   The moment
a guest enters Clarke's apartment she is on videotape without realizing
it.   Clarke continues to travel and explore videotape.   It is her passion. [81]

But will she return to films?   Only time has the answer.
Tony Rayns expresses his judgment, knowing that many share it with
him: "That Shirley Clarke has not made a film for so many years
is one of the tragedies of the American independent cinema; she has
more talent, it seems to me, than most 'independent' directors.   In
recent years she has worked exclusively in that most evanescent of
media, video. "[82]

Clarke knows what women have achieved in filmmaking.
Women have been film editors since the start of the moviemaking
business.   Women editors have really made the films the men have
shot and financed.   Women have written the original scripts that
have been filmed.   As editors and scriptwriters, women have not
earned the credit lines and earnings men have made.

Her plans? Clarke will pursue her conviction that she must search for a producer who will produce a film that she will write, direct, and edit. She will never forfeit her artistic freedom, her individual style.

As more and more women make films Clarke hopes their works will make meaningful statements. Women's films, she believes, should give audiences deeper insights into the whole human situation, not just feminist doctrine or male-oriented issues. In women's films, Clarke declares, we'll see and understand more than we've ever been permitted to perceive before. Including her own, of course.

FILMOGRAPHY*

Dance in the Sun (1953)

Bullfight (1955)

In Paris Parks (1955)

A Moment in Love (1957)

Loops (1958)

Skyscraper (1959)

Bridges-Go-Round (1959)

A Scary Time (1960)

The Connection (1960)

The Cool World (1963)

A Lover's Quarrel with the World (1964)

Man in the Polar Regions (1967)

Vosnesensky (1967); not completed

Portrait of Jason (1967)

NOTES

1. Susan Rice, "Shirley Clarke: Image and Images, " Take One 3:2 (1972), p. 20.
2. Marjorie Rosen, "Shirley Clarke: Videospace Explorer, " Ms. (April 1975), p. 107.
3. Ibid.

*Note: Release dates used are from Women's Films in Print: An Annotated Guide to 800 16 mm Films by Women, compiled by Bonnie Dawson.   San Francisco: Booklegger Press, 1975, pages 22-23. Also, the documentary about Robert Frost omits his name in the title (1964).

4. Ibid.
5. Storm De Hirsch and Shirley Clarke, "A Conversation, " in
    Women and the Cinema: A Critical Anthology, ed. by Karyn
    Kay and Gerald Peary. New York: E. P. Dutton, 1977, p.
    233.
6. Ibid.
7. Karen Cooper, "Shirley Clarke, " Filmmakers Newsletter 5:8
    (June 1972), p. 34.
8. Rosen, p. 107.
9. Bonnie Dawson, comp. Women's Films in Print: An Anno-
    tated Guide to 800 16 mm Films by Women. San Francisco:
    Booklegger Press, 1975, p. 23.
10. Ibid. , p. 22.
11. Rosen, p. 107.
12. "Films of Shirley Clarke, " Film Quarterly XIII:4 (Summer
    1960), p. 58.
13. Ibid. , p. 57.
14. Ibid. , p. 58.
15. G. Roy Levin, Documentary Explorations: 15 Interviews with
    15 Film-Makers. Garden City, N. Y. : Doubleday, 1971, p.
    223.
16. Henry Breitrose, " Films of Shirley Clarke, " Film Quarterly
    XIII:4 (Summer 1960), p. 58.
17. Rosen, p. 107.
18. "The New American Cinema Group, " Film Culture no. 22-23
    (Summer 1961), p. 130.
19. Ibid. , p. 131.
20. Ibid. , pp. 134-135.
21. Ibid. , p. 136.
22. Ibid. , p. 137.
23. Ibid.
24. Ibid. , p. 144.
25. Ibid. , p. 145.
26. Ibid. , p. 148.
27. George N. Fenin, "The Skyscraper Experiment, " Films and
    Filming (April 1961), p. 12.
28. "Filming 'The Connection, ' " Sight and Sound 30 (Spring 1961),
    p. 69.
29. Ibid.
30. Ibid.
31. Ibid. , p. 70.
32. Ibid.
33. Ibid.
34. Ibid.
35. Ibid. , pp. 192-193.
36. Ibid. , pp. 41-42.
37. Ibid. , p. 42.
38. Ibid.
39. Ibid. , p. 43.
40. Ibid. , p. 42.
41. Ibid. , p. 43.
42. Ibid.
43. Ibid.

44. Ibid., p. 45.
45. Colin Young, "Robert Frost: A Lover's Quarrel with the World," Film Quarterly 17 (Spring 1964), p. 45.
46. Ibid.
47. Ibid.
48. "Frost Bit," Newsweek 59 (January 29, 1962), p. 82.
49. Ibid.
50. New Republic (May 23, 1964), p. 26.
51. Ibid.
52. Judith Crist, The Private Eye, the Cowboy, and the Very Naked Girl. New York: Holt, 1968, pp. 71-72.
53. Dwight Macdonald, On Movies. Englewood Cliffs, N. J.: Prentice-Hall, 1969, p. 323.
54. Ibid.
55. Ibid., p. 324.
56. Ibid.
57. Ibid., p. 325.
58. Ibid.
59. Ibid., p. 326.
60. Variety 236 (November 11, 1964), p. 23.
61. Rosen, p. 110.
62. Karen Cooper, "Shirley Clarke," Filmmakers Newsletter 5:8 (June 1972), p. 35.
63. Rosen, p. 108.
64. John M. Smith and Tim Cawkwell, eds. World Encyclopedia on the Film. New York: Crowell, 1972, p. 47.
65. Crist, pp. 268-269.
66. Rosen, p. 108.
67. Ibid.
68. Tony Rayns, "Shirley Clarke," in Cinema: A Critical Dictionary, ed. by Richard Roud. New York: Viking Press, 1980, p. 221.
69. Rosen, p. 108.
70. Rice, p. 22.
71. Cooper, p. 35.
72. Ibid., p. 34.
73. Cooper, p. 34.
74. Ibid.
75. Ibid., p. 36.
76. Rosen, p. 110.
77. Ibid.
78. Ibid.
79. Rice, p. 21.
80. Ibid., p. 22.
81. Clarke's videotapes were included in a three-day show "Tokyo-New York Video Express," starting January 7, 1974. The name of the show is the title of the article about it by Kyoko Michishita in Women and Film, vol. 1 (5-6), 1974, pp. 86-87. No specific comments on Clarke's contributions appear in the article.
82. Rayns, p. 221.

11. AGNES VARDA: FROM AN UNDERGROUND RIVER

Born: May 30, 1928 Ixelles, Belgium

"It is the image (of women) that is important, not so much who is making the film. "[1]

" 'Watch out. I do not authorize you to use me against other women. . . . ' "[2]

Dubbed "Mother of the New Wave" (nouvelle vague) of French filmmaking, Agnes Varda has piqued the curiosity and admiration of film devotees and students of cinema since her first film, La Pointe Courte, was viewed in 1955. Film critics regard her with respect even as they are puzzled or pleased with the themes and techniques of her startlingly individualistic feature and documentary films.

Georges Sadoul, in his Dictionary of Film Makers (Berkeley: University of California Press, 1972), on page 261, characterizes Varda as "one of the most important filmmakers of the nouvelle vague, with a sharp, highly personal vision of both people and life. . . . " Varda is commended for her film works by P. Graham in his article "The face of '63-- France, " in Films and Filming 9 (May 1963), page 13: "At 34 undoubtedly the greatest woman director in the world. She has been photographer, painter, and sculptress, worked with the TNP (Jean Vilar's Theatre National Populaire) and been a journalist. All her films ... are idiosyncratic and experimental, with moments of startling beauty. . . . "

Charles Ford in Femmes cinéastes (Paris: Editions Denoël-Gonthiers, 1972, page 110), considers Varda a strong personality who has done distinctive and original cinematographic work.

Varda, as "Mother of the New Wave, " has generated 19 films in 23 years. In contrast to her persistent and productive career path, her entry into movie-making was cat's-paw casual. Current Biography 1970 quotes Varda on this facile first step. She admits she'd never even seen what a film studio looked like. When she wrote a scenario, a friend who had directed short films decided to film her scenario. Varda formed a co-operative society to make La Pointe Courte, contributing money of her own, borrowing what she needed, to complete the filming near Sète, where she had spent her childhood years. [3]

The diminutive director is described in Current Biography 1970, page 426, as five feet three inches tall, about 100 pounds weight, being "small, dark, intelligent, charged with energy...."

Born in a Brussells suburb, Varda was one of five children born to an engineer father of Greek descent and a French mother who was a native of Sète, a Mediterranean seaport, whose neighboring village La Pointe Courte became the locale of Varda's first film. After completing classes at the Sorbonne, Varda studied art for four years at the Ecole du Louvre. Her aspirations then inclined toward museum curatorship. Then she attended evening classes at the Vaugirard School of Photography and was awarded a diploma. When Jean Vilar, a former resident of Sète, founded the Theatre National Populaire in 1951 he appointed Varda his official photographer. She occupied that position until 1961. During her decade's tenure, Varda accepted assignments as photographer for several Parisian periodicals, and completed four films. Working for the TNP increased Varda's interest in theatre, as she tells it, "although at that time I didn't have any enthusiasm for movies. When I made my first film ... in 1954, I knew nothing about the rules."[4]

Yet, Varda's statement that a filmmaker must exercise as much freedom as a novelist became Rule Number One for all New Wave directors.

> "They still call me the grandmother of the nouvelle vague." She gives a kind of squirm as she recollects the familiar description, which sprang from the fact that Alain Resnais was her film editor for La Pointe Courte (by which time he had made a couple of shorts himself) and that the initial Varda essay in cinema has been regarded as a precursor of the first Resnais movie of feature length, Hiroshima, mon amour....[5]

Georges Sadoul confirms the accuracy of this film fact in his Dictionary of Films (Berkeley: University of California Press, 1972, page 288), in his comments on La Pointe Courte:

> This is certainly the first film of the French nouvelle vague.... Its interplay between conscience, emotions, and the real world make a direct antecedent of Hiroshima, mon amour.... In its concern for the ambiguous relationship between the apparent world of things and the interior world of feelings and thoughts La Pointe Courte reflected a theme that was to occupy many of the new French film makers of the Sixties.

In the film, Varda juxtaposed the personal problems of a married couple with the economic conflicts in the lives of the village fishermen. She planned a novel, not a film. When she showed line drawings as a story outline to an acquaintance who was an assistant film director, he suggested that her concept was ideally suited to filming. Varda's novel became a movie script. In the story, a man, Noiret, and his wife, Montfort, visit the village where he was born, La Pointe Courte. Staying there, they observe the rustic routines, the patterns of birth, marriage, death. Living this simple style of life draws the couple closer than ever before.

Richard Roud likens Varda to her peers, Chris Marker and Alain Resnais, tagging them "Three New Wave French Filmmakers" and indexing their shared characteristics. 6 The three are about the same age. They live on the Seine's Left Bank. Their films take place outside of Paris, with few exceptions. And all three made films long before the New Wave gathered momentum. All have made documentaries. They display a wider cultural background and broader artistic interests than the Right Bank clan (Godard and Truffaut, as examples). Roud believes that these Left Bank filmmakers have inherited the concerns of the thirties rooted in economic and societal problems and the desire to deal with these issues in the realm of artistic endeavor. But, as Roud further defines this trait, the threesome do not espouse the use of art to sermonize or to instruct. Contrary to the credos of Godard and Truffaut, Varda and her peers operate on the conviction that the emotions and conflicts of the individual must be placed and viewed in the context of society. This dilemma, Roud asserts, of filming the subjectivity of the individual as related to the objectivity of the environment had occupied Alain Resnais for some time. Varda solved this predicament in La Pointe Courte.

> What he sought ... was a form which would be able to express both social problems and emotional ones.... The solution to his problem was found by Agnes Varda; and, typically enough, she found her example in literature. Faulkner's The Wild Palms is a book made up of two short stories.... The stories are each split into five parts, and printed in alternate chapters. The effect Faulkner obviously aimed at was a kind of contrast or counterpoint; but it was the success of this form that gave Agnes Varda the hope that she might accomplish something along similar lines ... she filmed the struggle of a small fishing village ... against the economic domination of the big combines, side by side with the story of a young man from the village who has come home with his Parisian wife in a last attempt to sort out the failure of their marriage. The two stories are told side by side, but the two themes are never intermingled. It was up to the spectator to make the connections between these themes ... the idea worked--so well that when ... Varda asked Resnais to help her edit the film he was very reluctant to do so, precisely because she had succeeded in doing something he had been aiming at for a long time. He eventually gave in, and it is no exaggeration to see in La Pointe Courte the not very distant ancestor of Hiroshima, mon amour. 7

In fact, Varda is credited with inspiring Alain Resnais' Hiroshima, mon amour by Lisbeth Lindeborg in her article "Fostering Feminist Films, " in Atlas World Press Review 23 (April 1976), page 50.

Charles Ford expresses his viewpoint on La Pointe Courte
in Femmes cinéastes (page 110):

> The film employed professionals and some inhabitants of
> the town in a creation both personal and anti-conformist.
> The double thread of action in the film is new. In making
> the natives of the region take part, Varda used a method
> dear to Jean Epstein and other excellent filmmakers, such
> as Luchino Visconti in La terre tremble. ... The slow ac-
> tion, the imperfect rhythm, the refinement of the psycho-
> logical discussions excited the critics. Varda has a pene-
> trating feel for point-of-view, announcing a talented film-
> maker. ... Breaking certain conventions, La Pointe Courte
> holds up well in spite of the inexperience in its realization
> and its extremely modest budget. "8

Roud and Ford do not mention the stunning use of symbolism,
which, more than Resnais' editing and Varda's counterpointing the
narrative, propels La Pointe Courte into a class by itself. Gordon
Gow, in "The Underground River, " in Films and Filming 16 (March
1970), page 7, explains: "Miss Varda relied on symbolism to establish the relationship between her characters and objects: wood
symbolized the hero, and iron, the heroine. " When the married
couple are far apart, physically or emotionally, then wood and iron
objects take their place in the camera's eye. When they are, in
person or in feelings, close, they are on camera and the objects
have disappeared.

Varda explains her use of this personification of objects.

> "The girl ... is associated in my mind with steel. Be-
> cause she's from the city, you know, and that makes one
> think of trains and the railroad. And the man is asso-
> ciated with wood, because his father was a ship's carpen-
> ter. ... The reason I think like this is because of a pro-
> fessor of philosophy who had a very great influence on me
> when I was studying at the Sorbonne ... he had this dream
> of the material in people: a psychoanalysis of the material
> world related to people, wood, rivers, the sea. ... He
> taught us to study writers not by the stories they told but
> by the material things they mentioned. "

She claims an inherited appetite for the sea.   "'Because my father
was Greek. And I really need the sea. I need the smell of it. ' "9

Varda waited seven years until she found a financier to underwrite the costs of a feature film. While waiting, she made three
documentaries: O Saisons, ô Châteaux (1957), Du côté de la côte
(1958), and L'Opéra Mouffe (1958).

L'Opéra Mouffe, 19 minutes long, is the best of the three,
having won the International Federation of Film Clubs Prize in 1958
at Brussells. Made while Varda was pregnant, it demonstrates on

a small scale the singularly rich fusion of emotional experience and
exterior environment in which Varda films excel. In Women in Focus
(Dayton, Ohio: Pflaum, 1974, pages 90 and 91), Jeanne Betancourt
describes the "filmic metaphors and violent symbols" in the film, as
meshed with "documentary footage of the poor section of Paris. "
This was the Mouffetard district as seen by Varda, a pregnant woman. Each portion of the film is prefaced by a hand-written inter-
title announcing its balanced equation of metaphor with reality.

It opens with the back view of a woman. She turns to disclose a very pregnant body outline. A close-up of a full pumpkin
follows. It is then cut and scooped out, becomes market produce,
with people in the market talking and gesturing. "The Lovers" consists of nude lovemaking culminating in metaphors for sex: a branched
tree, a half cabbage that revolves, and a sliced lemon. Cinematic
ciphers for pregnancy appear next: the revolving cabbage begins a
sprout, a hen forms in a glass bubble, and a girl runs in slow motion.

Children wearing masks expressing the ugly and the absurd
dominate the "Holidays" segment. In "Drunkenness" a pregnant
woman's fears evolve: sleeping bums lead to a hammer breaking
light bulbs which shifts to a small chick in a glass, struggling, then
dying. In "Desires" which considers the cravings of pregnancy, various cuts of meat in a butcher shop are seen. Then a pregnant woman leaves a flower shop, eating two flowers in her hand.

For Susan Rice in "Some Women's Films, " in Take One 34
(Nov.-Dec. 1970), on page 31, L'Opéra Mouffe bears the impress
of Varda's still photography training. Rice finds a semblance of
the out-of-this-world qualities of Dali-Buñuel experimental works in
L'Opéra Mouffe. Provocatively, Rice comments that it "may be a
classic in an unexpected sense--were a 'woman's film movement' to
develop, it is a film that could only have been made by a woman in
that it is refreshingly chauvinistic and meaningful to other women...."

In an erudite and enlightening triptych comparison, Parker
Tyler in Film Quarterly 12 (Spring 1959, pp. 50-53, appraises the
values of L'Opéra Mouffe as experimental film while considering
Stan Brakhage's Loving and Dom by Walerian Borowczyk and Jan
Lenica. Dom had won the Grand Prix (around $10,000) at the Ex-
perimental Film Festival in Brussels in 1958. The Brakhage and
Varda films won runner-up awards. Tyler points out that Varda's
film did not use film clips as did the other two. "All black and
white, L'Opéra Mouffe probably photographed its sequences from
scratch, but they could have been film clips so far as their material
and approach go.... " Tyler explicates the pun in the film's title:
"a pun on 'L'Opéra Bouffe' and a poor Paris neighborhood nicknamed
La Mouffe, and dissects its documentary qualities as 'sensitive' ...
and, as such, 'experimental' to the extent that it introduces imaginative moods.... " He asks, "But is the method of showing these
things imaginative enough?" For him it is uneven, pretentious, arty,
banal. Sometimes the film drifts "by adding one image statistically,

rather than meaningfully, to another ... the montage-idea becomes
very diluted.   Image added to image without development or impetus
is not true montage but picture-magazine journalism. " He classifies
it.   "Technically, L'Opéra Mouffe is a 'suite, ' a series of facets,
but these facets possess no unifying principle either intellectual or
sensuous. " Yet this progression of phases,

> however interesting and well-photographed in the conven-
> tional sense, the "anthology" attitude that life is an end-
> less network of strange contradictions can never get in
> terms of meaning, beyond the stage of clever reporting;
> it can never reach the stage of meaning that is art as an
> efficient form; it falls apart into the scattered materials
> of potential art. ... L'Opéra Mouffe, with its air of a
> jaunty cafe ballad, is deceptively "chic" and highly irre-
> sponsible in every way.   The best reason for talking about
> it is that it represents a decided trend in ways of con-
> temporary thinking, insofar as these ways have a signifi-
> cant moral meaning.

In approaching conclusive comment, Tyler calls the film not art,
but a "stunt, " a documentary treatment of a moral psychology, and
"experimental" only in terms of montage imagery.   It "is only a reporter's visual notebook ... it is inadequately processed studio material, playing a charade as an experimental film. ... " L'Opéra
Mouffe was a stylistic exercise, similar to the two travelogue-type
films she made at this time.   O Saisons, ô Châteaux viewed the
chateaus of Loire with vivacious concern.   Gardeners on chateau
grounds dance in balletic style.   Du Côté de la Côte looked at the
French Riviera contrasting the Eden-like aspects of wealthy estates
there with the shops and streets frequented by tourists.

Using the binary skeins of the psychic and physical self employed in La Pointe Courte (with symbolism) and in L'Opéra Mouffe
(with moral psychology) as a pilot pattern, Varda created her second
feature film, Cleo from 5 to 7, not to be confused with Eric Rohm-
er's film, Cleo in the Afternoon.

As fate would have it, Georges de Beauregard who had
financed Godard's Breathless (1960) was searching for other unknown
French directors to underwrite.   Godard suggested Jacques Demy,
who suggested Varda (his future wife).   Beauregard decided to back
Cleo, about a pop singer who suspects that she has cancer.   The
film tracks two hours in her life as she waits confirmation of the
diagnosis.

Current Biography 1970 (page 425) records Varda's intentions
for Cleo.   She wanted to integrate the concept of death with Cleo's
fear of it at the same time that she is freeing herself of it.   Cleo's
two-hour restless walking and waiting takes her from the Rue de
Rivoli to the Salpêtrière Hospital, from self-conceited ignorance to
incipient understanding of private self and public image.

The co-ordinates of time and space dominate both the viewer's and Cleo's consciousness with increasing emphasis, from 5 p. m. (start of film) to 6:40 p. m. --100 minutes later. As Betancourt clarifies:

> The viewer is forced to wait, as Cleo must, the exact eighty-six minutes that the film recounts. The film is broken up into chapters that announce each segment of time as Cleo will spend it. We are told every minute that has passed of her waiting and of our watching--for example, "Cleo from 5:13 to 5:18. " This exact rendering of real time in film intensifies the suspense. 10

This time structure as Varda wrote it is unique. Allan Casebier explains physical time in Film Appreciation (New York: Harcourt Brace Jovanovich, 1976, page 53):

> When a film attempts to show all phases of events, another time order is introduced, namely physical time. Very few films are structured entirely according to physical time. Cleo from 5 to 7 ... is a notable example of one that is.... Physical time then, refers to a filmic structuring of events at the same rate at which they would occur in the world outside the movies.

Cleo's outlook upon Paris as she wanders through a cafe, strolls in a park, visits a friend, and her views of herself in the myriads of mirrors and shop windows in the city collide: her self-image of a lush, blond, shallow and spoiled singer shatters and the shards evidence an abrupt, painful maturation. The metaphor is clear, Betancourt asserts: "To see herself in the face of death, to see herself in any perspective other than that of a beautiful woman ... is to destroy her image of herself. Cleo says: When I think, which is seldom, I only have questions. Today everything is new, faces of others and mine. "11

To the subjective frame of physical time and the populace and geography of Paris as objective environment, Varda adds the element of the unknown--destiny--in the form of Tarot cards. "The huge, grotesquely ornate cards come down, one by one, against her; she is advised to change her lover and be prepared to face trouble. " As Roger Manvell depicts the opening scene of the film while the credits are running (Films and Filming, Dec. 1962, p. 38) Cleo's fortunes are played beyond and within herself: "everything that happens to her now is a heightened ... experience.... Everything is momento mori. Finally, she takes a cab to the Pargue de Mont-souris, and here by chance she finds what she needs, a stranger with ... humanity to understand her and help her find her bearings. " The young soldier on leave from Algeria helps her face the doctor's deadpan verdict on her future. Manvell finds fault only with "the repetition involved in Cleo walking short distances ... and taking taxi and bus rides which tend to seem interminable because they literally mark time in the story and reveal nothing new. " Manvell

finds "moments of cruelty and macabre shock" too and wonders
about the "insistent, recurrent images of the street entertainer
swallowing live frogs. " A vividly ugly symbol of a growing green
cancer inside the body, perhaps.   Nonetheless, the film "represents
a considerable achievement for Agnes Varda. "

Several reviews of Cleo are capsuled in Filmfacts 1962, p.
233.   Saturday Review (Aug. 4, 1962) critic Hollis Alpert found
that

> Miss Varda's method is not satisfactory, mainly because
> here it provides a diluted rather than an intensified experi-
> ence.... It may be that this talented young director's pur-
> suit of originality, her attempt to convey a more luminous
> reality, has led her to neglect her story ... it ... means
> that she hasn't brought off what she has tried in this first
> large film attempt.

The New York Herald Tribune (Sept. 5, 1962) didn't care for Varda's
"downright Swiss preoccupation with the time of day, which she
keeps flashing on the screen every few moments ... [but] a film
worth seeing.... " Time (Sept. 14, 1962) found Cleo "a spuriously
brilliant attempt to contemporize the legend of Death and the maiden
.... The cinematography is imaginative, if sometimes cute.... "
Variety (Dec. 20, 1961) reports: "This pic marks ... Varda as a
fine addition to French film ranks.   She is able to overcome the
banality of the situation by a knowing visual feel for revelation and
reflections of the girl's state via intelligent symbols.... "

Bosley Crowther in The New York Times (Sept. 5, 1962) issued a curiously flat diagnosis of Cleo:

> ... fairly glitters with photographic and cinematic "style, "
> yet fails to do more than skim the surface of a cryptic
> dramatic theme.... Varda is so absorbed with her cam-
> era stunts ... that the essential concentration on the
> heroine is neglected and the interest lost.   The character
> becomes incidental to the techniques by which it is being
> explained. ...

An excerpt from Cleo's script appears in Films and Filming
(Dec. 1962), on pages 22 and 23.   An unsigned preface reports that
Cleo, like L'Opéra Mouffe, is divided into chapters

> named after their predominant characters.   And sometimes
> a scene is seen as Angele sees it, another as Bob sees
> it....   The photography, the directorial style and even
> the tonal color of each chapter (although the film is black
> and white) are modulated so as to evoke each character's
> vision.   For example, Angele "sees" in fixed set-ups,
> straightforwardly, in clear and realistic images; Cleo
> "sees" in sinuous camera-movements, in images "woven"
> on pale, vague backgrounds.   The scenes were shot in nar-
> rative order, in real locations and in the streets of Paris.

This unsigned writer concludes: "The film is the meticulous and impassioned description of a personality."

The chapter notations and the divisiveness of time may have diluted the intensity and impact of Cleo as the immature pop singer developing a fresh vision of life when faced with death is portrayed clock-watching under the duress of waiting for a life-or-death decision. Yet, the techniques are psychologically honest and the unity of the film preserved.

Charles Ford, too, notes that Varda chose different styles of film shooting for each sequence and commends the choices while lamenting the excess verbosity, a fault typical of the cinéma vérité. However, Cleo evidences a pronounced taste for striking images, a remarkable facility with point-of-view lens-ability. He classifies Varda, while admitting that Cleo is an uneven work, as worthy of being estimated with men filmmakers. 12

Varda's Cleo echoes the films, especially Lola, of Jacques Demy, later her husband. Gordon Gow claims Demy's influence on Varda was established at the Tours Festival in 1958. 13 As indicators he lists the casting of Corinne Marchant as Cleo. She had appeared in Demy's Lola. Michel Legrand composed the musical scores for Lola and Cleo.

More probing criticism confronts the theme of the film. Vernon Young and Richard Roud assign an environmental footing to Cleo's import. Young's comment in On Film (p. 260) takes this view: "Some critics heavily deprecated Miss Varda's effort in the mistaken belief that she believed she was creating a tragedy, whereas, obviously, I should think, Cleo used mock tragedy as a subterfuge for a loving excursion into milieu." Roud underlines this opinion.

> Agnes Varda has beautifully succeeded in striking a balance between the frivolity of Cleo's little group and the outside world--the streets of Paris, its shops and parks.... The most important problem in making such a film was to render the visible world in all its beauty, thus increasing the poignancy of the idea of death, without falling into the trap of aestheticism. Largely shot in the street like a documentary, Cleo shines with some fantastically beautiful images.... Varda has made a sensational debut, and ... we may expect even greater things from her. 14

Opposed to the lilt of these laudatory grace-notes is the air of lampoonery with which Stanley Kauffmann in A World on Film (pp. 252-254), suffuses his disparagement of the film:

> How Do You Know You Can't Be a New-Wave Director?
> Have you tried? Follow these simple steps.... 1. Get
> a good cameraman.... 2. Get a story.... Your story
> need not be gripping or valid. 3. Cast the female lead

with a photogenic girl.... 4. Lay it on. "It" is the
New Wave repertoire of stunts, camera techniques, and
cutting.... Use freakish faces for minor characters....
Use a little nudeness.... Include long walks ... to show
that you are as free of plot contrivances as Antonioni....
Do not omit Resnais backward jumps.... Oh, yes. Your
female lead has to sing, in Judy Garland style, a sorrowful song to release your tears.

All these rules are important, Kauffmann insists, because
Agnes Varda, a New Wave director (one of just a handful of women
film directors anywhere) has made a movie called Cleo from 5 to 7,
about a blond entertainer who's afraid she'll die of cancer, and
Varda has followed all these rules so that Cleo will tug at your
heartstrings. On top of these rules, Varda has thrown in fortune-
telling cards--the Tarot kind--in color to contrast with the black-
and-white reality she faces. Cleo is waiting for a laboratory test
decision and Varda keeps track of every minute she waits by running
it along the bottom of the screen.

The whole thing, Kauffmann emits in a final blast, is a pot-
pourri of what Varda figured was the best techniques from her col-
leagues--Resnais, Truffaut and some others--and she got "Cleo-
realism, " an over-sentimental, overtly imitative, soap-opera-like
soupy tale.

The subject of Cleo? For Roger Manvell it is vulnerability,
the absence of armor against truth, crystallized in the moment,
which both mention, in which Cleo abruptly removes her blond wig
to face herself in the mirror with straight blond hair. Manvell
tenders this sentence: "... When we discover her she is pathetic
and vulnerable, facing a particular test of character...." Gow puts
it this way: "... Perhaps its most telling effect is Cleo's abrupt
removal of her wig.... This comes as a surprise ... and the action lends the character a certain vulnerability as well as strengthening the impression that delusions are being abandoned in the face
of reality...."15

In a discussion of Varda's documentaries and feature films,
William D. Routt in "One Man's Truth ... Another Man's Poison, "
Film Quarterly (Sept. 1971), p. 27, suggests that Varda's best
films have been about love (L'Opéra Mouffe, Cleo de 5 à 7, Le
Bonheur, and the loveliest parts of Les Creatures). " Although
Routt does not amplify his premise, the film student can safely do
so once the films have been viewed: love of child, love of self,
love of married and sex partners, and love of artistic creativity.

Betancourt circumscribes the dual skeins of self-infatuation,
or love, and recognition of reality revealing vulnerability in her
commentary: "Music is used very ironically. In a Judy Garland
tradition Cleo sings a sad new song ... a full orchestra breaks out
of the piano, and histrionically she sings, 'Dead, alone and ugly without you.... All my love is dying. There is no love to replace it. "

Then, "Cleo accepts the news that her doctor will give her two months of radiation treatment and see what happens, a clear diagnosis that there is nothing he can do..." (Women in Focus, pp. 90-91).

Unwilling to repeat the Cleo formula and unable to find funds for the film concepts she hoped to realize, Varda visited Cuba and took 4,000 still photos. From these she constructed a relatively non-political work annotating Castro's revolution-in-progress. Considered a successful effort in Cuba and France, Salute to Cuba (1963) won the Bronze Lion Award at the 1964 Venice Film Festival.

Varda's third feature film, Le Bonheur (1965), evoked the form of controversial criticism from the professional film critical echelon that presages a celluloid life in perpetuity for the film. If Varda made just this one film, she would justifiably be recalled by critics and historians as its author-director. Is Happiness a fairy-tale, animal fable, pastoral tone poem, amoral satire, a feminist tract, a French story-of-a-marriage? Each critic differs.

For Judith Crist it was "... one of the most beautiful films that I think you ever will see"(Womanhood Media Supplement, page 158). For Sadoul, the starting-line for controversy was Varda's title. In his Dictionary of Films (page 39), he suggests that this story of an "artisan milieu in the Paris suburbs" could have been named "A Great Misfortune." With this title the film would have stirred up less debate.

The immorality of Varda's premise for Happiness causes the debate. This is Charles Ford's opinion in Femmes-cinéastes, on page 112. The premise is as follows: If one loves, one has the right to abolish an obstacle to a new love. "In retrospect, it is the ecstasy and honesty of motivation transposed into the beauty of the images which recalls the brilliant works of the Impressionists." Later, Ford observes, Varda herself said the same thing. "'Le Bonheur was my first film in color; it is essentially a pursuit of the palette.... I tried, with a subject which I kept very simple, to obtain impressionism; it represents for me ... a taste which is not for the beatniks ... but of natural impulses, of social situations which call forth personal instincts. Psychology takes first place" (page 113).

The unsigned, cheerfully bland article, not review, on the film in Letter from France 9 (May-June 1965), pp. 3-4, interests the reader in the film's director, who is "one of the world's most eminent women directors, [who] proved her exquisite sense of color and chronology in 'Cleo from 5 to 7.'" Le Bonheur has won the 1965 Prix Louis Delluc, and

> is a hymn to happiness.... Filmed in Eastmancolor on the pastoral Ile de France ... Varda creates a subtle blend of realism and reverie. Claude Drouot, as the carpenter François, lives in perfect harmony with his wife and children. These are played with unaffected simplicity

by Drouot's real wife, Claire, and their two children.
François is like a beautiful domestic animal, whose pleasures are immediate and whose appetite for affection is
insatiable.   He meets and falls in love with a pretty post
office clerk ... and then takes her as his mistress.   When
his wife is tragically drowned, he is crushed.   But he is
soon reclaimed by his innate relish of life.   In the concluding scene he takes his mistress in his arms, closing the
gap in the family circle.   With characteristic detachment,
Miss Varda allows the film to develop almost independently
of the director, fulfilling a natural and logical destiny within its own given terms.   The natural gift of happiness
with which François is endowed is not shared by his wife,
his mistress, nor necessarily the director, and its morality is self-contained.   "Happiness," said Agnes Varda,
"is like the delicious combination of melon with smoked
ham, or grapes with roquefort cheese--always slightly
paradoxical. "

A. H. Weiler asks between the lines of his review in The
New York Times (May 24, 1966, 55:2): Is she kidding? The thrust
of the director's brushmarks upon the cinematic canvas may be more
irony than idyll.

> ... a seeming idyll sheathed in irony....   One must as-
> sume that ... Varda is not kidding in spinning her amoral
> tale.   But there is little in it to offset the gaps in logic
> or the absurdity of some of the situations.   But as a
> pioneer New Waver, she has cut her film as a slow-moving
> pastoral that also quickly switches from boudoir to boudoir
> to beautiful bucolic vignettes with artistic and technical
> grace ... mood and dialogue are secondary....   What is
> important is that Miss Varda, perhaps with tongue-in-
> cheek, has fashioned a simple fable for our time.
> [Weiler's overall impression is of] a memorable and ex-
> asperating view of male and female animals ... that makes
> it at once joyful and moving but crucially immature, dis-
> turbing and tragic....

The title of the Newsweek (June 13, 1966, p. 114) review,
"Plants and Animals, " is keyed to a pivotal statement made by the
carpenter to his mistress: "My wife, says the hero ... is wonderful in her way and you are wonderful in yours; she is a vibrant
plant while you are an uncaged animal...." To his wife, earlier in
the film, the hero has stated what most critics have elected as the
germinating seed from which the film developed: "Happiness may
be submitting to nature. "

> At first, Miss Varda seems to be trading in nothing but
> treacle.   Her hero ... spends a perfect Father's Day with
> his radiant wife and adorable children in the sunflowered
> sunshine of the French countryside.   The scene, which
> might have been lifted bodily from "Picnic in the Grass"

is a candid tribute to Renoir--both painter ... and movie-maker.

But then the carpenter sets up a new arrangement in which he "con-tinues to be candid with his mistress and loving to his wife." When his wife learns of his mistress at the picnic she accepts the knowl-edge with equanimity; later, though, she is found drowned in a pond. The widower mourns her but manages to establish a new household with his ex-mistress whom he has married.

Newsweek's diagnosis of this supplanting one wife with an-other in a picnic setting is this: "It is the case history ... of a seeming psychopath who claims ... to be in love with two women, when his emotional responses are so shallow that he cannot love even one. "

When told of this diagnosis by Newsweek's Joseph Morgen-stern, Varda said (in this same article):

"I'm astonished that this interpretation of the film should be possible.... I think he's completely capable of love in the fullest sense. For me the story is the coming of responsibility to a young spirit ... who has then to invent a personal morality.... He's normal.... Not adult but normal.... It's like Mozart, where there's always joy but also death.... Having said all this, I don't like the film too much. " When asked about the dearth of women film directors, Varda replied: "Prejudice, I suppose ... not men's, it's women's. Women think it's not feminine to be strong. How silly that is! A strong woman needs pro-tection just as much as a strong man does. "

Horticultural tropes and rustic overtones abound in Varda's pastorally pretty picture for John Simon (Private Screenings, pp. 228-232). Describing the film as "a Playboy joke ... rewritten as an erotico-sentimental novel, " Simon dubs and drubs the hero's ex-planation of his postmistress-passion to his wife:

"You, me, the children, we're like an apple orchard in-side a fence. Then I see an apple tree outside the fence, and it's in bloom too. There are more apple blossoms, more apples to add to ours ... do you see?"... By way of winning over his mildly jolted wife ... "It's as if I had ten arms with which to enfold you, and you too had ten arms for me.... You don't find that I love you less?" ... proceeds to make mad love to his stunned but obliging ... wife. While he sleeps ... she drowns herself in a near-by pond....

While granting the visual beauty of the film, Simon found it silly, and the musical (Mozart, no less) score annoying. The fruity image uttered by the hero quoted above is nonsensical. "Just as Mme. Varda's husband's movie The Umbrellas of Cherbourg was one

of the silliest films ever made, so Le Bonheur strikes me as the
most amoral and one of the silliest. " Yes, the film has style,
"most of it Godard's, every one of whose devices is present; the
rest of it Resnais', Truffaut's, and Antonioni's. "

The one exciting element in the sex scenes was that "it
usually takes a while before one can tell whether François is in bed
with wife or mistress (get the point?); otherwise, they are either so
static, or so artfully contrived ... as to deny us any illusion of
spontaneity or intensity. "

Simon signals one segment of the film's action for excellence.

> ... when François, with the two children, is looking for
> Therese in the woods, and stopping periodically to ask
> people whether they have seen her, the pacing of the action
> through both subject and camera movement ... is anguish-
> ingly and expertly accelerated toward the dreadful dis-
> covery.   But then Varda has to spoil it all by crosscutting
> from François holding the dead Therese to one frame
> flashbacks (à la Resnais) of her drowning--sheer gimmickry.

The basic blame for the film's lack of conviction lies in its characters: "... they are trifle too elaborate to be animals, and quite a
bit too simple to be human beings. "

Critic Elizabeth Sussex clobbered the film in her negative review in Sight and Sound (Autumn 1965), pp. 200-201: "fragmentation
is simply a method of varying the presentation of a series of pretty
pictures. It is style for style's sake: a symptom of all that is
wrong with Varda's picture. " Only the scenes between carpenter
and mistress hold conviction; the music is wrong, Mozart being incongruous with simple people's picnics in the woods--Legrand would
be fine--the film is slobberingly sweet, "Jacques Demy's kind of
sweetness, and the colour is almost as good as that of Les Para-
pluies de Cherbourg...." (Moral: Women film directors must risk
comparison of their films not only with rival directors but with
their husbands' movies!) "the worst aspect ... the feeling that it is
a kind of intellectual slumming...."

Le Bonheur's photographic proficiencies are analyzed in true
textbook fashion by Lincoln F. Johnson in Film: Space, Time, Light,
and Sound (New York: Holt, Rinehart and Winston, 1974) in three
categories: tonal contrasts, evocation, and a parallelism of action,
idea, and tone. Although no value judgments as such are made by
Johnson, his delineation of Varda's techniques affords a clinical dissection of a few scenes which may enhance the film student's appreciation of her accomplishment.

> Using a sequence shot rather than cuts ... Varda ... cre-
> ates a rhythm of tonal contrasts through camera movement
> ....   Observing a dance, she stations the camera behind
> a tree trunk, then pans from the bright, variegated hues

of the dancers on one side of the tree across the relatively
neutral and uniform tonalities of the tree trunk to the
dancers on the other side, crossing again and again, the
back and forth movement catching something of the rhythm
of the dance. Varda also uses tonal contrast to separate
one sequence from another ... (p. 138).

Varda's use of color to achieve what Johnson calls "internal
evocation" is exampled by "the closing sequence of Le Bonheur, in
which a young man, after the death of his wife, takes his children
and his mistress on a picnic. The mistress, who has been wearing
cold, bright blue tones through the film, now wears the warm tones
that have been associated with the wife, evoking her memory, suggesting the mistress' assumption of the wife's role ... " (p. 148).

In Johnson's detailed analysis of the major love scene between the carpenter and his mistress, which Johnson finds similar
to like scenes in Breathless and Ecstasy, he points out its departures from these two films in "spatial organization (which transforms anatomy into abstract forms), in action ... and in tone. "
Johnson explains Varda's use of tone in the love scene: "developed
largely through near static close-ups cut in an almost metrical manner. The tone is relatively high in key, with very low intensity
flesh tones arranged against white sheets to create a general sense
of coolness ... the palpable intimacy of their involvement is countered by detachment, abstraction, and coolness" (p. 151).

Johnson's most particulate scrutiny is applied to the aftermath of the love scene:

> the camera retreats to reveal a bowl of withering flowers
> that are dull in tone. There are significant ironies in
> these tones, not only as they affect the content of the se-
> quence itself, but also as they compare with other scenes
> in the film. For their pallor is in sharp contrast to the
> warmth that suffuses the screen when the wife is present
> ..., and to the tones that describe flowers and other ob-
> jects in her house, which are so bright and intense in
> tonality they sometimes seem to contain more energy than
> people ... " [(page 151)].

Yet another textbook commends the film for its painterly,
picturesque settings and its use of a narrative akin to the le nouveau
roman literary movement led by novelists Nathalie Sarraute and
Alain Robbe-Grillet. In this sense, Le Bonheur may be a cinematic
double-header because it exemplifies the New Wave of cinema and
the New Novel in literature, the latter keyed to "emphasis on expression rather than content and a rejection by an author of any
overt psychological, moralistic, or metaphysical comments on what
happens to characters that become as much "things" as the objects
that surround them. Le Bonheur can be considered as a cinematic
rendering of a 'new novel.' "16 But,

> It is the director's exciting use of the camera and color that makes us want to see it repeatedly and to study it ... from this perspective we believe that it has few rivals in the last two decades. There are three main settings in the work, and each is presented with consummate skill. In the scenes in the country, Varda focuses on the beauties of nature.... And we feel during such shots some of the sheer aesthetic pleasure evoked by looking at a still life by Monet, Pissaro, Sisley, or Renoir.... The colors in François's and Therese's home are drab ... with some objects that are vulgarly bright ... Emilie's apartment is modern in style and decorated in cool colors, particularly shades of white. There is an aseptic quality to the rooms that makes an effective contrast to the passionate love-making that occurs there ... when the film is recalled ... its lyric loveliness is what lingers most in memory 17

The passionate love-scenes concerned Variety's reviewer, (March 3, 1965) as cause for censorship in American theatres. "Film does not stump for polygamy but tries to show a case where love blossoms for two people.... Its stunningly filmed love scenes and nudity are always in proper perspective and never leering. All this may encounter censor troubles.... "

The Time (May 27, 1966) review specified an untenable basic premise as a structural weakness in an otherwise exquisitely fashioned work.

> The film's conceptual flaw is in the character of the carpenter, a prefabrication rather obviously nailed on to a thesis. [But Varda] merely accepts his behavior as an inexorable fact of life and dramatizes it bewitchingly in enforced New Cinema style, using abrupt cuts and soft focus to suggest the spontaneous electricity generated by lovers repeating one action several times to underscore the emotional impact of a scene....

Hollis Alpert's suspicious speculation on the film in Saturday Review (May 28, 1966) echoes that of Elizabeth Sussex's in Sight and Sound, as regards Varda's intellectual integrity.

> I feel it my duty to be just as suspicious of intellectual hokum as I am of the commercial variety.... Varda has made her people into puppets who obey neither their instincts nor their conscience, but instead the arbitrary intellectualized concepts of a film director ... substituting one kind of unreality for another, doesn't add up to either art or truth....

The forms of dance, painting, music are invoked by Max Kozloff in Film Quarterly (Winter 1966/67), pp. 35-36, who terms Le Bonheur a pastoral, "Imbued with a simple gravity, nymph and

shepherd ... [which] magically evokes an ancient pantheism ... alien
to tragedy.... Unlike The Umbrellas of Cherbourg by her husband
Jacques Demy, Varda's Le Bonheur does not announce itself as anything so hyper-stylized as operetta." Varda circumscribes the
"earthly cycle" in coming full circle from one wife to the second,
from the picnic in spring to one in autumn: "To obey that cycle
which appears here almost in sonata form...." For Kozloff, the
Saturday night dance "enacts the psychological ritual of the pastoral."
He lauds the "color lyricism" of the film:

> Every interchange between foreground and background in-
> stigates some small chromatic alteration, and it is pre-
> cisely this kind of short, mercurial shift that most links
> the film with Impressionist painting ... the many floral
> bouquets that flounce through countless shots are a kind
> of leitmotiv of the whole picture.... For this chromatic
> pavanne, we are indebted to a cameraman with the too-
> much name of Claude Beausoleil.

The latter, no doubt, is responsible for the memorable qualities of the wife-drowning scene mentioned by a majority of the critics. "Crouched over the drowned body of his wife, the husband ...
'sees' her white arm going underwater ... this device is not a
flashback so much as it is a fantasy inset, related to the differ-
entiated consciousness pioneered more radically by Resnais in Marienbad and Muriel...." Kozloff closes his commentary by a probe
of the so-called theme uttered from a television screen "Happiness
may be submitting to the order of nature." "For if these characters
... find happiness, it is largely in the context of a fairy tale...."

Another critique in the art-form groove is Gordon Gow's in
Films and Filming, (Sept. 1965), pp. 30-31, which asserts that Varda
wrote the script in three days, an "antithesis of the conventional
scripted film." Subsequent to a plot summary, he analogizes: "A
minor tone-poem then, about human nature ... a brave try at making
something fruitful of a wholly cinematic language.... It is the kind
of thing that would be accepted ... as a ballet." In a film which
makes subtle tributes to French artists, past and present, Gow labels the repeat action of the husband's holding his drowned wife's
body as a tribute to Resnais' Marienbad as affirmed by Kozloff:

> ... we see him lift her again and again and again, with
> two cuts back to mental images of her drowning, ... a di-
> rect homage to the passage in Marienbad where Delphine
> Seyrig reclined on a bed many times over ... more than
> anything else in the film it combines image with meaning,
> to a degree that revitalizes attention for what is to fol-
> low.... Despite shortcomings, ... an essential film for
> anyone who believes that the cinema can speak a language
> of its own....

The film student can ponder without reply the meaning of the
oft-mentioned scene of husband with drowned wife when trying to

equate John Simon's "gimmickry" with Kozloff's "fantasy inset" with Gow's "homage ... to Marienbad" and so on.   Again, the film student wonders if film critics influence one another unknowingly as filmmakers borrow, influence, etc. each other when confronted with an article such as Frederick Wellington's "Three Films from Paris, " in Film Comment 3 (Summer, 1965), pp. 30-33, in which he aligns the kinships of Le Bonheur with Truffaut's La Peau Douce and Godard's Une Femme Mariée.   Wellington believes the story-lines and themes are similar, but the development and style in each quite divergent.   Each film explores adultery, uses nudity and phys-ical love for dramatic exposition; none of the three "are moral in any conventional sense" and the characters are "victims, not exe-cutioners. "   Each filmmaker owes a debt to the others, because there is "a certain community of artistic concern. "   The films share a vantage point neither nihilistic nor sentimental; in effect, they form a trilogy and could be shown to audiences as such.

Claire Johnston finds fault-lines in the feminist posture of Varda's films, singling out Le Bonheur for chastisement in her article, "Women's Cinema as Counter-Cinema, " in Bill Nichols' Movies and Methods: an Anthology (Berkeley: University of Cali-fornia Press, 1976, p. 214).   Affirming that the European art film is "more open to the invasion of myth than the Hollywood film," Johnston sees

> The films of Agnes Varda ... a particularly good example of an oeuvre which celebrates bourgeois myths of women ....   Le Bonheur ... almost invites a Barthesian analysis! Varda's portrayal of female fantasy constitutes one of the nearest approximations to the facile day-dreams perpetua-ated by advertising that probably exists in the cinema. Her films appear totally innocent to the workings of myth; indeed, it is the purpose of myth to fabricate an impres-sion of innocence, in which all becomes "natural":   Varda's concern for nature is a direct expression of this retreat from history: history is transmuted into nature, involving the elimination of all questions, because all appears "natu-ral. "   There is no doubt that Varda's work is reactionary: in her rejection of culture and her placement of woman outside history her films mark a retrograde step in wom-en's cinema.

For the sake of fairness, Varda herself should be given equal space here to reply to this conclusion.   Here is Varda speaking in her interview with Barbara Confino, previously mentioned.

> When I started making movies I wasn't really thinking of that specific problem (the image of woman in films) ... it took me five to ten years before I started to raise my own consciousness.   Even feeling strong and complete, and liberated as I did, I was wrong because I had been buying a lot of the ordinary clichés.   It is only in the last three years or so that I have felt the desire to do very different films. ...

As yet another experiment in form, Elsa (1966) "is positively
reeking with the kinds of technical effects that originally made the
New Wave such a controversial happening.   There is a lot of jump-
cutting, a lot of repeated action, a lot of talking directly to the
camera, a lot of jiggling hand-held shots. "[18]   But Varda's technique
never occludes her subjects: here they are Elsa Triolet (1896-1970)
and her husband, novelist Louis Aragon.   As a "film portrait" Varda's documentary relates the most significant events in the lives of
this man and his wife, who herself was a novelist of substantial
reputation, born in Russia and sister-in-law of Mayakovsky.   But
Elsa is not about someone or something; it is not a tribute to the
novelist.   Varda's subject is love, her form is the cinematic essai,
and her techniques approximate the use of a camera as an author
uses a pen.   Her goal is to help the viewer see Elsa and Louis as
she, as filmmaker, does.   "Varda's technical subjectivity ... gives
a receptive viewer the opportunity to see an emotion in toto; in this
case as historic and literary fact (both Aragon and Elsa wrote poems
about their love) and as something personal, undefinable, alive and
ultimately mysterious.... " So, if an emotion can be captured on
camera, Varda has assuredly used an impressive battery of technical devices to render it live in its two real-life hosts.

Financing her films, happily, was no longer a frustration for
Varda after Le Bonheur's success at the box office and its top prize
at the Cannes Film Festival.   Les Creatures (1966) was written by
Varda before Le Bonheur.   Unlike the latter, The Creatures (its
American title) was not well received by critics.   Current Biography
1970 (page 426) describes it as a thriller and fantasy.   Its musical
score was orchestrated by a computer.   Its setting was an island,
Noirmoutier, situated in the Bay of Biscay.

An unusually detailed review in Variety 244 (Sept. 7, 1966),
page 18, reveals the rich mix of ingredients in what American audiences believed was a science fiction picture: black and white with
red colors, an inside/outside plot development, the mingling of real
and unreal events, and a mechanistic versus a deistic force struggling
for control.   Variety found it "somewhat overwrought and a bit pretentious and literary with patches of tedium.... "   As in La Pointe
Courte, a young couple retreats to a rural locale.

> An   accident has a writer's wife left mute.   They hole
> up on a little island where he writes his book.   But he
> begins to notice sudden strange actions of the inhabitants
> as he walks among them which he incorporates into his
> book.   The real and imaginative get intertwined.   He
> spies on a recluse who he finds has a machine that allows
> him to make people act as their subconscious, rather than
> their conscious, demands at times of crisis or change.
> He gets into a sort of chess game with the man with the
> various characters as the pieces.   A red-tinted screen
> marks when the characters are being manipulated from
> the game.   The writer rebels and in a fight kills the
> man.

The writer's wife then gives birth to their child and regains her speech. The writer hears that the old recluse had killed himself; this was

> the man of his imagination. So perhaps Miss Varda
> wanted to comment on creation ... trying to get this on
> film does not quite work. It waters down both the real
> and unreal and finally neither makes a comment on the
> problems of artistic creation, nor can the film quite build
> characters out of the ambivalent nature of the two sets of
> action. ... "

Howard Thompson in The New York Times (Sept. 16, 1966, 31:2) was confused and admitted it. "The confusion is compounded by footage spurts and sequences ranging from violence to slapdash comedy, and by the screen's abruptly turning red. It may be actuality, fantasy or a hint of things to come. ... "

The tuned-for-tourists Letter from France 10 (May-June 1966), pp. 4-5, praises it as an "ingenious double story of a writer who transforms the people around him into characters in a novel he is writing. " It is the people of Noirmoutier who are transfigured into the creatures of Edgar's imagination. "As the brightly colored chapters alternate with the black and white events, Edgar's vision begins to prevail. ... " Toward a crimson conclusion is implied.

The storyline is difficult to follow, Charles Ford agrees, in his Femmes cinéastes (pp. 113-114) because of the nebulous nature of the parallels established. Although this binomial premise is embossed firmly upon the spectator's mind, still he is led astray. The movie really gets exciting, Ford declares, when the Devil (or Evil) appears in real society, but the film is really a product of the director's ingenuity not of her sensibility--cool and cerebral, not evocatively emotional.

Ingenious as the film was, Gordon Gow in his article "The Underground River" differs. He tells us that Varda wrote the script from a recurring dream she dreamt in which she had lost her powers of speech. Her husband and daughter were figures in this night dream. In fact, Mr. and Mrs. Demy own a home in Noirmoutier, where they live and work. Gow admits, "This conceit gets rather out of hand, in my opinion ... relating humans very closely to inanimate objects ... Varda's preoccupations are manifest: 'My only regret is that I didn't have the guts to make it all more abstract.'" Which may signify that her sensibilities were firmly employed in The Creatures, ingenious as the red tinting process may have been, and that she retread specific tracks in her subconscious in writing and filming it: the proximity of the sea, the locale of a small village, the pairing of objects with subjects, the dual thread of action, the young married couple as protagonists--all reminiscent if not a replay of La Pointe Courte but this time as science fiction not socioeconomic realism.

The Demys visited the United States after the completion of
Les Creatures. Demy completed The Model Shop and Varda made
a documentary featuring her Uncle Janco (1967). Rex Reed puts
down both works in Big Screen, Little Screen (New York: Macmillan,
1971, pp. 147-149). Reeking of rancid vinegar, Reed's brief paragraph sourly recounts the fact that Varda's short subject was shown
with Model Shop, and both were no-count entities.

> While Demy was ... wasting Columbia's money, his wife
> was up in San Francisco shooting her own tedious little
> bore about a long-lost uncle of hers who lives in a house-
> boat in Sausalito. Miss Varda obviously considered her
> uncle a wonderful subject for a film.... She was wrong.
> All she proves is that people ... who shove their home
> movies down the throats of others should be arrested.

Uncle Janco was shown at the London Film Festival in 1968
as was her documentary appraising the Black Panther movement in
the United States, titled Les Pantheres Noires. Varda next participated in Far from Vietnam, a cooperatively made film which took
an anti-war stance upon the conflict in Indochina. Released and
viewed in the United States in 1967, Variety's three notices of this
anthology documentary reveal the nature of its segments but does
not peg the work of individual directors so that attribution, and thus
criticism, to and of each filmmaker, becomes impossible. The most
useful of Variety's reviews is dated Dec. 20, 1967 (page 4). The
caption reads: "Rabidly Anti-U.S. 'Vietnam' Opens in Paris, which
won't allow 'Algiers.'" The National Theatre was filled for the first
matinee. Chris Marker was the prime mover of the project. "He
and Miss Varda mobilized Parisian film people to donate their services ... over 150 film technicians donated services." The proceeds
were donated to the Red Cross.

Raymond Durgnat tried to make shrewd guesses as to which
segments of the film could be attributed to which directors in his
review in Films and Filming (Feb. 1968), pp. 20-21, while for him
the total piece was "a serious kaleidoscope, a thoughtful dazzle...."

Renata Adler disparages its "serene banality" which is "designed to enrage one cliché cast of mind against the administration
and another against the enragés...." These are the kindest words
she has in her New York Times (June 7, 1968, 32:1) review.

John Simon's evaluation in Private Screenings (pp. 381-2)
was surprisingly bland: "... a clumsy piece of agit-prop anti-
Americana...."

Employing an American locality for the first time, Varda
made her first feature film, Lions Love, with an American cast
speaking English. The setting was Hollywood, and the cast included
Viva and the co-authors of Hair, Gerome Ragni and James Rado,
and a friend of Varda's, filmmaker Shirley Clarke. Varda rented the
house which served as headquarters and site of the film. The para-

mount pieces in this jigsaw puzzle of a movie are a beach scene
cleared of hippies by the police; parts of a performance of a play
The Beard, and a repeat of this play to entertain children in the
drained swimming pool near the house; a vignette in which children
pass around a cigarette (not marijuana) from hand to hand; a fake
suicide scene acted by Shirley Clarke who couldn't complete it; and
the reception of the news that Andy Warhol was shot just as a TV
set blares forth reportage on Bobby Kennedy's assassination.

"Arguably ... Lions Love is the best of Varda's work, free-
ranging and perhaps self-indulgent.... In this film her 'underground
river of the instincts' is running fast and deep...." This is Gordon
Gow's reaction in his article "The Underground River," Films and
Filming (March 1970), pp. 6-13.

John Simon, writing in Movies into Film (pp. 386-7) this
time, is less acerbic than he usually is. "Varda's attempt at a
more sophisticated version of an Andy Warhol film ... a tiresome
pursuit of a kind of spontaneity not all that good...." Simon found
the TV news on Kennedy's death and funeral especially distasteful.

Jonathan Hoops in Film Quarterly 23 (Summer, 1970), on pp.
60-61, rates it as "among the year's film weirdities.... It should
be clear that Varda intends something serious, a philosophy underlying all her films. Unfortunately, she flops."

Writing in Deeper into Movies (pp. 30-31), Pauline Kael's
verdict is that the film displays a conspicuous lack of intelligence
and technique. Lions Love fared only a bit better in the judgement
of Arlene Gould in Take One 2 (Jan.-Feb. 1969), p. 21. "Tediously self-indulgent and obscure in implementation if not intention ...
it is difficult to tell just what Agnes Varda is trying to say about
Hollywood." What is the film about anyway? It

> concerns a female director who goes to Hollywood to make
> a movie [Shirley Clarke]. But Clarke ... has a singular
> talent for not emoting ... Shirley is supposed to gulp
> down an overdose of sleeping pills.... She cannot ...
> bring herself to take the pills on camera ... and so di-
> rector Varda slips casually into Shirley's mod gear and
> takes over her part for the scene. Then the real Shirley
> is whisked off to the hospital.... I ... object to Miss
> Varda's use of secondary sources either to amuse or
> bore.... In a recent interview with Village Voice critic
> Jonas Mekas she explained that Lions Love is simply a
> collage of her impressions of Hollywood in 1968.... I
> am just about ready to class films about directors trying
> to make films ... as tediously self-indulgent....

If nothing else, Lions Love (1969) provides subject material
for debates on the nature of the documentary film. The barely dis-
cernible line between the actual and the invented is scrutinized by
G. Roy Levin, who observes, "it's difficult at times to make that

distinction--Agnes Varda's Lions Love, for example. My point is
that it isn't always clear to what degree certain incidents in the film
are or are not documentary--that is, actual incidents.... "19 Exactly what Arlene Gould objected to, although Gould did not like being
forced to watch and listen to the Kennedy TV program in a film any
more than she protested the re-staging of The Beard (let's do it
again for the kids) and questioned the validity of the Clarke attempt
at suicide. The film student may naively wonder if the no man's
land of factual fiction and fictional fact is precisely what Varda
wanted to represent so that knifebladed queries would be thrust at
the viewers: What is real? Did that really happen? Is it important? When does an event stop and a pseudo-event start? Is Varda
looking for the types of realities which can be translated to the
screen, thence to the viewer?

    Writing in Femmes cinéastes, pp. 115-16 again, Charles
Ford found Lions Love an uneven work, made haphazardly. But,
"it is a bold film; it is clear that psychology is of no concern. It
is an existential film. " In it, Varda "wanted to depict the environment of avant-garde actors in Hollywood, to render the hippie mood
in certain parts of the former cinema capital and to grasp an epoch,
the evolution of American society.... " Ford claims the film was a
failure for French audiences. Further, the film had a reputation
as a comedy abroad. As a truly foreign product, the French found
Lions Love hard to understand. But then, Ford recalls, French film
audiences have reacted negatively to the unconventional hippie life-
style in Hollywood and probably would dislike Lions Love.

    Filmmaking itself is the subject of Lions Love, Richard Roud
theorizes, citing several scenes to ground his views. Among these
are Shirley Clarke's unsuccessful attempt to act out a suicide try.
Clarke, a friend of Varda's, bows out and Varda herself acts the
scene. Before the film's end, Viva laments that her dream of being
in an honest-to-goodness movie has been dashed--one more time.
But it is the startling, and to some very offensive, depiction of
Viva, James Rado, and Gerome Ragni in bed eating breakfast as
they watch scenes of Robert Kennedy's assassination on television
that most strongly persuades Roud that Varda was striving for a
"contrast and contradiction between public events and private viewing. " Roud is led from his initial premise of the film's subject toward a broader concept. Maybe, Roud deliberates, Lions Love
deals with twinning or doubling of realities that Varda is fond of
portraying: "reality and illusion ... private faces and public places,
a collage of America in the plague year of 1968. "

    In 1969, the Demys returned to France after a sojourn of
two years in Los Angeles. Varda's next film was a feature for TV
centering on Greeks living in France. Nausicaa (1970) was semi-
documentary; once completed French television authorities refused to
air the show, either privately or publicly. Varda had advised them
that her film about a contemporary Greek woman in France would
inhere political nuances, would be subject to political interpretation.
Why was it not shown? Varda replies that it was too openly against
military-ruled Greece. That's the reason, she is certain.

In 1971 Varda helped write the script of Last Tango in Paris with Bertolucci. The year 1971 marked the start of Varda's involvement and interest in the women's movement. My Body Belongs to Me (1972), a feature length musical derived from a woman's dream, reflects Varda's concerns regarding reproductive rights for woman, a concern which became stronger as the seventies waned. My Body considers the lives of three women who operate a contraceptive clinic for women in Nice. In this time phase, Varda's son, Mathieu, was born.

Varda herself told her intentions for the film to Barbara Confino for an interview in Saturday Review (Aug. 12, 1972), page 35. Varda was attending the First International Festival of Women's Films in 1972 at which Cleo was screened. "I am about to start a film, Mon Corps Est à Moi (My Body Belongs to Me) around the theme of abortion--a big problem here. It is not a documentary, it's not cinéma vérité, but it is related to real problems.... "

Varda made another film in 1975 expressing her stance on women's issues. This 8mm essay Reponses de Femmes (1975) has generated no criticism or annotation to date.

Shifting to less controversial subject material, Varda made a documentary, Daguerreotypes, released in 1976. Shown at the Second International Festival of Women's Films in September 1976, the film's classification was noted as "none" on the program, with this explanation: "There is no cast in this film. "

From the Film Review Digest 2:2 (Winter 1977), pages 132-133, Molly Haskell's review dated September 29, 1976, reads:

> The title, Daguerreotypes, like much of the film, is a play on words, with the 'types' of the Rue Daguerre where Agnes Varda lives comprising the subject of her affectionate tribute, to them, Paris, and the inventor of the 'photoportrait. ' It is a slight but lovely and evocative work, in which one enters into Varda's feelings and understands precisely what appeals to her about the musty store window with old corsets and beauty aids and an inventory that hasn't changed since the '50's.... "

Made for German television, Richard Roud reports that Daguerreotypes failed to reach the levels of excellence Varda had set and met for herself, and he wonders why. The decade 1967-1977, Roud reflects, was one of frustration and failure for Varda's films. In a recapitulation of her prolific and progressive career, Roud declares: "Varda had her biggest commercial hit with Le Bonheur and her biggest flop with Les Creatures. Then came Lions Love in 1969, and after that nothing. " Then, Roud adds, the year 1977 came along, a time of prestigious films for the Left Bank Threesome. Alain Resnais made Providence, Chris Marker made Le Fond de l'air est Rouge (Roud remarks that no acceptable idiomatic English translation can be used and that The Base of the Air

is Red does not convey the import of the film), and Varda made
L'Une chante l'autre pas (One Sings, the Other Doesn't). Surely a
triumph of its kind after Varda's decade of mishaps, unrealized projects, and half-finished efforts. Varda told Judith Thurman:

> In men's films women have almost always been presented
> in terms of love. . . . Men are shown in relation to their
> jobs. Some years ago I wrote a script about a woman
> math teacher and her problems on the job. At that time
> we were about to introduce the new math in France. I
> was never able to raise the money to make that film.

In 1971, while Varda was traveling in Iran she met a woman
who had had an abortion. The inspiration for One Sings as well as
her previous two reproductive rights films may partially have been
spurred by this encounter. When Varda finished the final draft of
One Sings screenplay, the customary protracted pursuit of a producer, actors, and musicians followed.

Not finding financial resources to film is a routine roadblock
in the life of a filmmaker. Varda responds stoically to this grim
fact: Free cinema has always been hard to achieve no matter who
does it. "I've been in a crisis for 20 years. I made all my films
with difficulty. "

One Sings did not appeal to would-be producers. Men had
minor roles and there were musical interludes in it, they objected.
Varda established her own production company Ciné-Tamaris to make
One Sings. The unconventional environment in which One Sings was
made contributed directly to the atmosphere of the film. In essence,
Varda created a "family" of workers to make a movie about new
forms of families. She selected an equal number of men and women
to work on One Sings. To Varda, this is a more human on-the-job
relationship.

> Usually there are twenty men on the crew, and one script
> woman, and all the men competing to see who'll screw
> her or the actress first. This time it was fifty-fifty men
> and women, a hierarchy of responsibility but not one of
> power. And the relations changed. The working friend-
> ships were stronger than any sexual attractions or an-
> tagonisms. 20

Varda discovered Therese Liotard for the role of Suzanne.
Therese discovered Valerie Mairesse for the role of Pauline-Pomme-
Apple, and the chain of discovery carried on, actors discovering
each other. Circumstances on the shooting sets and locations (Paris,
south of France, Amsterdam, and Iran) paralleled the film's action.
There were children and babies present, and all--grips, electricians,
actresses--feeding and caring for them. On the set and in the film
a new kind of family spirit was felt and formed.

As in previous Varda films (The Creatures, La Pointe Courte)

One Sings tells two stories.   Richard Roud sees in the title Varda's perennial preoccupation with doubling.   Even Lions Love doubled many story skeins and Varda's unrealized film Mélangite (1962) incorporated doubling into a tale about a woman who confused matters and persons.

One Sings begins in 1962.   Two young women are friends. Suzanne (Therese Liotard) lives with a married photographer.   They have two children and she is expecting a third.   Pauline (Valerie Mairesse) gives her money for an abortion.   When the photographer hangs himself, Suzanne must return with her children to her parents' farm.   Pauline decides to leave home, changes her name to Pomme (Apple) as more suitable for the singing career she pursues, with a group of musicians.   Their lives converge ten years later at an abortion rally at Bobigny in 1972 where, once again, circumstances part them.   Suzanne has learned to type, has worked as a secretary, and later sets up a family planning clinic, subsequently marrying a pediatrician she meets in her workplace.   Pomme marries an Iranian, bears his child, a son, then decides to leave him when she discovers his pro-feminist stance is false.   In the penultimate scenes, the two women, who have corresponded and kept in touch, are reunited.   Suzanne and her husband join Pomme and her musical combo on a picnic.   The camera's last shot lingers on Suzanne's daughter, a teen-ager (acted by Varda's daughter Rosalie), representing the next generation, already facing the ever old, ever new (the Pill vs. no contraceptive measures) issues of womanhood.

While One Sings poses more queries than the replies it provides, Varda does not inflict her personal views upon the audience. It is her best film, Roud concludes, because "This chronicle of parallel lives is both the story of a friendship and a dramatization of Simone de Beauvoir's phrase, 'One isn't born a woman; one becomes one.' Occasionally the film's ideological load threatens to swamp its dramatic impact, but Varda gets away with it by the skin of her teeth."21

Susan Stark, reporting from the New York Film Festival, recognizes in One Sings an "ideal yet to be realized." Her review in the Detroit Free Press, October 16, 1977, on page 7-C, commends the film as "a very contemporary piece with a wonderfully happy, if idyllic, ending." Pomme and Suzanne, after years of tribulation and accompanying maturation, rejoice in their womanliness.

Vincent Canby admits that his "tepid reaction ... is biased." "Chauvinist Game" captions his review of One Sings in The New York Times, September 23, 1977, III, 10:3.   The movie isn't honest, Canby asserts.   It has beautiful acting, well realized scenes, but "at key moments, it's as phony--as relentlessly schematic and upbeat--as Soviet neo-realist art.   It's of less interest as a movie than as a statement of position." Canby believes Varda has started her own feminist propaganda rally in One Sings.   The total effect on Canby is one of disbelief.   The fifteen years' friendship of Pomme and Suzanne maintained only by casual correspondence, and especially

that very sunny reunion at the film's close, just isn't credible. The
two women do not emotionally involve Canby's sympathies or interest. "If we were more aware of the toll taken of the two women in
their struggles, the film would carry more emotional impact. As
it is, it has a sort of high-toned perfunctoriness to it. "

Carrie Rickey's reaction is as tepid as Canby's. In psychologically probing critical terms, Rickey's review in Artforum 16
(December 1977), pages 53-54, titled "Tepid Yesterdays, " faults One
Sings for lack of character development and political scope. Rickey's
sub-title, "Some Make Movies, Others Don't" capsules her reaction.
But she knows why Varda's characters remain undeveloped. Varda
has "done an audacious thing" in narrating her tale of a long friendship by mail in a form disclosing the evolving feminist movement
in France. This format effectively excludes character delineation
or alteration. "Varda's images are of a sunny, carefully composed
and deep space, but the people in them are paper dolls flattened
against the screen. Dimensionless, they never hold or describe
the space they inhabit. " The men in One Sings "suffer cardboard
characterization. " Rickey guesses this was Varda's artistic decision:
to maximize the women's roles she had to reduce the men's. "But
this fails as a strategy because of its smugness. " Caricature results.

Rickey instances this caricature in Darius' response to
Pomme when she leaves him after their son is born. " 'You used
me. ... I was good for nothing but a little semen. ' " Pomme and
Suzanne tend toward caricature, too: they are vehicles traversing
feminist history, representing the required progression toward becoming deciders of their own destinies. Both women, Rickey observes, organize groups that function as consciousness-raisers:
Pomme a performing group and Suzanne a family planning center.

The audience must read the film as Varda narrates it, Rickey
discerns; her words close the breaks in the narrative. Audiences
perceive Varda's women as sex objects not love objects, because the
two women's friendship focuses on their reproductive powers. Rickey
frowns upon Varda's vision of the feminist movement as primarily
sisterhood and motherhood, while subtracting remaining major aspects of it. "This isn't a movie, it's an accretion of sentimental
language.... Some make movies, some make celebrations. "

The most glowing critique of One Sings is Stanley Kauffmann's
in New Republic 177 (October 8, 1977), pages 26-27. In this film,
Kauffmann purrs, Varda has discovered her own voice, her persona,
and themes. Each upholds the other. He prefaces his pleasure in
and praise of One Sings by listing the poverties of her previous
works. He finds One Sings a delight; in his estimation, the best
film so far about the new attitudes we may have toward men and
women both. Kauffmann confides his private measuring rod for
Women's Lib movies: If the film annoys him, it's poor. If it
makes him feel ashamed, it's good. One Sings made him feel
ashamed.

Varda as narrator separates the story of the film into three parts: 1962, 1972, and a brief afterword in 1976. The braided biographies of the two women as they mature do not form a traditional plot, Kauffmann notes. Instead, Varda chose the most universal events in the lives of most women on which to base her account of the individual development of her protagonists. The two are not "idealized, martyrized, sentimentalized. They are just two women who insist on questioning and experiencing, rather than accepting. " The film could be a bit shorter. Nevertheless, its men characters "are handled with truth and solicitude. " And overall One Sings is "a rich, life-filled work, accomplished in its making, engrossing in its humility and courage. "

Pauline Kael subtitled her review in her Current Cinema column appearing in the New Yorker 53 (November 14, 1977), pages 75-78, "Scrambled Eggs." Kael sums up the film: straightforward and all up-front, but shallow with no depth. "It's a cheery, educational feminism-can-be-fun movie. " Abortion dominates the first and second parts of the film's action. In part one, Suzanne has an abortion. In part two, when Pomme and Suzanne meet in 1972 at an abortion rally, Pomme confides that she has had one.

When the two friends part, Pomme goes to Iran with an Iranian, Darius, she met in Amsterdam. She had gone there for the abortion. When she becomes pregnant, Darius and Pomme marry. After their son's birth, Pomme discerns her husband's views becoming the traditional dominant male attitudes. She returns to France. Darius follows her: he wants custody of his son. Pomme decides not to return to Iran; she gives Darius a choice. He may have their son, if he will make her pregnant again so that she will have a child of her own.

Suzanne and Pomme differ in the lengths of time required for their consciousnesses to be made aware. They are contrasted to their own mothers who are "narrow, unloving housewives.... " But for Kael, the movie is unreal. Varda wrote the lyrics that Pomme sings while on tour in the provinces with her musical group: Kael deems these glad notes of liberation unconvincing: "'I'm neither a tough cookie nor a busy beaver nor a utopian dreamer--I'm a woman, I am me. '" The scenes in which Pomme performs her songs are "so laughable. " But, "you can't hate the picture. You just feel that some of your brain cells have been knocked out. " When Pomme's group celebrates the satisfactions of pregnancy, using cushions to stuff their costumes, chanting, "your choice and your pleasure" Kael is not amused but affronted. And when these pregnant pretenders release balloons "or sing about their 'ovules, ' Varda brings a Disney touch to women's liberation. " The feminism in One Sings "is a new form of asexual lyricism. " Kael finds this lyricism "trivializing. " Kael suggests, "If there were twenty seconds of footage of an actual abortion in the movie, Pomme's chirrupy songs would be chilling. It seems never to have occurred to Varda that her characters have no depth.... " Varda doesn't dramatize her narrative. Pomme and Suzanne do not engage audience sym-

pathy; their friendship is so fragile it does not connect them. "The
way Varda skims over their lives, they could be butterflies or
duckies." Varda is, in Kael's judgment, "a lively, sophisticated
film technician who thinks that this ode to superficiality is poetic
truth."

Richard A. Blake protests "The vulgar propagandizing intent
of Miss Varda's film. It represents to me what is most despicable
in the lunatic fringes of the women's liberation movement." Blake
can't understand why One Sings, "this pedestrian film [has] been so
kindly received, without any mention of the central theme, which is
a sustained argument for the benefits of free access to abortion...."22

In a three-paragraph review, Mark Ably in Maclean's 91 (November 20, 1978), page 67, believes the film fails because "it
doesn't make us care." Although, as an entirety, One Sings "sinks
under the weight of its worthiness" the picture's overall impression
is "so cool and passive that you long for any sort of passion....
The moments don't connect; there's no drive or fire."

Judith Thurman relates to the historical impact of One Sings,
because it is "a very clear and valuable account of a certain period." The lives of two women twine around the core of women's
history for fifteen years, 1962 to 1977. Thurman faults the over-
simplification of the problems and obstacles the characters encounter
in One Sings, but she sees its greatest strength in Varda's decision
not to use an all-is-well closure, with all situations completely
solved. Instead, Varda "has had the confidence as an artist and
the honesty as a woman to leave them unresolved."23

Varda replies to the criticism of One Sings eloquently. She
knows that critics have negated its too sweet optimism. She says
she wanted to project the fact that being a woman can be a happy
experience. "As an artist, I cannot situate myself among those
who complain. If we are going to create, or to re-create the
sources of women's self-expression, I believe they will not be
plaintive...."24

She wanted to hold as large an audience as possible with One
Sings. Her view is that a sunny, upbeat film will reach and hold
an audience better than a pessimistic, or radical-themed, picture.
Varda explains: "'I want to illuminate women's lives--not only
their hardships, although they're important, but also the light, the
transparence, the pleasure of being a woman.'"25

Varda will pursue this path of illumination by writing, directing, and producing her films. With more than a quarter century's roster of film works behind her, all signals show GO for this
Mother of the New Wave to continue her conquest of uncharted
cinematic seas inspired by her underground river of inspiration.

FILMOGRAPHY

Feature Films

La Pointe Courte (1954)

Cléo de 5 à 7 (1962)

Le Bonheur (1965)

Lions Love (1969)

My Body Belongs to Me (1972)

L'Une chante l'autre pas (1977)

Documentary Films

O Saisons, ô Châteaux (1957)

Au Côté de la Côte (1958)

L'Opéra Mouffe (1958)

Salute to Cuba (1963)

Elsa (1966)

Uncle Janco (1967)

The Black Panthers, or Huey (1967)

Far from Vietnam (1967) co-directed

Nausicaa (1970)

Reponses de Femmes (1975)

Daguerreotypes (1976)

Unrealized Film Projects

La cocotte d'azur (1961)

Mélangite (1962)

NOTES

1. Barbara Confino, "An Interview with Agnes Varda, " 55 Saturday Review (August 12, 1972), p. 35.
2. Judith Thurman, "One Sings the Other Doesn't ... " Ms. (January 1978), p. 28.
3. Current Biography 1970, p. 424.
4. Ibid.
5. Gordon Gow, "The Underground River, " Films and Filming 16:6 (March 1970), p. 7.
6. Richard Roud, "The Left Bank, " Sight and Sound 32 (Winter 1962/63), pp. 24-27.

7. Ibid. , p. 24.
8. Charles Ford, Femmes cinéastes, ou le triomphe de la volonte.
    Paris: Editions Denoël-Gonthier, 1972, p. 110.
9. Gow, p. 9.
10. Jeanne Betancourt, Women in Focus. Dayton, Ohio: Pflaum,
    1974, p. 30.
11. Ibid. , p. 32.
12. Ford, p. 111.
13. Gow, p. 8.
14. Richard Roud, "Cléo de 5 à 7, " Sight and Sound 31 (Summer
    1962), pp. 145-146.
15. Roger Manvell, "Roger Manvell sees a girl's two hours 'til
    zero... , " Films and Filming 9:3 (December 1962), p. 38.
16. Dennis DeNitto and William Herman, Film and the Critical Eye.
    New York: Macmillan, 1975, p. 511.
17. Ibid. , p. 512.
18. William D. Routt, "One Man's Truth ... Another Man's Poi-
    son, " Film Quarterly 20 (Spring 1967), p. 28.
19. G. Roy Levin, Documentary Explorations: 15 Interviews with 15
    Filmmakers. New York: Doubleday, 1971, pp. 286-287.
20. Thurman, p. 28.
21. Richard Roud, "Agnes Varda, " in Cinema: A Critical Diction-
    ary, ed. by Richard Roud. New York: Viking Press, 1980,
    p. 1022.
22. Richard A. Blake, "Women: Friends to Each Other, " America
    137 (October 22, 1977), p. 269.
23. Thurman, p. 28.
24. Ibid.
25. Ibid.